INDUSTRIAL POWER AND THE SOVIET STATE

Industrial Power
and the
Soviet State

STEPHEN WHITEFIELD

CLARENDON PRESS · OXFORD
1993

Oxford University Press, Walton Street, Oxford OX2 6DP
Oxford New York Toronto
Delhi Bombay Calcutta Madras Karachi
Kuala Lumpur Singapore Hong Kong Tokyo
Nairobi Dar es Salaam Cape Town
Melbourne Auckland Madrid
and associated companies in
Berlin Ibadan

Published in the United States
by Oxford University Press Inc., New York

British Library Cataloguing in Publication Data
Data available

Library of Congress Cataloging in Publication Data
Whitefield, Stephen.
Industrial power and the Soviet state / Stephen Whitefield.
Includes bibliographical references.
1. Industrial organization—Soviet Union. 2. Industry and state—
Soviet Union. 3. Soviet Union—Economic conditions—1965–1975.
4. Soviet Union—Economic conditions—1975–1985. 5. Soviet Union—
Economic conditions—1985–1991. I. Title.
HD70.S63W45   1993   338.947—dc20   93–15328
ISBN 0–19–827881–0 (acid-free paper)

Typeset by J&L Composition Ltd, Filey, North Yorkshire
Printed in Great Britain
on acid-free paper by
Bookcraft (Bath) Ltd
Midsomer Norton, Avon

To
my parents

PREFACE

THIS book originated as a doctoral thesis which I embarked on in 1985 and submitted in 1991. I began with little interest in industrial ministries; by the end, a distinguished scholar of the Soviet economy had accused me of making the error of all doctoral students—falling in love with the object of my study. It should be evident from the contents of the book, I hope, that my feelings are not pro-ministerial, but there are still those who will object that I attach far too much importance to them. I hope the argument and evidence presented below will convince all scholars that I am right to do so.

The credit for introducing me to ministries belongs to my supervisor, Professor Archie Brown, whom I must thank again for having the judgement to know a good topic. I am also deeply grateful for all the support and criticism he has given me over the years. The book would not have been as good without the penetrating and, occasionally, devastating comments of Mary McAuley, Ron Amann, and Bob Service. I will be surprised if I have yet fully convinced them, so they can take no blame for any of the remaining inaccuracies. Thanks also to the ESRC for the studentship which allowed me to undertake doctoral research; to Nuffield College for the provision of such a supportive academic environment; to the British Council which supported me in Moscow in the academic year 1988–9; to the Department of Administrative Law at Moscow State University, and in particular to my *nauchny rukovaditel'*, Yury Markovich Kozlov, for his patience, experience, and insight; and to the Institute of State and Law of the (then) USSR Academy of Sciences. Great appreciation is also due to my colleagues at the School of Slavonic and Eastern European Studies, especially during my first year when they virtually carried my work-load while I finished the thesis.

I must also give special thanks to the friends who helped me finish the thesis and the book. I will never forget the support of Fred and Masha Weir, and the rest of the family; of Nikita and Marina; of Sergei and Alyona Grigoriev; and of Joe Schull and Geoff Garrett.

As always, I must thank my parents, who got me going and whose encouragement did so much to keep me going. Most importantly, my thanks go to Emma who is the real reason it got done.

S.W.

CONTENTS

Introduction
Perestroyka in the long durée of Soviet Politics

PERESTROYKA was not a new departure in Soviet politics but the final phase of an endemic systemic crisis. Exogenous factors such as declining oil prices, rising costs of production, and the arms race certainly played their part in motivating *perestroyka*. But the problem of the Soviet system was inherently a political one which arose from a paradox. How were politicians, despite all the ostensible power at their disposal, to deal with the effective usurpation of their control by the very institutions that they themselves had created? It was the search for power by political leaders that accounts for the regular cataclysmic upsurges of reform throughout the Soviet period; and their failure to secure it that accounts for the long periods of apparent quiescence.

The principal argument of this book is that the relationship between political and industrial power, and, in particular, between leading politicians and industrial ministries in the period after 1965, is the key to understanding the stability and instability of the Soviet political system from 1917 to 1991. The struggle between political and industrial power is best conceived as a bargaining relationship, in which each side brought its resources to bear. It should not be thought that the resources of either side in this battle were negligible, nor that their powers were homogeneous or their interests uniform. However, on the basis of both theory and the balance of evidence, the power of industry and its institutions emerged as the ultimate and surprising victor. Their ability to import their economic power into the political sphere effectively emasculated the exercise of political authority. In a phrase, industrial ministries were the cuckoos in the nest of communist political power! Operating under the guise of political institutions, they starved the politicians of authority, and ended up holding the resources to make politicians do their bidding. The power of industrial ministries and the desire of the politicians to expel them lay at the heart of the decision by Gorbachev and other leading reformist politicians to launch *perestroyka*; and it was this power that did so much to defeat their efforts.

This position departs from most explanations of the Soviet political system and its demise, which focus on the dominance of the Communist Party and the popular struggle against it. Such a conclusion, therefore, will come as a surprise to some, but not all, students of Soviet politics. There has as yet been no comprehensive work devoted to studying these industrial institutions.[1] A considerable amount is already known about the power, behaviour, and interests of industrial ministries from empirical research conducted by economists, political scientists, and management theorists, but this research has focused primarily on other Soviet institutions—the Communist Party, the local soviets, the enterprises, and the planning agencies—and dealt with the ministries only as secondary phenomena.

Economists have devoted the most attention to ministerial power. Nove, for example, suggested that ministers were neither 'politicians' nor 'coordinator–planners'; instead, they were best thought of as the 'objects of planning coordination'. Paul Gregory used a principal–agent approach derived from the economics of regulation to characterize relations among Soviet economic institutions, and argued that the ministry was the 'agent' to Gosplan's 'principal'. For Alice Gorlin, at least, the bargaining position of ministries in the Soviet system created great difficulties for the planners seeking to regulate their activity. However, even she would probably also accept David Dyker's view that ministerial behaviour was simply a rational response to the system of targets established by their superiors.[2]

Political scientists to a large extent mirrored the position of Sovietological economists.[3] Though considerable attention was devoted to

---

[1] Archie Brown noted a number of years ago that, despite general recognition of their importance, industrial ministries remained under-researched in Soviet studies. See A. H. Brown, *Soviet Politics and Political Science* (London, 1974), 68.

[2] See e.g. D. Granick, *Management of the Industrial Firm in the USSR* (New York: 1954); P. Rutland, *The Myth of the Plan* (London, 1985); D. Dyker, *The Process of Investment in the Soviet Union* (Cambridge, 1983); Ed. A. Hewitt, *Reforming the Soviet Economy* (Washington, DC, 1988); P. Gregory, *Restructuring the Soviet Economic Bureaucracy* (Cambridge, 1990), 15–23; A. Nove, *The Soviet Economic System* (3rd ed., London, 1986), 49–50; A. Gorlin, 'The Power of the Industrial Ministries in the 1980s', in *Soviet Studies*, 3 (1985), 353–70; and D. Dyker, 'The Power of the Industrial Ministries', in D. Lane (ed.), *Élites and Political Power in the USSR* (Aldershot, 1988), 199.

[3] Among the many examples of political science literature are: J. Hough, *The Soviet Prefects* (Cambridge, Mass., 1969); L. Holmes, *The Policy Process in Communist States: Politics and Industrial Administration* (London, 1981); D. Hammer, *USSR: The Politics of Oligarchy* (Hinsdale, Ill., 1974); T. Gustafson, *Reform in Soviet Politics* (Cambridge, 1981); R. Amann, 'Searching for an Appropriate Concept of Soviet Politics: The Politics of Hesitant Modernisation', in *British Journal of Political Science*, 16 (1986), 475–94;

institutions other than the Communist Party, and recognition given both to 'bureaucratic pluralism' in the policy process and to the centrality of the interaction between politics and economics in the Soviet system,[4] the position of ministries as players in the political game did not receive a great deal of attention.[5] This may, in large measure, have been the result of the inheritance of the dominant paradigm and responses to it.

Though, as a political model, 'totalitarianism' concerned itself with questions different from those advanced by economists, questions less to do with securing economic performance than with securing political control, similarities to the economic model are none the less evident; ministries were considered to be medium-rank institutions and objects of political coordination. As with the economic model, considerable attention was paid to some of the manifestations of independence on the part of non-élite party institutions and groups. None the less, even where bureaucratic pluralism and ministerial power were recognized, the emphasis remained on the dominant role of the Communist Party.[6]

J. Hough, *The Soviet Union and Social Science Theory* (London, 1977); A. H. Brown, 'Political Power and the Soviet State: Western and Soviet Perspectives', in N. Harding (ed.), *The State in Socialist Society* (London, 1984), 64–5.

[4] Mary McAuley has recognized that the difficulties of operating party dominance over state and other institutions are among the main causes of continuing reform cycles in Soviet-type political systems. She does not, however, offer a detailed account of the importance of ministries as the main organizational factor provoking party reform. See M. McCauley, 'Soviet Political Reform in a Comparative Context', in *Harriman Institute Forum*, 2/10 (1989).

[5] Stephen Fortescue has been perhaps the most forceful advocate of the role of industrial ministries in the Soviet political system after 1965. In a series of highly informative and analytical articles, he has uncovered a wealth of information about the internal dynamics of ministries and attempted to generalize this to a view of the Soviet political system which he calls the 'sectional society model'. Much of what shall be argued below is clearly supportive of the line taken by Fortescue, but the evidence suggests that, along with other political scientists, he underestimates the power of ministries in the Soviet system. See S. Fortescue, *The Primary Party Organisations of Branch Ministries* (Washington, DC, 1985); id., *The Technical Administration of Industrial Ministries* (Birmingham, 1986); id., *Science and Technology Management Structures in Soviet Industrial Ministries* (Birmingham, 1986); id., *Building Consensus in Japanese and Soviet Bureaucracies* (Birmingham, 1987); and id., 'The Regional Party Apparatus in the Sectional Society', in *Studies in Comparative Communism*, (1988), 11–23.

[6] The same problem remains, unfortunately, in Peter Rutland's recent study, *The Politics of Economic Stagnation in the Soviet Union: The Role of Local Party Organs in Economic Management* (Cambridge, 1992). The difficulties inherent in drawing conclusions about the exercise of economic power from a study of local bodies is obvious enough in the context of the Soviet state but Rutland, citing space considerations, leaves the national picture out. While it may be a matter of interpretation whether Gorbachev was trying to preserve the old order or reform it, Rutland also seems to miss the point

The argument presented here challenges these points of view directly. Each part of the literature in its own way has tended to underestimate ministerial power, be it in the economy, in politics, or even over society. The bulk of the primary evidence which will be presented in defence of this overall claim is drawn from the period after 1965 when the industrial ministries were re-established. The argument is defended, however, on the basis of tendencies in Soviet history as a whole, though the Brezhnev period provides a focus because it represents the apogee of ministerial power. *Perestroyka*, for its part, contained virtually every form of anti-ministerialism—and more—that had been seen in the Soviet period.

However, the claim that ministries were the dominant players in the game played between various forces and institutions of the Soviet system is not only evidentially based, but underpinned by theoretical considerations as well. It is surprising to me, given reasonable assumptions about the nature of the resources of the participating actors, that the notion of political dominance ever gained such wide credence. Before moving on to the detailed evidence for these claims, therefore, it is essential to deal with the structure of the game of Soviet politics as a whole. No doubt this game was always arcane and difficult to decipher, in particular because the division between political and other forms of power was difficult to draw. Careful attention to the nature of the political, however, will be seen to provide the key to unlock its mysteries and allow the multitude of evidence to be brought into order.

POLITICS AND THE SOVIET SYSTEM

Understanding the nature of politics and political power is not just a semantic issue; it is about naming real phenomena on the basis of observed differences between them. If, for that reason, I say that political power was weak in the Soviet order, this is not a definitional fiat but a conclusion based upon the behaviour and powers available

by treating the totalitarian model, albeit in a revised form, as usable, when it begs the question of the contradictory relationship between the totalitarian—if you like—economic structure and the totalitarian political structure. When Rutland says that, despite repeated attempts after Stalin's death to reform the economic system, it remained unchanged, he somehow fails to draw the conclusion that this was due to a weakness in the very political structure that, he says, dominated economic rationality. Who, after all, was seeking economic change?

to actors at different levels of the system. The point is worth emphasizing; drawing the proper distinction between political and other forms of power allows us to model events in Soviet history which otherwise appear strange and contradictory.

The starting-point for an analysis of the Soviet system, therefore, has to be in the sharpening of conceptual tools. Michael Urban has suggested that it 'is rather ironic that for all the attention afforded students of the Soviet Union to "politics" or "power" as the salient or determining feature of the social order, conceptualising just what "power" and "politics" involve in state socialist societies has remained a relatively unattended project'.[7] The end-point for an analysis of the Soviet state system has often been the assertion that politics are impossible to separate from economics. Arguing from a Marxist perspective, for example, Wlodzimierz Brus stated that: 'Economy and politics are so intimately intertwined, especially when considered dynamically, that the continued use of the old conceptual apparatus of base and superstructure becomes more and more inadequate.'[8] Nove agrees, arguing that 'Politics and economics, political organs and managerial functions, do indeed intertwine.'[9] However, he does offer a way of delimiting the two spheres—'plainly, political choices are being made'—on the basis that political decisions have a strategic or macro character. This too seems to beg the question: in what respect are macro decisions, which all agents must make at some time, political ones? Other discussions have gone further without ultimately clarifying the issue. Hough, for example, quite rightly points to the need to defend the effectiveness of political action—which he identifies with the discretion and power of Gorbachev—against the economic determinists who would underplay its significance.[10] But, again, the political meaning of discretion is not explained.

---

[7] M. E. Urban, 'Conceptualising Political Power in the USSR: Patterns of Binding and Bonding', in *Studies in Comparative Communism*, 4 (1985), 208. Urban has offered a stimulating account of the problems of understanding and exercising power in the Soviet system. He also displays an awareness of the difficulties of conceiving the Soviet state as strong, or its politicians as powerful, but confuses the issue, in my view, by suggesting that the terms of the game put economic actors in a double-bind in which the politicians still dominated. My view is that the terms of the game provided a camouflage for industrial power.

[8] W. Brus, *The Economics and Politics of Socialism* (London, 1973), 88.

[9] Nove, *The Soviet Economic System*, 8–9.

[10] J. Hough, 'Understanding Gorbachev: The Importance of Politics', in Ed. A. Hewett and V. H. Winston (eds.), *Milestones in Glasnost and Perestroika: Politics and People* (Washington, DC, 1991).

As was suggested above, when the relationship between political and industrial institutions and actors is considered from the perspective of bargaining, the dominance of industrial bodies becomes evident. On this basis, we ought to examine political institutions as a form of resource possessed and utilized by certain actors. The question then is, what kind of resource is it, and which actors possess and use it?

At this point it is useful to consider the issue of political and economic power from a more comparative perspective. Much of this work, of course, is directed at the functioning of political systems under conditions of capitalist democracy and, therefore, it is not immediately applicable to the Soviet Union, though I will argue that it is far more relevant than the many *sui generis* models of the Soviet system might have us believe. Three types of social science literature are particularly relevant to attempts to explain ministry power: first, methodologies which model strategic behaviour and the patterning of interests, especially rational choice; second, theories of politics, bureaucracy, and the state, which clarify in general terms what is meant by authority, legitimacy, and political power; and, finally, research which combines the first two with a multidimensional model of capitalist democracy, as well as an institutionalist approach to the impact of organizations.

In modelling the power of political actors and industrial ministries it is useful to apply the methodological assumptions of a structurally constrained rational actor approach,[11] which consists of three criteria: first, that the test of an explanation should be its ability to account for data by the actions of agents, which in the end means individuals, even when they exercise powers which are attached to institutions; second, that rationality is defined as interested and goal-oriented action, where a rational actor will seek to maximize his interests within the constraints set by the interests of other agents; and third, that under normal circumstances the agent will find it most conducive to his interests, and thus most rational, to pursue them by means of the power which he possesses, whatever form this power may take.

These assumptions about rationality, constraint, action, and explanation are kept deliberately weak. The virtue of the approach lies in the way it allows these issues to be resolved in the course of empirical investigation. For example, no claims are made about what beliefs or

[11] See e.g. M. Olsen, *The Logic of Collective Action* (Cambridge, Mass., 1971); A. Downs, *An Economic Theory of Democracy* (New York, 1957); O. Williamson, *The Economic Institutions of Capitalism* (New York, 1985).

actions are rational in specific circumstances; neither are there in-built assumptions about the type of power available to actors, or their relative strengths. What is suggested, quite reasonably, is that the power exercised by individuals is often linked to their control over resources and other actors, and that these are often located in social institutions. For this reason, the definition of goals and interests by an individual is likely to be connected to the possibilities and methods available for achieving them.

The methodological criteria presented above help provide an answer to the question of how political decisions are to be distinguished from economic ones, or, more importantly, how political actors are to be distinguished from economic ones. The answer now appears deceptively simple: political actors are those whose interests are realized through the exercise of political power. The character of a political system will thus be given by identifying the strength of political actors and the range of matters over which political power is exercised, together with the interrelations and constraints placed upon these actors by those who exercise non-political power. If it is said that the power of the industrial ministries is thus at the heart of how the Soviet political system is to be characterized, then the question is: how able were the ministries to intervene in political processes and decisions?

The meaning of political power, of course, remains to be given. In general terms, power may be defined as the ability to affect resources and other actors. To have *direct* power over someone or something means to have that ability without recourse to being granted leave by other actors to use it as one chooses. In short, it is mine; I do not require the assent of other people in order to act with it in my interests. Clearly, in most cases of human action the range of resources under the direct control of a single actor is limited. Social relations are characterized by trade and bargaining, in which the items of trade are those resources under the direct control of a particular person, and the issue of power arises from their use to secure the compliance or participation of others. Understanding political power means investigating the resources the politician may use directly without requiring the assent of others; the politician is empowered, in other words, to act directly upon those resources and areas which are his.

What the politician has direct power over, therefore, are those things that he has managed to designate as being within his personal sphere of decision-making; and, in practice, this means that politicians have direct power over law-making and the state. The nub of the politician's problem, however, lies in getting other actors to accept the power of the politician to allocate the resources under their direct control and regulate their behaviour. How does the politician carve out a space in which to run his 'law-making business'?

The answer to this question has generally been given in moral or coercive terms; either the politician rules through legitimacy, or through the ability to use those resources which are directly at his disposal, especially force, to secure social compliance. Either way, political power may be treated empirically by the following suggestion; if politicians are defined by their interest in compelling assent from others through their direct control of the state, where politicians are able to get what they want they have *de facto* authority. Politicians are weak, on the other hand, where, because of a *de facto* authority failure, which may result either from a legitimacy crisis or the absence of marketable political goods—or commonly both, they are unable to allocate resources under the direct control of others or regulate their behaviour.

The key term here is authority which is the peculiar resource at the disposal of the politician and which, on my reading, may include either or both coercive and legitimizing components. The central point, however, is that authority allows the politician to intervene in the processes by which other actors directly dispose of resources which are theirs. As such, it is a testable and, indeed, in some sense quantifiable resource. To repeat, politicians are those actors who exercise direct power over the state through the law-making and coercive bodies. But the power of the state *vis-à-vis* other actors is best understood as an authority relationship in which the politician may succeed, by a variety of methods, in inducing other actors to accept his claims on their resources and behaviour.

Conversely, where an actor exercises direct power over physical resources, unmediated by authority relations, he should be considered an economic actor and not a politician. Again, in respect of the state, the politician acts directly; but the power of the state extends, via the authority claim, over resources which are in the immediate control of economic actors. Finally, where actors depend on the resources under their control, they are interested in maximizing that control and in expanding their capital; where politicians are primarily dependent on the political to realize their interests, they will seek to maximize the stock of political capital, by expanding the sphere, the range, and the efficacy of their authority.

Understanding the bargaining relations between politicians and other actors is improved by a comparative perspective. An analysis of capitalist democracy is, obviously, beyond the boundaries of this book, but a number of aspects of the complex bargaining relations which occur within it are of significance.

First, though politicians across systems are defined by the powers and interests outlined above, their market position—their ability to trade in resources under their direct control and to build their authority over resources at the direct control of others—in capitalist democracies exhibits particular constraints and possibilities. On the one hand, the range of issues within their authority or jurisdiction is generally limited by private property, rights, and the discipline of democratic competition. The last, for example, may constrain how a politician trades political goods for other resources. On the other hand, the public space created by open democratic competition allows the politician to gather support for his policies which, when then enacted in the characteristic form of law, carry more authority in virtue both of the added legitimacy attached to them and the underlying threat of social power which the publicity involved in aggregating interests makes clear. In other words, the politician may be constrained by the forced and clear delimitation of political and economic spheres in capitalist democratic systems, but he is also able to use it to gather support, attack enemies, and thus build authority.

Secondly, the resources of the politician—both physical and legal—in capitalist democracies are constrained by the power and interests of the other actors. Crudely put, no growth, no taxes, no re-election. What unifies much of the post-Marxist, post-functionalist, and post-pluralist analyses of capitalist democracies is precisely this recognition of the privileges which accrue to economic agents in this system. Perhaps the best example of such work is Charles Lindblom's classic attempt to model relations among politicians and various market actors, in which the relative powers of each are characterized and interrelated.[12] Dominant power, in other words, resides in the economy and with those actors who exercise direct control over its important economic resources, that is, capital. Capital's ability to determine the economic environment delimits the possibilities of state action and disposes the state to favour it in order to improve the position of the

[12] C. E. Lindblom, *Politics and Markets* (New York, 1977); for other examples of this kind of literature see A. Przeworski, *Capitalism and Social Democracy* (London, 1985).

mass of voters who are dependent on it for increased living standards. This is not at all to suggest that the interests of capital, state, and voters are identical, or that its dominance reduces other actors to mere obedience. Rather, a complex bargaining game occurs in which the interests of capital predominate, though they can be overruled.

At first sight, it is not clear how a model of bargaining based upon the market power of capital, the limitation of rights, and the possibilities of authority-building via the electoral process can be adapted to the strategic environment of a Soviet-type socialism where each of these is absent. Furthermore, it seems unlikely that the absence of these factors might have the effect of weakening politicians in comparison with their Western counterparts.

Where there is a separation between politics and economics, the account given of the power of politicians may be accurate. But, as Nove and Brus have pointed out, such a separation is precisely what is absent in the Soviet system. The reason that politicians are difficult to isolate and identify in the Soviet system is because they abolished the direct power of others over resources and subsumed all of it in the Communist Party and its *nomenklatura* state under their immediate control. Thus the Soviet system appears to give the politicians overarching and unconstrained power to the point where it seems barely sensible to talk about politics at all because the need for authority relations was abolished. Any difficulties that arise in comparing the power of politicians and bureaucrats with that of their counterparts in other systems may be explained by the fact that their power is based in large measure not on authority, and certainly not on legitimacy derived from the competition for social support, but on direct power over resources and people.

The fact that this interpretation contains some truth does not prevent it leading to important errors in explaining the character of Soviet politics. The problem is that the need for authority, and therefore for politics, is not abolished with markets, rights, and elections. This becomes evident as soon as the description of the system moves beyond the primordial to include its highly variegated institutional elements. At that point, the familiar spheres of politics, authority, legitimacy, economic power, and social support are put back into the centre of political explanation.

The need of some actors in the Soviet system for politics and authority arises from the bare fact that they cannot achieve direct control. The very effort to exercise control, in other words, necessitates politics. The problem facing any actor seeking to operate in a large complex society is that the co-ordination problem of direct control is immense. No single actor is capable both of assuming direct control and of regulating at a strategic level; and it is in the the trade-off between direct control and strategic choice that the need for politics arises. The problem of politics, therefore, is not just that strategic or macro-level decisions must be taken. The price of meat or steel, after all, is resolved in market societies without there necessarily being a sense that the methods to be used in deciding it are political. Problems arise when the actors who are charged with taking these decisions depend for the efficacy of their strategic decisions on the authoritativeness of their judgements. Where no single actor can manage the co-ordination problem of direct control over resources, there exists a tendency for those in strategic decision-making positions to seek to regulate by means of authority rather than direct power. The fact, therefore, that in the Soviet Union the politician cannot easily be separated from some other actor may not constitute the end of the matter; rather, it may simply suggest that political authority and bureaucratic authority are very strong or very weak—though it will be proposed here that it was the latter that was the case.

From this it follows that there were politicians seeking to maximize their interests through the exercise of authority either by legitimating their claims to take decisions or by trading political goods for co-operation from other actors. As a corollary of this, Soviet politicians also had to enter into bargaining relations with non-political actors who were themselves seeking to use their direct powers to secure political support or to marginalize politicians. A detailed exposition of the division of labour between strategic decision-makers who relied on authority and those who exercised direct control over resources will be given later in the book. At this point it is worth noting in general terms who the various actors were, and why it is difficult to separate one from the other.

The strategic role, reliant on the exercise of authority and political resources, was primarily located in the leading committees of the Communist Party and the highest bodies of the state apparatus—the Politburo, the Secretariat, the Presidium of the Council of Ministers, the higher echelons of the planning agencies, the coercive agencies, and the cultural institutions. This is not to suggest that these bodies exercised only authoritative functions. As is well known, the abolition of private capital allowed politicians to intervene directly in economic processes. However, as will be shown in the final section of this chapter, Soviet history demonstrates that the politician faced serious costs and resulting pressures when he chose to abandon regulation via authority in favour of direct control. Where he chose to intervene directly he sacrificed strategic interests and became, in a sense, the spokesman of the resources he administered. Where he chose to regulate authoritatively, he faced the problem of controlling subordinates. The pressures on politicians to move in both directions is observable throughout Soviet history, and the interplay of these pressures and the implications that authoritative versus direct power have for the political system since 1965 will be the main focus of this book. But the theoretical question to be addressed at the moment is why Soviet politicians should have faced an authority problem when they chose to regulate to any greater extent than, or in a different way from, their counterparts in capitalist democracies.

The Soviet political system exhibited three distinct and interlocking features, all of which affected the extent of authority of the political actors. First, the abolition of private capital, which allowed the politician to intervene directly in the economic process, actually weakened his authority and control rather than strengthened it. Second, the legitimation strategy designed to authorize the politician's powers to control and lead actually worked to disempower him. And, third, the nature of leadership selection and competition, from which the public was excluded, removed the space in which the politician could mobilize support and build authority. The paradox of the bargaining game of Soviet politics, therefore, is that it worked in quite the opposite way to the common-sense approach; far from being a game in which politicians could increase their power, it was one in which they were structurally inclined to lose it.

To explain why, it is necessary to bring in the third comparative element mentioned above—the institutional explanation. The central reason for doing this is that, where the politicians seek to exercise the maximum degree of immediate control over resources, the organs of control need to be institutionalized. The level of institutionalization may vary depending on the concrete circumstances but there are strong tendencies for at least functional specialization, and it is here that industrial ministries enter the stage. The ministries appear as nominally political bodies, operating as the instruments of the political leadership, on the basis of bureaucratic power, and comprising the centre-piece of state authority in the economy.

Appearances can be deceptive, however. The primary reason for this lies in the abolition of the private sphere of economic activity and its importation into the state itself. Ministries were the bearers of direct operational control over physical resources, and their dual position as members of the state and its institutions as well as the main direct economic actors radically transformed the game of politics. This is not to suggest, any more than was suggested of the power of capital, that the economic powers of the ministries were not susceptible to influence from the cards still remaining to other players. Clearly, the politicians had a considerable amount to play with, including their monopoly on legitimate violence and its institutions, as well as their ability to exercise power over other organizations which had few resources of their own to dispose of. However, it should be noted immediately that the position of ministries as nominal political players removed the monopoly of state power from the hands of the strategic actors; ministries also issued binding norms and decrees. In this sense, the politicians had already surrendered a bargaining chip. This indiscretion, however, was not the most important in the transformation in the nature of the game which resulted from the entry of politics into direct control of economic resources—or the introduction of direct control over physical resources into politics.

Power over the physical allocation and use of resources conferred on its possessor the ability to use such goods to influence those people who were nominally regulating them; in other words, not only did the ministries act as political players inside the state, but they also used the resources they controlled to affect the decisions of politicians. As institutions, therefore, not only did ministries pose difficulties for regulators, sit on the same political bodies as their supposed superiors, and exercise political power in association with their regulators, but they were actually given sufficient direct economic power over resources to be able to pay off the referee. Ministries were made strong enough by the politicians' initial strategy to be in a position to regulate the regulators! Communist politics thus appears as a self-defeating game in which the initial power which the politician achieved by abolishing the constraints imposed by capital, rights, and democracy was traded in for the recomposition of economic forces within the state in a form close enough to debilitate him.

Related institutional causes of political weakness were also in operation. First, the legitimation and authority strategy played by the politician was destined for defeat. This may appear strange at first sight in a system in which, until 1990, the major legitimizing principle for the rule of politicians was the 'leading role of the Communist Party' which, 'guided by the scientific world-view of Marxism-Leninism', acted as the 'vanguard in the development of Soviet society towards communism'. Again, the appearance of empowerment is deceiving. The leading role of the party required institutionalizing, and the main beneficiaries of this were once again the organizations which held direct control of physical resources. The terms in which interference in the economy by the party were couched,—planning, the abolition of markets, all-round economic and social development, equality and justice of distribution, etc.—and the organizations which were charged with institutionalizing these claims—Gosplan, the industrial ministries, the wage-regulating committees—effectively legitimized the activities of institutional actors whose powers and interests were often distinct from those of politicians. Michael Urban has rightly pointed out, in this regard, that there has been a pronounced dualism of perspective on the issue of power in Soviet politics; on the one hand, the Leviathan state, on the other the evidence of autonomy.[13]

The final aspect in the peculiar bargaining game of Soviet politics which reduced the power of politicians was the narrowness of the political sphere. In the discussion of capitalist democracy above, it was noted that democracy and open leadership competition provide the politician with possibilities as well as constraints. The politician is able, in the public space of democracy, to mobilize public opinion, publicize issues, aggregate interests, and achieve a mandate to run the state. Those who may be adversely affected by his decisions when in office are thereby weakened in their opposition not only by the level of legitimacy which the elected leader attains, but by the knowledge of the level of public support in the politician's favour.[14] The narrowness of the sphere of politics in the Soviet system, however, worked against the politician, not only for reasons implicit in the first two factors limiting his power, but also in virtue of the fact that ministers formed a central part of the leadership selectorate. The problem with authority and legitimation in the Soviet system, as Rigby has noted,[15] was that

[13] Urban, 'Concepualising Political Power,' 207–26.

[14] It is this, rather than the uncertainty of future outcomes, which must account for the need of players to carry on with the democratic game. In this sense, I disagree with the claim in A. Przeworski, *Democracy and the Market* (Cambridge, 1991).

[15] See T. H. Rigby, 'A Conceptual Approach to Authority, Power and Policy in the Soviet Union', in T. H. Rigby, A. H. Brown, and P. Reddaway (eds.), *Authority, Power and Policy in the USSR* (London, 1980), 9–31.

the leaders competing to secure it did so in a very narrow circle of participants. In addition to the restricted space for mobilization, the main interests to be aggregated by politicians seeking high office were the very ones which were most responsible for restricting the power of the politicians in the first place—the powerful economic actors, especially ministries. Furthermore, the organization of social groups and interests beyond the narrow confines of the selectorate had been entrusted to the very same institutions which exercised economic power, so that, even where the politician may have desired to find support and authority outside the inner circle, the groups and interests to which he might have appealed had been effectively organized out of politics before he could reach them.

The way is now open for advancing a number of hypotheses and arguments about the role of Soviet industrial ministries as political institutions, about the power of other actors, and about the political system as a whole.

1. Industrial ministries were the dominant players in the game of Soviet politics. Ministerial dominance—or rather the dominance of those actors who controlled the ministerial apparatus—was achieved on the basis of their broad powers in a range of areas: in decision-making within their own organizations; in the information, much of the codification, and implementation stages of the policy process; in the operational management of economic resources; through their participation in the political process, or, more accurately, through their membership in nominally political bodies where they were well placed to stifle genuine political activity; and in their relation to social interests and activities. Ministerial dominance lay in their success in realizing their interests—in high budgetary allocations spent according to the priorities of the institution; in the professional and personal development, and the security of the individuals in the apparatus; and in their prolonged success in defeating attempts by non-ministerial actors to alter the balance of power away from them. Because of their dominance, the position of ministries explains much of the interests, powers, and behaviour of the other actors in the political system. In this sense, the industrial ministries can be called the hegemonic actors in Soviet politics.

2. Politicians and bureaucrats, in the sense defined above, were weak and operated in a narrow and constrained sphere. Authoritative decisions based on law were unlikely to take effect unless they were also supported by ministry interests. In reality, the scope of bureaucratic

action was even more limited; the word 'bureaucracy' as a description of Soviet administrative behaviour is a misnomer: most of the so-called bureaucrats were actually primarily economic actors, working in ministries and operating on the basis of direct power rather than authority.[16] Even if Gosplan and the Presidium of the Council of Ministers are included in the list of bureaucratic organizations, their powers *vis-à-vis* the ministries were not sufficient to control them. To call the Soviet state powerful is a misconception for similar reasons, though not for the reason usually cited, that the Communist Party continuously interfered in its operation.[17] Indeed, the suggestion will be defended that the Communist Party itself was weak, and that political control at all levels was ineffective. The General Secretary, for example, could not rely on the branch departments of the Central Committee apparatus to act as authoritative instruments because of their captive relationship to the ministerial apparatus. The *nomenkla-tura* system of appointments worked ineffectively, at best, in the ministerial hierarchy, and political attitudes and behaviour were insignificant aspects of promotion decision-making. At the regional level, not only did ministry interests predominate, but regional secretaries were forced to act in concert with ministries in order to achieve their own interests and objectives.

This is not at all to suggest that political and economic interests confronted one another as homogeneous and opposed blocks, or that politicians were without power and resources. There was clearly a high degree of symbiosis between party and ministerial power, though my argument is that this symbiosis resulted from the dependence of the former, notably but not exclusively at the regional level, on the control exercised by ministries over resources. There was also, as Peter Rutland has argued, 'fierce competition among ministries and within individual ministries, between different layers in the administrative structure'.[18] Such competition certainly offered the politicians some opportunity to use their power over discretionary allocation to increase

---

[16] This point supports conclusions drawn by both Jan Pakulski and Paul Gregory, though for different reasons. See J. Pakulski, 'Legitimacy and Mass Compliance: Reflections on Max Weber and Soviet-Type Society', in *British Journal of Political Science*, 16 (1986), 35–56; and P. Gregory, 'Soviet Bureaucratic Behaviour: Khozyaistvenniki and Apparatchiki', in *Soviet Studies*, 4 (1989) 511–25.

[17] See R. Hill, 'Party–State Relations and Soviet Political Development', in *British Journal of Political Science*, 10 (1980), 149–65.

[18] Rutland, *The Politics of Economic Stagnation*, 27.

their control—though, as will be argued in Chapters 1 and 3, political discretion and ministerial competition were probably less prevalent than Rutland suggests. The amount of discretion available to the politicians was itself a function of prior decisions about resource allocation taken by the ministries. Politicians were clearly more powerful in some areas, such as control over culture, the press, and foreign policy, which were not organizationally linked to industry, or where they concentrated on a particular project—though the risk of concentration in one area was of loss of control in another. It is evident from the bare fact that anti-ministerialism occurred regularly in Soviet history that politicians sometimes had at their disposal the means to attack them, including the threat of dismissal—or worse—and the carrot of appointment. What is being argued, however, is that taking *all* these caveats into account, despite their undoubted weapons the politicians had no effective way to use them.

3. Social actors barely entered the political system, not only because the sphere of public debate and legitimization of political activity excluded them, but more pertinently because the politicians had little to offer them. To get what they wanted, social actors operated most rationally within the rules of the ministerial apparatus; social distribution and policy was largely occupationally determined and ministerially controlled. The social structure produced by ministerial distribution, however, involved further atomization and social disorganization. This in turn provided a buffer for ministerial interests in the event of attacks upon them from either political or social actors; the former could not reach the latter, while society, though deeply unimpressed by both its politicians and ministries, could not organize itself. At a more general level, therefore, we can conclude that ministerial power was the main source of stability in Soviet politics, in so far as it enabled society to be incorporated and delivered to the political system. It should be noted, however, that one of the important conclusions suggested by the approach outlined above is that social stability did not arise on the basis of any of the usual explanations. It was not based on force, a relationship between official and mass culture, a social contract, the success of the socialization programme, or a normative commitment to the legitimacy of the ideology; rather, it was organized by the manner in which ministerial power structured social interests, power, and rationality.

On the other hand, ministerial power was also the greatest source of instability in Soviet politics, because of the conflict it generated with the weak and constrained politicians. It is worth pointing out immediately that the characterization of powers, interests, and bargaining relationships given above should not be considered static; the game was one of ongoing crisis in which actors sought and needed to expand their resources and frequently were able to do so. When I say that ministries were dominant, it does not mean that other actors were powerless or accepting of their power, only that anti-ministerialism risked costs even to those who were most interested in opposing them, which made it a highly dangerous and potentially self-defeating strategy. Confronted with the dominance of economic power in the heart of the state, politicians faced a number of alternative courses of action. Doing nothing, acquiescing, was clearly one of them, and was often the preferred option. But the incipient contradiction between political and economic power and actors militated against this and in favour of one of the other alternatives.

Three possibilities were open to the politicians, each of which presented enormous costs and risks: first, they could deal with the constraints created by the institutions that had earlier been established by abolishing them and assuming direct economic control themselves; second, they could attempt to increase their regulatory powers—in other words, to treat the problem as soluble within the 'principal–agent' game; or, failing either of these, they could abandon the whole political strategy, and seek out new forms of legitimization and new institutions. The argument of this book will be that none of these alternatives afforded politicians a winning option, though an assessment and explanation of the failure of the final alternative will wait until the chapters on *perestroyka*. The other two alternatives, however, were tried at numerous times before 1985, and it is instructive to see how a theory which asserts the primacy of institutional conflict, especially between politicians and economic actors, in explaining both stability and instability in Soviet politics can fit the historical background.

The chapters which follow will deal in detail with the various aspects of ministry power and the evidence of how this power affected the interests and powers of other actors. Chapter 1 will examine ministry power in the economy, the basis of their bargaining relations with other actors, and the manner in which ministries sought to use economic power in their own interests. Chapter 2 will examine the prerequisite for ministry power, i.e. the ability of top ministry officials to control their own administrative environment in their own interests by examining the experience of the structural and personnel reform of the ministry apparatus from 1965 until 1985. Chapter 3 will investigate how ministry power operated in the political system by looking at relations between ministries and other nominally superior institutions. Chapter 4 will deal with the relationship of ministries to Soviet society, where the task of social regulation was accomplished. Chapters 5 and 6 will examine the rise of a radical anti-ministerial agenda under Gorbachev. Ministerial power will be shown to have been both one of the main motivations for *perestroyka* and one of the main reasons for its failure. The concluding chapter will examine new developments in the relationships between politics and industrial power in the post-Soviet period.

In the next section, however, an attempt is made to apply the model developed above to the realities of industrial and institutional developments in Soviet history before their reform in 1965.

INDUSTRIAL MINISTRIES IN SOVIET HISTORY[19]

Institutions assume a life of their own once established. Industrial ministries were established by politicians as agencies to act as their instruments; very quickly, however, the ministries acquired powers which made them potent actors in their own right. It is important to place the interaction between politicians and their economic agencies in the context of Soviet history. This is so because the conflict, first among politicians over the appropriate way to institutionalize economic activity, and then among the various agencies and politicians, is central to Soviet politics from 1917 onwards. Secondly, it is because the re-establishment of the ministries in 1965 with which we are principally concerned was not a start *de novo*, but built upon the powers and structures of the pre-1957 ministries, many of which had effectively continued to exist even under Khrushchev's system of regional economic councils.

In most historical circumstances politicians are in no position to reconstruct radically the institutional environment they inherit, or even to form governments based on new constituencies. As was suggested above, although it is within the formal power of politicians acting through the state to alter radically the existing system (the British

[19] Because the historical period to be discussed in this section lies outside the primary focus of the book, much of the support offered is derived from secondary sources.

Parliament could, if it so chose, pass legislation abolishing private capital), they are inhibited, among many other reasons, by their belief that such action would be politically unsuccessful, namely, that there exists no constituency for it, or that they know of no way of institutionalizing their power.

Revolutionary situations, however, occur when a (normally new) political leadership is both willing and able to alter radically institutions and replace them with new ones which they believe will either satisfy or build up a solid core constituency. This was the circumstance in which the Bolsheviks assumed (or seized) power in 1917.[20] The new leadership committed itself to pursuing a 'socialist' political strategy which, it believed, would enable it to solve the difficulties of staying in power in Russia. In particular, 'socialism' was a strategy which it hoped would safeguard Russian independence (and its empire), while modernizing, industrializing, improving living standards, and ensuring a measure of social justice which would attract support among the population. Indeed, these ends were meant to be mutually reinforcing.

However, as is often said, 'there was no blueprint for socialism'. From the start, the leadership was internally divided as to the most effective means of institutionalizing the regime, and about which social groups were to be its central elements. These disagreements themselves had an institutional bias, as trade unionists were far more likely to envisage the centrality of their own organizations in the political and economic structure of the new socialist state, while officials in the Supreme Council of the National Economy (VSNKh) were inclined to support a more ministerial alternative.[21]

The emergence of a fully fledged 'ministerial socialism', however, in which there was a predominance of politicians who saw the industrial ministries as the best way of institutionalizing their political strategy, and in which the ministries themselves occupied the foremost institutional position, took many years of Soviet history and even then remained the subject of ongoing political struggle. In prototype, ministerial socialism can be seen in the *glavki* (chief administrations) of VSNKh during the Civil War,[22] though War Communism, as this period is often called, can hardly be considered a regime in any stable

---

[20] Even then, however, the Bolsheviks were forced to rely on the old structures of state and its personnel. Cf. T. H. Rigby, *Lenin's Government* (London, 1979).

[21] See F. I. Kaplan, *Bolshevik Ideology and the Ethics of Soviet Labour* (London, 1969).

[22] S. Malle, *The Economic Organisation of War Communism* (Cambridge, 1985), 202–92.

sense, given the plethora of competing institutions and the general emergency atmosphere. As a more or less stable formation, ministerial socialism did not finally emerge until 1938.

There were as many socialisms in 1917 as there were leaders, strategies, institutions, and constituencies. The point was, however, that the initial emergence of the new regime occurred in conditions where politicians were undoubtedly the most powerful and dominant actors. The task here is to explain why, to those politicians, ministries should have been a credible way of institutionalizing a socialist regime, and why, despite this credibility, there should have continued to be opposition to them.

First, ministries appeared to satisfy the economic demands of the socialist form of industrial society by abolishing the imputed harmful effects of anarchic, market relations and substituting planned, non-commodity production. By being large and potentially all-Union organizations, the ministries were supposedly also able to realize socialism's presumed advantage in achieving beneficial economies of scale. Resources could be distributed on a rational basis and concentrated on the main priorities of the country's economic development; the ministries could act as the foundation for the discovery and dissemination of the latest technical advancements which could be introduced evenly throughout whole branches of industry under their control.[23]

Secondly, the ministry was a credible means for the realization of a socialist social policy, in both a broad and narrow sense. As distinct from direct workers' control, for example, the ministries seemed able to realize the pre-NEP (New Economic Policy) Bukharin's demand for 'administration of the enterprise that would accustom the workers to the viewpoint that each factory is the property not of the workers of that factory but of all the working people'.[24] In this sense, they were supposed to lead to the formation of integrated, solidaristic social relations, rather than ones where interests were defined by individual work collectives. More narrowly, the ability of ministries to centralize control of resources seemed to substantiate the leadership's claim to operate policies of all-round economic development among various regions and nationalities, and to support equalization of unfair economic advantages or disadvantages by the redistribution of enterprise funds.

[23] G. Kh. Popov, *Effektivnoe upravlenie* (Moscow, 1985), 161.
[24] Kaplan, *Bolshevik Ideology*, 212.

Thirdly, although the political persuasion of the personnel of ministries remained, in various ways, problematical throughout the Soviet period, the ministries were presumed to be appropriate instruments of the peculiarly partisan state created by the socialist political leadership. Through the effective functioning of the *nomenklatura* system of appointments, whereby ministry appointments were subject to the approval of a party committee, the loyalty of the Soviet state to the politician was theoretically greater than that of the quasi-independent bureaucracy of the capitalist state. The result ought to have been a set of effective, just, and loyal economic policy institutions.

However, the success of the ministries lay not only in advancing credible claims to be socialist institutions, but in transforming these claims into real power against rival claims to institutionalize the socialist strategy, and this power was contingent on a number of other factors in Soviet history. Most importantly, ministries or their predecessors already had power and were able to use it to defend their position even when the regime underwent its periodic transformations. Conversely, the ministries were able to use the subsequent institutional dependence on them of the leadership's strategy as a means of advancing their own organizational powers further. Because of their existing control over economic resources, they were well placed to succeed in this struggle against their institutional rivals. Secondly, as is evidenced in the improved rate of growth in the second plan, the ministries could plausibly be held to perform better than alternative means in the economy.

There were three important stages after 1921 in the transition to a fully fledged ministerial regime. First, the New Economic Policy represented a departure from the excesses of 'glavkism' which had been associated with War Communism.[25] As a regime, NEP was distinguished by the standing of Bukharin (though leadership instability was also characteristic of the period); the dominance of financial, indicative planning and market-based institutions, like trusts and later syndicates, and the presence of large numbers of highly skilled 'bourgeois' experts, often supporters of the old Mensheviks, in key positions relating to economic policy; and a concern for the peasantry as a core element in the regime's constituency. At the same time, however, much of the control of industry remained in the hands of the state, and institutions like VSNKh exerted a growing influence

[25] See M. I. Piskotin, *Sotsializm i gosudarstvennoe upravlenie* (Moscow, 1984) 58–84.

throughout the period. The question of the superiority or otherwise of NEP as a purely economic policy,[26] therefore, is moot to the issue of its instability as a regime *in toto*. Indeed, one of the reasons for the failure of NEP in regime terms, quite apart from its economic performance, which may well have been better than any alternative strategy, was that its supporters continued to rely on state institutions such as VSNKh to resolve crises in policy, such as the scissors crisis of 1923.[27] Competing politicians were thus afforded the opportunity at a later stage to advance these institutions as credible economic alternatives once NEP ran into difficulties; and the institutions provided a home for officials who themselves had an interest in increasing their operational control once the opportunity was offered. In short, in strategic, institutional, and constituency terms, the New Economic Policy was not sustainable.

The second stage in the transition to a ministerialized economy and polity came with the first five-year plan from 1929–1932, though this was dominated not by ministry officials and by ministry power, but rather by party leaders, especially Stalin, who operated through institutions like Rabkrin (the Workers' and Peasants' Inspectorate) and the NKVD (the People's Commissariat for Internal Affairs). The manner in which the complex structure of the game favoured economic officials over the politicians becomes evident here; what was in the first shot a winning blow for the politician, when played iteratively led to decreasing and finally negative marginal gains. The growth strategy of the first five-year plan was far more openly political in focus, relying heavily on a high level of exhortation, 'creativity', and uncovering of 'saboteurs'.[28] None the less, even then the political leadership and its strategy were highly dependent on the existence of bureaucratic economic management institutions, such as VSNKh, and frictions between the more directly political approach[29] and a more cautious, centralized one were evident very quickly.[30] The first plan, utilizing

[26] See R. Tucker, 'Stalinism as Revolution From Above', in id. (ed.), *Stalinism: Essays in Historical Interpretation* (New York, 1977), 88.

[27] E. H. Carr and R. W. Davies, *Foundations of a Planned Economy* (London, 1969), 351–84.

[28] See M. Lewin, *Political Undercurrents in Soviet Economic Debates* (London, 1975), 97–126.

[29] For an account of early Stalinism in the factory see H. Kuramiya, 'Edinonachalie and the Soviet Industrial Manager, 1928–37', in *Soviet Studies*, 36 (1984), 185–204.

[30] See S. Fitzpatrick, 'Ordzhonikidze's Takeover of Vesenkha: A Case Study in Soviet Bureaucratic Politics', in *Soviet Studies*, 37 (1985), 153–72.

overtly political motivation, failed to justify in performance its promise of high growth through enthusiasm.[31] The existence of ministerial-type institutions then became crucial, both in terms of their promise to deliver more rational and disciplined organization of growth, and in the importance their leaders had in the regime. Molotov, Ordzhonikidze, and Kuybishev, once Stalinist anti-bureaucrats, were by 1932 in charge of Sovnarkom (the Council of People's Commissars), VSNKh, and Gosplan respectively. It was in 1932 that the inexorable growth in the numbers of ministerial bodies began, with the division of VSNKh into three separate industrial commissariats, for heavy, light, and timber industries. The increased political importance of the commissariats, and the bureaucratization of the Communist Party, were quite evident at the XVIIth Congress in 1934, at which Stalin's position was noticeably weaker.[32]

The final stage in the transition to a ministerial regime occurred between 1934 and 1938, in the arcane and bloody internal battles which culminated in the Great Purges of 1937 and 1938.. At that point it was evident that efforts to challenge the ministerial way of doing things had costs which threatened the interests of all political participants.[33] At the same time, no actor was able (or willing) to advance a credible anti-ministerial means of institutionalizing the socialist economy. Rittersporn has commented on the enormous change that emerged in the status and style of ministers at that time.

In 1934, a People's Commissar could be censured for his 'professorial' manners. Five year later, it was not their allegedly 'proletarian' work-style but their diplomas for which the officials received loud praise. The way was free for the introduction of grades, insignia, and even uniforms for different categories of officials which began in 1938 and attained its apogee after the war when it was proposed that university graduates wear a specific badge.[34]

By 1939 there were twenty industrial commissariats, and a huge expansion occurred in the immediate post-war period, when the power of ministries also increased. Such, indeed, was the power of the ministries, even in the period of so-called 'high Stalinism', that Stalin's decisions were only implemented when they were also in the ministries'

[31] H. Hunter, 'The Over-Ambitious Soviet First Five-Year Plan', in *Slavic Review*, 2 (1973), 237–57.
[32] W. J. Conyngham, *Industrial Management in the Soviet Union* (Stanford, Calif., 1973), 40–2; Dunmore, *The Stalinist Command Economy*, 147.
[33] G. Rittersporn, 'Stalin in 1938: Political Defeat Behind the Rhetorical Apotheosis', in *Telos*, 46 (1980–1), 6–42.   [34] Ibid. 21.

interests. As Dunmore has argued of the late Stalin period, 'to ensure the implementation of an economic policy the Politburo had either to make sure that it accorded with the majority of ministerial interests or change those interests by restructuring the ministries'.[35]

However, as generations of Soviet politicians before and after were to discover, controlling the ministries by restructuring was to prove a far more formidable task than they initially expected. Or as Khrushchev put it:

The main force was administrative action, from one centre, all over the country. It was really incredible. A minister used to be higher than God ... The Party, the trade unions, and the members of the Young Communist League were only like auxiliaries.[36]

This last point is central to understanding the failures of Khrushchev's dramatic experiment in anti-ministerialism via the regional economic councils (*sovnarkhozy*) between 1957 and 1965. At the same time, however, Khrushchev's decision to abolish the ministries is an indication of the deep problems of ministerial socialism as a stable regime form. This raises the fundamental question: why should politicians in the Soviet Union be anti-ministerial?

I have already used the term regime in a loose way above. In general terms, if a political regime is identified as consisting of a political leadership, pursuing a strategy, through institutions, and directed at a constituency, then it can become unbalanced by a number of internal contradictions among its component elements. Leaders compete and can change, or they can revise their strategy and/or the best means to institutionalize it, especially when the strategy or institutions fail to deliver economic performance to important constituencies. The constraining power of central economic institutions, or their capture of figures who are supposedly loyal to the politicians, can give an incentive to rivals to make radical institutional changes. Finally, constituencies themselves can change over time, either in respect of their size or relative clout, or internally as regards the salience of certain desired goals.

Khrushchev's *sovnarkhoz* reforms, in which most industrial ministries were formally abolished and regional economic councils created, occurred as a result of only a few of these factors, and this narrow

[35] Dunmore, *The Stalinist Command Economy*, 147.
[36] Interviewed in *The Times* (1 Feb. 1958), 5. My thanks to Bill Tompson for bringing this to my attention.

basis for radical change was the main reason for its failure to stabilize. The reforms were directed on three fronts. First, they sought to avoid the economic irrationalities of the branch ministerial system by devolving economic decision-making down to territorial units where, it was hoped, local initiative and knowledge would improve performance.[37] Second, Khrushchev hoped to deal with the deficiencies of leadership control over ministries and the economy—which were already evident during the Stalin period—by increasing political control through the expanded representation of Gosplan on the Council of Ministers,[38] and by increasing the power of party–state control agencies.[39] Khrushchev himself became chairman of the Council of Ministers.[40] Finally, of course, Khrushchev pursued anti-ministerialism as a means of removing the power base of his rivals in the so-called 'anti-party group'.

Khrushchev's *sovnarkhozy* reforms demonstrated an awareness of deep-seated problems in the economy and were significant in their recognition of the need for institutional change to curb the weakness of the state and politicians *vis-à-vis* the ministries. As was the case under Stalinism, however, despite their anti-ministerial appearance the Khrushchev approach to economic reform did not go so far as to represent a radical break with the old regime. First, institutional change did not imply strategic change. The socialist strategy which the ministries had plausibly encapsulated remained. One commentator has suggested that Khrushchev's intention in creating the *sovnarkhozy* may have been to preserve the strategy by avoiding genuinely radical reform.[41] However, given the strongly anti-ministerial tenor of his programme, this cynical view misses the mark. Yet, giving powers to regional bodies to operate and to fulfil functions similar to those of ministries was not likely to overcome the deficiencies of state and political control over economic power, despite the increase in Gosplan representation. Secondly, the reforms took place without being based

[37] A. Vedishchev, 'The Territorial System of Economic Organisation', in H. G. Shaffer (ed.), *The Soviet Economy* (London, 1964), 193–200.

[38] O. Hoeffding, 'The Soviet Industrial Reorganisation of 1957', in F. O. Holzman (ed.), *Readings on the Soviet Economy* (Chicago, 1962), 475–87.

[39] G. Hodnett, 'Khrushchev and Party–State Control', in A. Dallin and A. F. Westin (eds.), *Politics in the Soviet Union* (New York, 1966), 113–64.

[40] G. Van den Berg has gone as far as to say that the Council of Ministers under Khrushchev 'became in practice the highest political body, and the meeting of the Politburo became a formality'. See 'The Council of Ministers of the Soviet Union', in *Review of Socialist Law*, 6 (1980), 301.

[41] A. Katz, *The Politics of Economic Reform in the Soviet Union* (New York, 1972), 63.

on any significant broadening in the leadership's constituency. As Gavril Popov has argued, even among ministry officials who might have been most affected, the reforms were not seen as especially damaging.[42] Third, the reform did not abolish the branch principle, but rather retained it in conjunction with other overlapping economic authorities. In many cases, the personnel of the old ministries went to work in an expanded Gosplan, and a further degree of organizational continuity was achieved by the concentration of the old technical personnel in the *tresty*, or trusts. As the Khrushchev period developed, one result was the increasing *de facto* re-establishment of the ministries.[43] Finally, the *sovnarkhozy* failed to deliver in economic terms, and substituted their own deficiencies, especially of *mestnichestvo* (localism), in place of the old ones, despite Khrushchev's decision to make failure to meet interregional delivery schedules a criminal offence.[44]

Khrushchev's term in office, however, did improve the functioning of Soviet political and state institutions,[45] and it enabled his political successors to take formal decisions about the nature of economic and other institutions.[46] It also marked the beginning of deep divisions in the CPSU, which persisted into the Gorbachev period, about the proper direction for a socialist economy and society.[47] However, it did not yet significantly alter the nature of the regime itself or the contradictions and constraints within which it operated. Nor did it lead to a significant reduction in the power of economic actors in the political system.

The Brezhnev–Kosygin succession remained committed to the strategic value of socialism, and, within these terms, given the economic disruption of the late *sovnarkhoz* period, had little choice but to restore industrial ministries as their political instruments in the economy. By early 1965, the administrative chaos caused by the

---

[42] G. Kh. Popov, 'S tochki zreniya ekonomista', in A. Bek, *Novoe naznachenie* (Moscow, 1987), 187–213.

[43] J. Hough, 'Reforms in Soviet Government and Administration', in A. Dallin and T. B. Larson, *Soviet Politics Since Khrushchev* (Englewood Cliffs, NJ, 1968), 23–40.

[44] Conyngham, *Industrial Management*, 112–13.

[45] A. Brown, 'The Power of the General-Secretary of the CPSU', in T. H. Rigby, A. H. Brown, and P. Reddaway (eds.), *Authority, Power and Policy in the USSR* (London, 1980), 135–57.

[46] Especially important was the ability of the post-Stalin leadership to deal with the NKVD, if not with 'Beria-ism'. See G. Kh. Popov, 'Sistema i zubri', in *Uroki gor'kie, no neobkhodimye* (Moscow, 1988), 93–105.

[47] S. F. Cohen, 'Gorbachev and the Soviet Reformation', in id. and K. vanden Heuvel (eds.), *Voices of Glasnost* (London, 1989), 13–33.

overlapping economic powers of various agencies had led to calls for the re-establishment of ministerial control over sectors of the economy. It is evident from Kosygin's impatient remark to an expanded Gosplan meeting in March 1965 that the constituency for 'give us a ministry and the proper order will be restored' stretched widely from high officials to at least the enterprise management level.[48] Brezhnev and Kosygin's continued hesitancy about seeing ministries as a panacea in economic or political affairs remains clear, however, both from the speech delivered by the former to the Central Committee meeting which replaced Khrushchev where he spoke of the need to increase the role of party organs in all spheres of economic and social life,[49] and from the terms on which the ministries were eventually re-established in September 1965. The new leadership, despite its strategic conservatism, was aware that the power and performance of the ministries were constraining both politically and economically, and that their restoration ought to be accompanied, so far as possible, with controls designed to ensure that they operated differently from their 1957 predecessors.

[48] A. Katz, *Politics of Economic Reform*, 119.
[49] See W. J. Tompson, 'The Fall of Nikita Khrushchev', in *Soviet Studies*, 6 (1991), 1115.

Industrial Ministries and the Soviet Economy, 1965–1985

INDUSTRIAL ministries occupied a peculiar and powerful position in the Soviet economy. The most notable and consequential feature of this position was that the ministries straddled both state power (*vlast'*) and economic functions. On the one hand, ministries were nominated by the political leadership as the instrument of the state in the economy, while, on the other, they physically controlled resources in the way that their exercise of power was more akin to that of an economic organization. On the basis of their control over resources and on account of their presence in the heart of the state, which prohibited the emergence of a clear demarcation between politics and the economy, industrial ministries were able to act in their own interests, undermine the control, and even dominate the agendas, of other institutions, and function both directly and indirectly as the most powerful, hegemonic political forces in the Soviet system.

This chapter will describe and analyse the sweeping nature of ministry powers in the economy, and their use in the interests of the ministries themselves. Despite the fact that the political leadership clearly perceived the negative consequences which resulted from ministry interests and autonomous action, decisive measures were not taken to create new economic or state institutions. This was the consequence both of the very ministry powers themselves, which allowed them to override alternative institutions in the state or the economy, and of the negative effects of reform within conditions which the ministries themselves were in large measure responsible for creating. Indeed, one of the ironies of reform attempts between 1965 and 1985 was that, when translated into practice, the political leadership often, despite their clear worries, actually strengthened ministerial power in the economy.

None the less, despite the consolidation of the ministries' position in the Soviet system during this period, there emerged towards the end a broad consensus that the anomalous position of the ministries, straddling both state and economy, stood as a major obstacle to further development of the Soviet system. Interestingly, this consensus embraced both right and left, though, as will be shown, the position of the ministries in some measure makes the application of these terms problematical. The general tenor of the debate, however, formed around programmes calling for the emergence of either, or sometimes both, autonomous economic and state spheres. In so far as the ministries straddled both, they must be regarded as the hinge on which the Soviet political and economic system hung until 1985.

THE TASKS AND FUNCTIONS OF THE RECONSTITUTED MINISTRIES, 1965–1985

Following the failures of Khrushchev's overt anti-ministerialism, the new leadership put its faith in expanding the sphere of effective regulation of economic agents as the best method of improving its authority. The concerns of the leadership are demonstrated in Kosygin's speech to the plenum of the Central Committee September 1965[1] which set out to delineate the precise tasks and functions of the ministries which were to be re-established. The speech is worth examining in detail because it expresses the hopes that the leadership retained for a ministerial socialism, while highlighting most of the concerns and methods which Soviet politicians were to exhibit and utilize in seeking to control the behaviour of the ministries for the next twenty years.[2]

In a reference to the deficiencies of the *sovnarkhozy*, Kosygin noted that industrial ministries were being re-established to deal with the technical problems of industry, where 'effective guidance can be exercised . . . only if full account is taken of the specific features and tasks of each branch . . . Therefore the ensuring of the industrial-branch principle of guidance is an indispensable element of economic management.' However, Kosygin emphasized that the territorial and inter-branch deficiencies of the old ministries, which the *sovnarkhozy* had been created to overcome, were to be eliminated by combining with the branch principle 'inter-branch tasks of the integral development of the national economy as a whole and of the economies of the country's republics and regions'. None the less, Kosygin claimed,

---

[1] Brezhnev's speech to the same body is slightly more pro-ministerial than Kosygin's but agrees with it in the most important respects.

[2] All references to Kosygin's speech are from *Pravda*, (28 September 1965).

the overall institutional superiority of the branch principle had been demonstrated by the development of the branch production associations under the *sovnarkhozy*. Kosygin spelled out the tasks of the new ministries.

> The ministries will carry out planning, will guide production and will decide questions of technical policy, material and technical supply, finance, labour and wages. The research institutes of the branches of industry will also be under their jurisdiction. This will ease the production and economic work of the enterprises, since all major questions of principle in the productive and economic activity of enterprises will now be decided in one agency—the ministry.

However, the ministry was not to utilize a large staff for these functions; 'on the contrary, it must be reduced.' It was necessary 'to work out a simple structure for the ministries'.

Enterprises and associations were to be given substantially increased autonomy and rights. Ministries should not exercise petty tutelage over them.

At first glance it may seem that a simple return to the former ministries is being proposed. But to think this means to ignore a number of new circumstances, to make a mistake. The ministries that are being organized will work in wholly different conditions when the functions of the administrative management of industry are combined with a considerable increase in methods of economic accountability and economic incentives, when the economic rights and the initiative of the enterprises are substantially broadened.

In fact, Kosygin mentioned the prospect of putting sub-units of the ministries themselves on an economic accounting basis. It was necessary to 'abandon the customary notion that in the relations between the guiding economic agencies and the enterprises, the former have only rights and the latter only obligations'.

Kosygin concluded by insisting that the 'creation of branch ministries require[d] a strengthening of Gosplan's role'. The role of other state committees, such as Gossnab (the State Committee for Material and Technical Supply) and GKNT (the State Committee for Science and Technology), was to be expanded in an effort to provide a framework for all-round development and control of the economy.

Some of the tasks, functions, and concerns mentioned by Kosygin, particularly those relating to economic performance, will be discussed in greater detail in later chapters. It is important to note the general features of the balance of power and control among the ministries and other institutions which Kosygin envisaged: small staffs with simple structures; reduced interference with subsidiaries; a greater role for supervisory bodies. In no way can the intentions of the leadership at that time be considered more than lukewarmly pro-ministerial.

The joint Central Committee and Council of Ministers resolution, of 30 September 1965, spelled out the tasks and nature of the ministries in greater detail. Two types of Moscow-based ministries were created. The resolution called for the establishment of eleven Union–republican ministries, which had a republic-level administrative tier operating under the dual subordination[3] of Moscow-based ministries and republic-level Council of Ministers.[4] Enterprises of Union–republican ministries were to work on the basis of regulations worked out by the union ministry.[5] These ministries would have jurisdiction over coal, metal, oil and chemicals, forestry and paper, construction materials, light industry, and parts of the food industry. Nine all-Union ministries, which, as the name implies, exercised sovereign decision-making power over all enterprises within their jurisdiction regardless of territorial location, were created in the machine-building sectors to supply equipment to all other sectors of the economy.[6] In addition, a number of industrial agencies from the sovnarkhoz period were transformed into ministerial bodies of either all-Union or Union–republican status: the former, for the gas industry, transport construction, and the medical industry; the latter, for energy and electrification, the fishing industry, design and special construction work, and for water economy.[7]

The resolution charged the ministries with: securing with the

[3] See V. G. Vishnyakov, Dvoynoe podchinenie organov upravleniya (Moscow, 1967).

[4] The initial large number of Union–republic ministries reflected the concentration of technical specialists in the republics during the sovnarkhozy period. Criticism of the small-scale nature of Union–republican ministries developed quite quickly, however, and there was a continuous movement towards all-Union ministries from 1970 onwards. Whereas in 1965 there were 16 all-Union ministries, by 1974 there were 27. See A. S. Petrov, 'Ekonomicheskaya reforma: tendentsii organizatsii otraslevogo upravleniya promyshlenost'yu', in Sovetskoe gosudarstvo i pravo, 3 (1971) 12–21; and V. Vorotnikov, 'O neobkhodimosti i zadachakh dal'neyshego sovershenstvovaniya organizatsii upravleniya otraslyami promyshlennost'yu', in Planovoe khozyaystvo, 5 (1971), 29–39. There is evidence, however, that even in the early stages, the Moscow branch of the Union–republic ministry was the dominant one. See S. B. Baysalov and V. M. Levshenko, 'Kompetentsiya otraslevykh organov upravleniya promyshlennost'yu', in Sovetskoe gosudarstvo i pravo, 3 (1969), 71.

[5] KPSS v rezolyutsiyakh i resheniyakh s'ezdov, konferentsii i plenumov, 10 (1986), 449.
[6] Ibid. 450.   [7] Ibid. 451–52.

minimum expenditure the highest quality of production for satisfying industrial and consumer demands; fulfilling the tasks of the state plan; rationally utilizing capital investment, raising its effectiveness, and introducing and mastering new productive capacities as quickly as possible; the conduct of a single, unified technical policy and the achievement of a high technical-economic level of production; securing for the enterprises and organizations under it a qualified staff and their proper utilization, and for taking measures designed to ensure an improvement in the organization of their labour, and for improving the living and cultural situation of their workers and employees.[8] To achieve all this, the ministries were to be given sufficient resources as well as technical expertise, the latter to be present through the inclusion of scientific, research, and design organizations within their jurisdiction.[9]

The period from 1965 to 1985 was characterized by ongoing efforts by the leadership to achieve the agenda for the ministries and the economy outlined above, but, despite these efforts, these years saw the continuing failure of the ministries to perform satisfactorily the tasks and functions assigned them. Though, as will be shown, the almost continuous activity of the leadership to realize their agenda suggests that failure occurred not through lack of effort or lack of awareness of the need for change, there can be no doubt that it was politically blinkered in its efforts by its unwillingness (or inability) to confront the narrow base of state and political power. The result of this blinkered, constrained approach was that ministries were simply able to ignore or, in the course of the reform-implementation process, to undermine central leadership directives which were directed at improving ministry performance.

THE ECONOMIC POWERS OF INDUSTRIAL MINISTRIES

Before examining the dynamics of ministry economic behaviour in the period from 1965 to 1985, and the nature and fate of efforts to overcome some of the deficiencies which resulted, it is useful to outline the general shape that the economic powers of ministries took. The main economic powers of industrial ministries lay over planning

---

[8] Ibid. 450; N. G. Kalinin (ed.), *Organizatsiya upravleniya v sisteme ministerstva* (Moscow, 1974), 89.   [9] *KPSS v rez.* 450–1.

and supply, investment and construction, in the establishment of economic norms, in pricing, control (*kontrol*), law-making, and property. Though these elements can be separated analytically, in practice they comprised an interwoven panoply of powers which enabled the ministry to control subordinates and expend resources according to its own interests. The debate which occurred in Soviet literature on the role of the ministries, which is presented in a later section of this chapter, in large measure reflects the complexity of this interwoven pattern of powers. However, the combination of these powers was such as to make ministries the most important economic institutions in the country, able in practice to override competing economic and political institutions and to ignore the economic responsibilities with which they were also nominally charged.

Planning and supply

Clearly, in economies like the Soviet Union, planning functions often overlapped with other aspects of the production process; the demarcation between operative-planning and economic-stimulative activities was never clear in practice, and other ministry powers were important in explaining the economic behaviour of enterprises. However, ministry power in the widest sense was broadly defined by the decrees of the Council of Ministers of 1967.[10] Ministries were to 'study the needs of the national economy in the production of the branch' and plan their sector accordingly. More specifically, they were to work out schemes for the distribution of enterprises within the branch, and to secure the rational utilization and renewal of natural resources. All-Union ministries were to define control figures of perspective and annual plans for the Union–republic ministries, as well as enterprises and other subordinates, to organize work on the drafting of perspective and annual plans, and to work out norms for expenditure, supply, and other aspects of the production process. In accordance with central plan indicators handed down from the State Planning Commission (Gosplan), the ministry was to work out and hand on to subordinates directive and accounting indicators.

[10] 'Obshchee polozhenie o ministerstvakh SSSR', *SPPSSSR* 17 (1967), 371–87; and 'O dopolnitel'nom rasshirenii prav ministrov SSSR', ibid. 387–97. For a discussion of the laws see K. E. Kolibab, 'O pravovom polozhenii ministerstv SSSR' in *Sovetskoe gosudarstvo i pravo*, 1 (1968) 15–23; and Yu. S. Tsimmerman, 'Promyshlennie ministerstva v usloviyakh khozyaystvennoy reformy', in *Sovetskoe gosudarstvo i pravo*, 10 (1969), 76–82.

Though, as shall be shown below, the ministry was supposed to work from 1965 onwards on the basis of increased utilization of economic levers, the use of directive indicators to enterprises was still within the ambit of the ministries' powers in planning, and widely used. Directive indicators fell within the framework of so-called organizational-directive methods of administration, founded on state power [vlast'] and characterized by non-commodity [bezvozmezdno] relations of the subject and object of administration, by the direct action on the will of the executor by the employment of administrative commands. Organizational-directive methods of administration were realized on the basis of direct orders, obligatory for the subordinate organization.[11]

Ministerial relations with subordinates took place in terms of such indicators as: the general volume of realized production, including new production; the production of important types of products specified in physical terms; profits and profitability; the general wage fund; growth in productivity of labour; the volume of centralized capital investment including construction–assembly work; the volume of new technological processes and automated mechanisms of especial importance to the branch; and the volume of deliveries of raw and other materials and equipment for distribution to superior bodies.[12] The 1967 legislation also gave ministries rights, which in some cases required the approval of Gosplan and other state committees, both to raise and lower within certain limits enterprise plan indicators for output, profits, and other variables.[13]

The supply powers and functions of ministries were equally widely defined. Ministries 'defined the need' of enterprises for raw materials, energy, equipment, and other material resources, and directed (rasporyazhaetsya) material resources earmarked for the ministry. As explained by the Chief of the Material-Technical Supply

[11] K. I. Taksir, Upravlenie promyshlennost'yu SSSR (Moscow, 1985), 33.
[12] N. G. Kalinin, Organizatsiya upravleniya v sisteme ministerstv, 127.
[13] In addition must be mentioned the legal obligation of ministries to fulfil certain operative tasks at an enterprise and ob'edinenie level, e.g. in allowing the personnel of these bodies the right to kommandirovki (business trips) outside the system of the ob'edinenie (see Pravda (18 Mar. 1975), 2), and in resolving certain small-scale property disputes. See Yu. S. Tsimmerman, 'Promyshlennie ministerstva v novykh usloviyakh otraslevogo upravleniya', in Sovetskoe gosudarstvo i pravo, 8 (1976), 21; and A. M. Rubin, 'Sovershentsovanie struktury apparata promyshlennykh ministerstv', in Sovetskoe gosudarstvo i pravo, 5 (1978), 31. The problem of the illegal use of ministry power to effect changes in enterprise plans, however, was never dealt with in this period. See EKO 6 (1975), 116–47; and the editorial, 'Otrasl' i ministerstvo', Planovoe khozyaystvo, 11 (1982), 36–8.

Administration of Moscow City, 'the industrial ministries have become the agencies in charge of the material and technical resources of the branches of industry. They are charged with an important task—the ensuring of complete co-ordination between the plan for production and the plan for supply.'[14] Supply was handled in the ministry by its Chief Supply Administration and the *glavki*. By 1975, despite repeated calls for their strengthening, regional supply depots handled only 2 per cent of even extra-departmental supply.[15]

In practical terms, ministry planning powers had grown considerably since the 1950s, as is especially clear in the case of planned commodity supply. (Here planning and supply functions and powers overlap.) For example, whereas in 1953 there had been 2,390 'funded commodities', that is, those the output and distribution of which were controlled by Gosplan direct, by 1971 the number had fallen to 277. This compares with about 26,000 decentrally funded commodities supplied and distributed within the ministerial apparatus in 1969.[16] Slightly different figures are offered by authors in 1983. A vice-chairman of Gosplan, for example, claimed that ministries had responsibility for the planning of 24 million commodities as compared with only 6,000 by Gosplan itself. In a round-table conference the same year, Abel Aganbegyan, at that time Director of the Siberian Academy of Sciences' reformist think-tank, the Institute of Economics and Organization of Industrial Production, claimed that while Gosplan drew up 2,000 single product balance sheets, and Gossnab (the State Supply Committee) drew up 15,000, the industrial ministries were responsible for over 50,000.[17] Despite these differences in the figures, however, it should be evident that the broadness of the powers given to ministries over planning would allow them considerable scope for manœuvre.

Economic norms

One of the breakthroughs of the 1965 reform, at least theoretically, lay in the expectation that ministries should utilize 'economic levers' of management in dealing with subordinates rather than simply direct

---

[14] *Pravda* (22 August 1966) 2. The important part played in the supply power of industrial ministries is not, however, as new as the author suggests. See T. Dunmore, *The Stalinist Command Economy* (London, 1980).

[15] Cited by A. M. Belyakov, in *EKO* 6 (1975), 116–47.

[16] P. R. Gregory and R. C. Stuart, *Soviet Economic Structure and Performance* (London, 1972), 137.   [17] *EKO* 8 (August 1983), 16–49.

plans. 'This is a method of administration realized not by means of direct instruction . . . but by means of indirect influence on conduct through interests and other economic levers such as wage payment, prices, bonuses, etc.'[18] The main focus of the introduction of economic methods into ministerial work after 1965 lay in their ability to control both the distribution of funds and deductions from enterprise profits. This, in turn, worked at two levels; in terms of the use by the ministry of its own funds, and through its control over the formation and size of enterprise funds.[19] Among the most important of the ministry funds were those for science and technology,[20] and those for capital construction.[21]

Economic levers were expressed in the form of norms and indicators to enterprises, and among the most important of those decided by ministry departments were: labour indicators, cost price, price and profitability which were handled by the Economic Planning Department; profits, payments to budgets and assignments from budgets, normatives of payment to production foundation funds, and normed working assets, which were the responsibility of the Finance Department; norms of deductions to the fund of material incentives and for the fund of socio-cultural measures and housing construction, and the accounting and distribution of these funds, which were handled by the Labour and Wages Administration; indicators for the

---

[18] M. I. Piskotin, 'Izmenenie kompetentsii i sovershenstvovanie form i metodov raboty ministerstv v usloviyakh ekonomicheskoy reformy', in *Organizatsiya raboty ministerstv v usloviyakh khozyaystvennoy reformy* (Moscow, 1969), 23–4. See also Taksir, *Upravlenie*, 32.

[19] Ministry funds themselves must be divided into two kinds: those to cover the costs of the ministry apparatus itself, and to pay wages and bonuses to ministry employees; and those for stimulation of enterprise activity and for branch-level investment. See Z. M. Zamengof, 'Vzaimootnosheniya po imushchestvu v sisteme promyshlennykh ministerstv', in *Organizatsiya raboty ministerstv v usloviyakh ekonomicheskoy reformy* (Moscow, 1972), 189–94. In order to maintain the fiction that ministries were state rather than economic bodies—see the discussion below—expenditure on the ministry apparatus was nominally paid out of state budgets until 1986. The absurdity of the position of ministries was made even clearer after this. See A. V. Siginevich, 'Stiral'nye mashiny iz dvenadtsati ministerstv', in *EKO* 8 (1989), 50–2. See also V. V. Popov, 'Ekonomicheskaya rol' tsentralizirovannykh fondov i rezervov ministerstva v upravlenii otrasl'yu promyshlennosti', in *Materialy po voprosam planirovaniya i upravleniya proizvodstvom* (Moscow, 1972), 11–21.

[20] For an excellent discussion of one of the latter kinds of ministerial fund, for science and technology, see S. Fortescue, *Science and Technology Management Structures of Industrial Ministries*. (Birmingham, 1986).

[21] For the capital construction functions of the ministries see, 'Obshchee polozhenie o ministertsvakh SSSR', *SPPSSSR*, 381–2.

introduction of new technology and norms for the deduction from profits to the fund for production development which were handled by the Technical Administration; and, finally, the putting into operation of basic funds and production possibilities which was the responsibility of the Capital Construction Administration.[22] In the event of non-fulfilment, the use of economic levers could take the form of monetary sanctions to be applied against the enterprise.[23]

The significance of the list of ministry powers cited so far lies in the broad range of possibilities afforded the ministries to intervene and control the production process by means of either directive or economic powers. Interference in the operational activity of enterprises had a legal basis in the enormous number of normative acts on which the ministries operated.[24] There was almost no area where a ministry was completely powerless and, though it was expected to realize these powers in accordance with the integrity of its subordinates and the directives of its superiors, it is clear that, in an operational sense, a ministry was left with enormous scope for subverting the rights of subordinates and for adjusting the directives of superiors. These powers were enhanced by other aspects of ministry economic activity.

Control

Control (*kontrol'*) in the Russian denotes supervisory or checking powers. Though ministries were not the only bodies to exercise this function in the economy—it was also the job of some state committees, the State Bank, the People's Control Commission, and the procuracy—their powers were by far the most important in any given branch of industry. As with all the powers discussed in this section, they need to be considered as supplementing and supporting the others. Control functions, however, added a further dimension to the ability of a ministry both to affect the interests and performance of its subordinates, even in circumstances where the ministry might not have had formal directive or economic powers, and to control the

---

[22] Kalinin *Organizatsiya*, 207.
[23] See V. K. Mamutov, 'Otvetstvennost' vyshestoyashchego organa v khozyaystvenno-upravlencheskom pravootnoshenii', in *Sovetskoe gosudarstvo i pravo*, 3 (1966), 44.
[24] For a widely read discussion of this, see G. A. Kulagin, *EKO* 2 (Mar.–Apr. 1975), 82–95.

information and accounts which a ministry presented to its nominal superiors.

The main control functions of ministries were: checking on the fulfilment of directives; checking on the adoption of prices and tariffs, standards, measurements, and tests; control over quality of design and over estimates in documents; checking that confirmed estimates were adhered to, and supervising the quality of construction–assembly work and equipment; checking on the formation of funds in raw materials, energy, equipment, etc., and checking on the conclusion of delivery agreements and fulfilment of contracts; and control over finances and accounts, as well as expenditures and wages.[25] In addition, the ministry exercised control over the staff sizes of subordinate enterprises.[26] The responsibility for control, however, tended to be lodged in the department with the prime responsibility for a given area of activity.[27]

Pricing

In correspondence with the shift to economic levers, the General Statute on the Ministry declared that the ministry should 'affirm or present for affirmation [to the State Prices Committee], in correspondence with acting legislation, prices and tariffs for products and services of enterprises and organizations of the ministerial system, and realize control over the employment of prices and tariffs ...'. In addition to working out prices for the goods of Union-level production, ministries set prices for intra-ministerial products. This involved the ministries in agreeing over 1,000 prices with the State Committee, in addition to the intra-ministerial ones. In practice, due to the length of time required to affirm prices with the latter body, ministries had considerable powers to set prices on their own. For example, the Inspectorate of Goskomtsen (State Committee for Prices) found that

---

[25] N. I. Pobezhimova, 'Nekotorye voprosy organizatsii kontrolya v deyatel'nosti promyshlennykh ministerstv', in *Voprosy sovetskogo administrativnogo prava* (Moscow, 1970), 66.
[26] Rubin, 'Sovershentvovanie', 32. The abuse of their control functions by ministries anxious to cut back on certain categories of employees at the enterprise level in order to preserve employment in the ministry is discussed by G. Slezinger, *Pravda* (17 October 1974.
[27] This led to calls for the establishment of 'independent' control departments within the ministry.

a machine-building ministry in 1968 had been responsible for setting over 131 temporary wholesale and 2,311 special prices.[28]

Norm-making powers

As with other aspects of their power, the ministries' ability to issue binding legal norms on the authority of the state, backed up with sanctions applied against law-breakers, is difficult to isolate from their powers in planning and economic norm-making. None the less, as pointed out above,[29] the legality of ministry actions highlighted their appearance as state institutions. In Soviet juridical parlance, the norm-making (*normotvorchestvo*) or quasi-legislative powers of ministries were rated formally below the legislative acts of the Supreme Soviet and decrees of the Council of Ministers, though in practice they had as much binding force on subordinates. The ministries' power in this area related to their ability 'to attach to adopted decisions a normative character, to invest these decisions in the form of an act, obligatory for those to whom it is addressed'.[30] In the Soviet legal system, laws made by the ministry had the status of 'sub-law normative acts' (*podzakonnye normativnye akty*), issued in accordance with the constitution on the basis of the orders (*prikazy*) and instructions of the minister himself. The sphere of ministerial legal competence was set very widely, in a way that allowed the ministry a high degree of legal manœuvrability. Law in the Soviet Union was often sectoral in the sense that it applied to branches or ministries rather than to all affected citizens. There was no single trunk of law. This allowed ministries to have large blocks of legislation at hand with which to deal with subordinates, and led to a proliferation of legislative acts.

The law-making activity of the ministry has as its aim to secure: (a) the juridical strengthening of existing relations in the branch and their legal regulation; (b) the forming of new relations, absent at a given moment, but

---

[28] N. G. Kalinin, 'Kompetentsiya ministerstva v voprosakh tsenoobrazovaniya', in *Organizatsiya raboty ministerstv v usloviyakh ekonomicheskoy reformy* (Moscow, 1972), 116–22. See also *Pravovye problemy rukovodstva i upravleniya otrasl'yu promyshlennosti v SSSR* (Moscow, 1973), 326–56. For a discussion of the manipulation of their influence over price policy by the ministries with the aim of increasing branch profitability see B. Parrott, *Politics and Technology in the Soviet Union* (London, 1983), 227.

[29] L. M. Rutman and Yu. S. Tsimerman, 'Normotvorcheskaya deyatel'nost promyshlennogo ministerstva i upravlenie otrasl'yu', in *Sovetskoe gosudarstvo i pravo*, 4 (1972), 88.   [30] Ibid. 89.

desirable or necessary from the point of view of realizing productive or economic perspectives; (c) the liquidation of relations and situations which are outdated or hinder the development of new progressive tendencies in social production.[31]

Clearly, though there were examples of the use of legislative powers by ministries to affect purposes which were consistent with other legislation, there were many more cases where ministries operated without the use of the legal mechanism.[32] However, the significant point about the ability of, and in many cases the legal need for, ministries to pass *podzakonnye akty* in the form of enabling legislation was that it allowed them scope for the application of sanctions against subordinates which effectively went against the grain of government policy, while avoiding the charge of being *ultra vires*. Indeed, there is considerable evidence that this was in fact the case, especially, as shall be shown, against the law on the state enterprise. Ministerial success in using legal means to subvert higher legislation must have been heightened by the absence or weakness of higher authorities of appeal and supervision in the conflict.[33] This situation persisted, despite the recognition after 1970, with the re-establishment of the Ministry of Justice, that departmental law was so complex as to allow for virtually any ministry activity.[34]

Property

Defining property rights and relations is extremely complex in the Soviet context. Whereas in Western liberal-capitalist states, rights of property, including state property, are defined by court-enforceable

---

[31] Ibid.

[32] R. O. Khalfina, 'Khozyaystvennaya reforma i razvitie teorii prava', in *Sovetskoe gosudarstvo i pravo*, 10 (1967), 79–87.

[33] The main bodies responsible were the People's Control Commission; the Procuracy, which investigated only criminal proceedings and not infringements of administrative law; and the arbitration service, which, according to the precepts of administrative law, under which the ministries operated, was considered as a primarily departmental rather than judicial body concerned with the public rather than the private interest. See A. E. Lunev, 'Puti sovershenstvovanie deyatel'nosti apparata upravleniya khozyaystvom', in *Pravovedenie*, 6 (1970), 29–38.

[34] Among many articles on this subject over the years see S. Bratus, N. Klein, and E. Polonsky, *Izvestiya* (31 July 1966), 5; V. V. Laptev, in *EKO* 6 (1975), 116–47; and M. Nikolaeva, 'Sistematizatsiya vedomstvennykh normativnykh aktov', in *Khozyaystvo i pravo*, 5 (1977), 47–53.

relationships among legal individuals, in the Soviet Union, at least in respect of the 'means of production' which was in the sole possession of the state (and which is of primary interest with regard to industrial ministries), there existed no independent authority to resolve disputes between the state and juridical persons such as enterprises. Relations between the ministry and the enterprise were not based on contracts, and enterprises could not appeal to an independent court in the event of an alleged violation of their legal rights. The use of the term 'state property' in the context of ministry relations with enterprises, therefore, must be treated carefully.

None the less, property was a consideration in a variety of circumstances of relevance to the power of ministries. First, however problematical the conceptual and legal position may have been, where the state was not, in respect of its 'property', a legal individual, the term functioned politically to define, and narrow, the possibilities open to private individuals and enterprises. Secondly, where the state held industrial property, the ministries were the effective executors of these rights. This is clear from the above discussion of ministry powers to control not only their own funds but those of subordinate enterprises which had no judicial redress in the event of disagreement. Thirdly, therefore, while in a sense the overarching power of ministries in relation to their subordinates is already overdetermined, and property rights supervened on their operational and other powers in planning, and over funds, etc., none the less the ability of ministries to defend themselves and their interests through the existing definition of property, and the institutional arrangements which supported it, must be considered as an additional factor in their pre-eminence.

With the passage of the 1965 enterprise law which conferred a degree of legal authority on the enterprise with respect to its funds, however, there developed an essential vagueness about the division of property rights among Soviet organizations. Certainly, after 1965, there is little sign of consensus within Soviet juridical circles on the nature of ministry property.[35] Indeed, the issue was often a smoke-screen in which political platforms competed. In short, it may be that only in conditions of highly established and fixed private property relations is it possible to determine the precise division of property. It

---

[35] For contrasting views see e.g. V. K. Mamutov, 'Otvetstvennost' vyshestoyashchego organa v khozyaystvenno-upravlencheskom pravootnoshenii', in *Sovetskoe gosudarstvo i pravo*, 3 (1966), 44–52; L. M. Borshchevskii, 'Peredacha prav vyshestoyashchykh organov upravleniya nizhestoyashchim', in *Sovetskoe gosudarstvo i pravo*, 8 (1969), 58–63.

is useful in the Soviet context, however, to examine how the various rights which are usually associated with property in capitalist systems— 'the right of use, the right of disposal, and the right of possession'[36]— were distributed among institutions.

In the Soviet legal lexicon there were a very large number of words which describe aspects of property relations. *Sobstvennost'* referred to property as in *gosudarstsvennaya sobstvennost'*, or state property; *imushchestvo* had the connotation of 'being in possession of'; *rasporyazhenie* was the equivalent of management or direction; *operativnoe upravlenie* (operative management) referred to those rights which the state delegated to enterprises as juridical subjects to take decisions regarding the use of their fixed and other capital. Using these terms, it may be reasonably accurate to characterize property relations between ministries and higher and lower bodies as follows. Ministries did not hold property in the sense of *sobstvennost'*, given that the means of production were the sole possession of the state; neither did ministries hold the right of disposal, if by that is meant the power to enter into contractual relations to sell state property outside the state sector, though they were empowered to dispose of enterprise assets, or, more importantly, allowed to prevent the distribution of their assets to other parts of the state sector. Ministries certainly had rights of use consequent on their operative control; since ministries were not, even in the most advanced case of Minpribor (Ministry of Instrument Making, Means of Automation, and Administrative Systems), juridical persons, however, there is no sense that they were liable for their funds, even in cases where their activities were damaging to the contractual relations of subordinates. The ministry held the right to intervene and redistribute what might have been considered as enterprise *imushchestvo*, though, for reasons which will be discussed in a later section, this subject was itself a matter of considerable debate.[37]

REGIME POLITICS AND MINISTRY ECONOMIC POWER, 1965–1985

These powers of the industrial ministries to intervene in economic relations did not exist in a vacuum. It was the economic behaviour of

---

[36] M. Braginsky, *The Soviet State as a Subject of Civil Law* (Moscow, 1988), 71.
[37] See Zamengof, 'Vzaimootnosheniya', 189–94.

ministries in relation to subordinate combines (ob"edineniya) and enterprises which must now be considered. This section will relate ministry economic powers to the bargaining game of Soviet politics from 1965 to 1985. It is suggested that there were three cycles of reform in the period, coming at roughly six to seven year intervals. At the start of each reform cycle ministries were faced with attempts by politicians to assert and increase their authority by placing on ministries demands which affected their powers as outlined above. The first attempt lasted from 1965 to 1968 when ministry power was not regarded as the principal tool for improving economic performance; however, when the alternative economic institutions proved to exhibit behavioural defects in a broad sense, it was logical for leaders to support a return to ministry power as the best means of restoring order. The second attempt, from 1973 to 1975, involved efforts to establish ob"edine-niya as a means of overcoming some of the perceived deficiencies of the 1965 reform; however, the interests of the ministries and the new institutions themselves were such as to make the reform ineffective. Finally, in 1979, planning reforms were introduced which sought to effect another shift in the manner in which ministerial power was exercised, though again, in practice, the panoply of powers of the ministries was preserved and there were no significant changes in their performance.

It will be shown, therefore, that, despite pressure from the political leadership, in the main ministries were able to consolidate their position as the main regime institutions in the economy. However, the manner in which the economic power was exercised also raised questions about the damage imposed by ministry interests on economic performance. And this, together with the experience of political failure at reform, led to the search for other alternative institutions and broadened into a critique of ministry power which laid much of the basis for the economic debates of *perestroyka*.

The enterprise reform of 1965

Alongside legislation which restored the industrial ministries in 1965, the political leadership introduced substantial reforms aimed at in-creasing the autonomy and responsiveness to economic stimuli at the enterprise level.[38] As well as a drastic reduction in the number and

---

[38] Kosygin seems to have favoured enterprises over ministries; Brezhnev emphasized his preference for the latter. See Parrott, *Politics and Technology*, 216–18. The ultimate

form of planned indicators, there was also provision for the establishment of direct ties at agreed prices, for an expansion in wholesale trade, and for the application of economic discipline through economic incentives and sanctions. In addition, the enterprise was to have the right to form funds out of profits which would enable it to increase decentralized investment, stimulate incentives, give managers leeway in production, and so on.[39]

There is evidence to suggest that the growth rates experienced in Soviet industry between 1965 and 1970 were improved by the reform. At the same time, however, there were a number of negative aspects in the behaviour of the enterprises which raised strategic and practical questions for the leadership. Strategically, the reform suggested a move away from the 'principles of socialism' which in general terms the leadership continued to believe offered the best hope for their political position.[40] For example, a Gosplan official reacted to proposals to extend to enterprises rights to wholesale trade and to find suppliers freely by saying:

This proposal, harmless at first sight, in fact contains within itself the abandonment of centralised planning, a move towards market relations . . . This would mean the user will choose the supplier who is most advantageous for him . . . This would lead to elemental (stikhiynyy) search for the best suppliers and customers, would disorganise the enterprises, and increase their costs.[41]

The spectre of sanctions applied to enterprises which might lead to bankruptcy was equally antithetical to conceptions of the strategic interest.[42] A suggestion in 1967, that 'the national economy . . . must go through this not very long but painful period so that inexorability of payment might untangle all the snags that have formed in the ramified system of commodity circulation in the country',[43] brought a strong negative response from management theorists who in

success of the latter in assuming pre-eminence, however, was partly the result of the deficiencies in the performance of enterprises to be discussed below.

[39] For a full account see Ed. A. Hewett, Reforming the Soviet Economy (Washington, DC, 1988), 227–45.

[40] See L. I. Abalkin, 'Trudnaya shkola perestroyki', in Uroki gor'kie, no neobkhodimye (Moscow, 1988), 260–3.

[41] Quoted in A. Nove, The Soviet Economic System (3rd edn., London, 1986), 30–1.

[42] Since Aug. 1954, according to the economist Birman, enterprise insolvency had been possible with their assets being sold at auction. No auctions were ever held, however. See Literaturnaya gazeta, 2 (1967), 10.   [43] Ibid. 11.

other respects had reforming reputations: 'The logic of economic management has and can have nothing in common with the logic of depersonalized and callous materialism.'[44] Baybakov, the chairman of Gosplan in 1968, rejected as 'alien to socialism the principles of competition and the inevitability of liquidating enterprises ... experiencing financial difficulties'.[45]

Strategic difficulties might not in themselves have defeated the enterprise reform, had there not been other difficulties and substantial negative practical consequences.[46] The latter, however, cannot be separated from the problem of ministry power, as the interests of enterprises were formed in conditions of ministerial domination. Among the perceived problems arising from the enterprise reform, the following were widely cited. Enterprises were too small and unconcentrated, and the poor capabilities of their managers failed to make reforms feasible. In any case, the terms of the reforms placed too many tasks on the shoulders of the enterprise management, with staffs that were far too small to cope. Furthermore, the new indicators on which the enterprises operated allowed them the opportunity to cheat on deliveries and sales, while the funds obtained were not used for purposes of innovating technically, and incentive funds were abused.[47]

Faced with these strategic and practical deficiencies, the leadership had in the industrial ministries a ready and willing instrument at hand for reasserting control.[48] The ministry was an institution which could deliver on the strategic promises of socialism to avoid bankruptcies, generalize profits, and override the detrimental effects of the markets by organizing plans, supplies, and investment. In any case, ministries had had, from the very beginning of the reform, little confidence in

[44] S. Kamenitser and B. Milner, in *Literaturnaya gazeta*, 5 (1967), 10.

[45] Quoted in M. Ellman, *Planning Problems in the USSR* (Cambridge, 1973), 143.

[46] The Soviet invasion of Czechoslovakia in 1968 is often cited as an external political cause of the failure of economic reform at home. See D. Dyker's article in id. (ed.), *The Soviet Union under Gorbachev* (London, 1987).

[47] See e.g., B. P. Kurashvili, 'Gosudarstvennoe upravlenie narodnym khozyaystvom', in *Sovetskoe gosudarstvo i pravo*, 6 (1982), 38; M. I. Piskotin, 'Problemy kompetentsii i metodov raboty ministerstv v usloviyakh ekonomicheskoy reformy', in *Organizatsiya raboty ministerstv v usloviyakh ekonomicheskoy reformy* (Moscow, 1972), 82–4; Petrov, 'Ekonomicheskaya reforma', 14–15; S. Pomorski, 'The Soviet Economic Associations: Some Problems of Legal Status and Organisation after the 1973 Reform', in *Review of Socialist Law*, 2/3 (1976), 137; *Pravda* (20 Sept. 1966), 2; *Izvestiya* (24 July 1969), 1.

[48] Council of Ministers resolution, 'On the work of enterprises transferred to the new system of planning and economic incentives and measures for the further transfer of branches of industry to the new system', *Izvestiya* (24 Aug. 1967), 4.

enterprise management.[49] Before being called on to recentralize, they had, in their own interests, ensured 'manœuvrability of supplies' to meet branch targets by forcing enterprises to conclude delivery orders on the basis of 'pre-emptive orders'.[50]

The intention of the leadership to utilize the ministries to re-establish control was signalled by a Council of Ministers' resolution as early as 1967. Although the ministries were criticized for failing to allow enterprises sufficient autonomy, they were none the less called upon to strengthen enterprise science and technical policy, to make better use of capital and construction capacities, to improve the efficiency of enterprise funds, and to take measures to increase enterprise specialization.[51] Ministerial control was quickly re-established. It should be evident from the first section of this chapter that their powers were sufficient for effective interference. Ministries dealt with the stockpiling of reserves in enterprise funds by rechannelling them for use in areas outside their nominal purpose.[52] It became impossible for enterprises to use their production development funds without ministry permission.[53] Indeed, it is clear that ministers took the opportunity to press the advantage for even more powers, claiming that they were overly restricted from above and below.[54] Ministerial power reached its apotheosis in Brezhnev's speech to the 1971 Party Congress.[55]

The ob″edinenie reform of 1973–1974

Though the ob″edinenie reform seems to exhibit all the dullness of mid-Brezhnev technocratism, especially in comparison with the drama of the enterprise reform of 1965, it none the less contained much of interest to an appreciation of the position and powers of ministries in the Soviet regime, and of their relation to other institutions. The

---

[49] See B. P. Kurashvili, *Bor'ba s byurokratizmom* (Moscow, 1988), 32. A. E. Lunev cites this as an example of the conservatism of the apparat, 'Sovershenstvovat', 31.

[50] *Pravda* (2 Feb. 1966), 2.

[51] Council of Ministers resolution cited in *Izvestiya* (24 Aug. 1967), 2. For a full account of measures taken to give ministries power over the enterprise see H.-H. Hohmannn and H.-B. Sand, 'The Soviet Union', in H.-H. Hohmann, M. Kaser, and K. C. Thalheim (eds.), *The New Economic System of Eastern Europe* (London, 1975), 78.

[52] Parrott, *Politics and Technology*, 218.

[53] See article by N. Drogichinsky in *Planovoe khozyaystvo*, 11 (1970).

[54] K. N. Rudnev (Minister of Minpribor), 'Otrasl' vstupaet v reformu', interview in *Kommunist*, 1 (1967), 57–63.   [55] *Pravda* (31 Mar. 1971), 2–10.

reform represented a continuation, in both strategic and technical terms, of some aspects of the 1965 reform,[56] consolidated ministry power, and demonstrated the ability of the ministries to affect the environment of other economic institutions in such a way as to make their interests to a significant degree coincident with their own.

As well as introducing economic stimuli into the behaviour of enterprises, the 1965 reform was important for establishing the principle that enterprises were founded on their own rather than the state budget. As was mentioned above, this implied the possibility, if not the reality, of contractual relations between the state—and its organs—and juridical persons. Though there was no sign of a renewal of emphasis on the use of economic levers in the 1973 reform,[57] it was highly significant that this principle was established further by the 1973 *ob"edinenie* reform, though again, for reasons which will emerge below, the practice turned out to be vastly different from the theory.[58]

The industrial associations (*promyshlennye ob"edineniya*) were to be created out of the old ministerial *glavki*, on the basis of limited *khozraschet* (cost accounting) principles. Though the industrial association itself had no property and *khozraschet* applied only to its components, the management of the association was separated in law from its ministerial superiors, operated with its own balance sheet having the status of a component of the association, held rights and obligations, was in possession of funds to stimulate enterprises, could conclude contracts, and had the status of juridical persons. As 'commodity producers', in Soviet juridical parlance, the industrial associations might in theory have been brought before arbitration.[59] At the same time, renewed emphasis was placed on the strategic tasks of ministries, encouraging a greater separation between the directive, authoritative tasks of the state, to be realized by the ministries, and the economic tasks to be accomplished by subordinates. The 1973 reform also sought to deal with some of the technical deficiencies in

[56] Pomorski is right when he criticizes Gorlin for suggesting that the 1973 reform abandoned the goals of 1965—but for the wrong reasons. See Pomorski, 'Soviet Economic Associations', 138.

[57] This defeated the hopes of such Soviet writers as V. Vorotnikov, 'O neobkhodimosti i zadachakh dal'neyshego sovershenstvovaniya organizatsii upravleniya otraslyami promyshlennosti', in *Planovoe khozyaystvo*, 5 (1971), 33. For a list of recentralizing directive measures taken in contradiction to that, see Gregory and Stuart, *Soviet Economic Structure and Performance*.

[58] In fact, in 1970 many *ob"edineniya* were established in the way generalized in 1973.

[59] Pomorski, 'Soviet Economic Associations'.

the earlier reform. These were summarized neatly by Brezhnev in his speech to the 24th Party Congress in 1971.

The intensified concentration of production is becoming a necessity. Accumulated experience shows that only large associations are able to concentrate a sufficient number of specialists, to ensure rapid technical progress and to make better and fuller use of all resources . . . In creating associations, it is especially important that administrative boundaries and the departmental subordination of enterprises not serve as obstacles.[60]

The result of the reform, however, was a general strengthening in the position of the ministries. The next section will discuss the defeat of the practical proposals outlined by Brezhnev. From an early stage, however, it was clear that the ministries wished to retain control over the funds of the associations, citing again their alleged inefficient use.[61] Ministries, in any case, retained in law their right to determine the fund formation of subordinates.[62] It became clear, therefore, that in practice *ob"edineniya* would not possess funds independently of the ministries.[63] Furthermore, it was argued that real economic exigencies made it imperative that ministries retain operational control over subordinates rather than divest them on to the associations.[64] The clear acceptance by the leadership of the extension of ministry power can be illustrated by the 1978 Council of Ministers' resolution which broadened the rights of ministries to determine the transfer of subordinates' jurisdiction.[65]

Finally, however, it is important for an understanding of the power of the ministries to note that the 1973 reforms failed to achieve even

[60] L. I. Brezhnev, Speech to the XXIVth Congress, *Pravda* (31 Mar. 1971), 14. For a detailed account of the hoped-for benefits of the *ob"edinenie* reform see L. Holmes, *The Policy Process in Communist States* (London, 1981), 119–26.

[61] See the article by the First Deputy Minister of Finance, V. V. Dementev, in *Ekonomicheskaya gazeta*, 25 (1975), 8.

[62] Tsimerman, 'Promyshlennye ministerstva v novykh', 21.

[63] See D. Gvishiani, 'Klyuchevye rezervy upravleniya narodnym khozyaystvom', in *Kommunist*, 4 (1984), 42.

[64] A. N. Komin, 'Glavk obyazan i komandovat' i menyat' plan', in *EKO* 6 (1975), 137–8; and Yu. S. Tsimerman, 'Khozyaystvennoe ministerstvo i ob"edinenie', in *Khozyaystvo i pravo*, 8 (1979), 49–50. Given that a ministry maximized its advantage by fighting for new resources rather than using existing ones more efficiently, it had an interest in planning enterprise perfomance from 'the achieved level'. See Yu. V. Sukhotin, 'Khozyaystvennyy mekhanizm v usloviyakh intensivnogo sotsialno-ekonomicheskogo razvitiya', in *Sots. iss.* 4 (1985), 34–5.

[65] M. Yukov, 'Novoe postanovlenie o poryadke peredachi predpriyatiy, ob"edineniy, organizatsiy, uchrezhdeniy, zdaniy i sooruzheniy', in *Khozyaystvo i pravo*, 1 (1980), 49–52.

the relatively constrained aims of the leadership because the interests of the actors most affected were more coincident than divergent. Powerful informal links existed at all levels for the purposes of plan fulfilment.[66] As Leslie Holmes has documented, opposition to the ob"edinenie reforms came not only from inside ministries, glavki, and state committees, but from managers, local party officials, and even local soviets.[67]

The planning reform of 1979

Finally, brief mention must be made of the 1979 reforms.[68] Though there is general agreement that on balance the measures passed had a recentralizing effect,[69] and there is certainly no evidence that those parts of the reforms, on stable norms and counter-plans, which emphasized enterprise rights and autonomy were observed,[70] the decrees none the less took a small further step towards defining the role of ministries as economic rather than state bodies by extending khozraschet principles—though not practices. The beginning of this definition, to be discussed in greater detail in the last section of this chapter, had come with the conversion of Minpribor to a khozraschetnoe ministerstvo (cost accountable ministry) in 1970. In a far from radical way, the 1979 reform reaffirmed the separation of the ministries' economic functions from their state ones, by announcing accounting procedures in which ministry contributions to the state budget from their profits were set at a fixed amount regardless of whether the branch profits plan was fulfilled.[71]

In summary, the various reforms from 1965 to 1979 were important in the way they established important principles, though they failed to alter the reality of ministry interests or powers. Instead, many of the measures resulted in a strengthening of that power. However, the reforms do give an indication of the development in thinking of scholars and political leaders on economic and state functions, and the

---

[66] V. Shubkin, 'Byurokratiya: tochka zreniya sotsiologa', in Uroki gor'kie, no neobkhodimye (Moscow, 1988), 121–2.   [67] Holmes, Policy Process, 219–35.
[68] For a full account of the details of the reforms see Nove, Soviet Economic System, 82–4.
[69] Ibid. 83; Dyker, 'Introduction', in The Soviet Union under Gorbachev, 15. The reform increased the number of centrally determined indicators. See S. A. Sitaryan, 'Tsentralizatsiya i samostoyatelnost'', in EKO 2 (1980), 3–13.   [70] Izvestiya (6 Feb. 1983), 2.
[71] See G. Bazarova, Ekonomicheskaya gazeta, 17 (1980), 10.

continuity in the cycles of reform showed an awareness by the political leadership of the damage that ministry interests had for the economy as a whole.

INTERESTS AND *VEDOMSTVENNOST'*

The concept of interests: state, department, and individual

The classic characterization of Soviet socialist society admitted of no 'antagonistic contradictions' among the various interests of classes and organizations. It defined a strict order of preference in the event of occasional disharmonies between the general interest and particular interests, in which the former was to be preferred to the latter.[72]

Socialist property, subject to the state power of working people, and the leading role of the Communist Party, creates the basis for the harmonic combination of various interests, for their deep internal unity. The system of public administration is built taking into account all these interests and secures their combination, which by the best method makes possible the further forward development of society.[73]

Given this impoverished sociological inheritance, the emergence in the 1960s and 1970s of theoretical and empirical studies of concrete instances of interest-motivated behaviour which contradicted the fiction about Soviet society was of great significance. For example, some research suggested to the leadership that reform of public administration was likely to be ineffective unless it was founded on the real interests of ministry personnel.[74] Most importantly, from the point of view of this book, these studies raised two issues: first, the concrete behaviour of industrial ministries; and, arising from that, the implications of ministry behaviour for the theory of the state.[75]

The pursuit of departmental interests (*vedomstvennost'*) was not

[72] See B. P. Kurashvili, *Ocherk teorii gosudarstvennogo upravleniya* (Moscow, 1987), 158–63.
[73] B. M. Lazerev, 'Sotsial'nye interesy i kompetentsiya organov upravleniya', in *Sovetskoe gosudarstvo i pravo*, 10 (1971), 86.
[74] F. T. Selyukov, 'Obshchie i osobennye interesy v sovremennom khozyaystvovanii', in *Sovetskoe gosudarstvo i pravo*, 11 (1973), 108–10.
[75] At this point it is interesting to note the beginnings of a convergence of interest among jurists, economists, and sociologists about the relationships between the state, other institutions, especially ministries, and society.

always regarded as essentially detrimental to the public interest.[76] Indeed, in some ways it was considered to be positively beneficial, both as a sign of the commitment and preparedness of ministry officials, and as a means of contradicting the departmental interests of *other* ministries: 'many high-level officials often regard *vedomstvennost'* and localism as a sign of enterprise, as economic resourcefulness, as a manifestation of organizational preparedness, although all this is accomplished at the expense of general societal interests or with damage to the interests of other departments.'[77]

Rassokhin cites a number of circumstances in which the pursuit of departmental interests could be of public benefit: for control purposes when the enterprise was not directly subordinate to the ministry and thus had different interests; when the ministry was a consumer it could discipline the producers; finally, ministries could react well in emergencies when involved in large-scale projects.[78] But the existence of ministry interests contradictory to those of the state and individuals none the less became undeniable. Theoretically, the ministry was asked to act both in the general interest and, within its branch competence, to take care of 'the all-sided development of the branch subordinate to it as a component part of the national economy'.[79] However, contradictory behaviour not only led to questions being begged about the state functions of the ministries, but about the appropriate methods and institutions to be adopted to restore harmony. For some, the redefining of the state—in a narrower sense than one which included the ministries—led by the party, was the appropriate means to overcome disharmonies;[80] for others, the solution to the harmonization of interests would come through the fuller application of economic levers and the recognition of ministries as economic bodies.[81] The important thing, however, was the growing recognition that ministries could not simply be regarded as state institutions.

---

[76] V. F. Sirenko, *Interesy v sisteme osnovnykh institutov sovetskogo gosudarstvennogo upravleniya* (Kiev, 1982), 56. For M. Mikhaylov, 'Po povodu vedomstvennosti', *Kommunist* 8 (1981), 106, branch patriotism was a precondition of any general state patriotism.

[77] Sirenko, *Interesy* 56.

[78] See V. P. Rassokhin, *Mekhanizm vnedreniya dostizheniy nauki: politika, upravlenie, pravo* (Moscow, 1985), 74–90. Some doubt must be cast on these claims, however. For example, ten consuming ministries awaiting the production of precision alloys were not unduly concerned by the delays of the Ministry of Ferrous Metallurgy in meeting their order because of the availability of imported alternatives. See *Pravda* (7 May 1980), 2.

[79] Lazerev 'Sotsial'nye interesy', 87.   [80] Sirenko, *Interesy*, 56.

[81] Ya. V. Vorobel' and V. V. Efrelov, 'Ekonomicheskie interesy i upravleniya', in *EKO* 4, (1978), 141–2.

Before considering this aspect in greater detail, however, let us look at the actual interests of ministries in practice and the meaning and forms of manifestation of *vedomstvennost'*.

The interests of ministries

A very large literature exists on the nature of economic interests in the planned economy. Within this, the position of the ministry is quite well defined. Because it was responsible for the development of its branch, the ministry's prime interest was in meeting the target established for it by Gosplan. Given plausible assumptions for which there is evidence in reality, it follows that the ministry sought to minimize the size of the target,[82] to maximize the resources allocated it for plan achievement,[83] and, as far as possible, to conceal the true state of its performance. A great example of the willingness of ministries to apply for large resources irrespective of the economic use to which they are put can be seen in the commissioning of a factory in Siversky producing 14,000 tractor engines per year. 'The only trouble is that no such plant exists. If you go out to Siversky, what you find is a bearded duffer with an antiquated rifle guarding a deserted construction site.'[84] Most importantly, for an understanding of the behaviour which follows from ministry interests, was their willingness to abandon criteria other than those beneficial to the achievement of the above. In a sense, therefore, a prime cause of the existence of departmental interests, which contradicted the totality of state interests, was the effort to establish state-led criteria for ministry performance in the first place.[85] The desire and responsibility to meet aggregated targets for growth meant a diminution in ministry concern for such factors as resource use and waste processing,[86] and encouraged a willingness to manipulate indicators,[87] to countenance low qualifications,[88] to seek autarky, and to pervert organizational principles.[89] Though departmental interests had a certain legitimacy in Soviet thinking, therefore,

---

[82] See Tsimerman 'Promyshlennye ministerstva', 27.
[83] Rassokhin, *Mekhanizm*, 65–6.   [84] See *Pravda* (30 Jan. 1980), 3.
[85] Sirenko, *Interesy*, 56.
[86] See V. N. Leksin, 'Narodnokhozyaystvennaya effektivnost' i interesy otrasli', in *EKO*, 4 (1977), 58–60.
[87] For a good example of how ministries manipulated indicators see *Pravda* (16 Dec. 1981), 1.   [88] See Shubkin, 'Byurokratiya', 119.
[89] These and other aspects of departmentalism will be discussed in greater detail below.

the totality of these and similar phenomena in which ministries pursued interests in contradiction to those of the states was known in the Soviet lexicon as *vedomstvennost'*, and it is in their actual behaviour, where they had the ability to use the framework of control to their own advantage, that the power of ministries is most firmly evident.

Vedomstvennost'

Economically, the essence of the phenomenon was defined as 'a negative quality in the activity of an administrative apparatus, which unjustifiably allows unnecessary labour, opposes group interests to those of the state, and uses legal means to secure an undeserved share of material and other wealth'.[90] *Vedomstvennost'* was often considered alongside other 'deviations against the state', such as 'localism' (*mestnichistvo*) and 'technocratism' which went under the collective name of 'bureaucratism'.[91] As suggested above, the source of *vedomstsvennyy* behaviour resided both in the economic demands placed on ministries and in their own interests and abilities to maximize their advantages within this system. The point was not that politicians had no abilities within the bargaining game to affect the strategic environment; only that the powers left in the hands of ministries were sufficient to allow them to override political control and to continue to exercise dominance and pursue their interests.

On the one hand, the very existence of the branch principle of economic organization created the conditions for the emergence of an apparatus with sufficient degree of *esprit de corps*, a sufficient level of internal cohesion, to organize *vedomstsvennyy* practices.[92] On the other

---

[90] Mikhaylov, 'Po povodu vedomstvennosti', 37–8.

[91] Kurashvili includes under bureaucratism: multi-leader, multi-written replacement of law by instruction and other sublegal forms; predominance of administrative over elective bodies; regimentation; *vedomstvennost'*; and localism. See Kurashvili, *Bor'ba s byurokratizmom*, 5–6.

[92] For those who hold that the organizational factor is sufficient to explain *vedomstvennost'* see Sirenko, *interesy*; and Yu. V. Subotsky, 'Ekonomicheskie problemy organizatsii upravleniya v otrasli promyshlennosti', in Organizatsiya raboty ministerstv v usloviyakh ekonomicheskoy reformy (Moscow, 1972), 39–50. As will be clear from the discussion in the next chapter, the possibility of organized *vedomstsvennye* behaviour arose from the ability of high officials in the ministry to arrange collective action by their use of selective incentives and sanctions against subordinates.

hand, however, as has been pointed out by other authors,[93] the mere existence of an organizational factor is not sufficient explanation without locating the ministry in the framework of certain interests and objectives. Bad plans, which placed impossible demands on the ministries unless they had recourse to *vedomstsvennyy* practices were one further source of motivation.[94] At the same time, the indicators which were handed on to a ministry both compelled and allowed it to act in its own interests. There existed

a contradiction between the responsibility of the ministry for the satisfaction of the demand of the country in all aspects of the work and services of the corresponding branch, and the responsibility of subdepartmental enterprises and organizations for profitable productive-economic activity; these two directions of activity cannot always be made to agree without damage to one or the other.[95]

The result was that 'good economic indicators are occasionally achieved by means of affirming reduced plans, the unfounded raising of prices, the production of expensive items in place of ones with low profit margins'.[96] These tendencies were heightened further by the fact that only the consumer felt the result.[97]

A further incentive for *vedomstsvennyy* behaviour was located in the very existence of *vedomstvennost'* itself. Where a ministry found itself in a position where it might expect other organizations to favour their own interests first, especially when the first ministry was in the weak position of consumer *vis-à-vis* the second, the ministry had a strong reason to respond in advance by defecting from co-operation. This had a knock-on effect which further strengthened these tendencies. A good example of this deficiency in practice was in the supply and production sphere where the need to secure adequate certainty about inputs led to strong autarkical tendencies in order to gain self-sufficiency in inputs at all stages of the production process.

Vedomstvennost', then, may be summarized as the result of a structure of interests and constraints, in the form of resources, indicators, and responsibilities, which both compelled and allowed ministries to maximize their own advantage, while permitting only a minimal possibility of other interests, including state interests, being able to override them. The existence of widespread departmentalist

[93] See Mikhaylov, 'Po povodu vedomstvennosti'.
[95] Mikhaylov, 'Po povodu vedomstvennosti', 36.
[97] Rassokhin, *Mekhanizm*, 42.
[94] Sirenko, *Interesy*, 55–6.
[96] Ibid.

practices, therefore, implied the superior power of a body which though nominally charged with state functions practically pursued its own interests.

Organizational vedomstvennost'

The problem of the application of organizational over economic criteria for the subordination of productive units was evident in both the reorganization of ministries after the abolition of the *sovnarkhozy* in 1965, and in the *ob"edinenie* reform of 1973. In both cases, the power of the ministry to determine the jurisdiction of its own enterprises led to organizational criteria overriding rational economic criteria based on product mix, and overrode the explicit aim of the 1973 reforms to promote technological specialization.[98] Perhaps the biggest victim of this organizational *vedomstvennost'* was the so-called Scientific Production Association, whose *raison d'être* lay in bringing together non-departmental affiliates.

Productive vedomstvennost'

As with ministry powers, ministry behaviour may be analysed in its various aspects but needs to be seen as a totality. The organizational factors of *vedomstvennost'* outlined above were both a source of, and response to, the autarkical tendencies of ministries in production, which in turn were simultaneously the result of pressure on the ministries and their method of maximizing their advantages in a strategic environment.

Productive *vedomstvennost'* had a number of features. First, it involved a strong, and between 1965 and 1985 growing, separation between the administrative boundaries of the ministry and the actual production it was engaged in. Figures on the non-correspondence vary, but on average one-fifth of the output of a ministry lay outside

---

[98] For a study of enterprise subordination after 1965 see A. M. Birman, 'Otraslevoy printsip upravleniya: problemi, perspektivi' in *EKO* 5 (1970), 60–8; on *ob"edinenie* see G. Kh. Popov, *Sovershenstvovanie otraslevoy i territorial'noy struktury upravleniya proizvodstvom* (Moscow, 1986), 1–40. For example, the construction of metal-cutting lathes was subordinated to 20 ministries; centrifugal pumps to 13; equipment for the food industry to 18.

its nominal specialization, and for some ministries the figure was much higher.[99] The defence sector provides a good example of this. As I. S. Belousov, vice-chairman of the Council of Ministers and chairman of the State Military–Industrial Commission, noted in 1989, the defence sector ministries turned out 20 per cent of all non-food commodities in the country; 100 per cent of all-Union output of televisions and sewing machines; 97 per cent of refrigerators and tape recorders; 50 per cent of motor cycles; 70 per cent of vacuum cleaners and washing machines. They were also involved in the production of medical equipment and wheelchairs.[100]

Because of the tendency to autarky, the voluntaristic creation of ever more narrow ministries had the paradoxical effect of strengthening the discrepancy between production and nominal responsibility yet further.[101] The interest of ministries in maximizing inputs and their responsibility for meeting plan targets, in conditions of supply uncertainties and the existence of perceived *vedomstvennyy* practices, had important consequences for the physical structure of the enterprise, for enterprise relations within ministries, and for types of output. Enterprises tended to be small-scale, with many so-called 'dwarf workshops' attached, in response to the need of the ministry to produce as many products internally as possible, in order to enable it to live in its own universe.[102] Enterprises were united in intra-ministerial *ob''edineniya* regardless of their territorial proximity, increasing cross-hauling, and in defiance of economic efficiency.[103]

The output of ministries thus spread widely, though it is also important to distinguish the defensive aspect of ministerial protectionism from more entrepreneurial forms. For example, there were cases where ministries entered into forms of production in order to increase their likely future appropriations and prevent the growth of other ministries, even though they were incapable of making the product itself.[104] An example that would have been farcical, were it not in Soviet conditions of scarcity so tragic, concerns the decision of the

[99] R. G. Karegadov, in *EKO* 8 (1983), 50–69.   [100] *Pravda* (28 Aug. 1989), 1, 4.
[101] See I. O. Bisher, 'Sovershenstvovanie otraslevogo upravleniya', in *Sovetskoe gosudarstvo i pravo*, 4 (1984), 28.
[102] See V. G. Olyanskii, 'O sisteme spetsializirovannogo obsluzhivaniya v otrasli', in *EKO* 1 (1973), 60–4; and, with regard to the machine-building sector, S. A. Kheinman, 'Organizatsionno-strukturnye faktory ekonomicheskogo rosta', in *EKO* 5 (1980), 32–52.
[103] Popov, *Sovershenstvovanie*, 16.
[104] One case concerned the Ministry of Machine-Building for Construction, Road Building and Civil Engineering. See *Sovetskaya Rossiya* (16 Jan. 1973), 2.

Ministry of Building Materials to produce glassware: 'The only problem is that artistically and aesthetically the glassware is not very satisfactory.'[105] Just as serious was the refusal of the Ministry of Ferrous Metals to commission a factory producing corrosion-resistant pipe for use in other branches, despite almost twenty years and 3,000,000 roubles of investment.[106] Vast resources were spent on creating branch automated management systems,[107] though here, where information was concerned, there is a suspicion that ministries wished to maintain a virtual monopoly on knowledge about the workings of the branches. Finally, a priority of any ministry in conditions of uncertainty was to secure its own supplies. Evidence of strong efforts by ministries to replace completely territorial supply depots with their own emerged quickly after their re-establishment.[108] Attempts to deal with the refusal of ministries to meet intra-departmental deliveries were limited in success.[109]

Among the most significant results of the levels of waste, duplication, low quality, and poor efficiency which resulted from these practices was that they swallowed up virtually all increases in gross national product.[110] By the evaluation of specialists, there were '1,100 enterprises in the country which were the only producers of a product (almost 1,800 aspects of production with a total value of 11 billion roubles). An even greater number of products were produced by only 2–3 enterprises.'[111] In machine-building, according to research by Gossnab, the weight of monopolism in production was 80% of output, from seventy-seven enterprises.[112] The economists Zhydkov and Yakovlev linked monopolism to the combination of concentrated industry and departmental decision-making, and noted that the Ministry of the Forestry Industry in 1988 fulfilled their plan for one item only by 88.2% so far as outside consumers were concerned, but by 109.6% in terms of intra-branch needs.[113]

[105] *Izvestiya* (26 Mar. 1975), 3.   [106] *Pravda* (27 May 1975), 2.
[107] Ibid. (25 Feb. 1976), 2.   [108] Ibid. (15 Dec. 1965), 2–3.
[109] Rassokhin, *Mekhanizm*, 42. Even after being attacked in the press for issuing instructions to subordinate enterprises to refuse deliveries to other ministries and to Gossnab, the minister in the Ministry of Ferrous Metals allowed the practice to continue, on what Gosplan officials described as illegal grounds. See *Pravda* (3 June 1977), 3, and a follow-up ibid. (20 Dec. 1977), 2.
[110] S. Andreev, 'Prichiny i sledstviya', in *Ural*, 1 (1988), 106.
[111] V. V. Maslennikov and V. I. Slobodnik, *Gosudarstvennyy zakaz* (Moscow, 1990), 76.
[112] V. Il'in and A. Gorodetskiy, 'Kak vyrvat'sya iz tiskov monopolizma?', in *Khozyaystvo i pravo*, 8 (1989), 7–15.
[113] O. Zhidkov and L. Yakovlev, 'Monopolizm i pravo', in *Khozyaystvo i pravo*, 10 (1989), 102.

Researchers on the problem of monopolism blamed not so much the structure of production as the branch–departmental form of administration. 'In our situation, monopolism in production is closely bound up with the administrative lobby in the ministries.'[114] One commentator noted, in accordance with the view of ministry power and interests noted above: 'A curious observation. If competition existed in our country, then it was between ministry-monopolists. Competition for allotment of funds, and imports, for influence in the highest echelons of power, for their significance at the highest state level.' Anti-monopoly policy, he thought, meaning anti-ministerial policy, was problem number one for the economy.[115]

This was true even of those sectors which were normally associated with strong political control, like the defence sector. In 1989, V. Avduyevsky, the chairman of the Soviet National Commission to Facilitate Conversion, disputed the claim that the military industries were so much superior to the others, or immune from departmentalism.

Is it normal that today the military–industrial complex, like the notorious Ministry of Land Reclamation and the Water Industry, determines its own requirements and plays the role of its own client? This is where the urge to produce more and receive more money comes from . . . Moreover, the entire hypertrophied system of secrecy and the departmental barriers have meant that even within the military-industrial complex the best advances were not allowed to circulate freely, since they were held back by invisible but very strong boundaries . . . Monopolization and efforts to gain various privileges have been the high road of development for the defence industry. For example, our Ministry of the Electronics Industry has transformed itself into a super-monopolist by snapping up practically all production of basic components for electronic and radio equipment. And as a result, we have fallen catastrophically behind the world level. There is no reason whatever to labour under the illusion that our military industry today can ensure a high-level civilian industry.[116]

Technological vedomstvennost'

Though ministries had large responsibilities for branch science and technology,[117] technological *vedomstvennost'* remained a strong feature of their

[114] Il'in and Gorodetsky, 'Kak vyrvat'sya', 8.
[115] *Pravitel'stvennyy vestnik*, 11 (1990), 4–5.   [116] *Izvestiya* (29 June 1989), 1–2.
[117] Popov lists: conducting a unified technological policy; the prognosis of main strategic developments of the branch; raising the effectiveness of production; operative

behaviour. This occurred despite a broad awareness among politicians and experts that, with declining numbers of new workers, technological progress would become the main source of improved economic performance.[118] There were a number of factors involved in causing technological departmentalism. First, despite the recognition of the growing complexity of scientific and technological processes, attempts to deal with it by creating new ministries failed for the reasons mentioned above: poor supplies, organizational barriers, etc. As will be shown below, creating new ministries in fact only complicated things further.[119] Secondly, however, ministries and their subordinates had a low level of interest in the achievement of technological innovation. It cost more to introduce new technology than to continue with the old, plan indicators favoured *val* (volume) rather than quality,[120] and their monopoly position in any case made their products saleable regardless of quality, technological sophistication, or unit costs.[121] The results, in conditions where *vedomstsvennyy* practices were already widespread, were a low priority for, and poor organization of, technological development,[122] ministerial secretiveness about dis-

control over the creation of new aspects of production from scientific research to proper utilization in enterprises; and raising quality. Ministries planned indicators for the fulfilment of the science and technology programme, for working out and introducing new technological processes and for the technical level of production. The list expanded substantially after the 1979 reform. For much of the period, the ministries controlled the technological side by means of a unified fund created from profits deducted from enterprises. See G. Kh. Popov (ed.), *Upravlenie nauchno-tekhnicheskim progressom* (Moscow, 1982), 133–8.

[118] The Russian buzz-phrase for technological innovation in this period was 'vnedrenie dostizheniy nauchno-tekhnicheskogo progressa'. Because of the utter failure of the ministerial economy to deliver technological improvement, Stanislav Shatalin, the radical Soviet economist, after being asked many times by foreign translators how he would translate the phrase replied: 'Gentlemen, I DON'T KNOW!' After he delivered to Gosplan a report on the economy from TsEMI in 1969, he was only narrowly saved from expulsion from the party by the president of the Academy of Sciences. See *Ogonek*, 20 (1990), 6–7, 24.   [119] Popov, *Sovershenstvovanie*, 17.

[120] In an apt phrase, David Dyker referred to ministries as 'the organisational focus of the cult of the gross. See D. Dyker, 'The Power of Industrial Ministries', in D. Lane (ed.), *Élites and Political Power in the USSR* (Cambridge, 1988), 188.

[121] For a detailed discussion of these factors see Rassokhin, *Makhanizm*, 12–42.

[122] Leadership of technological development was concentrated in the ministries. In the crucial machine-building sector, however, organization was often ill-coordinated among small departments. See B. A. Kogan, 'Novoe v upravlenii instrumental'nim proizvodstvom', in *EKO* 5 (1971), 67. In another memorable phrase, Stephen Fortescue called the Scientific and Technical Council, a collegial body within the ministry, a body to give 'authoritative justification to *vedomstvennost'* '.

coveries and very low levels of technological transfer,[123] low and declining levels of innovation,[124] defensive branch-oriented research establishments,[125] and immense bureaucracy in the technology and innovation decision-making process.[126]

Inter-ministerial vedomstvennost'

Finally, mention must be made of the evidence for *vedomstsvennyy* practices in more formal inter-ministerial relationships. The clearest example of this arises from the failure of the so-called *golovnoe* (head) ministry system as a means of governing inter-ministerial relations.

The 1967 law on the ministry contained two clauses (Nos. 1 and 9)[127] which stated both the responsibility of the ministry for the condition of the branch over which it had jurisdiction and for the products of its titular responsibility, regardless of the departmental subordination of enterprises producing them. The effect was to make an industrial branch the responsibility of numerous ministries.[128] The legal form whereby ministerial responsibilities were regulated was never made very clear. In some cases, the matter was dealt with by *ad*

[123] In 1970 the Central Committee and the Council of Ministers adopted a resolution instructing ministries to share inventions, which they had been hitherto failing to do. See *Izvestiya* (26 Sept. 1970), 3. The absence of any accompanying change which would give the ministries an interest in behaving differently, however, makes the success of this measure doubtful, to say the least, especially in the context of inter-ministerial relations. On technology transfer see Rassokhin, *Mekhanizm*, 46.

[124] For figures on the declining number of patent applications see *Pravda* (7 Jan. 1986), 2.

[125] Research assistants had a strongly low-risk attitude in their research, according to Rassokhin. See V. P. Rassokhin, 'Nauchno-tekhnicheskiy potentsial: tsentralizatsiya i svoboda tvorchestva', in *Sovetskoe gosudarstvo i pravo*, 1 (1987), 24. Some explanation was given by G. Lakhtin, *Pravda* (23 Jan 1981), who claimed that only 10% of topics worked on by institutes were decided by researchers—the rest came from the ministry. The problem of the monopoly position of the head institute of the ministry, especially in the machine-building sector, and its consequences for *vedomstsvennye* practices is discussed by Rassokhin in *Pravda* (12 July 1982), 7.

[126] According to Fortescue, the process of *soglasovanie* for new technological processes could take as many as 400–500 signatures and as long as 7–9 years. See S. Fortescue *Building Consensus in Japanese and Soviet Bureaucracies* (Birmingham, 1987). The most comprehensive discussion of technological development in the Soviet economy is found in R. Amann and J. Cooper (eds.), *Industrial Innovation in the Soviet Union* (London, 1982). [127] *SPPSSSR* 17 (1967), 371, 374.

[128] See A. S. Petrov, 'Ob osnovnykh napravleniyakh sovershenstvovaniya sistemy ministerstv', in *Organizatsiya raboty ministerstv v usloviyakh ekonomicheskoy reformy* (Moscow, 1972), 93.

hoc instructions from the Council of Ministers,[129] in others the ministries were expected to enter into agreements.[130] In many other cases, however, the relationship was meant to be defined by naming a *golovnoe* (head) ministry, which was intended to be the leading producer of a particular product range, with *vlastnyy* (state) powers over enterprises under the jurisdiction of other ministries. In such cases, the supra-departmental powers of the ministry included jurisdiction in planning, normative regulation, technical policy, quality control, co-ordination, and supervision.[131]

The Council of Ministers in 1968 named twenty-four *golovnoe* (head) ministries.[132] For example, the Ministry of Light Industry exercised state control over the quality of textiles and raw materials regardless of the subordination of enterprises which used them. Similar powers were held by the Ministry of the Gas Industry.[133] Despite often high-level support for the institution of the head ministry, however, there is a great deal of evidence for the predominance of departmental interests over the powers of the nominal supervisor, or the refusal of the supervisory ministry to accept its nominal responsibilities. The problem was the monopolistic behaviour of head ministries, which held up production of goods developed by outsiders. For example, the Ministry of the Automotive Industry forbade the Ministry of Transport Machinery to produce the Skif automobile trailer. The Ministry of Ferrous Metallurgy insisted on its responsibility for tableware. One hundred different head organizations in thirty ministries were in charge of 180 types of product.[134]

Often, given the pressures for autarky and budgetary allocations, ministries refused to accept the supra-departmental powers of the head ministry. In the town of Surgut the Ministry of the Petroleum

[129] See examples cited by Yu. S. Tsimerman in 'Osobennosti mezhotraslevykh funktsiy ministerstva', in *Khozyaystvo i pravo*, 8 (1980), 28.

[130] E. S. Frolov, 'O kharektere vzaimootnosheniy ministerstv SSSR', in *Vestnik MGU*, 3 (1973), 35. In the case of contractual agreements, no *vlastnyy* (state-legal) powers were attached to one ministry over the other beyond contractual ones, though, as Kozlov has pointed out, the ministries involved were empowered to issue joint legal instructions. See Yu. M. Kozlov, 'Gorizontal'nye upravlencheskie otnosheniya', in *Sovetskoe gosudarstvo i pravo*, 12 (1973), 67.

[131] See V. V. Vasil'ev, 'Nadvedomstvennye polnomochiya ministerstv SSSR', in *Sovetskoe gosudarstvo i pravo*, 4 (1977), 11; Kozlov, 'Gorizontal'nye upravlencheskie otnosheniny', 63; and E. Spiridonov, 'Zaboty golovnogo ministerstva', in *Khozyaystvo i pravo*, 11 (1981), 42.   [132] Spiridonov, 'Zaboty', 41.

[133] Kozlov, 'Gorizontal'nye upravlencheskie otnosheniya', 63.

[134] *Moscow News*, 30 (1989), 12.

Industry had been named as the head ministry, co-ordinating construction activity. Despite instructing other ministries to hand over funds for building work, they refused.[135] In another example, the Ministry of Motor Vehicles refused to accept responsibility for any servicing of its vehicles once they left the factory.[136] As Brezhnev said at the 1976 Party Congress:

Dozens of industrial branch ministries and thousands of enterprises are taking part in the creation of . . . complexes and systems. In these conditions, the effective organization of work calls for an integrated—or, as it is now called, a systems approach to planning and management . . . It appears that the assignment of head ministries for this purpose does not fully resolve the question since such ministries do not have adequate planning and administrative functions or economic and financial levers to apply to the co-operating ministries. Besides, the head ministries will be affected by their own departmental interests and we should not close our eyes to them . . . Life requires that we substantially expand the boundaries of the programme-goals principle of planning and management, which amplifies the branch and territorial structure of management.[137]

This awareness of the failure of the head ministry system and of the failure of the *ob"edinenie* reform, combined with knowledge of the other features of *vedomstvennost'* discussed above, led the politicians to create other institutions outside the ministerial system to deal with the pressing problems of inter-branch production and research; this also formed part of the development of a broader critique of the value of ministries in the economy.

THE SEARCH FOR ALTERNATIVE ECONOMIC INSTITUTIONS

The range of the powers and practices of ministries described indicates their pre-eminence in the economy and provides the reason behind the slow and hesitant search by the political leadership for alternative economic institutions and approaches. For most of the period 1965–85, these alternative institutions operated on the margins of the main system, and naturally were themselves subject to ministry

---

[135] *Pravda* (24 July 1975), 3. [136] *Izvestiya* (12 Mar. 1974), 2.
[137] For Brezhnev's speech see *Pravda* (25 Feb. 1976), 2–9; other notable speeches on inter-branch matters came from Kosygin, and the first secretaries of the Ukraine and Byelorussia.

resistance. With the accession of Yury Andropov as General Secretary of the Communist Party in November 1982, however, the search for alternatives deepened at a theoretical and practical level, and the political cleavages among commentators became more open. The effect of ministerial power, however, was to prevent the emergence in practice of serious alternative means of institutionalizing economic power.

Alternative approaches and bodies

Given the evidence about *vedomstvennost'*, it is not surprising that the main tasks in terms of industrial organization were defined from 1975 by politicians as creating structures over and above the basic head ministry system for inter-branch production. Highlighting inter-branch and territorial tasks and the need for a systems approach to their solution was very much the language of the day among party leaders at the 1976 Congress. A number of new forms of industrial organization emerged.

Programme-goal management

Programme-goal management was distinguished by scholars from the line or functional forms of industrial administration characteristic of the ministries. Politically, it was presented timidly as an *ad hoc* measure; as the name implies, 'administration possessing a programme-goals character exists for the achievement of defined, consciously chosen aims'.[138] It was intended to cut across the branch principle which many considered to be the organizational basis of *vedomstvennost'*, and the cause of the negative economic consequences, by substituting a new form of operational control, which 'carries a temporary character; hierarchical connections in this case, as a rule, are created only in the period of deciding a particular task ... Each structural unit fulfils a planned complex of multi-form measures for the achievement of this or that result.'[139] One body should see a single subject through from start to finish; the most common examples cited initially were in the

---

[138] D. N. Bakhrakh, 'Programmno-tselevye struktury v sovetskom gosudarstvennom upravlenii', in *Sovetskoe gosudarstvo i pravo*, 1 (1980), 36.   [139] Ibid. 35–6.

space and atomic programmes, which had been examples where the concentration of attention and resources by the political élite had allowed a measure of success in realizing their goals.[140] However, the politicians were to find that the successes in these areas were difficult to duplicate and generalize.

Organizationally, a number of institutions competed to be the focus of the programme-goals approach. Inside the ministries themselves, for example, commissions were established to investigate the introduction of such methods. The success of such bodies, comprised of twenty to thirty ministry officials and headed by the minister or one of his deputies, with all their other interests and responsibilities, must be highly doubtful.[141] Given its anti-ministerial bias, however, the more common focus of the approach was to locate it in either Gosplan,[142] a special department of the Council of Ministers,[143] or other special management agencies.[144] A number of examples in which programme-goals structures were created can be cited: for the preparation of all-Union and republican legal codes, for the Olympic Games, for the census, for the building of BAM and KamAZ, for the formulation of territorial production complexes, and for dealing with emergencies.[145]

Territorial production complexes

The concept of the territorial production complex (TPC) had been around in Soviet industrial administration since the third five-year plan. Its main aim was to combine branch with regional administration.[146]

---

[140] See e.g. A. A. Trofimuk, 'O mezhotraslevykh nauchno-tekhnicheskykh kompleksakh', in *EKO* 5 (1972), 105.

[141] See L. F. Konavalova, 'Ispol'zovanie programmno-tselevykh struktur v promyshlennom ministerstve', in *Planirovanie i proektirovanie razvitiya sistem upravleniya proizvodstvom* (Moscow, 1977), 85. The system was introduced in some departments of the Ministry of the Chemical Industry and the Ministry of the Coal Industry; see Rubin, 'Sovershenstvovanie', 37–8.   [142] *Pravda* (31 Jan. 1981), 3.

[143] See D. N. Bakhrakh, 'Sovet Ministrov SSSR i sovershenstvovanie apparata upravleniya', in *Pravovedenie*, 1 (1980), 16–17.

[144] B. Milner, *Pravda* (1 June 1979), 2–3, called for the establishment of a single inter-branch programme management agency.

[145] D. N. Bakhrakh, 'Programmno-tselevye struktury v sovetskom gosudarstvennom upravlenii', in *Sovetskoe gosudarstvo i pravo*, 1 (1980), 38.

[146] It will not prejudice the case for the TPC to note that despite plans to combine branch with territorial plans in the Volga region, which had existed since 1965, this had not been accomplished by 1984. See V. Ikonnikov and S. Krylov, 'O sochetanii otraslevogo i territorial'nogo upravleniya', in *Kommunist*, 4 (1984), 55.

The favourable publicity for it suggested that it allowed for a 'complex and unified approach to a wide variety of forms of production, technology and integration, allowing for the creation of a single complex of productive and social infrastructure, to combine in a complex enterprises of different specialization, and to utilize combined and co-operative production'.[147] By 1985 there had been established eight territorial production complexes, mainly in the north, in central Asia, and Siberia.[148] As with programme-goal organizations in general, the institutional bases of the TPCs were complex and unclear. Bodies with responsibilities for their operation included: a commission of the Presidium of the Council of Ministers to which was subordinated regional bodies and an advisory group of enterprise directors;[149] a sector of the *kray* or *oblast'* executive committee; the inter-departmental commission of Gosplan and territorial subdivisions of the Ministry of Finance, Gossnab, and Gosstroy (the State Committee for Construction); and then the various industrial ministries.[150]

In the end, however, the list of defects of the TPCs caused by ministerial involvement was as damning as the supposed list of advantages was long: breaches in established dates for completion of construction and changes in the volume of financing by the ministries involved; refusal by ministries to build agreed projects; the absence of development of construction collectives; the neglect of social infrastructure; underestimation of the importance of agriculture in development zones; groundless development of light industry; untrue estimation of resources; the isolated concern with the problems of a single branch; and the absence of decisions on principal questions.[151] One difficulty was that the powers of the TPC to rule on matters connected with ministerial power were not firmly established, nor were there any clear guide-lines about decision-making. Despite the interest that had been shown in them at the Party Congress in 1976, at the next Congress in 1981 it was still necessary 'to work out a uniform legal basis for creating TPCs and industrial conglomerates (*uzly*) and for the inter-branch administration of them'.[152]

---

[147] 'Kak upravlyat' TPC', in *EKO* 4 (1985), 56–7.
[148] For a full list see ibid. 65.
[149] See B. I. Fomin, 'Sovet direktorov . . . mezhdu otrasl'yu i territoriey', in *EKO* 2 (1982), 62–71.   [150] *EKO* 4 (1985), 75.
[151] Ibid. 62.
[152] V. A. Pertsik, 'Organizatsionno-pravovye problemy territorial'no-proizvodstvennykh kompleksov', in *Pravovedenie*, 1 (1984), 66.

Special projects

Finally, brief mention should be made of a variety of special projects with *ad hoc* administrations which also developed in response to the departmentalist tendencies of the branch system. Ironically, of course, these were also located sometimes inside ministries themselves, as with the special department of Minvodkhoz (the Ministry for Water Amelioration) under the control of the Council of Ministers of the RSFSR for supervising the development of irrigation in the non-black earth zones. Calls were heard for the creation of special commissions for supervising the transport industry; and for the development of plasma technology. Examples of the creation of special project commissions, in addition to those for the Olympics and BAM, include the Orenburg Gas Complex, a shock construction project involving nine ministries; two inter-departmental commissions for the petroleum complex, one under Gosplan, the other under the Presidium of the Council of Ministers; as well as a burgeoning number of experimental bodies in different parts of the country.[153]

The ministries' response

As with all other initiatives which ran contrary to their interests and involved a diminution in their powers, the reaction of the ministries to these new, albeit timid, efforts to create inter-branch institutions and forms of management was designed to minimize their losses and, effectively, to sabotage the operation of the new. Sergey Andreev, a political scientist who had worked in an oil research institute in Tyumen, in a celebrated article in an otherwise unnotable Sverdlovsk journal, succinctly expressed the strategy and tactics of ministries faced with change, be it of their structure, personnel, or powers. In the chess match with superiors, three forms of resistance were favoured: first, introduce tiny amendments against the major instructions to make the latter unworkable; then, utilize any lack of clarity in the instruction to wriggle out of commitments; finally, use powers over resources to make things worse![154]

The existence of departmental barriers to the development of the

---

[153] *Ekonomicheskaya gazeta*, 3 (1982), 15.
[154] Andreev, 'Prichiny i sledstviya', 122–4.

West Siberian oil fields had been noted and criticized by Brezhnev at the time of the Party Congress in 1976.[155] As mentioned above, the absence of any legal basis on which the various commissions operated must have allowed the ministries room to defeat it by small measures. Plans of the TPC did not have a directive character for the organizations involved; the *ad hoc* commissions were often understaffed and underorganized.[156] The continuation of the departmentalist problems Brezhnev dealt with in 1976 can be seen, for example, in the fact that it took the South Yakut TPC over two years to get the Ministry of Coal and the Ministry of Energy to agree to build enterprises there.[157] At the Kansk-Achinsk TPC there was no administration to 'lead the orchestra'. Even the two commissions for the petroleum complex, which were based in the highest institutions, had no normative basis and faced 'the complicated task' of finding their place in the ministerial system.[158] Such complaints could be heard time and again; however, one result of the experience of the operation of TPCs, special commissions, and programme-goal management was a deepening in the criticism of ministries at a much more general level.

New circumstances and the search for alternatives

The arrival of Yury Andropov as General Secretary in 1982 advanced the criticism of ministries and the further establishment of alternative institutions. Theoretically, the debate was opened by Andropov's article in *Kommunist* in which he affirmed collective ownership but argued that the forms and methods of industrial administration were lagging behind.[159] High-level anti-ministerialism, however, had already been voiced the previous year by Shevardnadze, then first secretary of the Georgian Party, who, though noting that ministries had been effective at one stage in the country's development, suggested that 'today almost every branch has become so territorially dispersed and has assumed such a scale that many enterprises, especially those that are not very large, are in point of fact ignored by ministries'.[160] Again in Georgia, a research survey of the opinions of high-level political

[155] See G. Kh. Popov, *Effektivnoe upravlenie* (Moscow, 1976), 96.
[156] Ikonnikov and Krylov, 'O sochetanii', 55–6.
[157] *Pravda* (30 May 1981), 2.   [158] Ibid. (3 Mar. 1982), 2.
[159] Yu. Andropov, *Kommunist*, 3 (Feb. 1983), 9–23.
[160] *Ekonomicheskaya gazeta*, 21 (May, 1982), 7–8.

and state leaders on barriers to technical progress and the role of *vedomstvennost'* indicated that nearly a majority of those interviewed favoured a radical reform of the administration of industry.[161]

At a practical level, a number of notable innovations were attempted. First, yet another economic reform package was introduced which reversed the centralizing direction of the 1979 reform, which had notably strengthened ministry power while increasing their financial manœuvrability. The 1982 package reduced the plan indicators which the ministry was to set for the enterprise, tried to lay stress on final results, and gave enterprises themselves a say in their production profile through the so-called counter-planning procedure.[162] Other experiments included a more radical reform package for self-financing in five ministries;[163] the creation of a State Committee in Georgia on Automated Transport Systems which dealt with all aspects from innovation to realization;[164] cases of the direct subordination of research–production associations to the Council of Ministers rather than to the ministry, as in Byelorussia and the RSFSR;[165] again, in Georgia, the Poti experiment united enterprises regardless of departmental affiliation under the first vice-chairman of the city soviet executive committee in a regional body operating on *khozraschet*;[166] and, finally, the creation of sixteen inter-branch science and technical complexes which, though operating alongside the ministerial system, were headed by Academies of Science rather than branch research institutes.[167] As one commentator put it, 'a many-tiered structure of inter-branch organizations is already becoming evident ... A system for the management of these inter-branch organizations by high-level agencies is also taking shape now.'[168]

[161] T. M. Dzhafarli, Sh. L. Kistauri, B. P. Kurashvili, and V. P. Rassokhin, 'Nekotorye aspekty uskoreniya nauchno-tekhnicheskogo progressa', in *Sots. iss.* 2 (1983), 58–63. The precise figures were: 36% favoured a 'stabilization programme'; 28% a policy of moderate reform (*umerennaya perestroyka*); and 16.5% a programme of radical *perestroyka*. The authors derive their conclusion about the desire for change in the branch system by adding groups two and three together.

[162] For fuller details see Nove, *Soviet Economic System*.

[163] These were the Ministry of Heavy Machinery, the Ministry of the Electro-Technical Industry, the Ministry of the Food Industry, the Ministry of Light Industry of the Byelorussian Republic, and the Ministry of Local Industry in Lithuania. See O. Yun, 'V pyati otraslyakh', in *Khozyaystvo i pravo*, 5 (1984), 21–6.

[164] *Izvestiya* (7 Oct. 1983).   [165] Ibid. (30 Sept. 1983), 3; (6 Oct. 1983), 3.

[166] See *Pravda* (18 Feb. 1983), 2; see also D. Slider, 'More Power to the Soviets? Reform and Local Government in the Soviet Union', in *British Journal of Political Science*, 16 (1986), 495–511.   [167] *Izvestiya* (17 Dec. 1985), 3.

[168] Ibid. (7 Oct. 1983).

However, as important as these *ad hoc* changes were in developing non-ministerial structures for the administration of industry, equal importance must be given to the sharpness of debate which ensued in this period about the appropriate response to deficiencies in the ministerial system. These can be summarized as falling into two camps: those who perceived the problem to lie in the absence of clear state leadership over the ministries and in the manipulation by the latter of value indicators, and who favoured strengthening planning bodies; and others who favoured a far-reaching reform of industrial administration, substantial cuts in the number of ministries,[169] and the creation of new, especially inter-branch and territorial institutions, along with a strengthening of economic levers.[170]

Two of the most well-known proponents of the former view were Yakushev and Ignatovskii, the latter being editor of the Gosplan journal *Planovoe khozyaystvo*. These authors shared the view that the problems in the economy originated from the practice of introducing commodity–money relations which led to the isolation of enterprises and branches and the development of *vedomstsvennyy* practices. The administration of the economy should recognize the priority of politics over economics, and, contrary to widespread belief, the development of specialization in production under socialism entailed the diminution in economic incentives rather than its increase. The solution for them lay in finding the correct cadres, improving control mechanisms, and strengthening 'democratic centralism'.[171]

The second view was perhaps best expressed by the radical economists Popov and Abalkin, though a number of other authors were supportive of their position.[172] The essence of their argument

---

[169] An intriguing variant of this proposal came from two Lvov scientists who suggested forming ministries around the International Classification of Inventions, which would have cut the number of ministries to 21, *Pravda* (19 Dec. 1980). The level of anti-ministerialism may be judged from the debate this touched off, with one of the more notable comments coming from F. Karkayev of Orenburg, who had been influenced perhaps by the magnitude of vedomstvennost' in the development of his region. 'These days it seems to me that in terms of numbers of ministries per capita, the USSR holds first place in the world', *Pravda* (2 Feb. 1981), 2.

[170] Of course, there were many who continued to argue for perfecting the existing system. See e.g. Gvishiani, 'Klyucheveye rezervy', 37–47.

[171] See V. M. Yakushev, 'Demokraticheskiy tsentralism v upravlenii narodnym khozyaystvom', in *Sots. iss.* 2 (1984), 52–61; and P. Ignatovskiy, 'O politicheskom podkhode k ekonomike', in *Kommunist*, 12 (1983), 60–72. For a reply to Yakushev, see K. A. Ulibin, 'Tovarno-denezhnye otnosheniya; iskusstvenno ustranyat' ili umelo ispol'zovat'', in *Sots. iss.* 4 (1984), 45–54.

[172] See e.g. Bisher, 'Sovershenstvovanie'; R. G. Karagedov, in *EKO* 8 (1983), 50–69; and Kurashvili, 'Gosudarstvennoe upravlenie narodnym khozyaystvom', 38–48. Kurashvili favoured the re-creation of an organ like VSNKh to run industry.

concentrated on the fact that the development of the ministerial structure had nothing in common with the branch for which each ministry was nominally responsible, but concluded that rather than cut the range of institutions operating on a commodity–money basis, these should instead be widened to include ministries operating on real *khozraschet* principles. The transformation of ministries would in practice only recognize *de jure* that they functioned as *de facto* sub-branch economic organs. At the same time, a new system of super-ministries should take on the job of branch management, especially of technological development, which would not possess operational responsibilities or powers. Since attitudes were determined by interests rather than politics, in their view, only a proper restructuring could be effective, including giving workers the feeling that their enterprise was their own.[173]

The two approaches illustrate the hinge on which the ministries turned. On the one hand, they were nominally state bodies which actually functioned on their own account; on the other, they effectively prevented the emergence of genuine economic bodies operating in civil law. The result was a neither/nor situation, in which the powers of the ministries predominated over both those above and those below; and this directly raised important questions about the nature of the Soviet state and economy which had been preoccupying Soviet scholars since the mid-1960s.

STATE BODIES OR ECONOMIC BODIES?

Given the huge position in the state and the economy which the ministries spanned and dominated, to the detriment of both, it is not surprising, as the cleavage between the two camps suggests, that there should have been a division of views between those who considered that state control should be stronger and those who thought the economy should be more independent (though it might also be argued that there is nothing inherently incompatible about these viewpoints); indeed, for this reason, the issue of whether, for example, ministries should be on *khozraschet* cut across other cleavages on the use of the market or plan.[174] The important thing to note is the tacit admission

[173] See L. Abalkin, in *Kommunist*, 14 (1983), 28–38; and G. Kh. Popov, in *Kommunist*, 18 (1982), 48–59.

[174] e.g. Birman, who was clearly a proponent of the market, was also opposed to putting ministries on *khozraschet* because he favoured their state regulatory functions (Birman, 'Otraslevoy printsip', 65–6).

in the terms of the debate itself that for neither camp were ministries state bodies in any significant sense of the phrase.

The debate about the nature of the socialist state often took arcane forms, which may explain why it has not received the interest it deserves.[175] But the discussion continued unabated with clear lines of demarcation throughout the whole period from 1965 to 1985, despite the clear political messages which the different viewpoints expressed.[176] Neither can its seriousness be underestimated; as one scholar pointed out as early as 1972, the heart of the matter was about the boundaries of state control, and that the problems of the Soviet state and economy could only be tackled once these boundaries were seriously redrawn.[177] The debate arose from the recognition of the duality of ministry functions, as being simultaneously organs of state leadership and of economic management. Clear problems, such as the concomitant responsibility of Minvodkhoz for both water use and water conservation, arose from this duality.[178] On the one hand, it was argued, the supra-departmental powers of ministries could only be understood if they were political state bodies.[179] At the same time, the idea of state control, as a means of wilful intervention in the development of society, was clearly identified as the heart of socialism.[180] On the other hand, however, it was evident that their dual nature had led to the ministries'

[175] Within the Marxist discourse, for example, it was necessary for authors to address the question of whether the state, which clearly exercised economic functions, was part of the base or the superstructure. See A. D. Kan, 'Otnosheniya po upravleniyu promishlennost'yu v SSSR', in *Pravovedenie*, 6 (1975), 26–33; and Yu. G. Basin and A. G. Didenko, 'Imushchestvennaya otvetstvennost' i operativnye sanktsii v sisteme khozyaysvennogo mekhanizma', in *Pravovedenie*, 3 (1984), 24–34. In a manner typical of the 'dialectic approach' of Soviet Marxism, the latter authors suggested that it was part of the superstructure but that this did not imply that it could act subjectively or wilfully. For a further discussion of some of this esoteric literature see A. H. Brown, 'Political Power and the Soviet State: Western and Soviet Perspectives', in N. Harding (ed.), *The State in Socialist Society* (London, 1984), 51–103.
[176] The potential political fall-out after 1968 may be gauged from the fact that the suggestion that the socialist state was part of the base as well as the superstructure was associated with the 'revisionist' Czech economist Ota Šik.
[177] V. K. Mamutov, 'Ekonomicheskie problemy organizatsiya upravleniya v otrasli promyshlennosti', in *Organizatsiya raboty ministerstv v usloviyakh ekonomicheskoy reformy* (Moscow, 1972), 51–5. Mamutov's own view was that ministries needed to be seen not just as political bodies but as economic ones as well.
[178] Lazarev, 'Sotsial'nye interesy', 89.
[179] Vasil'ev, 'Nadvedomstvennye polnomochiya', 4–5.
[180] See Yu. M. Kozlov, 'Kharakter deyatel'nosti ministerstv v svete teorii upravleniya', in *Organizatsiya raboty ministerstv v usloviyakh ekonomicheskoy reformy* (Moscow, 1972), 26–33.

role as a government organ being seriously deformed.[181] By 1984, therefore, it was clear that the real practice of ministries contradicted the view that they were organs of state leadership which reflected the state's interests.[182]

This conclusion has clear implications for the nature of the Soviet state itself, for other institutions like Gosplan, and for the role of the Communist Party. If the ministries were, as this chapter suggests, both the most powerful actors in the economy, controlling vast resources and directing huge numbers of workers, while at the same time operating on the basis of direct power and not under the control of the politicians and the authority of the state of which they were supposed to be part, then it is vital to appreciate how they related to the remainder of the political and state system. This is the subject to be addressed in Chapter 3. Before that, however, it is necessary to tackle the question of the manipulation of power within the ministry itself; for, if the claim about the organization of ministry activity in its own interests is to be sustained, then it must be shown that leading officials in the ministry were in a position to control their own organizations in a way that their superiors were unable to control them.

[181] Bisher, 'Sovershenstvovanie', 32.   [182] Rassokhin, *Mekhanizm*, 50–1.

2

Structure, Personnel, and Power
Inside the Industrial Ministry, 1965–1985

A s was shown in the last chapter, the attitude of the politicians towards the ministries they re-established in 1965 was sceptical from the outset. Ministries were enjoined to behave differently from their predecessors with regard, among other things, to their structure, personnel, and style of work. This chapter will examine the nature and fate of efforts by the politicians to control ministry behaviour in these areas. The question of who controlled structure, personnel, and style of work is an important one for Soviet politics and for the argument of this book: the ability of both ministries and politicians to act effectively in their interests, after all, depended on who controlled the administrative environment. The prerequisite for the ministerial power I am advocating was surely its ability to act as a unit on its own behalf, and the test of its abilities in this regard can be observed in the ability of its leading officials to control internal power. The point is highly important, for the converse argument, that politicians exercised effective authority over their subordinates via such institutions as the *nomenklatura* system of appointments, rests on the politicians' ability to dominate ministerial behaviour. It will be observed, however, that though the politicians retained formal powers to enact legislation which instructed ministries to alter aspects of their internal behaviour, in practice the complexity of ministry structure, the weakness of regulatory or checking bodies in the face of this, the consequent complexity of work arrangements and job requirements, the insider nature of appointments, and the input granted the ministry in the implementation stage of the policy process practically defeated political control inside the ministry itself. The failure of politicians to control the internal structure and behaviour of ministry personnel, however, did not mean that these were ungoverned organizations; rather, the high officials in the ministry were quite firmly in command.

THE STRUGGLE OVER MINISTRY STRUCTURE

As can be seen from the list provided in Chapter 1, in 1965 the industrial ministries were given a very broad and complex range of tasks and responsibilities and were enjoined by the leadership to achieve these by means of a simple structure without undue interference in the affairs of their subordinates. Many Soviet commentators and politicians between 1965 and 1985 regarded structural reform inside the ministries as central to efforts aimed at ensuring that the ministries achieved these targets.[1] In a sense, the politicians needed to have a regulatory policy towards ministry structure; they could not, after all, leave ministry power over its own internal organization entirely unchallenged.[2] However, the very complexity of the tasks assigned them made it possible, and probably necessary, for ministries to consist of complex structures which went beyond the regulator's ability to control. Indeed, quickly following their re-establishment, the ministries were once again the subject of the very complaints which had been made against them previously for over-complex, over-blown structures which exercised petty tutelage over their subordinate enterprises. Despite a further twenty years of efforts to change this situation, these complaints continued.[3]

Although all industrial ministries had common features, their internal structure and the technical demands of the particular industry they supervised meant that in practice they differed markedly. Each ministry was headed, not surprisingly, by a minister who, according to the established Soviet administrative practice of *edinonachalie*,[4] or one-man management, was authorized and required to pass important decisions of the ministry into law. In the Soviet legal hierarchy, this had the status of *prikaz* (order), which was law binding on all

[1] See V. V. Tolstosheev, 'Sovershenstvovanie apparata ministerstv', in *Sovetskoe gosudarstvo i pravo*, 3 (1970), 75–82. For commentary on this 'unbalanced approach' see G. Kh. Popov, *Sovershenstvovanie otraslevoy i territorial'noy struktury upravleniya proizvodstvom* (Moscow, 1986), 8–12.

[2] This is not to dispute the validity of the criticism of those who regarded structural reform as impossible to obtain unless the functions of ministries discussed in the last chapter were changed as well. See I. L. Bachilo, 'Funktsiya upravleniya: soderzhanie i pravovoe oformlenie', in *Sovetskoe gosudarstvo i pravo*, 12 (1969), 76–82.

[3] For an example of the view that the structure of the ministry conformed to no known principle and that personal power governed relations with subordinates, see D. N. Bakhrakh, 'Organizatsionnye struktury gosudarstvennogo upravleniya', in *Pravovedenie*, 6 (1981), 34.

[4] See K. I. Taksir, *Upravlenie promyshlennost'yu SSSR* (Moscow, 1985), 26–8.

subordinates, but having less formal authority than an *ukaz* (decree) of the Council of Ministers, or *zakon* (law) of the legislative authority. Under the minister, and appointed by him and ratified by the Council of Ministers, there were generally two first deputy ministers and a variable number of deputy ministers, who oversaw the ministry's sub departments. The minister, his deputies, and other important departmental officials, together collectively comprised the *kollegiya* of the ministry, which, as its name implies, was a collegial body intended as a forum for discussion of general branch development and for the supervision of ministerial decisions. Decisions of the *kollegiya* were put into effect on the authority of the minister, though the *kollegiya* was formally entitled to appeal against the decision of the minister to the Council of Ministers.[5] Other collegial bodies in the ministry included the Scientific and Technical Council.[6] Ministry departments, following their re-establishment in 1965, were divided into two general types: line production departments, formally called chief administrations or *glavki*, which were responsible for the operational supervision of enterprise activity, and, like the ministry, had direct administrative power over them; and functional departments, which exercised guidance and control over areas of production, development, and other activity, but, like the state committee, required a ministerial decision for their recommendations to become mandatory for the enterprise. All of this taken together comprised the ministry, which oversaw the activity of subordinate enterprises, research institutes, and production associations. Formally from 1973 onwards, and in some ministries from 1970, when the *glavki* were abolished, they also oversaw the supposedly semi-autonomous industrial associations.

The precise subdivisions of the ministry and the responsibilities of its officials, however, varied considerably from one to another. Before looking at the various efforts at structural control exercised at the ministries after 1965, it is worth examining the complexities with which any regulator was faced when confronted with an actual industrial ministry.

Among the factors cited by the Moscow State University economist

---

[5] In formal terms, this was one of the defining differences between state committees and ministries. See V. S. Pronina, 'Sootnoshenie kompetentsii gosudarstvennykh komitetov i ministerstv', in *Problemy sovershenstvovaniya sovetskogo zakonodatel'stvo* (Moscow, 1976), 89–98.

[6] For a full discussion of the role of the Scientific and Technical Council see S. Fortescue, *Science and Technical Management Structures in Soviet Industrial Ministries* (Birmingham 1986).

Nikolay Kalinin as reasons for variation between ministries were: the volume of work of various departments, the capabilities of officials, the scale of administration, the degree of centralization of rights of decision-making about scientific and technical matters, the nature of the productive structure of the branch, the size of enterprises, the labour-intensity of branch output, the complexity of the technology, the level of branch specialization, the degree of mechanization of administrative labour, and the numbers of workers, materials suppliers, and consumers.[7] As figures cited by Kalinin show, the level of variation between ministries in respect of numbers of *glavki*, subdepartments, enterprises, and workers would make accounting for efficiency and control over the internal branch arrangements extremely difficult for any extra-ministerial agency.[8]

Further structural differences between ministries can be observed in the division of responsibilities among ministers and their deputies in the Ministry of Instrument Making, Means of Automation, and Control Systems (Minpribor), the Ministry of Tractor and Agricultural Machine-Building, and the Ministry of the Coal Industry. In the first, the minister held responsibility for the all-Union Industrial Associations (VPOs), the Scientific-Technical Council (STC), the *kollegiya*, the branch Inspectorate, and for general questions of branch development. In the second, the minister was held responsible for the Planning and Economic Administration, the STC, the *kollegiya*, the Administrative Department (*Upravlenie Delami*), the Accounts Department, and the Inspectorate. In the third, the minister attended to the Planning and Economic Administration, the Finance Administration, the Administration for Perspective Development of the Coal Industry and Capital Investment, the Administration for Computing Technology and Organizational Structure, the Control and Auditing Commission, the *Kantselyaria* (the department in charge of preparation of documents and correspondence), and the *Pervyy Otdel* (which monitored branch figures). Similarly broad discrepancies can be seen in the responsibilities of first deputy ministers, who controlled functional departments in the first case, and line departments in the second, while, in the third, one first deputy supervised exclusively functional while the other dealt exclusively with line matters. The same variation

---

[7] N. G. Kalinin (ed.), *Organizatsiya upravleniya v sisteme ministerstva* (Moscow, 1974), 67.

[8] Ibid. 68. Although Kalinin does not name the ministries, the context and the figures indicate that they are real.

may be seen in the responsibilities of the other deputy ministers as well.[9]

The level of complexity and variation in all branches of industry, and in the ministerial structure which coexisted with it, presented a problem to the supra-ministerial regulator in terms of control. Not only does the above picture suggest that the structure was highly idiosyncratic, it demonstrates the possibility which recalcitrant ministry officials, seeking to preserve their independence in the face of pressure from above, must have had to obfuscate, conceal, shift responsibility, and resist. Even when formally obeying instructions—a fact which must, in itself, have been extremely difficult to verify in the welter of paperwork produced by a multitude of departments—the minister or his subordinates could find ample opportunity for practical opposition. Similarly, even had a regulatory body wanted to advance detailed proposals for restructuring the apparatus, it would have had little possibility, in the face of bureaucratic opposition, to discover the true state of affairs to be reformed. This is not to mention the sheer scale of problems attached to discovering real efficiency criteria for the operation of various apparatuses, operating in different industrial circumstances with enormous scope for concealing costs. To hope for the creation of a simple structure, malleable to the interests of leaders rather than bureaucrats, therefore, represented little more than the wishful thinking of political leaders in the face of the near impossibility of regulation.[10]

None the less, as suggested above, the politician was faced with little choice other than to try to regulate since he could not leave the ministry entirely to determine its internal arrangements. In light of this, it is worth examining efforts to introduce ministry general schemes (*general'nye skhemy*) from 1973.[11] Legislation governing the introduction of general schemes was passed in 1973 and 1974 aimed

[9] Ibid. 71–2; R. D. Migachev, *Opyt sovershenstvovaniya upravleniya otrasl'yu* (Moscow, 1975), drawing 32; and *O strukture tsentral'nogo apparata minugleproma SSSR* (Prikaz ministra, 23.10.74.) no. 370, *passim*.

[10] This is not even to mention the issue, to be discussed in Ch. 3, of the political connections between ministries and their regulators which tended to make the supervisory function rather less than rigorous in any case.

[11] Another structural reform which met with little success was the effort to improve the functioning of the ministry *kollegiya*. Among the early proponents, see A. E. Lunev, 'Puti sovershenstvovanie deyatel'nosti apparata upravleniya khozyaystvom', in *Pravovedenie*, 6 (1970), 29–38. The extent to which the task had been accomplished by 1981 can be judged from the continued criticism heard at the XXVIth Party Congress. See 'XXVI s"ezd KPSS i organizatsionno-pravovye voprosy gosudarstvennogo upravleniya', in *Sovetskoe gosudarstvo i pravo*, 9 (1981), 9.

at reducing the number of ministerial links.[12] The idea was that the line administrations (*glavki*) of the ministries, which had been strongly criticized for excessive tutelage on the one hand, and superfluity on the other, would be reformed on an independent, so-called *khozraschet* (cost-accounting) basis, into either industrial (*promyshlennye*) or production (*proizvodstvennye*) associations (*ob"edineniya*).[13] At the same time, there would be a corresponding strengthening of the functional administrations,[14] though the dangers of 'functionalism'—in which responsibility for fulfilment of decisions and control over the enterprise was diffused among a variety of bodies—would be avoided through the subordination of functional departments to a deputy minister.

The implications of the introduction of the reform for actual power relations inside the ministry will be considered later. It is clear, however, that in practice the reform did not lead to simplified, common structures for all ministries. Evidence of this kind of difficulty comes from Viktor Vishnyakov who worked as part of a Council of Ministers group investigating the introduction of the proposed new *general' nye skhemy* in the ministries which had been transferred to the new system on an experimental basis in 1970. The practical result of the introduction, in ministries like oil refining and petrochemicals, forestry and wood-working, and construction of enterprises for heavy industry, where the schemes had been nominally introduced, was very far from the intentions of those who drafted the original plan. In these ministries, for example, 'there was not a single functional or service department subordinate to the minister or one of his deputies', which was at complete variance with the government's proposals for a general structure to serve all ministries.[15] Similar problems attended the transition to the system on a broad basis. Each ministry introduced the

[12] The number of links varied from ministry to ministry. A two-link system would be comprised of ministry-enterprise or ministry-production association relations, while a three-link system could entail Union ministry-republic ministry-enterprise or ministry-industrial association-production association relations, and so on.

[13] See L. Holmes, *The Policy Process in Communist States: Politics and Industrial Administration* (London, 1981).

[14] See A. M. Rubin, 'Sovershenstvovanie struktury apparata promyshlennykh ministerstv', in *Sovetskoe gosudarstvo i pravo*, 5 (1978), 30–8.

[15] V. G. Vishnyakov, 'Sovershenstvovanie struktury promyshlennykh ministerstv', in *Pravovedenie*, 4 (1975), 26–35. Vishnyakov told me in an interview that the commission had been unsuccessful in subsequently altering the ministries' ability to design its own substructure. He also said that, for the publication of materials in the article, he was formally reprimanded along with the journal's editor.

scheme according to its own priorities.[16] The intention of the legislators had been to introduce the new general schemes by 1975. The difficulties in getting ministries to draw up acceptable plans meant that structural reform was continuously put back. From 1975 to 1979, twenty-seven ministry general schemes were introduced, but they were often conceived as 'one-shot documents'.[17] The Ministry of Electrical Equipment was the first to introduce a general scheme, but showed no rush to put it into practice.[18] The desire of policy-makers that inter-branch considerations form part of the general plans was ignored. In fact, most ministries dealt with inter-branch issues only when they wanted the transfer of an enterprise of another ministry within their jurisdiction.[19] The extent to which the new schemes altered the nature of the ministry can, perhaps, be judged from the fact that the number of ministerial sub-units dropped very little, if the new industrial associations are included.[20]

A second important reason for the failure to secure a simple ministry structure after 1965, however, was that the ministries themselves were largely entrusted with introducing the reform measures. The potential difficulties in this were apparent to scholars at the time, who pointed out that with the abolition of the State Staff Commission and the transfer of its functions to the Ministry of Finance, any systematic supra-ministerial review of ministry structure had virtually ended.[21] A similar lack of power over the ministries applied to the Inter-Departmental Commission on Economic Reform of Gosplan (the State Planning Commission). Responsibility for introducing reform in administrative structure varied from ministry to ministry. The self-regulation of structural reform can be seen, for example, in the case of the Ministry of the Coal Industry where the task of introducing the general plans for introducing the industrial associations fell to the Administration for Computing Technology and Organizational Structure under the minister, Bratchenko. Furthermore, the department was responsible for the 'rationalization of all levels and links of administration in the branch'.[22] However, in other ministries

---

[16] Yu. S. Tsimerman, 'Promyshlennye ministerstva v novykh usloviyakh otraslevogo upravleniya', in *Sovetskoe gosudarstvo i pravo*, 8 (1976), 19–20.

[17] *Pravda* (10 June 1979), 3.

[18] Ibid. At the time of the report, it had been postponed until 1980.   [19] Ibid.

[20] Holmes, *Policy Process*, 202–5. He also notes that the structure of the industrial association itself changed little in comparison with its predecessor, the *glavk*.

[21] A. E. Lunev. 'Sovershenstvovat' pravovoy status i koordinatsiyu deyatel'nosti ministerstv', in *Sovetskoe gosudarstvo i pravo*, 1 (1966), 10. The author favoured the re-creation of a body similar to Rabkrin.

[22] *O strukture tsentral'nogo apparata minugleproma SSSR*, 39.

reform was the responsibility of the Technical Administration, the Administration for Labour and Wages, or sometimes of branch research institutes (where it must have had a very low priority). However, for each of these administrations structural reform was only one task among many.[23] The failures of the industrial and production association reforms of 1973 and 1974 can in large measure be explained by the control of the ministry apparatus over its fulfilment, and their ability to put responsibility for fulfilment on organs which were more or less openly recognized to have no competence to do so.

The general argument of this section has been that the complexity of the ministerial structure and the control of the ministerial apparatus over the implementation process made the introduction of malleable and simple structures unlikely. The structures of the ministry were probably inefficient (though it would be impossible to arrive at an exact costing) but were highly conducive to the ability of ministries to achieve functional independence from outside regulation; indeed, their resistance to anything other than the most formal structural reform may be seen as good evidence for the desire of ministry officials to use structure to enhance their independence. The desires of the political leadership to curtail the ministries' ability to control structure is, for this reason, completely intelligible, though it may be a mark of the naïvety of official thinking that it was thought possible under the circumstances.

THE STRUGGLE OVER PERSONNEL

One reason that is often cited for the ability of the political leadership to enforce its will on its institutional subordinates is its formal power over personnel.[24] Control over personnel—its numbers, quality, training, etc.—was the leadership's "second front" against the ministries in the period under scrutiny. At the same time, however, it must be noted that the conclusions reached above about structure also afford a prima-facie reason for believing that personnel policy was likely to differ markedly in practice from theory; ministry officials who

[23] G. Kh. Popov, 'Organizatsiya raboty po sovershenstvovaniyu upravleniya sotsialisticheskim proizvodstvom', in *EKO* 1 (1973), 77. Popov himself worked at that time in the Laboratory of Problems of Administration at Moscow State University which was tied to the Institute of Planning and Normatives of Gosplan.

[24] e.g. A. Nove, *The Soviet Economic System* (3rd edn., London, 1986).

controlled the structure would, if they so chose, possess additional capabilities in subverting personnel policy.

Control over state personnel has been a central feature of party policy since the earliest days of the Soviet Union. The Soviet Marxism of the Bolsheviks was very ambiguous towards the state and its functionaries. On the one hand, the state was a necessary organ, both for repressive and constructive purposes;[25] on the other, immanent in the state, was the constant danger of 'bureaucratism', a deviation wherein the bureaucrat appropriated the state as his private property.[26] To combat these tendencies, the Bolsheviks, after consolidating their power, developed a series of institutions and practices, the most important of which was the so-called *nomenklatura* system of appointments wherein only those on an approved list held by the party could be placed in specified state functions. The general pattern of these institutions and practices formed the basis for the claim of Soviet politicians that they had founded a distinct new type of state. Its features were: avowed partisanship wherein the state itself was guided by the party policy, as opposed to liberal states where the state and the government were quite separate; a guarantee that the partisanship of the state was given both legally (and constitutionally from 1977) by the party's leading role; the penetration of the party of the state through its membership and organization, which was strengthened in 1971 by the extension of *pravo kontrolya* (right of control) to primary party organizations in the state apparatus;[27] control by the party over personnel policy inside the state apparatus. The vigour with which these institutions were supported varied considerably throughout Soviet history.[28] Though the period after 1964 cannot be regarded as strongly anti-bureaucratic (in the Soviet sense and by Soviet standards), strong emphasis was none the less placed upon improving the

[25] See further, R. Theen, 'The Idea of a Revolutionary State: Tkachev, Trotsky and Lenin', in *Russian Review*, 31 (1972), 297–323; T. H. Rigby, *Lenin's Government* (London, 1979), 11–14.

[26] Among the many examples of this kind of argument see V. Martov, *Pravda* (1 July 1983); B. P. Kurashvili, *Bor'ba s byurokratizmom* (Moscow, 1988); and A. Obolonsky, 'Byurokraticheskaya deformatsiya soznaniya i bor'ba s byurokratizmom', in *Sovetskoe gosudarstvo i pravo*, 1 (1987), 52–61.

[27] S. Fortescue, *The Primary Party Organisations of Branch Ministries* (Washington, DC, 1985).

[28] D. Christian, 'The Supervisory Function in Russian and Soviet History', in *Slavic Review*, 31 (1982), 73–90.

performance of state and ministry officials, especially through rationalization, the scientific organisation of labour, attestation of officials, and
so on.

One of the central arguments of the book is that politicians in the
Soviet Union proved to be highly ineffective in controlling the
behaviour of ministry and other officials despite this battery of means;
and it will be argued in Chapter 5 that this failure lay behind the
interest of the post-1985 generation of politicians in creating a new
kind of state. Further evidence of this ineffectiveness can be found in
the failures of party personnel policy from 1965 to 1985. The
institutional aspects of the relationship between party and state will
emerge in later chapters. This section will examine the following areas:
the functioning of the appointment mechanism, that is, the list of
officials fit to be appointed to ministry positions; the attestation and
training of officials, designed to certify and improve their qualifications; and the attempt to limit the growth of bureaucracy through
control over personnel numbers.

In his article, 'The Regional Party Apparatus in the "Sectional
Society"',[29] Stephen Fortescue has argued convincingly about the
limits on the direct power of the party to impose its preferred
candidates on enterprises over ministry opposition. Evidence of a
different kind, however, appeared in a series of articles and responses
in the newspaper *Literaturnaya gazeta* in 1975–6,[30] entitled 'How to
Become a Minister', giving some indication of how ministry appointments actually occurred, and raising questions about the likelihood of
any serious political control being exercised over this process.[31] The
dominant impression obtained from these accounts of the placement
of officials and managers by ministries is of informality, confusion, and
inefficiency. Differences between ministries on methods of personnel

[29] S. Fortescue, 'The Regional Party Apparatus in the "Sectional Society"', in
Studies in Comparative Communism, 1 (1988), 11–23.

[30] The articles referred to are: A. Levikov, *Literaturnaya gazeta* (5 Nov. 1975, 28 Jan.
1976, 1 Feb. 1976, 19 May 1976); for discussion of Levikov, see the same journal (21
July 1976).

[31] Lowenhardt divides the *nomenklatura* into three types: basic, requiring a party
committee to make the appointment; registration, where the party's approval was
needed; and 'promotion reserve'. See J. Lowenhardt, 'NOMENKLATURA and the Soviet
Constitution', in *Review of Socialist Law*, 1/10 (1984), 36–55. Though the evidence in
this section concerns what is officially a reserve list, it is clear that the party had an
interest in its functioning as well. See J. Hough and M. Fainsod, *How the Soviet Union
is Governed*, (London, 1979), 431–2.

placement were also quite pronounced. Perhaps revealing his techno-cratic leanings—a viewpoint shared by many influential advisers to the leadership itself— the journalist, Levikov, at one point almost wistfully refers to the efficiency of the GDR's appointment system, based on an 1,100 strong, fully computerized, reserve list, where the right candidate could be found in a matter of seconds. In the Soviet Union, there were no objective criteria for advancement—not even, as some of the respondents indicated, clear political ones; reserve lists were formed haphazardly—sometimes openly, sometimes not—and personal acquaintanceship with a ministry official was cited as often the most likely means of promotion[32]—a view confirmed by the Minister of Oil-Refining and Petro-Chemical Industry since 1985, Nikolay Lemayev, who agreed that his success as an enterprise director lay in getting his superiors to give him scarce supplies.[33]

The continued prevalence of non-political factors favouring appoint-ment and promotion was supported by a study of 828 ministerial officials upgrading their qualifications who entered the Academy of the National Economy of the Council of Ministers between 1980 and 1986.[34] The authors allude to the almost wholly formal character of 'moral–political qualities' in promotion prospects. No one would have been foolhardy enough at that time to propose their abolition, and candidates were required to have a clean record. But their real importance, even at the stage of entry into the *nomenklatura* (referred to by the authors as *rukovodyashchaya rabota*) was evident from the relegation of 'social–political activeness' to sixth place in factors influencing their appoint-ment. Even more interesting, once appointed, 'social–political activity' became a negative factor influencing career prospects for all but the highest ministry officials, who assigned it no influence at all.[35]

---

[32] The need to improve the functioning of the apparatus of ministries and their subordinates was a common theme from 1965. See also V. Vishnyakov, 'Povyshenie effektivnosti raboty apparata upravleniya promyshlennost'yu', in *Sovetskoe gosudarstvo i pravo*, 3 (1966), 33–43   [33] *Moscow News*, 12 (1987), 13.

[34] I. F. Sokolova and M. A. Manuil'skiy, 'Kak stat' ministrom', in *Sots. iss.* 1 (1988), 16–25. Perhaps not surprisingly, the respondents in their survey do not cite family connections as a reason for their career rise (see table 3). However, their testimony is strongly contradicted by a further survey of ministry workers conducted by the Academy of Social Sciences of the Central Committee of the CPSU in 1988 in the Ministries of Finance, Cereals, Chemical Industry, and Water Amelioration. Of the officials 31.8% had no real qualifications for working there—the Ministry of Finance was the exception. They had got there, the report concluded, by protectionism or family ties. Cited in L. Ponomarev and V. Shinkarenko, 'Kto kogo? Chem silen byurokrat?', in *Uroki gor'kie, no neobkhodimye* (Moscow, 1988), 155–9.

[35] Sokalova and Manuil'skiy, 'Kak stat' ministrom', 21–4.

The accounts given in the articles in *Literaturnaya gazeta* suggest that officials generally rose to their level of incompetence, after which they were shifted sideways. A converse consequence of the secrecy of the reserve appointments list was that managers and officials were able, and often willing, to keep their good people hidden—often, no doubt, to the detriment of the efficient worker's career. There were no legal norms governing advancement.[36] In any case, many appointments did not come from reserve lists at all. In Minpribor, for example, in 1973–4, of ten new research institute directors only five came from the reserve list. In the Ministry of Construction of Heavy Industrial Enterprises in the same period, of thirty-five executive appointments only eighteen came from the reserve list. In the Ministry of Electrical Equipment only 36 per cent of directors appointed were from reserve lists.[37] These appointees were often referred to as 'Vikings', who dropped in on areas unprepared, unexpected, and not carefully selected. The prevalence of these occurrences is an indication that local officials were in no position to oppose Viking appointments, even if they wanted to. The very secrecy, inefficiency, and informality of the cadre selection process worked to the advantage of ministry officials who were able to utilize their control over information and their ability to strike first with appointments against local officials who were in no position to judge candidates. Not surprisingly, however, according to Levikov, ministry officials did complain about the existence of too much democracy, which hindered their ability to move people around the country as they saw fit.[38]

Informality and a similar lack of control also characterized the procedures surrounding the certification (*attestatsiya*) of officials on which the party and Council of Ministers passed legislation in 1969 and 1973. Ministries were instructed to draw up certification norms for work efficiency, responsibility for assigned tasks, qualifications, and ideological and cultural standards. The periodic attestation of fulfilment of these norms for personnel was to be completed every three

[36] Attempts to introduce a standard legal norm for management by Goskomtrud in 1969 came to nothing.   [37] Levikov, *Literaturnaya gazeta* (28 Jan. 1976).

[38] At the same time, the evidence from readers' letters indicates that the system of *nomenklatura* appointments had a wider political significance which had an effect in a number of directions. Some readers were in favour of formalizing the system by introducing competitive open exams. Others suggested that this would merely favour the educated who were able to memorize while excluding manual workers from promotion. Levikov noted that this issue was increasingly important in a period of declining mobility prospects. The lack of political consensus on the issue probably strengthened the ministries' ability to carry on as usual.

to five years by a ministry certification commission, and a list of positions subject to certification was to be drawn up by ministries in conjunction, in relevant cases, with republican Councils of Ministers.[39] Evidence from a study published in 1979, however, points to fundamental deficiencies in the implementation of these directives.[40] The number of times certification took place varied from ministry to ministry; in some it was done annually, in others only once every four years. Regardless of the number of times, however, in the vast majority of cases certification was treated completely formally and investigation was superficial. In 98–9 per cent of cases, those examined received identical marks, and the author suggested that the failure of ministry officials to obtain certification was used by (and probably the result of) his superiors as a means of getting rid of otherwise unwanted staff by legal means.[41] As A. V. Obolonsky put it, lamenting the inability of formal means to deal adequately with the real processes of life in the apparatus:

In practice, the evaluation of this or that colleague takes place under the influence of the collective opinion of members of the work collective, and at the time of the procedures of certification, there mostly occurs the affirmation and juridical formulation which comprises the informal opinion of colleagues.[42]

A similar picture emerges from an examination of efforts to improve the training of ministry officials. Already in the period immediately after their restoration, it was clear to scholars that there was a substantial difference between the training of technical workers and that of leading cadres.[43] At the same time, however, the distinction was blurred in practice by the operative code for the classification of employees.[44] In 1970, the Institute of the National Economy of the Council of Ministers opened for the purpose of raising the qualifications of ministry and other personnel. (No basic training school for managers followed.) In the aftermath of this, ministries themselves

[39] *Izvestiya* (22 Aug. 1973), 3.

[40] L. Okun'kov, 'Periodicheskie attestatsii upravlennogo personala', in *Khozyaystvo i pravo*, 1 (1979), 21–4.   [41] Ibid. 22.

[42] A. V. Obolonskiy, 'Formal'nye i neformal'nye gruppy v apparate gosudarstvennogo upravleniya', in *Sovetskoe gosudarstvo i pravo*, 5 (1983), 33.

[43] V. G. Vishnyakov, 'Podgotovka i povyshenie kvalifikatsii gosudarstvennykh sluzhashchikh', in *Sovetskoe gosudarstvo i pravo*, 6 (1971), 73–81.

[44] Yu. A. Rozenbaum, 'K ponyatiyu upravlenshskikh kadrov', in *Pravovedenie*, 6 (1975), 24–5.

followed suit in creating branch training institutes. The successes, however, of branch or national institutes in raising the qualifications or in training a new type of official were minimal. In the period 1965–79, 74 per cent of high officials had engineering backgrounds;[45] by 1988, the figure had risen to 80 per cent and only 20 per cent were specialized administrators.[46] Furthermore, according to the study of graduates of the Institute of the National Economy, even of those with technical qualifications, the level tended to be low. 'The system of preparation and qualification of cadres was highly immobile.' Though the majority of entrants had diplomas, 22 per cent of them were obtained either at night school or at extra-mural departments of *Vuzi* (technical schools). There were evident large discrepancies between rises in levels of responsibility and corresponding improvements in qualifications. The main reason for promotion was not educational, but success in achieving targets set by the existing economic mechanism.[47] The situation inside the branch training institutes was likely to emphasize even further the formal nature of educational attainment. A report of a department of the Central Committee in 1983 was highly critical of the performance of the Ministry of Heavy and Machine Transport Machinery. Although, each year, more than 300 officials of the ministry's apparatus studied in the ministry's education system, the composition of the group changed only slightly so that the vast majority of ministry personnel received no training at all. The syllabus was attacked as irrelevant to the needs of training people for the new system of economic rather than administrative management; no course was offered on economic reform, nor were there any specialist seminars.[48]

The general conclusion to be drawn from looking at training, promotion, and assignment of ministry officials, which accords well with the other evidence presented in this chapter, is that there is little sign that superior bodies, including the Council of Ministers both nationally and at republic level, were able to operate effective control over ministry personnel, in large measure because the ministries themselves were charged with the process.

The organization of work inside the ministry, in any case, would have rendered any superficial criteria of job parameters or efficient

[45] K. Ryavec, 'The Soviet Bureaucratic Élite from 1964 to 1979', in *Soviet Union/ Union Soviétique*, 12/3 (1985), 332.   [46] *Pravitel'stvennyy vestnik*, 5 (1989), 4–5.
[47] Sokolova and Manuil'skiy, 'Kak stat'ministrom'.
[48] *Ekonomicheskaya gazeta*, 7 (1984), 11.

performance wholly irrelevant. The appearance of working life inside a ministry is that of chaos.[49] In the Ministry of Machine Tool and Tool Industry in 1969, for example, a thousand people came to work each day, to supervise 300 enterprises, 36 research institutes, 44 design bureaux, all of which employed over 30,000 scientists, engineers, technicians, and office employees.[50] A continuous daily stream of petitioners from enterprises decamped in the corridors, and too many people crowded into cramped offices. One *glavk*, the Chief Administration for Manufacture of Forge and Press Machinery, by no means the biggest in the ministry, logged 15,000 incoming and 7,000 outgoing documents for the first six months of 1969.[51] By 1983, the problem of the paper flood had not noticeably improved. Over 80 billion documents were generated a year, 90 per cent of which circulated without any interest to their recipient.[52]

Various ethnographic and time-and-motion studies of work in ministries confirm the view of an apparently chaotic and inefficient use of work time, though these latter-day Taylorists' efforts to improve the style of work met with little success.[53] Almost half the ministry workers, asked in a 1970 questionnaire about their job description, answered that it was defined only in the most general way, and more than 60 per cent said that they spent time on tasks that were unrelated to their official responsibilities. Although there was evidence in the report of formal success in introducing departmental plans of work, on daily, weekly, monthly, and quarterly bases—only 4.5 per cent were to have no plan at all—the situation with regard to individual ministry workers was very different. The majority had no plans for the following day's work. Among the factors cited for the lack of work rhythm were the changing demands at different parts of the production cycle, *sezonnost'*, which was the main cause of employees taking work home— a common practice—as well as delays in receiving documents, the need to present work for the appropriate signature, and the absence of proper conditions of work, including boring, repetitive tasks, background conversation, noise, etc.[54]

[49] *Pravda* (25 Dec. 1969), 2.   [50] Ibid. (21 Dec. 1968).
[51] Ibid. (25 Dec. 1969).   [52] *Trud* (12 May 1983).
[53] See B. I. Levin, 'O nekotorykh aspektakh izucheniya raboty sluzhashchikh promyshlennykh ministerstv', in *Organizatsiya raboty ministerstv v usloviyakh ekonomicheskoy reformy* (Moscow, 1972); K. S. Kryukova, 'Analyz chislennosti rabotnikov apparata promyshlennykh ministerstv', in *Trud i zarabotnaya plata*, 1 (1970), 16–22; and *Nauchnaya organizatsiya truda rabotnikov apparata ministertsv i vedomstv* (Moscow, 1973).
[54] V. Kazimirchuk and Kh. Shneyder, 'Sotsiologiya upravleniya', in *Problemy sotsiologii prava* (Vilnius, 1970), 15–25.

Many Soviet politicians and scholars from 1965 onwards considered that the problem of poor organization of the work process in the ministries could be solved by the introduction of branch automated management systems.[55] In 1976 15 million people were cited as working on the processing of 10 billion documents, and the branch automated management system seemed a possible way of cutting through the excess of paperwork. In the main, however, it was hoped that the management system would not be based on a high degree of departmentalism within the bounds of the ministry.[56] Between 1966 and 1979, 1,335 automated management systems were created, of which 1,257 were in enterprises and 247 were located in ministries and state committees.[57] However, even when correctly installed, the plans worked out by the system were ignored,[58] and, by 1974, the familiar and predictable problems of ministries introducing the system to meet their own needs were evident. The design of the systems varied between ministries, as did the departments responsible for introducing them.[59] Although another article in 1974 suggested that the best way forward for introducing the system was to let the ministry have control over the process, including staffing,[60] by 1983 it was clear that because of ministerial control, the great improvements in the quality of the computers, and large increases in the number of staff operating them, had resulted in little improvement in their economic yield and their use for trivial purposes.[61]

Such findings are confirmed by research on the attitude towards innovation of officials in three separate ministries. It seems that 70 per cent of them spent their time filling in forms and informational materials. In many cases, there was little difference in the work of leading and ordinary officials. Only 6 per cent of those questioned were involved in introducing new technology, and only 2.3 per cent were involved in new organizational structures—despite the fact that this matter had been formally put before all the ministries. A third of respondents felt they were unable to assess properly the work of research institutes; 0.7 per cent thought they were using scientific

---

[55] For an indication of the different political positions and diverging hopes concerning the introduction of automated management systems see *EKO* 2 (1970), 151–6. In the event, no one's hopes were realized.   [56] See *Pravda* (28 Oct. 1971), 3.

[57] 'XXVI s"esd KPSS i organizatsionno-pravovye voprosy gosudarstvennogo upravleniya', 4.

[58] I. V. Zhezhko, 'Pochemu upravlencheskiy rabotnik korrektiruet ... optimal'ny plan', in *EKO* 3 (1979), 85–93.   [59] *Pravda* (25 Feb. 1974).

[60] *Izveztiya* (3 Jan. 1974), 2.   [61] *Pravda* (23 Aug. 1982), 2.

achievements properly, and 43 per cent thought they were using them badly. In all, 65 per cent of respondents said they were doing mainly current work; only 29 per cent reckoned that they achieved an optimal combination of current and strategic work, and only 2 per cent thought that they spent the basic part of their time on strategic work.[62]

Finally, it is useful to examine the evidence concerning the success of the leadership in achieving their declared target for controlling the growth in ministry staff sizes. Kosygin had emphasized in his 1965 speech, that the ministries should not become large organizations. Controlling the numbers of white-collar staff in all spheres of the economy had been a continuous concern of Soviet politicians,[63] since the early days of the Soviet state, in large measure because of the view of bureaucracy outlined above. Managerial personnel were often considered unproductive.[64] Resolutions of the party and the government were passed on a number of occasions between 1965 and 1985 which were designed to reduce the size of the ministerial apparatus,[65] and return employees to production. However, these target reductions were not met.[66] Figures show that in the period 1975–85 there was a trend towards increasing personnel numbers, which continued despite the Council of Ministers resolution which had deplored and supposedly controlled it in 1981. Taking ministries and state committees together,[67] (*apparat organov upravleniya ministertv i vedomstv*), the number of workers in the apparatus rose from 1,356,000 in 1975, to 1,531,000

---

[62] V. Amelin, 'Smogut li otraslevye ministerstva stat' sub"ektami innovatsiy', in *Voprosy ekonomiki*, 10 (1989), 25–32.

[63] e.g. at the Central Committee Plenum in Dec. 1956; in a joint resolution of the Central Committee and Council of Ministers in 1973; and again at the June 1983 Plenum of the Central Committee. See S. Andreev, 'Prichiny i sledstviya', in *Ural*, 1 (1988), 114.

[64] See V. G. Vishnyakov, 'Sovershenstvovanie struktury i shtatov organov upravleniya v usloviyakh khozyaystvennoy reformy', in *Organizatsiya raboty ministertv v usloviyakh ekonomicheskoy reformy* (Moscow, 1972), 108. One irony of the drive to cut white-collar staff, pointed out by Vishnyakov, was that, not surprisingly, specialists on the 'scientific organization of labour' were among the first to be dismissed (114).

[65] *Pravda* (24 Oct. 1969). See also the resolution 'On Measures for Limiting Increases in and Reducing Personnel in Administrative Jobs and in Certain Branches of the Nonproductive Sphere', in *Izvestiya* (24 Nov. 1981).

[66] Evidence of the failure of the ministries to meet the Oct. 1969 resolution of the Central Committee and Council of Ministers is given in a report of the People's Control Commission in 1971. Of 14 *glavki* investigated, 12 had overfulfilled their maximum allocations for personnel numbers. Rather than reducing them the ministry had tried to deceive the higher authorities by transferring budgets to other sources and laying off production personnel rather than administrators. *Pravda* (9 Dec. 1971).

[67] Unfortunately, no detailed breakdown was given.

in 1980, to 1,623,000 in 1985. Of those, in the apparatus of all-Union and Union–republican organs, the figures were 96,000 in 1975; 104,000 in 1980; and 107,000 in 1985. At the republican level, the figures were 122,000, 134,000, and 140,000 respectively. (The remainder were working in lower regional bodies.)[68] Indeed, as the figures show, the tendency towards an overall acceleration in personnel growth can be observed, though after 1980 the biggest rates of growth were experienced at the lower levels.[69]

Not only had there been a general trend for the number of ministries to increase across the board, within each ministry the number of high officials grew. The number of deputy ministers had increased: by 1983 there were twelve in the all-Union Ministry of Timber, Pulp and Paper and Lumber Industry, eleven in the Ministry of Coal Industry and the Ministry of Finance, and twelve in the Ministry of Power and Electrification. Ministry *kollegiya* contained around thirty members. The problem was that this increase was duplicated all the way down the regional ministerial structure, which explains why the increase in overall personnel was located at the lower levels.[70]

Under the control mechanism developed by the Ministry of Finance, the indicator for reducing personnel numbers was given to ministries in terms of planned rouble savings.[71] The ministries, however, passed these on down the line without taking too much of the pain themselves. An immunity process (of a typically ministerial style) developed whereby, first, all auxiliary personnel—typists, messengers, etc.—were cut, leaving the engineer to type using one finger at a time, or the designer to function as a delivery boy. Office personnel, for example, constituted only 3.8 per cent of total white-collar staff. Secondly, a system of 'dead souls' developed, wherein only vacant jobs were made redundant, and ministry officials desperately tried to create vacancies in advance of presumed cuts. Thirdly, the system encouraged 'staff reduction through progress' wherein, through reforms like the creation of industrial associations out of the old *glavki*, the ministry was able to double the size of its staff, or where whole ministry departments were transformed into research institutes.[72] At the same time,

---

[68] *Argumenty i fakty*, 11 (12–18 Mar. 1988).

[69] Another source suggested that the number of administrative personnel increased by 3 million in 1983 compared with 1975. See *Izvestiya* (12 May 1984), 2.   [70] Ibid.

[71] Around 1 billion roubles for 1984. Ibid.

[72] Ibid. Evidence for this was available as early as 1975.

other evidence makes it clear that plans for cutting personnel numbers were not carried out at all if the result was a reduction in average income of those who remained behind.[73] The practical effect of staff cuts and personnel control on the work process itself, therefore, indicates that it operated against the grain of other attempts to improve work organization. The case of the Ministry of the Gas Industry, investigated by the People's Control Commission in 1975, may have been typical. It had lied about savings from industrial reorganization and claimed for changes which had not then occurred. The reorganization which did take place increased staff costs by 762,000 roubles; the money was obtained under the pretext that it was being used for building work.[74]

POWER INSIDE THE MINISTRY

The evidence presented above points to a number of conclusions which need to be drawn about the difficulties political and state leaders faced in seeking to regulate. First, the structure of the ministry, and the work process inside it, were mutually reinforcing elements in the ability of ministry officials to resist control by their supervisors. The irregular, chaotic, over-complex, overlapping departmental arrangements, the highly fluid form of work organization with flexible task assignments and low development of responsibility, the huge staff sizes and budgets, spread over a multiplicity of sub-units with few clear cost-effectiveness criteria, the arcane and lengthy procedures[75] through which decisions were taken—all these factors together created the space for ministry officials to defeat the efforts to impose arrangements which were unacceptable or unsuitable. Indeed, the complexity and chaos apparent in the various ministries is probably explained as much by the interests of officials in maintaining control as any technological factor associated with the production process.

---

[73] Vishnyakov, 'Sovershenstvovanie', 29.   [74] *Izvestiya* (18 Sept. 1975), 3.

[75] For a full explanation of the complex process by which documents are circulated among concerned departments for the purpose of securing a stamp of agreement (*vizirovanie* or *soglasovanie*) see B. M. Lazerev (ed.), *Upravlencheskie protsedury* (Moscow, 1988), 182–202. The issue of *kontrol'*, for example, was important in some ministries for relations between the minister and his *kollegiya*. In the Ministry of Road-Building Materials, *kontrol'* was exercised by the *Upravlenie Delami*; for an assessment of the political implications of procedural matters see S. Fortescue, *Building Consensus in Japanese and Soviet Bureaucracies* (Birmingham, 1987).

Secondly, however, though efficiency probably declined with the increase in the fluidity and complexity of administrative work,[76] the informality of the process need not necessarily have resulted in a decline in the power of leading officials in the ministry. Though ministry officials were not property owners, their operational control of state property gave them equivalent powers. Clearly, ministers themselves were faced with problems of control over their own subordinate enterprises, but it is essential to make a qualitative distinction between the powers of the individuals in ministries exercising operative control over subordinates, as the ministries were empowered to do, and the regulatory powers of those bodies charged with supervising the ministries. Ministry officials, on the basis of their local knowledge, and working with formal instruments and within informal groups,[77] were in a position to manipulate various levers of intra-ministerial power to their own advantage while defying the efforts of their nominal superiors to control the behaviour of their institutions. Evidence about the mechanisms of decision-making in the ministries suggests that power was concentrated among the top officials, at the level of the minister and his deputies (though some of the latter were more powerful than others).

A study of the Ministry of the Coal Industry,[78] for example, lists seven types of rights and responsibilities: decision-making powers, preparation of decisions, preparation of decisions by specially created commissions, participation in the preparation of decisions, mandatory agreement at stages in the preparation of decisions and in its adoption, the introduction and fulfilment of decisions, and control (*kontrol'*) over execution. These rights and responsibilities were then broken down by department. While the formal decision-making power of the minister is clearly shown—and should not be underestimated in conditions where the minister wished to exercise his operational powers—of equal or greater significance must be the enormous control he exercised in conjunction with some of his deputies over the agenda of departmental decision-making. Most preparatory functions were concentrated in the hands of special commissions under the minister's supervision, as were the strong mandatory agreement

---

[76] This is only in comparison to some optimally functioning bureaucracy. The ministry as it actually operated may have been more efficient than it would have been had the naïve plans of the regulators been introduced.

[77] Obolonsky, 'Formalnye i neformalnye gruppy v apparate gosudarstvenogo upravleniya'.   [78] Migachev, *Opyt sovershenstvovaniya*, 24–7.

(*soglasovanie*) rights of the Administration for Perspective Development of the branch.

The other departments most notable for their formal rights to affect outcomes were concentrated under only one deputy minister for economics, who supervised the mandatory agreement rights of the planning and economics administration, the finance administration, and the accounts department, and the administration for labour-norming and wages. The formal powers of the juridical service and arbitration, whose agreement was required at different stages, must surely have been compromised by the fact that the department was supervised by the deputy minister for supplies and transport. Power over the industrial associations was exercised directly by other deputy ministers. The deputy minister for coal machine-building, for example, had decision-making powers over the raw materials, energy, equipment, wages, and finances of the supposedly independent industrial associations Soyuzugelmash and Zarubezhugol. The industrial associations, as noted above, had been established to replace the old *glavki* which had been rendered largely superfluous by the tendency for subordinate enterprises to deal directly with the deputy minister or his functional apparatus. However, the evidence suggests that in terms of intra-ministerial power, the industrial associations made little difference. Enterprises continued to apply directly to the deputy minister.[79]

Similar difficulties befell the arbitration service of the ministry. From 1970, when the Ministry of Justice was re-established with, among others, the aim of increasing the role of contracts in the economic sphere, there had been some hope that the juridical and arbitration departments of the ministries would strengthen legality in ministry activity, especially with regard to enterprises.[80] Placing the department under the supervision of the deputy minister for supplies, for that reason, was the Soviet equivalent of putting the fox in charge of the hen-coop. The evidence tends to support this argument. An inquiry in 1979 by the supra-ministerial State Arbitration Service (Gosarbitrazh) into the work of arbitration in the Ministry of the

---

[79] V. G. Vishnyakov, 'Problemy sovershenstvovaniya tsentral'nogo apparata promy-shlennykh ministerstv', in *Konstitutsiya SSSR i pravovya problemy sovershenstvovaniya rukovodstvo narodnym khozyaystvom* (Moscow, 1979), 14.

[80] See N. N. Gorbunov, 'Yuridicheskaya sluzhba otraslevogo ministerstv', in *Sovetskoe gosudarstvo i pravo*, 4 (1970), 84–9.

Fishery Industry revealed a catalogue of blunders.[81] The fact that guide-lines on the work of the arbitration service were determined inside the ministry was also a factor most negatively influencing its work. Legislation on the arbitration system qualified it as an administrative as well as judicial organ, and its primary economic tasks were defined by the primacy of state over enterprise interests; in practice, given the way in which state interests were institutionalized in ministries, this meant the primacy of departmental interests over any other.[82]

There is other direct evidence of the domination of the ministry by its leading officials exercising operational control. Complaints surfaced in the early 1970s about the amount of time ministry officials spent on operational matters.[83] Only 10.5 per cent of ministry time was spent on planning; the rest was spent on operational tasks, including over 50 per cent of the work time of the so-called functional apparatus.[84] However, little changed up to 1985. In 1975, for example, a report on the Ministry of Building Materials indicated that the minister or his deputy signed a vast number of telegrams authorizing movements of enterprise managers and officials (though there was also evidence of widespread enterprise circumventing of this power).[85] Another article spoke of the increase in the power of the deputy minister for the economy of the Ministry of Cellulose and Paper Industry in 1976.[86] Finally, in 1984, Gvishiani, deputy chairman of the State Committee for Science and Technology (GKNT), wrote that not only were the general schemes introduced from a departmental point of view, but that, inside the ministries, the department head took all decisions while functional administrations sought to transfer all decisions to the top to reduce their responsibilities.[87] A balanced assessment of the various

[81] P. Kharchikov, 'Arbitrazh ministerstva. Ego oshibki i upushcheniya', in *Khozyaystvo i pravo*, 8 (1979), 41–3.

[82] See A. Ya. Maksimovich, *Arbitrazh v sisteme ministerstva i vedomstva* (Moscow, 1987), 18–23.

[83] M. I. Piskotin, 'Problemy kompetentsii i metodov raboty ministerstv v usloviyakh ekonomicheskoy reformy', in *Organizatsiya raboty ministerstv v usloviyakh ekonomicheskoy reformy* (Moscow, 1972), 81.

[84] A. S. Petrov, 'Ekonomicheskaya reforma: tendentsii organizatsii otraslevogo upravleniya promyshlennost'yu', in *Sovetskoe gosudarstvo i pravo*, 3 (1971), 18–19.

[85] *Pravda* (13 May 1975), 2.

[86] R. A. Kanunova and V. G. Sharkovich, *Osobennosti formirovaniya organizatsionnoy struktury otrasli i obshchey modeli upravleniya* (Moscow, 1976), 38.

[87] D. Gvishiani, 'Klyuchevye rezervy upravleniya narodnym khozyaystvom', in *Kommunist*, 4 (1984), 40–1.

claims of a shift of power to or from functional bodies therefore would suggest that this misses the point; power in the ministry always belonged to the leading officials, who rewarded with promotion those who were most able to meet the success criteria which they themselves pursued.[88]

This chapter has tried to show how ministers and high officials, heading institutions with enormous budgets, output, and employees, were able to avoid the declared efforts of their superiors to alter the structure of their institutions, the behaviour, and even the number of their personnel, while the minister and his high officials were able to operate the decisive levers of power within the organization. Though nominally agencies of the party political leadership, therefore, their potential power was clearly enormous and the next chapters will be concerned with elaborating on how this power was used to pursue other ministry objectives.

[88] A view confirmed in discussion with Soviet specialists.

3

Industrial Ministries in the Soviet Political System

INDUSTRIAL ministries were political bodies in so far as they were created by politicians as instruments of state, took decisions in its name, and then participated themselves in the very selection of political and state leaders. However, because their interests were essentially economic, their place in the political process had the effect of undermining the space for the exercise of authority; they were able to use their economic power to exert influence on political and state leaders and institutions in support of themselves. Four main kinds of ministerial power were evident: allocative power, through their ability to control the direction of resources; direct political power, as agents able to affect and override the influence of other institutions; integrative power, as institutions able to deliver the population, or at least structure the activity of social forces to render them politically controllable; and hegemonic power, as actors who were able to impose costs on change which outweighed the benefits.

The issue of the ministries' relationship with society will be taken up in the next chapter. This chapter will deal with the use and exercise of ministry power as it affected the operation of the other state and party institutions. The main conclusion to be drawn from the evidence that will be presented is that the power of ministries had the effect of creating a *weak* state rather than a strong one, as is often wrongly assumed; and, as a corollary, the weakness of the state meant equally weak control by politicians. The result was that, as distinct from the notion of the statization of the economy which is implicit in the dominant paradigm of the Soviet Union, the power of the industrial ministries paradoxically led to the economization of the state and politics. To paraphrase Marx, when the state is but the executive committee of economic interests, little is left for it as the institutional basis for the exercise of political power.

These general conclusions will be supported by examining evidence about the relationship of ministers and ministries to other political and state institutions: state committees and the apparatus of the Council of Ministers; republican level bodies, including the republican Council of Ministers and the Union–republic ministries of the republic themselves; and, most importantly of all, the Communist Party at its various levels. In each case, it will be argued, the power and behaviour of the ministries suggests not only that they were far from the pliable instruments of Communist Party rule, but that they were effectively dominant *vis-à-vis* other institutions.

MINISTERS, THE STATE, AND THE ECONOMY

In the introductory chapter of this book it was suggested that state officials—bureaucrats— were rational actors seeking to maximize their own interests. In itself this assertion is a truism. More important is the claim that actors functioning as state officials—those, in other words, whose interests depended on their attachment to the structural position of state employee—were distinguished by their use of a particular form of power. This power was based upon the execution of authority, which closely linked the state official to the politician.

Whether those who occupy nominally state or political roles actually realize their interests by means of the exercise of legitimate authority, however, is an empirical question. As shall be shown below in the discussion of corruption, bureaucrats, and politicians for that matter, may find it easier to realize their private and institutional interests by utilizing their position in various ways for illicit gain, or by exercising direct control over resources, rather than relying on the acceptance of the authority of their instructions. These corrupt forms of rational advancement of private and institutional interests were especially present in the ministerialized political and state system of the Soviet Union.

In an important sense, it has always been difficult to answer with an unambiguous affirmative that the Russian, and then Soviet, state system had a bureaucracy which operated on the basis of legitimate authority. Writing about the durability of the autocracy Hans Rogger has commented that it

remained strong and rigidly conservative not so much because of excessive bureaucratization but because there was no homogeneous, efficient, alert, and politically conscious policy-making bureaucracy comparable to the Prussian, French, or even Austrian. The Russian bureaucracy was unable to create a *rechtstaat*, the *sine qua non* of orderly bureaucratic government, and, as a result, the arbitrary capricious power of the Russian autocrat remained undiminished until 1905.[1]

This does not imply, however, that the idea of an efficient, legally based, and rationally recruited, authority was absent from the ambitions and hopes of reform-minded politicians and statesmen of both the pre- and post-revolutionary eras. The emergence of a Western-type bureaucracy would have been as much a threat to the rule of the emperor as revolution itself, which may help explain the autocrat's willingness 'to undermine the ministerial bureaucracy as the lawful foundation of government, political innovator, and potential mediator between the Tsar and society'.[2] One reason why ministries may have been seen by the Bolsheviks as more natural ways of modernizing the country, in comparison to the spread of corporate capitalist bodies in civil society, was that this view had had a long tradition among progressives in Russia.

One of the features of the failure to establish an efficient *rechtstaat* in the Tsarist period, of which there are many similarities in the successor Soviet state was, as Sabel and Stark have put it, that 'no particular bureaucracy ever escapes the circumstances of its own creation'.[3] Officials were not only poorly trained and recruited, but often inherited from their institutions the dubious character which is to be expected when their interests were not primarily connected with the exercise of state authority. Though to some extent there did occur a rationalization of the recruitment of the civil service in the late Tsarist period, the minister continued throughout to be known for his lack of character and will, and for his mediocrity, greed, and corruption. This was plausibly connected with the institutions in which they operated, and learned their trade; Tsarist ministers frequently emerged from within the departments in which they began their careers. By and large they were regarded as little more than high-grade *chinovniki*.[4]

---

[1] H. Rogger, *Russia in the Age of Modernisation and Revolution 1881–1917* (New York, 1983), 47–8.

[2] D. T. Orlovsky, *The Limits of Reform: The Ministry of Internal Affairs in Imperial Russia 1802–1881* (London, 1981), 198.

[3] C. F. Sabel and D. Stark, 'Planning, Politics and Shop-Floor Power: Hidden Forms of Bargaining in Soviet-imposed State-Socialist Economies', in *Politics and Society*, 4 (1982), 444.

[4] Meaning literally 'official', the word carries a strongly negative connotation in Russian. See W. B. Lincoln, 'The Ministries of Nicholas I: A Brief Enquiry into their Backgrounds and Service Careers', in *Russian Review*, 34 (1982), 308–23.

As has been attested to elsewhere, however, the power of the state to affect social change was highly regarded by the Bolsheviks, whatever the rhetoric of works like Lenin's *State and Revolution* may indicate, and the creation of an efficient administrative machine, comprised of partisan and trained personnel was a priority.[5] The desired features of the peculiarly Soviet statesman is well expressed in the character of Aleksander Bek's fictional minister Onisimov, who was nothing if not the model Soviet statesman. Gavriil Popov summarizes his traits as follows:

Onisimov was 53 years old. Under his eyes were dark shadows, the result of many years of lack of sleep. The motto of his life was irreproachability. He always tried to act in such a way that he was beyond reproach. He always exacted the most from himself. The first person to whom he refused the least pampering and the fewest excuses was himself. But any remark from above, even the most mild and tender, was the cause in him of the sharpest pain, such that he couldn't rest until he had managed to get rid of what had called forth the dissatisfaction of his superiors. The basis of Onisimov's activity? 'I will fulfil the directives of above; you fulfil mine.' 'Ours is not to reason why . . .' was his favourite dictum. He worked like a precision machine, exemplified administrative techniques, knew the whole labyrinth of the administrative mechanism, the full depth of interdepartmental relations . . . To be exact, Onisimov had no interests besides those of his work. And these interests he understood as the efficient execution of commands [*ispolnitel' nost'*]. Now, as with his sixteen years in the underground, he remained a party member, he never sought to deviate or to elude the fulfilment of party and state decisions.[6]

It is possible to abstract from this description certain key features which ought to be present in the ideal Soviet bureaucrat. First, his right to take decisions was inextricably linked to his personal credibility; corruption effectively undermined his authority. Secondly, to be effective the activity of the bureaucrat needed to be based on the application of rules, not only to others but to himself; informality was also the enemy of authority. Finally, the connection between the ability of the bureaucrat to take decisions and the authority of the politician is emphasized; the former derived his power from his acceptance of the latter.

Of course, in large measure the character of Onisimov was established

---

[5] See e.g., R. Theen, 'The Idea of the Revolutionary State: Tkachev, Lenin and Trotsky', in *Russian Review*, 31 (1972), 297–323.

[6] G. Kh. Popov, 'S tochki zreniya ekonomista', in A. Bek, *Novoe naznachenie* (Moscow, 1987), 191–2.

by Bek as a literary device against which to compare and criticize reality. It is evident from the novel that it is precisely the introduction of corruption into politics and the state which most concerned Bek. This corruption was personified in Beria, who headed the MVD, an organization which, though nominally a state body, was essentially an economic organization of the most brutal kind, running large areas of the economy on the basis of slave, prison labour. Popov, however, makes it clear that such selfless and devoted statesmen as Onisimov, dedicated to fulfilling decrees and subordinate to the politicians, were by no means only fictional. Indeed, this vision of the minister as ideal statesman, acting in his ministry as Onisimov did with almost charismatic authority—but authority none the less—could still be encountered in fiction in the 1970s.

Iron self-mastery had made the minister a minister. In resolving any question, even a very urgent one, the minister was thoughtful and never hurried. He was noted for his extremely methodical approach. Sometimes it even overwhelmed those around him. But his methodicalness expressed his devotion to strict logic, consistency and conclusive proof. It was the mode of thinking of a man who had to keep in mind a great many things—thousands of employees, enterprises, product lists . . . His brain was incessantly categorising everything and creating systems. In every word he uttered, one sensed an inspired will, a charge of energy. He was utterly lacking in impetuosity.[7]

Of course, as Popov points out, in the corrupted and brutal circumstances of the *Beriyashchina*, the very characteristics of the minister, his absolute obedience to, and reliance on, the instructions of his superiors, were the cause of the peculiar personal psychological sicknesses which were a general condition among the administrative class faced with the indefensibleness of their own *ispolnitel'nost'*.[8] At the same time, the need for the minister to control the reins of power inside his department in order to realize the demands of the political élite may have both undermined the skill and character of the next generation of statesmen who had been raised in this bureaucratic environment, while at the same time affording its members the bureaucratic levers to realize their own corrupt ambitions, should they be that way inclined—as exemplified by the deputy minister in Kolesnikov's novel. It has been pointed out how reliant was such a

[7] From Mikhail Kolesnikov's novel *School for Ministers (Shkola ministrov)* quoted in *CDSP* 2 (1979), 11.

[8] What Popov, following Pavlov, calls a *sshibka*, arising from the contradictory impulses of those who operate the 'Administrative System'. See Popov, 'S tochki', 195.

centralized state system on the personal characteristics of the administrators.[9] By the dawn of *perestroyka*, therefore, another sketch of a minister, this time by Tatyana Zaslavskaya, may have been more accurate not only of popular imagination but of the reality of Soviet statesmanship itself.

When I was in Novosibirsk, the minister of the Ministry of Medium-Machine Building[10] Slavsky came—he has been replaced now.[11] It was interesting just to listen to him. He never mentioned 'in our ministry'; he just said 'mine'. The identification was personal. 'I have 330 state farms, my cows give 6,000 litres of milk, so my milk maids . . .' etc. And another interesting thing he said was—'By volume of production, my ministry is between the Ukraine and Kazakhstan.' That's third in the USSR. He is an emperor. This is an empire. Now suppose we tell him he is supposed to look after scientific and technical policy and he shouldn't pay the wages of milk maids.[12]

As with the Tsarist administrative élite, the issue of the background and career patterns of the top Soviet ministerial bureaucrats from 1965 is important in understanding their political position. It should be expected that where the high officials were poorly trained, especially in administrative or political skills, they would be less capable or inclined to exercise legitimate authority. Where officials were recruited from within an apparatus and inculcated with its methods, where power was exercised primarily through allocative functions, these tendencies were likely to be emphasized further. There is evidence that such theoretical considerations were reflected in reality. In Karl Ryavec's study of those between 1964 and 1979 who had achieved high positions in the ministerial system, it is noted that 74 per cent had engineering educational and training backgrounds, as opposed to only 11 per cent with any kind of administrative background;[13] that though 'institutional isolation' is too strong to describe career patterns, none the less 'once in the oil industry, for example, one can move to gas or leave extraction for refining or even petrochemicals but not for coal or automobiles';[14] and of those who had achieved the status of minister,

---

[9] T. Zaslavskaya, 'Chelovecheskiy faktor razvitiya ekonomiki i sotsialnaya spravedlivost'', in *Kommunist*, 13 (1986), 62.

[10] A euphemism for one of the main defense sector ministries.

[11] Slavsky resigned towards the end of 1986 on 'health grounds'. He was replaced by his first deputy.   [12] Interview with Tatyana Zaslavskaya, Moscow July 1989.

[13] K. W. Ryavec, 'The Soviet Bureaucratic Élite from 1964 to 1979' in *Soviet Union/Union Soviétique*, 12/3 (1985), 332.

[14] Ibid. 335. Furthermore, almost all changes in post occurred in key years: 1934–9, 1947–58, 1953, 1955, 1957–8, 1964–5, and 1969.

73 per cent had no experience of party work, compared to 50 per cent for the first deputy minister, and 62 per cent for the deputy ministers. Of those who had held party posts, only 13 per cent had occupied as many as two; 'the "dual executive" exists in a sense, yet early Party work left behind may not be ... meaningful ... except perhaps as a "legitimating factor" and source of informal contacts and knowledge about how the Party works, which bureaucrats can use to their advantage. It can strengthen the state as well as the Party.'[15]

Many of these findings are confirmed in Jon Richardson's study of biographical information on all heads of organizations belonging to the Council of Ministers between October 1964 and November 1982. Richardson notes that despite the broad variety of ministries in the economic sector, recruitment patterns differ to an insignificant extent among them.

Indeed, the dominant pattern has not changed from that established in Stalin's day, whereby most ministers had worked their way up from the shop-floor in one ministry or groups of closely-related ministries, usually acquiring a highly specialised technical tertiary education along the way. The main difference between the late Stalin period and the present is that now such education usually takes place before beginning work ... [16]

Again, in 1964 only two ministers had had any significant party experience. Of the sixty-nine new ministers appointed in the Brezhnev period, only nine had worked in the party apparatus. In five of these cases, the ministries involved were

new, reorganized or recently created bodies, which suggests that organizational coherence would not necessarily have been greatly affected. Of course, the dominant long-term pattern of infrequent lateral mobility does reinforce the organizational differentiation explanation, in so far as it emphasizes that persistent organizational affiliation is the prime determinant of personal identity.[17]

Both the educational and organizational integrity of the top ministerial apparatus is clearly important in establishing their distinctiveness and possible *esprit de corps*, and in training officials to achieve their aims by applying certain types of force. Analysis of forty-five ministers appointed in the 1960s or 1970s shows that they spent on

[15] Ibid. 338.
[16] J. Richardson, *Organisational Affiliation and Leadership Selection in the Soviet Union: The Ministerial Élite under Brezhnev*, paper presented to the 25th Annual Conference of the Australasian Political Studies Association, (Sydney, 1982), 8.   [17] Ibid. 9.

average eighteen years in the job, and every third minister and every second deputy was in his post for twenty-three years or more. In all, 70 per cent made their careers entirely in one ministry. As one commentator put it,

This practice inevitably led to a situation in which every minister ever more deeply was imbued with the interests of his branch, including those of his apparatus, and started by all means to widen his departmental sphere. This came to be the most important aspect of his activity. Among ministers there arose a natural tendency to try to obtain the maximum material resources at their disposal, to increase staff and production funds, to begin new projects and so on.[18]

The merging of economic functions and state activities at the level of recruitment must have been a further factor in undermining the latter, particularly since state power was typically only achieved by an official at the middle or end of a successful career of non-bureaucratic work, in the legitimized sense explained above. *Esprit de corps*, and the merging of state and economic activities, may have been supported further by the existence in many ministries of branch uniforms and insignia, which were designed to heighten departmental loyalty and status,[19] while by their quasi-military implications may have further blurred the state–department boundary. Clearly, also, the coherence of ministerial personnel and promotion patterns must have made an impact on the functioning of the *nomenklatura* system at the highest level, when the circle of candidates deemed suitable for a particular appointment was limited to those with the skills required to operate effectively within an organization with proven coherent self-interests.

The important point being argued here, however, is not so much that their relative organizational isolation afforded ministerial officials the possibility of acting in their own interests—though it was probably a condition of this—but that in conjunction with all of the other facts presented in the previous chapters, ministry officials ceased to exhibit the character of Soviet statesmen of the Onisimov type, but used their powers and independence to wield economic power through their virtual private ownership of the main resources. Ministers, in other words, were not so much bureaucrats as a peculiarly Soviet type of economic actor operating in conditions where their simultaneous occupation of the posts of state and industry, and take-over of the powers of the state, reduced the latter to a husk.

[18] Pavel Lebedev, 'Chto my znaem o ministrakh?', in *Ogonek*, 31 (1988), 7.
[19] *Ogonek*, 39 (1989), 14–15.

The result of the power of ministry officials to control the operation of their departments and dispose of large resources—as was shown in Chapters 1 and 2—was the emergence of a peculiar structure of decision-making in which the economic official decided, or set the agenda for deciding, the most important political questions. This operational power, or what other writers have referred to as the manner in which, through *vedomstvennyy* practices, social property was eaten away and political control undermined, allowed for the separation of property from control in conditions of socialism,[20] and created what Boris Kurashvili has called the 'material base of bureaucratism',[21] by which he meant the manner in which the institution of social property allowed for the subversion of political power by economic administrators, who were then empowered to utilize their control for their own private and institutional benefit.

The issue of the use of their official positions to achieve private or institutional benefit is clearly related to the question of corruption.[22] What is interesting about the case of the ministries is that an analysis of the behaviour of officials reveals the presence of corruption in all its forms, but in many cases illustrates the reverse order of influence to the one typical of Western societies. The form of corruption most prevalent among ministry officials, therefore, provides a useful guide to the type of power they exercised and to the political system as a whole.

Though he locates it in the context of a market society, the definition of corruption which seems most suitable to understanding the power of ministry officials is given by van Klaveren:

A corrupt civil servant regards his public office as a business, the income of which he will . . . seek to maximise. The office then becomes a 'maximising unit'. The size of his income depends upon the market situation and his talents for finding the point of maximal gain on the public's demand curve.

The concept can be adapted to Soviet conditions if, in place of 'market' with its assumption of the disposal of property, is substituted

[20] V. Dement'ev and Yu. Sukhotin, 'Sotsialisticheskaya sobstvennost' i upravlenie ekonomikoy', in *Obshchestvennye nauki*, 6 (1988), 66–72. See also A. V. Buzgalin and A. I. Kolganov, *Anatomiya byurokratizma* (Moskow, 1988), 16.

[21] B. P. Kurashvili, *Bor'ba s byurokratizmom* (Moscow, 1988), 38–40.

[22] For further discussion of the phenomenon of corruption in the Soviet state see: K. Jowett, 'Soviet Neotraditionalism: The Political Corruption of a Leninist Regime', in *Soviet Studies*, 3 (1983), 275–97; N. Lampert, *Whistleblowing in the USSR* (London, 1987); V. Shlapentokh, 'The XXVII Congress—A Case Study of the Shaping of a New Party Ideology', in *Soviet Studies*, 1 (Jan. 1988), 5; and K. Simis, *USSR: Secrets of a Corrupted Society*, (London, 1982).

'the administering of material resources'. This does not imply that the same officials may not have been open to other forms of corruption as well. For example, Leff defines the concept as an 'extra-legal institution used by individuals or groups to gain influence over the actions of the bureaucracy'. Ministerial officials, in this sense, may comprise either the corruptor or the corrupted—and were probably both in so far as it was to their advantage. Friedrich argues that

the pattern of corruption can be said to exist whenever a power-holder who is charged with doing certain things, i.e., who is a responsible functionary or office holder, is by monetary or other rewards not legally provided for induced to take actions which favour whoever provides the rewards and thereby does damage to the public and its interests.

Though Soviet ministries do provide examples of the last two forms of corruption,[23] it is highly significant to my general argument that it is the first definition which best captures the reality. This is principally because the ministries were themselves already in possession of the resources, and did not need to be bribed with the promise of them. If anything, the ministry official was more likely, using the resources in his possession, to seek to corrupt other officials in the last two senses.[24]

There is plenty of evidence concerning the attainment of high-living standards by ministry officials, their private use and disposition of state property and production for their own benefit, their manipulation of the non-market principles of the pricing system in the command economy to achieve high levels of profit, and their intimidation of those likely to expose what were essentially corrupt practices. Though formal sociological investigation into these questions remains limited, research by Borodkin indicates that in the social sphere, of those studied, heads of enterprises did best in all areas. Borodkin comments:

It is possible that leaders of higher levels, responsible workers of the party–state apparatus, of ministries and departments, may have less social advantages. However, one is led to conclude that the secretiveness about research into the life position of their families, either not conducted or not published, is due to

---

[23] e.g. a minister in the North Ossetian Autonomous Republic Ministry of the Food Industry was sacked for bribe-taking in 1985. See *Izvestiya* (29 May 1985), 3.

[24] The extracts from van Klaveren, Leff, and Friedrich are cited in M. Philp, 'Politics, Markets and Corruption', in R. Nick, M. Philp, and M. Pinto-Dushinsky (eds.), *Political Corruption and Scandals* (Vienna, 1990), 16–30.

reasons not of modesty or the lack of desire to advertise their material weakness.[25]

Writing in *Novy mir*, Men'shikov describes how ministry officials were able to manipulate resources to create deficit conditions favourable to the extraction of special prices or favours in return for deliveries. This worked in all branches of the economy, but as might be expected, where producer monopoly power was strongest, it worked most effectively.

Workers in state enterprises, not being the juridical owners of the means of production or its products, none the less have the ability to dispose of them as if they were their own and utilize them for their own enrichment—individual or collective. Those who practically control the use of resources which belong to another (in this case the state) have the possibility to use them for their private aims (either personally or with others) if the juridical owner does not realize effective or sufficient control. Hence, the very possibility of the black economy arises from the alienation of state means of production and in the command system of administration which renders adequate control impossible ... The participation of [departmental and local officials] is especially important in so far as *only they possess the power* to create deficits by using the levers of planning and distribution of resources. (Author's italics)[26]

The evidence presented in earlier chapters about how high ministry officials were able to control operationally the resources and, therefore, the behaviour of subordinates, at least to a significant extent, is backed up by the evidence in the italicized portion of the quotation about their impact in the formation of deficits. The result according to Men'shikov was a huge black economy that comprised not just the most obvious consumer products but all branches of the economy, even including iron and steel.[27] The case of the criminalization of the entire Uzbek cotton industry is well known. For his part in the scandal, Usmanov, the former minister of the Uzbek republic cotton ministry, was sentenced to death in 1986.[28] The giving rather than receiving of bribes for favours was exemplified by the case of a deputy minister in the Ministry of Tractors and Farm Machinery who had arranged a marriage in order for a colleague to be transferred to head his supply department. It was suggested that the situation arose out of a 'total

[25] F. M. Borodkin, 'Sotsial'naya politika: vlast' i perestroyka', in *Postizhenie* (Moscow, 1989), 258.

[26] S. Men'shikov, 'Ekonomicheskaya struktura sotsializma: chto vperedi? Opyt prognoza', in *Novyy mir*, 3 (1989), 197–8.   [27] Ibid. 198.

[28] See *Moskovskaya pravda* (28 Aug. 1986), 3.

confusion in the assignment of ministry duties'; however, this is the viewpoint of someone who fails to see the clear logic in having a reliable supporter in the department most in control of the assignment of materials.[29] The case of a criminal syndicate exposed in the Karaganda bus administration stretching all the way up the Kazakh Minister of Motor Transport also highlights the issue.

Under the system, inter-city bus drivers regularly pocketed a portion of passenger fares. They had to pay for this opportunity to enrich themselves by making large pay-offs to their immediate superiors for protection and continued employment. These officials, in turn, paid off their own superiors for the same privilege. And so it went on, up the chain of command—the higher the official, the larger the bribe.[30]

Cases of report padding are numerous and reflect both the ability of the ministries to avoid fulfilling plan tasks, which represents a hidden bonus in terms of work per unit of income,[31] as well as their ability to allow hidden reserves of materials to remain at the private disposal of the allocators. In the Ministry of Machinery for Light Industry, the Food Industry, and Household Appliances, losses were written off as production expenses and reports were altered.[32] The deputy minister in the Ministry of the Petroleum Industry was sacked for faking reports; indices were pure inventions, and no work had been done in five years to try to improve yields.[33] Where reporters sought to expose these widespread practices, a pattern of persecution of newspaper editors by ministry officials emerged, as was the case with both the Ministry of Civil Aviation and the Russian Republic Ministry of Inland Shipping.[34] As the sociologist Tatyana Zaslavskaya put it in an interview: 'Take the Ministry of the Water Industry and Amelioration. It has a budget of 2 billion roubles annually, with projects costing 16 billion roubles and 50 billion roubles. My God, if you run such projects, 2, 3, 4 million is bound to get stuck to people's hands!'[35]

These examples of corruption of the kind described by van Kleveren are intended to indicate how officials with ostensible state functions acted to secure their personal and institutional advantage by utilizing

[29] See *CDSP* 40 (1987), 16.
[30] See *Komsomol'skaya pravda* (24 Feb. 1988), 4,
[31] Sergei Andreev provides figures which suggest that to compensate for a declining share in gross national income, economic administrators were able to do substantially less work. See S. Andreev, 'Prichiny i sledstviya', in *Ural*, 1 (1988), 114.
[32] *Pravda* (14 Dec. 1984), 3.
[33] Ibid. (13 Oct. 1984), 3.
[34] Ibid. (11 Feb. 1986), 1.
[35] Interview with Zaslavskaya.

resources and behaving primarily as economic agents. It can be reasonably concluded that at the level of rational agency—what made the official act—the statesman and the politician were seriously short of support in the exercise of political or bureaucratic power, and were consequently at a structural level weak in relation to their nominal subjects. Soviet politicians and statesmen, in so far as they existed in the sense defined in this book in other words, were generals devoid of staff or army. In such circumstances, as shall be shown, it suited many of them to join the rationality of the ministry official rather than oppose it.

The point can be demonstrated further, however, by adding, to the personal case histories given above, evidence about institutional relations between the industrial ministries and other political institutions. The pattern of these relations indicates that the ministries' economic powers not only overrode the control of their political and state superiors but actually dominated the activity and functioning of these bodies. To quote Zaslavskaya: 'Yes, the ministries are the most powerful state within the state ... The ministries are the most important element in the structure of state power.'[36]

THE CONTROLLING POWERS OF THE COUNCIL OF MINISTERS

In the chapter on the economic powers of the ministries, attention was devoted to the functioning of many inter-branch organs of economic management which were designed to overcome deficiencies in the branch ministerial structure. It was noted that despite the location of the administration of these organs in the highest-level government bodies, such as Gosplan and the Council of Ministers, and despite the clear support of party leaders, the ministries managed to retain their operational control and to defeat inter-branch activity which was not also in their departmental interests. This section will seek to develop further the discussion of the impact of the ministries on the functioning of the state system by examining evidence about the relations of ministries with Gosplan, the apparatus of the Council of Ministers, and with other state committees, which relates to the ability of statesmen in these latter bodies to compel ministries to accept their

[36] Ibid.

authority to make decisions. Conversely, it will examine how the economic concerns of the ministries penetrated the functioning of these nominally state bodies, and corrupted them in the sense suggested in the previous section. Occasionally, sections of state committees themselves acted as ministries exercising economic power rather than as regulators of those operating on resources. Where they did so, they also behaved like ministries and the consequences for their interests, powers, and the state system itself were identical—or arguably even worse. Where the politicians sought to deal with the weakness of their authority by using their regulatory agencies to exercise operational economic management powers, the result was merely the importation of ministerial interests even further into the heart of the state. In either case, by ministerial force or calculation of self-interest, the predominant rationality of the official of the state committee was defined not by advancing his position by means of politics or bureaucracy in opposition to the ministries, but by supporting the interests of the organizations with physical control of resources.

Even operating on the official Soviet definitions, state committees and ministries are in some ways often difficult to distinguish. For example, in so far as state committees had direct subordinate institutions attached to them, their relationships were governed by the General Statute on the Ministry and state committees had the same rights as ministries. Industrial ministries, as was mentioned in the discussion of the *golovnoe ministerstvo* earlier, may also have had super-departmental powers of co-ordination, which made them close to some aspects of the jurisdiction of state committees.[37] In addition, there were some organizations which, though they bore the name of ministry are more properly thought of as state committees; for example, the Ministry of Finance, Ministry of Health, etc.

The administrative lawyer Pronina defined the difference as follows:

The ministry is an organ of branch administration, in whose competence is a great volume of powers which ensure the subordination of their objects of administration. They possess rights of resolving *operational* questions, allowing them to dispose [*rasporyazhat'sya*] of the finances and material resources of

---

[37] See B. M. Lazerev, 'Sotsial'nye interesy i kompetentsiya organov upravleniya', in *Sovetskoe gosudarstvo i pravo*, 10 (1971), 89–90. Ministries not only functioned as state committees in cases of head ministries. The Ministry of the Water Industry and Amelioration had both branch economic responsibilities and conservation duties more appropriate to a state committee; many ministries had production and inspection tasks.

enterprises and other subordinates, and to go deeply into their subordinates' activities . . . The state committee is the basic organizational form for securing co-ordination activity of organs of administration and for realizing *super-departmental* control. The co-ordination-regulatory-control activity of the state committees corresponds to the great volume of inter-branch functions and powers which are conditioned by the necessity of realizing administration over organizations not subordinate to them, many of which have equal legal powers to the state committee—for example, the ministry. (Author's italics)[38]

From the perspective of this book, the most important feature which distinguished the state committee from the ministry relates to the operational versus super-departmental powers italicized in the quotation. Where only the latter existed, the individuals in the institution were only able to achieve their will by exercising authority, or by being corrupted in the exercise of their authority. In these terms, it is evident that state committees were more like what we would recognize as state bodies than were the ministries, a fact which was reflected in their higher formal standing within the state system. This standing and closeness to the state was demonstrated by the large representation of state committees in the inner apparatus of the state structure, the Presidium of the Council of Ministers. Whereas all officials of ministerial rank obtained membership in the Council of Ministers itself, this was, as Hough put it, 'an extremely large body, and, as such, [could] hardly function effectively as a working cabinet'.[39] The Presidium, however, was comprised of officials drawn either from the state committees—Gosplan, the State Committee for Science and Technology (GKNT), the State Committee for Construction (Gosstroy), the State Committee for Supplies Procurement (Gossnab), and the Ministry of Finance—or from the permanent apparatus of the Council of Ministers, including officials with the task of overseeing branches of ministries.[40]

Because it lacked operational control, except in those cases where it functioned as a ministry, the state committee was forced to realize its will by means of normative acts; in other words, the state committee was able to realize its functions only on the basis of the authority of the state. In order, however, for the inter-branch normative acts passed by state committees to be made effective they needed to be

---

[38] V. S. Pronina, 'Sootnoshenie kompetentsii gosudarstvennykh komitetov i ministerstv', in *Problemy sovershenstvovaniya sovetskogo zakonodatel'stvo*, (Moscow, 1976), 89–90.
[39] J. Hough and M. Fainsod, *How the Soviet Union is Governed*, (London, 1979), 381.
[40] Ibid. 382.

passed into law by the decision of the minister of the branch concerned. The extent to which the minister accepted the authority of these norms, which were theoretically binding on him, provides a clear indication of the real level of political or state authority. However, there were numerous examples of ministries acting to subvert legislation passed by both the Presidium of the Council of Ministers or the state committees.[41]

The Presidium of the Council of Ministers and the state committees faced a dilemma when seeking to increase their power over institutions within their jurisdiction. Because they lacked operational powers, the control of the ministries over material resources effected the capture of the state; and where the state sought to rectify this by assuming operational control, it defeated its purpose by becoming ministerialized— in other words, by acting primarily as economic agents with all of the deficiencies outlined earlier. These factors tended to leave those in the heart of the state somewhere between two stools; not exercising operational power, while continually responding to the material agenda set by those who did exercise it. Real power over material resources in the hands of ministries, in other words, left the statesmen, and, as shall be shown below, the politicians too, in the absence of a defined sphere for the exercise of state authority with little to do but follow the ministries' rump.

This argument can be supported historically by evidence from the period from 1953 to the refounding of the industrial ministries in 1965, during which time the apparatus of the Council of Ministers and state committees like Gosplan were far more involved in operational activity than subsequently.[42] The role of Gosplan was increased after 1957 but the effectiveness of this, and the decline in the state-supervisory functions it exercised when given operational control, can be gauged from the fact that in November 1962 a new body was created within the Council of Ministers called the All-Union Sovnarkhoz, which was to take over the operational control which Gosplan had inherited from the old ministries. The immersion of Gosplan in the daily business of running the economy had had the effect of weakening the control of the statesmen and politicians over 'perspective tasks'. Within the new body, however, there very quickly appeared branch-based bodies—the ministries—which had, in any case, been alive more

---

[41] See A. V. Lobashev, 'Ponyatie i priznaki zakonnosti normativnykh aktov ministerstv i vedomstv', in *Pravovedenie*, 3 (1987), 28.
[42] See Yu. A. Tikhomirov, 'Razvitie funktsiy upravlencheskykh organov', in *Sovetskoe gosudarstvo i pravo*, 1 (1966), 28–9.

or less intact inside Gosplan since 1957.[43] State committees under the *sovnarkhoz* reform functioned more or less like ministries, though without the requisite legal base for subordinating enterprises—which often made it seem that they were subordinate to no one. The nadir of this period of state weakness came in 1962 when, in the midst of a profusion of state bodies, a new branch of Gosplan was formed, Glavkomplekty, designed to co-ordinate the activities of the multitude of *ad hoc* bodies running·the economy. The form of power exercised by this body, and the further constraints it imposed on the actions of politicians and those in the state who sought to exercise normative control over subordinates, can, perhaps, best be estimated by the positive reception given to the reformed ministries, which must for a while have seemed in comparison organizationally malleable despite their chequered past.

In comparison to the quixotic efforts of Khrushchev to establish the control of politicians and statesmen, the Brezhnev–Kosygin leadership was moderate and sensible. None the less, their acceptance of the basic rules of the system left them with the same difficulties in securing effective control. The debate throughout the period from 1965 to 1985 about the relative merits of state committees versus ministries reflected the fundamental dilemma pointed out above.

The argument being presented is not that ministries were the only actors with power or clout, only that this clout was ultimately the most significant. The influential radical economist and adviser to Gorbachev, Nikolay Petrakov, has described the dual nature of Gosplan as both operational controller—a quasi-ministry with all of the consequences for the state system evident in other ministerial bodies—and regulator:

Gosplan in reality combines the functions of planner and executor of economic plans. Those circumstances, that the five-year and annual plans are studied and affirmed by the Supreme Soviet, changes little in practice, so far as after the plan finds the status of law, the resources are with Gosplan. Without its sanction the ministries and departments cannot realize their right to make use of resources, reserved for them in the plan. Moreover, Gosplan can, without the knowledge of the Supreme Soviet, bring in operative changes and corrections to already agreed plans. To speak exactly, 'corrections' can often mean hundreds of millions and even billions of roubles. Finally, Gosplan has the wide possibility to effect intra- and inter-branch redistribution of resources

---

[43] See Ryavec, 'Soviet Bureaucratic Élite', 342.

for capital investment . . . For that reason, the ministers and directors of large combines 'walk with Gosplan', and not only in the period of working out the five-year plan but constantly. For this reason Gosplan resembles a railway station.[44]

There is obviously a considerable amount of truth in what Petrakov argues—though, as shall be seen in Chapter 5, he also argues a slightly different point—but the main rejoinder is that if plan changes were frequent it was because of ministerial pressure. In any case, Gosplan itself was obliged to compile plans with the participation of the ministries.[45] Of course, Gosplan interference did take place. K. N. Rudnev, minister in the defence-related Ministry of Instrument Making, Automation Equipment, and Control Systems (Minpribor) was strongly critical of the degree of supervision of his ministry by the planners and called for ministries to be largely sovereign within the constraints of their budgets, and to have more powers in the area of pricing.[46] Rudnev's programme should be seen as an aggressively entrepreneurial position on behalf of his ministry. He went even further in 1974, attacking not only the 'petty tutelage' (*podmena*) of Gosplan, GKNT, Gossnab, the Ministry of Finance, and the State Bank, but advancing a plan for strengthening economic performance which included provisions for: (1) more long-term planning; (2) full provision of financial resources by the branch itself with state credits for branches in difficulty, e.g. with high levels of capital investment and low short-term rates of profit; (3) an expansion in the ministries' functions, an elimination of duplication in planning functions between the ministry and the state, and the concentration of all distribution and supply functions in the hands of the ministry.[47] In other words, the proposal would have strengthened the operational control of the ministries, which in context implied a real increase in their *de facto* powers, an area, as Chapter 1 has shown, in which they were largely successful between 1965 and 1985. Another ministerial contribution to opposition to the perceived excesses in the power of state committees came from Busyatskaya, first deputy-head of the planning-economic department of the all-Union Ministry of Heavy, Energy, and Transport Machine-Building. She attacked ministry-state committee relations as

---

[44] N. Petrakov, 'Ekonomika i gosudarstvo', in *Ogonek*, 10 (1989), 15.

[45] See P. R. Gregory, *The Institutional Background of the Soviet Enterprise: The Planning Apparatus and the Ministries* (Cologne, 1989), 15–16.

[46] K. N. Rudnev, 'Otrasl' vstupaet v reformu', interview in *Kommunist*, 1 (1967), 59–60.   [47] K. N. Rudnev, *Trud* (15 Aug. 1974), 2.

being 'overly administrative', involving too little discussion and too many instructions which hindered branch development. Gossnab was singled out both for having too much power and using it ineffectively.[48] Essentially, Busyatskaya was calling for ministry independence.

Other evidence, however, suggests that Rudnev's criticism of the excessive power of state committees was self-seeking and Petrakov's exaggerated. In his excellent study of the testimony of *émigré* former ministry and Gosplan employees—which certainly points to the complexities in the bargaining relationship—Paul Gregory notes the very different rationality of *khozyaystvenniki* located in the ministries and *apparatchiki* in Gosplan, based principally on the different power and responsibilities attached to each. Clearly, as Gregory notes, a problem of control existed in their interrelations.[49] Indeed, most Soviet politicians and scholars in the period under examination called for quite the opposite kind of redefinition of power between the ministries and the state committees. In 1971, for example, Minpribor itself was criticized indirectly; ministries on *khozraschet*, it was argued, would have a departmental interest in resisting the creation of multi-branch *ob"edineniya*. The solution was to transfer power *to* the state committees and other extra-departmental agencies.[50] Gavriil Popov in 1976, when he was a member of the Economics Faculty of Moscow State University, argued even-handedly that the large number of competing state committees was itself a cause for concern. For example, Gosplan decided the overall needs in the sphere of technical progress, though GKNT had responsibility for finance. Popov was also well aware of the problem of increasing the responsibility of the apparatus of the Council of Ministers in that it would simply become another organ of current leadership. His preferred solution to the problem of departmentalism, however, would have none the less created either bureaux of the Council of Ministers to deal with groups of ministries, such as had existed in the immediate pre-war period, or the formation of blocs of state committees, including Gosplan, GKNT, and the others. Despite the experience of the Khrushchev period, at this time Popov

[48] 'Ministerstvo SSSR i khozyaystvennaya reforma', in *Sovetskoe gosudarstvo i pravo*, 1 (1970), 82–5.

[49] See P. Gregory, *Restructuring the Soviet Economic Bureaucracy* (Cambridge, 1990). Gregory's respondents suggest that Gosplan was able to arrange effective inter-ministerial co-operation. This seems highly unlikely given the facts presented in the previous chapter and in subsequent sections; indeed, this work would suggest that it is not true. Some doubt about other testimony of this sort must therefore be noted.

[50] *Izvestiya* (2 June 1971), 3.

even proposed the recreation of a VSNKh to co-ordinate the co-ordinators.[51] As the previous chapter showed, the growth in the salience of inter-branch problems in the economy conditioned the popularity of calls for a strengthened role for co-ordinating agencies throughout the period. At the XXVIth Congress in 1981, the need for an increased role for existing state committees was a dominant theme; while there were also calls being heard for the creation of new ones, for example, a State Committee for Questions of Improving State Administration.[52] However, at the same time the reality of the outcome of the debate was far closer to Hohmann's prediction in 1975. 'The ministries are therefore preparing to fight to obtain powers from Gosplan, Gossnab, the State Pricing Committee and other committees. There is no reason to doubt that these attempts will have considerable success.'[53]

The reasons for the strength of the ministries *vis-à-vis* the state committees and the apparatus of the Council of Ministers can be summed up as follows: first, the size and complexity of the ministerial system effectively overwhelmed the coping powers of the state controllers; secondly, the structure of the state committees in many ways led them to function poorly as controllers or aided their co-option into the ministry networks; thirdly, the ministries operated a very effective lobby system inside the higher bodies of state which was supported by a high degree of coincidence of interest between the two kinds of bodies; and, fourthly, the state committees were simply not sufficiently empowered to counteract the ministries when the latter chose to act independently. Evidence about the overload of the apparatus of the Council of Ministers and of the state committees is not hard to find, belying the prospect of their acting as sectoral co-ordinators. The overload on Gosplan, which harkened back to the *sovnarkhoz* period, for example, was cited by Kosygin in his speech to the XXVth Congress of the CPSU in his call that it should be 'freed from the many current tasks which could be dealt with by Gossnab, ministries and other organs'.[54]

[51] G. Kh. Popov, *Effektivnoe upravlenie* (Moscow, 1976), 99.
[52] 'XXVI s"ezd KPSS i organizatsionno-pravovye voprosy gosudarstvennogo upravleniya', in *Sovetskoe gosudarstvo i pravo*, 9 (1981), 3–12.
[53] H.-H. Hohmann and H.-B. Sand, 'The Soviet Union', in H.-H. Hohmann, M. Kaser, and K. C. Thalheim (eds.), *The New Economic System of Eastern Europe* (London, 1975), 8.
[54] See Yu. S. Tsimerman, 'Promyshlennie ministerstva v novykh usloviyakh otraslevogo upravleniya', in *Sovetskoe gosudarstvo i pravo*, 8 (1976), 25.

Petrosyants noted that the sheer number of all-Union and Union–republic level ministries made the job of co-ordination by the Council of Ministers extremely difficult. His suggestion, however, for relieving the overload by amalgamating ministries and putting at the head of the new groups a deputy of the Presidium only seems to beg the question.[55] Conyngham has also made the very valid point that even where the apparatus of the Council of Ministers did weigh in effectively, their action carried huge opportunity costs.[56] Nor was the situation in other state committees likely to afford them the capacity to cope more easily with the work imposed by the ministries. After the introduction of a new indicator for enterprise prices and profits in the early 1980s, the so-called 'normed net output', the volume of petitions to the State Pricing Committee overwhelmed them, while in practice the ministries manipulated the new indicator with the collusion of enterprises in the opposite direction from that intended. In relation to the power of producers Gostsen was 'one-on-one against tens of thousands of petitioners'.[57]

The degree to which the ministries set the agenda for the activity of the state committees and other supervisory bodies can be measured by the fact that, structurally, the state committees tended to duplicate the branch system. The branch departments of state committees originated in the *sovnarkhoz* period and carried on afterwards. As a result, branch subdivisions were to be found in Gosplan, GKNT, Gossnab, the State Committee for Labour and Wages (Goskomtrud), the Ministry of Finance, and others.[58] Gosplan, for example, contained two kinds of department: *svodnyy*, or co-ordinating administrations, which dealt with Gosplan's own affairs; and *otraslevyy*, or branch departments, which supervised the various ministerial sectors. Gosbank established branch departments after 1965, and a component of the bank's credit plan was directed through the ministries. The result was, as Kurashvili has pointed out, that instead of functioning as the 'general staff', state committees 'duplicated branch administration'.[59]

In corroboration of the argument made above about the rationale for officials in state committees faced with the impossibility of realizing

[55] A. Petrosyants, *Kommunist*, 8 (1983), 100–1.
[56] W. Conyngham, *The Modernisation of Soviet Industrial Management*, (Cambridge, 1982), 252.   [57] V. Selyunin, *Sotsialisticheskaya industriya* (1 Mar. 1983), 2.
[58] A. S. Petrov, 'Ob osnovnykh napravleniyakh sovershenstvovaniya sistemy ministerstv', in *Organizatsiya raboty ministerstv v usloviyakh ekonomicheskoy reformy*, (Moscow, 1972), 93–4.
[59] B. P. Kurashvili, *Ocherk teorii gosudarstvennogo upravleniya*, (Moscow, 1988), 290.

their aims through bureaucratic means, Krylov has suggested that the branch departments of Gosplan began to function as small ministries of their own.[60] More important, the interests of the branch departments became linked to ministries they were nominally charged with supervising. There is considerable evidence of successful lobbying by ministries of state committees, especially Gosplan, producing a co-incidence of interest. The Gosplan office, as the Petrakov described it, resembled a railway waiting room the whole year round.[61] Although only 3,500 people worked in the Gosplan building, over 6,000 used the canteen facilities daily.[62]

The Inter-Departmental Commission on Economic Reform established inside Gosplan in the late 1960s to establish methodological guide-lines for the implementation of the 1965 enterprise reform was not to interfere in the direct activity of the ministries.[63] It became, in the words of Gavriil Popov, 'a commission of departments for mutual aid in diminishing the casualties in departments as a result of the reform'.[64] In 1967 the economist Birman insisted that reform would only be successful if measures were taken to prevent Gosplan coming to the defence of ministries in difficulty.[65] Another reforming economist, Abalkin (at least until he became a deputy chairman of the Council of Ministers under Ryzhkov), however, was to note years later that every ministry continued to have its representative in Gosplan, comprising the Soviet Union's 'own sort of lobby'.[66] Mostly, as Alice Gorlin has suggested, the ministries sought to obtain, and were successful in achieving, reductions in plan targets.[67] Men'shikov suggests that

for the previous twelve years [i.e. from 1977], for example, of the plan tasks for 170 of the most important aspects of production, located under the control of Gosplan and the ministries, none (!) have been fulfilled, and what's more, the non-fulfilment has been as high as 20–30% and beyond. Is it necessary to be surprised that the range of deficit goods—not only consumer but

---

[60] C. A. Krylov, *The Soviet Economy* (Lexington, Mass., 1979), 51.

[61] N. Petrakov, 'Ekonomika i gosudarstvo', in *Ogonek*, 10 (March, 1989), 15.

[62] *Moscow News*, 47 (1987), 12. Not only because of the quality of the sausages.

[63] *Izvestiya* (22 July 1970), 2.

[64] G. Kh. Popov, 'Perestroyka upravleniya ekonomikoy', in *Inogo ne dano* (Moscow, 1988), 624.   [65] A. Birman, *Literaturnaya gazeta*, 2 (11 Jan. 1967), 10.

[66] L. I. Abalkin, 'Strategiya obnovleniya', interview in *Ogonek*, 13, (March, 1989), 18.

[67] A. G. Gorlin, 'The Power of the Industrial Ministries in the 1980s', in *Soviet Studies*, 3 (1985), 361.

producer—has systematically grown, so that the goods deficit has become by degree universal?[68]

Finally, however, even where there might have existed a non-coincidence of interest, where the lobby failed, and where the state committees were not overloaded, there was a high likelihood of the ministry's will prevailing by simple *force majeure*. A number of examples can be provided to support this. Lebedinsky, a vice-chairman of Gosplan, blamed ministries for delays in producing the plan, and argued that the planning commission was unable to punish ministries for this.[69] The responsibility for that, however, lay with the already overloaded apparatus of the Council of Ministers. The practice of simply changing plans without informing Gosplan, the Central Statistical Administration, or other bodies was also long standing.[70] Even for Petrakov, the state budget deficit revealed the inability of the Ministry of Finance to control spending, as well as institutional confusion in tax collection.[71] Quoting from various sources, Sergey Andreev notes

Effectively up to now [the end of 1985] the economic mechanism and system of administration has not only not guarded against but spread yet further departmentalist [*vedomstvennyy*] psychology ... The structure of Gosplan today is such that in the main it facilitates the strengthening of *vedomstvennyy* partitions. Practically every ministry has reserved a branch department or sector, where, as a rule, work former ministry employees. Often, they are the vehicles of departmental interests ... One of the main difficulties about which local representatives of Gosplan complain is the enrootedness in the central apparatus of the *vedomstvennyy*-branch approach to business.[72]

MINISTRIES AND THE REPUBLICS

In looking at the relations of ministries to the republics, two important issues will be addressed. First, how powerful were the ministries in relationship to other high governmental agencies, such as the Council of Ministers of Union–republics? Relatedly, given their powers, how much difference could the central economic authorities make to the development of republic priorities? The answers to these questions

---

[68] Men'shikov, 'Ekonomicheskaya structura', 196.
[69] *Pravda* (21 Sept. 1983), 2. [70] Ibid. (25 Feb. 1974), 2.
[71] Petrakov, 'Ekonomika', 15. [72] Andreev, 'Prichiny i sledstviya', 126.

should not be too surprising given the weight of evidence presented above. Ministries were able to dominate republican authorities and impose their own interests.

As mentioned in Chapter 1, three types of ministries existed in the industrial sector. First, there were the all-Union ministries, which exercised control over subordinate enterprises across the country regardless of their territorial location. In this sector were located ministries in the areas of oil, gas and chemicals, not including refining; and all the machine-building ministries. Secondly, there were the Union–republican ministries, located in Moscow with subordinate ministries of the same name in each republic. These ministries exercised jurisdiction over the light and food industries as well as some areas of heavy industry: coal, construction, electricity, ferrous and non-ferrous metallurgy, land reclamation and water resources, timber, pulp and paper and wood-processing, and petroleum and petro-chemicals. Union–republican ministries were under the dual subordination (*dvoynoe podchinenie*) of both the ministry and the republic level Council of Ministers. Finally, 'arising from the concrete circumstances of given republics, the republic Council of Ministers can create ministries subordinate to it'.[73] For example, in the RSFSR there were ministries for local industry and the fuel industry. Union ministries controlled 57 per cent of output; Union–republican bodies controlled 37 per cent; only 6 per cent was under republican or local control. As the list suggests, the areas of economic development which fell under the sole jurisdiction of the republics tended to be less important, with the exception of the Kazakh Ministry of Cotton implicated in the scandals mentioned above. By and large republican ministries were in the area of light or local industry. However, the list of ministries under dual subordination included highly significant branches of the economy in which, if they had been able to exercise their theoretical powers, the republican Councils of Ministers would have been important political bodies.

The tendency throughout the Brezhnev period was for a growth in the number of all-Union ministries rather than Union–republic ones, and for a growth in the latter at the expense of purely republican organs. The reason for this may well have lain as much in a desire by central state and political authorities to increase their hold over Union-level ministries as over the republican authorities. Ministries, however,

[73] K. I. Taksir, *Upravlenie promyshlennost'yu SSSR* (Moscow 1985), 76.

were able to utilize the confusion which a two-tier administrative system allowed to increase yet further their independence. In practice, the situation was much as Fil'shin described it in 1971 (when he was working with Zaslavskaya and Aganbegyan in the reformist Novosibirsk Institute of Economics), in that the 'basic directions of the national economy of the country are being worked out under the decisive influence of the branch ministries and departments'.[74]

The formal relationship of the all-Union and Union–republic ministries to the republic Council of Ministers was defined by the 1967 Statute on the Ministry. Ministries were required to submit perspective and annual plans for work within their branches to the republic Council of Ministers and to take account of their suggestions. Any decisions about the creation, reorganization, and liquidation of enterprises or other organizations under ministerial control was to be adopted by the ministries only after the issue had been reviewed in the Council of Ministers. In the case of Union–republican ministries, the local Council of Ministers was given the right to affirm structures and personnel of the republican-level ministerial apparatus. Though the Moscow ministries had broad rights over their subordinate republican organs, they were instructed not to override the budgetary rights of the republic.[75] It should be noted, however, that the same factors which impeded control over the ministries by all-Union state agencies applied in the republic case, and was compounded by the absence of any operational hold. Ministries in Moscow not only set the general tasks and affirmed the output of their republic-level counterparts in terms of the infamous 'natural expression' (*natural'noe vyrazhenie*), but they controlled the essential material supplies to republic enterprises as well as capital investment and other norms. As Shabaylov put it, 'it would be wrong not to notice that such centralization lowers the responsibility of the republic [Council of Ministers] for the development of the Union–republic branch, which secures the population with goods'.[76] By 1981, and despite further legislation being passed in the meantime to increase the power of republic Council of Ministers, 'none the less the branch vertical remained predominant'.[77] The

---

[74] G. I. Fil'shin, 'Sochetanie otraslevykh i terri torial'nykh interesov pri formirovanii investitsionnykh programm', in *EKO* 2 (1971), 50.

[75] K. E. Kolibab, 'O pravovom polozhenii ministerstv SSSR', *Sovetskoe gosudarstvo i pravo*, 1 (1968), 18–19.

[76] V. I. Shabaylov, 'Soyuzno-respublikanskie ministerstva soyuznykh respublik', in *Sovetskoe gosudarstvo i pravo*, 9 (1984), 27.

[77] 'XXVI s"ezd KPSS i organizatsionno-pravovye voprosy gosudarstvennogo upraleniya', 6.

amount of time spent by republican leaders at ministry headquarters is suggestive of this. As Makhkamov, first secretary of the Tadzhik Party, put it in 1988, 'for the previous year and five months, deputies of the chairman of the republic council of ministers were in the capital for almost a year, ministers and first-deputies of republic departments were in Moscow for almost 900 days, not to mention their assistants'.[78]

Moscow-based ministries were able to treat dual subordination as a formality. The Union-level ministry 'carried responsibility for the branch as a whole, it answered also for the situation in enterprises and other organizations which were within the jurisdiction of the republic-level ministry. Therefore, the union ministry was given broad rights in relation to the republic ministry. Orders, instructions, and decrees of the minister are obligatory for execution by republican ministries.'[79] On the issue of approval of structures suitable to the republic, Yury Tikhomirov, one of the first Soviet scholars to move into political science, noted that there was a 'mechanical coincidence of the structures of some all-Union ministries and their counterparts in the republics, although among them there is no similarity in the weight of work in administering enterprises'.[80] The resulting over-complexity and over-employment at the republican level placed policy-makers in a quandary. In some cases, there were strong calls for increasing the rights of republican Councils of Ministers, particularly in Kazakhstan and Uzbekistan.[81] On the other hand, while recognizing the need for republican bodies as a response to the political imperatives of a balanced national policy and republican sovereignty, the impulse for effectiveness pulled in the opposite direction.[82] Ministries in Moscow and the local centre frequently duplicated work.[83] The position of the republic-level ministry was not at all clearly established.[84] Also, as might be expected given their overall branch responsibility, the all-

[78] *XIX vsesoyuznaya konferentsiya Kommunisticheskoy Partii Sovetskogo Soyuza* (Moscow, 1988), 46.   [79] Kolibab, 'O pravovom',19.

[80] Yu. A. Tikhomirov, 'Sovershenstvovanie struktury i upravlencheskoy deyatel'nosti apparata ministerstva', in *Organizatsiya raboty ministerstv v usloviyakh ekonomicheskoy reformy* (Moscow, 1972), 135.

[81] See the article by M. A. Binder and M. A. Sharif in *Sovetskoe gosudarstvo i pravo*, 11 (1965).

[82] Yu. V. Subotsky, 'Sistema upravleniya: tendentsii razvitiya i puti sovershenstvovaniya', in *Sovetskoe gosudarstvo i pravo*, 1 (1971), 69.

[83] I. V. Shiryaeva, *Sovershenstvovanie struktury i shtatov v otrasli promyshlennosti* (Moscow, 1975), 8.

[84] See S. B. Baysalov and V. M. Levchenko, 'Kompetentsiya otraslevykh organov upravleniya promyshlennost'yu', in *Sovetskoe gosudarstvo i pravo*, 3 (1969), 71.

Union ministry would break the rights of its republic counterpart,[85] although there is also some evidence that republic level ministries operated outside the control of *any* supervisory body.[86] The relationship of republican bodies to economic ministries, therefore, especially those at the all-Union level where most industry was anyway concentrated, confirms the thesis that political authority was weak and that reliance on ministerial allocation to secure republican development was enormous.

THE LEADING ROLE OF THE PARTY?

The relationship of the industrial ministries to the Communist Party is the central one in assessing the political power of the ministries in the period up to 1985. This section will seek to demonstrate how ministerial power side-stepped party control and how ministerial interests effectively set the party's agenda.

Evidence about the power relationship between ministries and the party emerges in a number of areas: from resolutions of the party in relationship to the ministries, and their impact; from the operation of the *nomenklatura* system and the exercise of *pravo kontrolya* by primary party organizations (PPOs) inside the ministries; from the structure of the party and the personnel who occupied its leading organs; from evidence about what virtues were required for political success; and from direct and indirect testimony by party workers and scholars about party–ministry relations. In each of these areas, it will be argued, there is strong reason for believing that ministries were the dominant institutions and that the real position of the party differed markedly from its self-definition as the 'leading and directing force' in Soviet society, which tended to be shared, albeit in less congratulatory terms, by much Western literature.

The evidence presented above strongly suggests that ministries were disinclined to pay great attention to party resolutions concerning their activity. For example, in 1975 the Central Committee passed a resolution calling attention to inadequacies in the work of the Ministry

---

[85] M. I. Piskotin, 'Izmenenie kompetentsii i sovershenstvovanie form i metodov raboty ministerstv v usloviyakh ekonomicheskoy reformy', in *Organizatsiya raboty ministerstv v usloviyakh ekonomicheskoy reformy* 22.

[86] See B. A. Mukhin, head of the chemical *glavk* Volokon, in 'Ministerstvo SSSR i khozyaystvennaya reforma', in *Sovetskoe gosudarstvo i pravo*, 1 (1970), 92.

of Chemical and Oil-Machine Building;[87] in the Ministry of Ferrous Metals in the same year;[88] in the Ministry of Construction of Enterprises for Heavy Industry in 1976;[89] and, specifically on the inadequacies in fulfilment of party decisions, in the Ministry of Oil Refining and Petro-Chemicals in 1980.[90] Indeed, an awareness is evident in party resolutions of the general problem of both lack of fulfilment, and lack of control over the fulfilment, of party decisions.[91] Typically, despite Brezhnev's strong criticism of ministry officials for ill-discipline in fulfilling party resolutions made at the December 1969 Central Committee plenum in 1972, the People's Control Commission was able to report that in the Ministry of the Building Materials Industry there had been no change in style of work and that party resolutions were only raised in the most cursory fashion.[92] Evidence of Gosplan–ministerial collusion is available in the Central Committee resolution on serious violations of party and state discipline by officials in the Ministry of Machine Tool and Tool Industry, the Ministry of Electrical Equipment Industry, Minpribor, and the Gosplan machinery manufacturing department, both for failing to meet plans and for allowing plans to be reduced.[93]

A similar disinclination to follow instructions from the highest bodies of the party can be see in the failure of a second means of theoretical party control over ministries, the right of control (*pravo kontrolya*) which was extended to primary party organizations in 1970. As Fortescue has argued, the right of control allowed the PPO: (1) to hear reports from management when necessary; (2) to establish permanent and temporary commissions; (3) to study affairs on the spot and to be acquainted with relevant information; (4) to offer suggestions and recommendations, which must be taken into consideration by management and to strive for their implementation.[94] However, this was a poor solution to the problem of *vedomstvennost'*.

---

[87] 'Postanovlenie TsK KPSS' (4 Feb. 1975), in *KPSS v rezolyutsiyakh i resheniyakh s"ezdov, konferentsii i plenumov*, 12 (Moscow, 1986), 521–5.
[88] 'Postanovlenie TsK KPSS' (30 Oct. 1975), ibid. 558–62.
[89] 'Postanovlenie TsK KPSS' (8 June 1976), ibid. 13. 110–13.
[90] 'Postanovlenie TsK KPSS' (21 May 1980), ibid. 458–63.
[91] See e.g. 'Postanovlenie TsK KPSS "O dal'neyshem sovershenstvovanii kontrolya i proverki ispolneniya v svete resheni XXVI s"ezda KPSS"', (11 Aug. 1981), ibid. 14. 179–86.   [92] See *Izvestiya* (22 July 1972), 2.
[93] *Pravda* (9 July 1986), 3.
[94] Quoted in S. Fortescue, *The Primary Party Organisations of Branch Ministries* (Washington, DC, 1985).

Finding the right balance between a PPO with a sufficient degree of expertise to know what is going on while not under the thumb of the management, and at the same time keeping the institution manageable, was simply too difficult.[95]

The problems of central party control over the ministries and the difficulty faced by its PPOs in the ministries are illustrated by the number of resolutions passed by the Central Committee criticizing PPOs themselves, and by their predictable content. Resolutions were passed and conferences held on the subject of the activity of PPOs between 1965 and 1985. In 1966, a conference of party secretaries of ministries and state committees of the USSR and the RSFSR was held in Moscow to prepare these cadres 'to perfect the work of party organizations of ministries and departments in fulfilment of the decisions of the XXIII Congress'.[96] The party was held to have a large role in retraining personnel in the new conditions and in reconciling the interests of various departments in conditions of greater economic autonomy.[97] In 1970, however, the Central Committee passed a resolution on the work of the party committee of the Ministry of Meat and Dairy Industry,[98] which was criticized for everything from the number of its personnel and the size of its budget, to the level of introduction of new technology, the state of centre–local relations, and the poor level of ideological development of ministry workers. Further resolutions were passed in 1974 on the work of the party committee in the Ministry of Communications,[99] and on the Ministry of Chemical and Oil Machine-Building.[100] In 1970 and 1971, articles were published calling for a greater role for PPOs.[101] Criticism of the actual performance of these party bodies, however, continued to be forthcoming. In 1975, the work of the PPO of the Ministry of Power and Electrification was criticized.[102] The party committee in the Ministry of the Petroleum Industry, where the deputy minister had been dismissed for faking reports, was strongly criticized for inaction in 1981.[103] Finally, in 1985 the PPO in the Ministry of the Machine Tool and Tool Industry was heavily criticized by the Central Committee

[95] Ibid.
[96] See 'Partiynye organizatsii ministerstv v novykh usloviyakh' in *Partiynaya zhizn'*, 24 (1966), 25–36.
[97] See *Izvestiya* (14 May 1967), 5 and *Pravda* (27 July 1967), 2–3.
[98] 'Postanovlenie TsK KPSS' (3 Feb. 1970), *KPSS v rezolyutsiyakh i resheniyakh s"ezdov, konferentsy, i plenumov*, 11 (Moscow, 1986), 519–24.   [99] Ibid. 12. 476–9.
[100] Ibid. 521–6.
[101] See e.g. *Pravda* (25 Aug. 1971), 2, and ibid. (29 Nov. 1971), 2.
[102] Ibid. (3 March 1975), 2.   [103] *Sotsialisticheskaya industriya* (4 Oct. 1981), 2.

for making no changes in its way of working, for failing to make any use of its powers of *pravo kontrolya*, and for failing to report to the Central Committee apparatus which supervised the ministry about negative features of the ministry's work.[103]

Nomenklatura powers are often cited as the most important means of party control over the state.[105] By controlling appointments of top officials in the ministries, it is held that the party's policies could be implemented. The evidence already presented in this and earlier chapters suggests a number of reasons why this assumption about the value of the *nomenklatura* should be doubted, not least of which was the evident lack of success in implementing party policy. As has been shown in Chapter 2, the reserve *nomenklatura* lists operated in a ramshackle fashion, with information held informally and party officials in the regions in some cases only hearing about appointments after the fact. The failure of the party to control the number of personnel is a further indication of weakness in making the *nomenklatura* effective. Finally, the practice of recruiting top officials in the ministries primarily from those who had made their careers inside the ministry bureaucracy and with technical rather than political backgrounds tends to confirm further the view that either *nomenklatura* appointments at the top tended to be purely formal or that non-political criteria were more important.

In an excellent article on the power of regional party secretaries, Stephen Fortescue has cast further doubt on the efficacy of party control over ministries by means of the *nomenklatura* system. Fortescue makes the point that ministry appointments at the regional level were probably confirmed by the party at the centre, at the level of the central committee department, rather than *in situ*, and that the relationship of the ministry to the central committee apparatus was probably a close one.[106] Regional party officials were certainly heard to complain about the 'all-powerful ministries'.[107] The activity of regional secretaries in supporting the economic reforms of 1965, though formally focused on the preparation of cadres, consisted in little more than holding seminars.[108] Further evidence to support this assertion about the

[104] *Pravda* (13 Dec. 1985), 1–2.
[105] See e.g. A. Nove, *The Soviet Economic System* (3rd ed. London, 1986), 6.
[106] S. Fortescue, 'The Regional Party Apparatus in the "Sectional Society"' in *Studies in Comparative Communism*, 1 (1988), 16–17.   [107] *Pravda*, (6 Apr. 1989), 3.
[108] See V. K. Pokrovskiy, *Deyatel'nost' KPSS po osushchestvleniyu ekonomicheskoy reformy v promyshlennosti v 1965–1968 gg.* (Moskow, 1970), 15.

relative impotence of party power will be offered below. However, as Sergey Andreev has put it,

The Party appears to be the power which is in principle capable of realizing ... action in relationship to administrative personnel. 'In principle', however, does not mean in reality. From that perspective, in such an organizational structure as the party has today, it—and this must be emphasized—cannot introduce even one-tenth of the necessary measures in this direction.[109]

The reason for the failure of the PPOs, and for the lack of interest of regional secretaries, was that they were effectively part of the process of administration, and their secretaries' interests tied to the success of the ministry in meeting targets. At the regional level, this point has been made by Hough.[110] However, as was alluded to by Fortescue, the duplication of the central party apparatus of the structure of the branch ministries meant not only a tendency towards identity of interest, but also that central party bodies became, as Boris Yeltsin put it,

so immersed themselves in economic affairs that they lost their role of political leadership. It was no accident that the structure of the departments of the central committee became almost a copy of the ministries. There is complete duplication of Gosplan, the Council of Ministers.[111]

My point is that in defining the relationship of party bodies to the ministries the politicians faced a choice: either the relationship was regulatory—in which case the operational power of ministries over resources was overriding and the regulators were tied to the ministries' agenda; or these bodies took over the operational control—in which case they were *de facto* ministries in their own right. Yeltsin also makes it clear in his autobiography that the real decisions were not taken in the Central Committee. Describing his time as a regional party secretary, he attests that normally he only ever went to the Central Committee 'for form's sake', 'out of a sense of politeness. Real substantive problems had to be solved in the Council of Ministers.'[112] Given what has been argued above, the role of ministries here was certainly decisive.

Jerry Hough has also suggested that the head of a Central Committee

---

[109] S. Andreev, 'Struktura vlasti i zadachi obshchestva', in *Neva*, 1 (1989), 159.
[110] J. Hough, *The Soviet Prefects* (Cambridge, Mass., 1969).
[111] Quoted in Nove, *Soviet Economic System*, 7.
[112] B. Yeltsin, *Against the Grain: An Autobiography* (London, 1990), 55.

department would have had difficulty in supervising the minister because the latter was considered to have a higher status.[113] Though Archie Brown, quoting the former Czechoslovak Politburo member during 1968, Zdenek Mlynar, on the position in Czechoslovakia, has quite rightly pointed out that the formal position of an official should not be the sole criterion for judging his relative importance, he concedes that the 'more technical ministries in the Soviet Union appear to acquire a significant degree of control within their area of functional specialisation'.[114] The central point being made is well expressed by the sociologists Sokolova and Manuil'skiy in their study of the qualities required for success in the ministerial bureaucracy. While noting that political activism was mostly a formal criterion for promotion for the official, the authors observed that

participation of leaders in elected bodies [including the party] was by no means empty formalism. And not only because materials, means, limits, and so on, of which there was an eternal lack in the city soviet and social organizations, were distributed in the main through *vedomstvennyy* channels, and that to receive, as they say, 'deficit bricks' [*defitsitnyy kirpich*] was possible exclusively through economic administrators [*khozyaystvenniki*]. There is also another important factor. *In the hands of economic administrators is concentrated real power [real'naya vlast'], with the help of which can be introduced the decisions of social organizations, of the collegial organs of administration.* (The latter probably refers to state committees; author's italics)[115]

In other words, the power of the ministerial apparatus, through its control over material resources, allowed them to determine the success or otherwise of those who were nominally in the position of supervising them. To get something done required the co-operation of the people with real power, the ministerial allocators. For this reason, it was necessary to ensure their presence on the party committees at all levels: not, as is often assumed,[116] in order to discipline the members

[113] Hough and Fainsod, *How the Soviet Union is Governed*, 440–1.
[114] A. H. Brown, 'Political Power and the Soviet State: Western and Soviet Perspectives', in N. Harding (ed.), *The State in Socialist Society* (London, 1984), 64–5. Testing Brown's contention that 'in comparative terms, there is vastly more central direction and co-ordination within the Moscow bureaucratic establishment than in Washington' is clearly beyond the remit of this work. However, given the theoretical limitations to leadership mobilization of authority in the Soviet system compared to public American politics, and the empirical evidence of leadership weakness in relation to industrial power, the contention is certainly worthy of further investigation.
[115] I. F. Sokolova and M. A. Manuil'skiy, 'Kak stat' ministrom', in *Sots. iss.* 1 (1988), 22–3.   [116] See Nove, *Soviet Economic System*.

of the ministries through their party membership, but rather the reverse, in order to allow the party access to the influence of the latter. The coincidence of personnel at the highest level of the ministry and of the party, for this reason, takes on a new significance.

The evidence presented so far in this section is intended to support the case for two kinds of ministry power: their direct influence over the party, as a result of their membership in party bodies and their privileged relationship with party committees; and their hegemonic influence, arising from the need of other political institutions, including the Communist Party, to tie their success to the interests of the ministries. It is to these factors that Gorbachev alluded at the January 1987 Central Committee plenum when he talked about the tendency for the weakening in the political levers of power over economic interests which occurred in the pre-*perestroyka* period.[117] As Andreev put it,

party power functionally in so far as it grew up with economic power is such that it is already indistinguishable from it, as if they were Siamese twins . . . Of course all questions can be viewed as political, but this also means that the functions of the apparatus of the party and of the apparatus of economic power were identical. The consequences of this situation entail a complete about-turn in emphasis. *Already it is not politics which dictates to the producer where to direct his efforts, but the economic administrator, using party organs as political mouthpieces which dictate to society how to behave itself.* The accountability of party organs (and this means the careers of party workers) is founded on the whole on the economic indicators of the region. The interests of the administrators of the system of production and of the party apparatus prove to be the same; at the same time, the organizational structure of the CPSU was subordinated to the new class, in so far as it (as we have shown) turns out to be directly dependent on it. (Author's italics)[118]

A similar distinction between political and economic power to that drawn in the introductory chapter is evident in Andreev's analysis; economic power, held by ministries, took over and dominated the political sphere to the extent that the latter was itself economized, or ministerialized.

The result was a curious irony in the Communist Party's position. Sirenko has defined the role of the party as being the force which stood above social antagonisms, and studied and reconciled all the non-identical interests in society, especially in the state administration

---

[117] See Kurashvili, *Bor'ba s byurokratizmom*, 36.
[118] S. Andreev, 'Struktura vlasti i zadachi obshchestva', 155–6.

of the economy. Though he did not discount the influence of *mestnichestvo* or *vedomstvennost'* on particular party organs, for Sirenko, the peculiarity of the party's position was that it was not directed at one class at the expense of another but rather placed the general interest above the particular.[119] In practice, as has been shown, the influence of economic administrators on party organs was a general phenomenon. The issue of the classless nature of the Communist Party will be dealt with below. However, it is important to recognize the penetration of the party by social interests, especially those of the ministries, and the irony is that this penetration did make it into a 'party of a new type', though hardly in the sense generally expressed in old-style Soviet propaganda, such as Sirenko's. As Zaslavskaya put it,

We don't know what this party is. It is not a party—if we take 'party' from the word 'part' [said in English—author] like the Liberals, Democrats or Conservatives who represent part of the population. The 'party of the whole people'—it is a very strange phenomenon indeed. That is why the party is *organically part of the general power system*. The fact that this symbiosis of party and state was not touched, that reforms were limited to the economy, meant that they had no chance of succeeding. (Author's italics)[120]

In the sense that it was part of the general power system, that is, dominated by large economic powers, the absence of party political domination does not justify the interpretation put on it by those inclined to 'pluralist' analyses of the Soviet system. In this context, none of the frequent complaints about the real practices of the party can be seen to be surprising. *Podmena*, or the involvement of the party in the affairs of state, arose from the symbiosis of personnel, structures, and interests. Similarly, criticism of ministers for failure to display a party approach should be considered a quite normal and expected feature of the political system, though, given the number of determinants which went into causing their aberrant behaviour, it is doubtful whether the prescribed cure, an increase in the study of Marxism-Leninism by high ministry officials, would have any effect.[121] The penetration of the party by economic administrators in any case would have raised the question of who educates the educators; and the party itself was commonly criticized for relying on administrative

[119] V. F. Sirenko, *Interesy v systeme osnovnykh institutov sovestkogo gosudarstvennogo apravleniya* (Kiev, 1982), 41–2.   [120] Zaslavskaya interview.
[121] See *Pravda* (16 Feb. 1974), 2.

rather than political techniques.[122] In the same sense, the attempt to solve problems of producer–client imbalances by holding joint meetings of the PPOs of each ministry probably had a double edge; on the one hand, there is no evidence that producer–client relations improved, while, on the other, there is every reason to believe that the circle of collusion which resulted from the close relations which did occur between the party committees and the ministerial executive would have been spread even wider.[123] As one commentator put it: 'The transformation of the ruling party into the main subject of economic and political power deformed the system of economic relations, and converted the party leader into a "minister" of a sub-departmental territory, not infrequently utilizing methods, occasionally very far from the methods of proper party leadership.'[124] In this lay the basis of the poor behaviour of party officials.

INDUSTRIAL MINISTRIES AND THE SOVIET POLITICAL SYSTEM

The limits presented by the ministries to the exercise of political and state power arose from three factors: their organization, their social cohesion, and their ability to set and manipulate the rules of the game. The three factors should not be seen as entirely independent one from the other; rather, they were mutually supporting and strengthening. First, as Evgeniy Ambartsumov has argued in his preface to Parkinson's Law, 'One of the reasons for the longevity of bureaucracy as an institution is that it is built on the durable foundation of impenetrable compartments. As is well known, such compartments secure the ship's stability even if one of them is punctured.'[125]

Because of the domination by ministries of the interests of other bodies, they, together with Gosplan and the other state committees, including the bulk of party organizations, comprised a single large network of power founded on the principle of *vedomstvennye* organization. As Andreev put it:

---

[122] See *CDSP* 18 (1984). [123] See ibid. 15 (1982).
[124] I. A. Glebov and V. G. Marakhov (gen. eds.), *Novy sotsial'nyy mekhanizm*, (Moscow, 1990), 115.
[125] Quoted in V. Shubkin, 'Byurokratiya: tochka zreniya sotsiologa', in *Uroki gor'kie, no neobkhodimye* (Moscow, 1988), 110.

Besides this, it should not be forgotten that Gosplan, the Ministry of Finance, Gosbank and the rest of the super-departmental structure comprise in totality with the ministries a mutually interconnected system . . . Everyone understands that with the help of *vedomstvennost'* it is possible to keep society and the government in close bridle. That is why every attempt to break the corporate organizational structure of bureaucracy, the branch principle, is bound to come up against opposition from those struggling for existence . . . Today, when the economic apparatus has already achieved for itself a monopoly of power, the basis of which is founded on extensive, decelerating development of production, for which *vedomstvennyy* reserve and branch interests is the essence, in order to carry on . . . [126]

Corroborating this, Rassokhin has argued that the depth of inadequacy of the state and politicians, which was founded on the dual nature of ministries as both nominally state institutions and as economic agents, would not have been plumbed had Gosplan not also functioned as a departmental and economic, rather than authoritative, body itself.

However, *vedomstvennost'* would not have shown such a deep influence on social and economic life had it been limited to the framework of the branch departmental structure. By stages there appeared a system of relations in the economy when every closed departmental structure had a dual centre which disposed of resources of the branch and simultaneously fulfilled the other functions of owner. This centre consisted of the ministry together with the branch departments or sectors of Gosplan. To the last days of their existence, the branch departments of Gosplan played the role not so much of state curators of the branch (which they ought to have done by means of planning and distribution of the resources to carry out the economic policy of the state, founded on the interests of all the people), as the factual role of a necessary part of the departmental-branch structure.[127]

In such circumstances, with all levels of the political and state system organizationally wedded to ministerial power, it is not surprising that the politician and the statesman would not only feel weak, but, as suggested by Sokolova and Manuil'skiy above, see their best chances of political and state success not in exercising their authoritative power to control and regulate the ministries but in co-opting the economic administrators into the political system, and paying the price in terms of a further strengthening of their position.

[126] Andreev, 'Struktura vlasti i zadachi obshchestva', 152.
[127] V. P. Rassokhin, 'Vedomstvennost' kak istorichesky fenomen Sovetskoy ekonomiki', in *Postizhenie* (Moscow, 1989), 469.

The second factor which is attested to by Soviet writers as allowing ministries to subvert the power of the politicians and the state was the social cohesion of their members who shared common interests as distributors and effective owners of state property and huge material resources. As ministries dominated their subordinate organizations, and formed one organizational network with their supposed supervisors, there was a framework for the transmission of these common interests into common action. It is not proposed to enter into the complexities of whether this group comprised a class in the Marxist sense, as Andreev has argued.[128] The important point is rather that their objective powers and interests, as well as evidence about their actual behaviour, gives strong reason for believing that they had a great deal in common. At the highest political level, in the Council of Ministers, Zaslavskaya has argued that the ministers were sufficiently coherent to share a political strategy and tactics.

If we take the Central Committee, it contains all the main ministers. Also take the Council of Ministers. So, of course they have the opportunity to form connections with one another and evolve some unified strategy. But I don't think it has such an open character as saying 'so come on lads, let's derail this train'. Anyway, they understand each other with half a word—they are all in the same position.[129]

Andreev has suggested that as a group the economic administrators comprised the biggest obstacle to democratization of the political system. He calls this social group the 'production-administrative apparatus' (*proizvodstvenno-upravlencheskiy apparat*), which is defined by its

general role in the process of social production, the factual merging of the functions of its members, the inter-meshing of members in relation to cadre promotions, the independence of their incomes on the concrete results of their work, their distinct share of national income and its equal development among both engineering and administrative personnel—this makes them a single

---

[128] See Sergei Andreev, 'Prichiny i sledstviya' and 'Struktura vlasti'. In a similar vein, Akhmeduev has argued that 'The state by means of the redistribution of the product of labour of one worker or labour collective to the use of another, in essence counterposed the work of one member of society to another. This was not capitalist exploitation of man by man, but in its economic content it was also exploitation, only with worse social and economic consequences.' See A. Akhmeduev, 'Gosudarstvennaya monopoliya: osnovnoe soderzhanie i puti preodoleniya', in *Voprosy ekonomiki*, 6 (1990), 27.   [129] Interview with Zaslavskaya.

social group which may be referred to as the production-administrative apparatus.[130]

There existed, in other words, a range of common interests among this category of state employee, which inclined them to the perpetuation of the existing system; by implication, those who nominally appeared to be politicians or bureaucrats preferred to retain a system which entailed the diminution of the specifically political or bureaucratic power.

The final factor which resulted in the demise of the power of politics and the state arose from the functioning of the economy and the ability this gave ministers and economic officials to control the rules of the game to their own advantage. This has been discussed to some extent in previous parts of the book, but the points made have been succinctly generalized to the political system by the economist Kosals in a discussion on monopolism. Three aspects of the position of the monopolist conditioned his ability to act as the decisive influence in the political system. First, he was protected from external factors by the fact that consumers had no choice but to accept his goods, and by the impossibility of bankruptcy. As mentioned in the discussion above, this protection from external factors applied also to control from state bodies at a higher level.

Even if some *vedomstvo* or organization produces a significant quantity of production for which there is no real demand, this need not result in a serious position: the *vedomstvo* has just the same an office on Kalinin Prospekt, Gosplan also will continue to extend its limits in capital investment, and its enterprises no one will declare bankrupt.[131]

Secondly, the monopolist was able to control his external environment, and thus ignore state or party demands.

An example which can serve to illustrate this is the history of the project to divert part of the flow of the Siberian rivers to the south which began to be realized in practice on the initiative of Minvodkhoz SSSR, notwithstanding the decision of the XXVII Congress of the CPSU in which was foreseen the deepening of research into the project.[132]

Even where the monopolist did not write the rules entirely on his own, he was able to 'conceal from central organs of administration,

[130] Andreev, 'Prichiny i sledstviya', 114.
[131] L. Ya. Kosals, 'Monopolizm—tormoz razvitiya Sovetskogo obshchestva', in *Postizhenie* (Moscow, 1989), 123.   [132] Ibid. 125.

from controlling organizations, socially harmful information about itself—mistakes, miscalculations, decisions which carried damage to the environment, about those things which it is not recommended to write'.[133] Thirdly, the monopolist was in a position to control his internal environment. When

a kind and rich state uncle gives Minvodkhoz billions from the state budget backed up by material resources, Minvodkhoz itself decides how to use it most profitably . . . This situation is not the result of 'bureaucratic plots' or 'lack of understanding of *vedomstvennyy* leaders in economic tasks'—it is the natural and inevitable result of the special position of the monopolist.[134]

It should be emphasized that not all forms of competition were eliminated in conditions of the ministerial economy. In such circumstances, ministries competed among themselves for resources; ministers competed for status in order to achieve resources; but, most importantly, consumers competed for the privilege of receiving the monopolist's output. These conditions, which defined the structure of economic power, gave the minister 'the possibility to become a blackmailer (*shantazhist*) in relation to the political leadership, as in relationship to society'.[135]

It is another irony of the Soviet political system as it emerged especially under Brezhnev, that in completely the opposite way to the intention of the Communists, the 'withering away of the state' was largely achieved. Leonid Abalkin has noted how 'political leadership of the country in the sphere of economic decisions is found in the apparatus . . . The political leadership can only ratify the suggestions of the apparatus, changing nothing in essence.'[136] The reality of the political system has been well expressed by Kurashvili, according to whom by the 1970s under Brezhnev a system of dual power, *dvoevlast'ye*, between the politicians and the apparatus, had emerged on an amicable basis; though the apparatus had not wanted to hold power openly, they none the less assumed the 'historical initiative' from the politicians.[137] Neither did the apparatus rule on the basis of their own distinctive ideology, preferring instead to use the existing one, as in the case of its attraction to state property.[138] The camouflage of the

---

[133] Ibid.   [134] Ibid. 127.   [135] Ibid. 129.
[136] Interview with L. I. Abalkin in *Ogonek*, 13 (1989), 19.
[137] Kurashvili, *Bor'ba s byurokratizmom*, 35; and *Moscow News*, 23 (1988), 13.
[138] See L. Ponomarev and V. Shinkarenko, 'Kto kogo? Chem silen byorokrat?', in *Uroki gor'kie, no neobkhodimye* (Moscow, 1988), 163.

domination of the politician and the statesman, the appearance of totalitarian or authoritarian power structures, in other words, perfectly hid the reality of the direct rule of those exercising economic power. Law was the form; corruption the content.

As predicted in theory, the withering away of the state took some time to occur. The first shots in the game were fired by the politicians against the power of the market; only once the new state institutions were in place was political power subverted. Kurashvili notes that the bureaucracy, especially the economic apparatus, was kept under greater control in the 1930s by a powerful and ruthless Stalinist élite.[139] And it should not be thought that the top leaders of the party were in a position of total weakness, that their interests were absolutely identical to those of the economic administrators, or that the economic apparatus could do entirely as it wished. For example, when the politicians worked most effectively they were able to create at least the rudiments of a non-departmental governmental structure. 'In Leningrad and Moscow by the strength of party organizations was co-ordinated a perspective plan for territorial and branch development. However, it is hardly likely that such a method could become a general state system.'[140] Furthermore, the politicians and statesmen retained the ability to pass resolutions and legislation even if they had no power or strong interest between 1965 and 1985 in ensuring its passage into reality. Finally, without postulating the existence of a separate sphere for the statesman and the politician, however weak it may have been, it is impossible, as later chapters will show, to explain the changes which have occurred since 1985.

However, the overall nature of the Soviet state and political system between 1965 and 1985 was, as Rassokhin has suggested, a situation in which, despite the appearance of state property,

the state is nothing more than a symbol, in the name of which the rights of possession, use and disposal are realized by the branch ministries, and in the most important cases, by the above mentioned dual centres of the *vedomstvennyy*-branch structure.[141]

As was mentioned in the introductory chapter, there exist numerous difficulties in finding historical comparisons to this form of state. Rassokhin mentions two fascinating possibilities.

---

[139] See Kurashvili, *Bor'ba s byurokratizmom*, 33–4.
[140] See A. M. Birman, 'Otraslevoy printsip upravleniya: problemiy, perspektivy', in *EKO* 5 (1970), 67.   [141] Rassokin, 'Vedomstvennost', 470.

In ancient Rome, the land was held in the private ownership of the citizens of the republic; however, the supreme owner was reckoned to be the republic itself. In the medieval feudal society the supreme owner of the land was reckoned to be the suzerain, (the prince or king), but his vassals had the right of property on their holdings [*udel*].[142]

Rassokhin's comparison of the Soviet Union with Roman and medieval society is focused on the discrepancy between the appearance of ownership and supremacy which disguised the realities of power which lay elsewhere. Rassokhin concludes with a comparison which entirely supports the argument of this book.

Ministries in the Soviet Union concentrate in the hands such monopoly power such has never been seen, not even with *the most powerful companies in the West*. *Vedomstvennye*-monopoly structures form, if you please, the most grave obstacle on the road to *perestroyka* in the economy. (Author's italics)[143]

As well as obstacles to *perestroyka* in the economy, the ministries, as this chapter has tried to prove, formed also the most severe obstacle to *perestroyka* in the political sphere; they were more powerful, and exerted an even greater influence, to paraphrase Rassokhin, than even capitalist corporations in Western democracies. Before looking at the period after 1985, however, it is necessary to chart the relationship of the ministries to broader sections of Soviet society.

[142] Ibid.   [143] Ibid. 471.

4

Industrial Ministries and Soviet Society

PREVIOUS chapters of the book have concentrated on demonstrating how ministries were able to dominate the economy and the élite institutions of party and state. To complete an analysis of ministries as political institutions, however, their impact within society as a whole needs to be considered. Any account of a political system is constrained by its ability to explain how the public is organized to accept the rule of the dominant institutions. Where societies are relatively stable, as was the case in the Soviet Union until 1985, the public is being 'delivered' in some sense; but the form and methods by which public behaviour is structured to allow for stability are empirical issues, the answers to which will vary greatly between states.

The aspect of Soviet politics that has probably been least explored is its social basis. This is, of course, in part the result of the even greater than normal difficulties in obtaining reliable data. Social groups have been studied as influencing factors in Soviet politics, but few political models have incorporated social behaviour as an integral part of their explanatory framework.[1] There were exceptions to this rule, though not all of their conclusions are supported by the evidence presented in this book. David Lane, for example, has argued that a political sociology of the Soviet Union revealed an acceptance among the population of the legitimacy of what he thought was the dominant institution, the Communist Party. It will be argued here, however, that, despite Communist illegitimacy, stability was achieved via ministerial domination of the social system. Given this, it becomes clear that a study of the importance of the industrial ministries on the Soviet

[1] Most famously in H. Gordon Skilling and F. Griffiths (eds.), *Interest Groups in Soviet Politics* (Princeton, NJ, 1971); D. Lane, *The Socialist Industrial State* (London, 1976); C. F. Sabel and D. Stark, 'Planning, Politics and Shop-Floor Power: Hidden Forms of Bargaining in Soviet-Imposed State-Socialist Economies', in *Politics and Society* 4 (1982), 439–75; and P. Hauslohner, 'Gorbachev's Social Contract', in *Soviet Economy*, 1 (1987), 54–89. The evidence of the relationship of ministries and social groups, however, points to a far less legitimized and solidaristic commitment to social norms than Hauslohner supposes, and it will be argued that it is the very illegitimize and inegalitarian practices of ministries, and the weakness of both political legitimacy and social solidarity which were more important in structuring social stability.

political system may cast doubt on explanations of social stability and instability which have focused on the success or weaknesses of official socialization or political culture.[2]

This is all the more obvious given the clear social functions which ministries exercised in housing, health, leisure, transport, consumer supply, etc. The complex impact of the involvement of ministries on the daily lives of many Soviet citizens needs to be measured if the ministries are to be properly understood. Evidence about the relationship between ministries and the Soviet public, when added to what has already been established above, supports certain important conclusions about the political system as it existed up until 1985. Furthermore, as the next chapter will argue, these conclusions are also important for understanding the politics of *perestroyka*.

The absence of political and state power, or authority as it has been defined in the Introduction, was a consequence not only of the ability of the ministries to control the economy and thus impose their agenda on their nominal superiors. There is an additional factor, once widespread coercive measures directed by politicians and the security services at ministerial personnel had been forsworn.[3] The failures of political power also resulted from the absence of a public space in which politicians and statesmen could operate to gather the social support required to make their decisions effective and verifiable. Most commonly, this public space is achieved through the existence of democratic discussion and decision-making, in which the politician has a force behind the law he passes which is derived from an awareness in the minds of those who might oppose his decision of the social forces which support it. Where politicians have effective power, society itself is, as it were, organized for democracy. The paradox of totalitarianism resulted from the fact that the more the politicians sought to control, the less powerful they became; by abolishing the independence of society and establishing economic agencies of the state in the industrial ministries through which they appeared able to realize their wills, politicians in fact cut off the basis for the exercise of political and state power. Politicians, therefore, are *more* powerful

---

[2] See e.g. S. White, 'Propagating Communist Values in the USSR', in *Problems of Communism*, 6 (1985), 1–17; A. H. Brown (ed.), *Political Culture and Communist Studies* (London, 1984).

[3] These were not in any case very effective means of dealing with the problem of ministries in the Soviet economy. See T. Dunmore, *The Stalinist Command Economy* (London, 1980); and G. Kh. Popov, 'S tochki zreniya ekomomista', in A. Bek, *Novoe naznachenie* (Moscow, 1987), 187–213.

when operating in an environment in which social groups have interests which are articulated and organized independently.

Public power, like any other form, needs an organizational basis to be effective; ministerial power, however, organized the Soviet public out of politics. By verticalizing the most important formal and informal channels of improving living standards in an apparatus whose apex was the minister, by ministerializing social inequality, and by dominating alternative institutional forms of social organization, the ministries effectively reduced public political action in pursuit of distributive benefits to terms that they themselves set, and in so doing turned social groups into private individuals seeking to maximize their qualifications according to the criteria of the branch. The social by-product of their dominance was the destruction of other forms of horizontal social organization, and the subordination of alternative political institutions which might have structured society in other ways, including the local soviets and even the market. The social result was the depoliticization of social life, in the sense that pursuit of state power to effect distributive choices in the interests of independent social groups was neutralized. As society was depoliticized, however, so too were the politicians disempowered.

The rest of this chapter will seek to demonstrate this argument by looking at: first, the social functions of industrial ministries, to establish the scope ministries had to verticalize rewards; secondly, the relationship of ministries to the alternative horizontal organizing body, the local soviet, to establish that horizontal, organizational bases for distribution were dominated by ministry power; thirdly, the impact of industrial organization on social interests, to establish the empirical responses of social groups and individuals in a reward structure dominated by ministry power; and, finally, at the consequences of these factors on the overall nature of political power in the Soviet system.

THE SOCIAL FUNCTIONS OF INDUSTRIAL MINISTRIES

The 1967 General Statute on USSR Ministries defined their social functions rather broadly and in little detail. Under the heading 'Main Tasks of the Ministry', the law spoke of ministries 'improving the housing and socio-cultural (*kul' turno-bytovyy*) situation of workers and employees, and creating safe conditions of work in production'.[4] Further legislation was enacted consolidating the mechanism of ministry activity in the sphere of social policy through its affirmation and authorization of enterprise deductions from revenues into the social fund.[5] Indeed, the evidence suggests that in the system of payment to workers, the role of the social fund grew as a proportion of total wages from the late 1960s, following aspersions cast on the ideological soundness of individual wage payments.[6] Despite the envisaged growth in the applicability of enterprise funds in the social sphere, however, it is clear that ministerial control meant that real expenditure in the non-productive sphere actually declined.[7]

The centrality of ministries to overall thinking on social policy has been noted by a number of Soviet commentators. 'It is possible to produce a huge number of examples to show that branch economic structures in the social sphere were more powerful [*vlastnyy*] than any other.'[8] The noted Soviet economist Stanislav Shatalin expressed the situation well when he said:

Among economic leaders there is a widespread stereotype. If the enterprise has everything of its own—housing, crèches, polyclinics and so on, then the collective will work better. Today, this stereotype is the subject of great doubt ... Today the departmental funds of GAZ [a large industrial enterprise], or, for example, certain industrial ministries, form a special source of additional income, reflected in better medical services or holiday hostels, sanatoriums or in the perspective of more rapid obtaining of housing or places in crèches without queues. To many people it must seem, that *their best route is by this road*.[9] (Author's italics)

The political importance of variations in ministerial social policies will be explained below; the main point being established at present

---

[4] *SPPSSR* 17 (1967), 372.   [5] *Izvestiya* (Jan. 30 1966), 2.

[6] In any case, the ideological soundness of the social fund must be doubtful when seen in practice. Research into the distribution system by Rutkevich suggests that the concentration of remuneration into the social fund, so favoured by certain socialists for its egalitarian character, in practice increased inequality by rewarding the middle classes disproportionately. In the post-war period, payments into social funds rose faster than wage funds. When used for the upkeep of theatres, and other forms of 'educated consumption', they can be seen to be disposed disproportionately. See M. N. Rutkevich, *Voprosy istorii KPSS*, 1 (Jan. 1986), 37–52.

[7] L. Abalkin, 'Khozyaystvennyy mekhanizm i stil' myshleniya', in *EKO* 2 (1981), 13.

[8] F. M. Borodkin, 'Sotsial'naya politika: vlast' i perestroyka', in *Postizhenie* (Moscow, 1989), 254.

[9] See interview with Stanislav Shatalin, 'Skol'ko stoit dom postroit'', in *Ogonek*, 43 (1987), 10.

was that the ministries were immensely powerful in social planning, and if they did not use these powers, it was because they could not be forced to, or had no interest of their own in doing so. However, whether they chose to use their power effectively or not, its concentration in their hands constrained the resources of any alternative institutions, and, as Shatalin suggests, dominated the rationality of those seeking to advance their social position.

The extent of ministry power in the social sphere is explained by the sociologist Leonid Kostin.

The ministry is given the necessary administrative power and has at its disposal great material, technical, and financial resources. Such planning at the branch level on the whole defines the basic directions of activity of the labour collective, its technical-economic and social organization . . . Today, almost three-quarters of resources allocated on consumption and infra-structure are expended on the branch principle.[10]

Despite the relative vagueness in the general legislation, therefore, ministries and their enterprises operated over a sweeping range of functions which made a huge difference to the daily life of Soviet citizens: they had wide powers in housing and town planning, in transport and social infrastructure from sewers to roads, and in supplying medical and recreational facilities, foodstuffs, and scarce consumer goods. As Moskvichev put it:

The basic part of the financial and material resources going into the social development of towns is concentrated in the hands of industrial ministries, although there have been undertaken attempts in experimental cases to transfer these functions into the disposition of some local soviets.[11]

The real picture of ministerial social policies, of course, will show considerable variety. The power of industrial ministries in the social sphere did not imply anything about the quality of their social performance; despite some progress in the sphere of social planning in general up to 1985, 'on the level of the branch . . . social planning has not yet received the necessary emphasis'.[12] Other authors laid the

[10] L. A. Kostin, 'Sotsial'nye rezervy otrasli', in *Sots. iss.* 3 (1985), 5. Note that these are official figures only; as shall be shown below, there is good reason to believe that the actual share of ministry spending in the social sphere may have been proportionately even greater.

[11] N. P. Moskvichev, 'Gorod, predpriyatiya i zhil'e', in *EKO* 7 (1982), 171.

[12] Kostin, 'Sotsial'nye rezervy', 4. For example, in the Ministry of the Industry of Means of Communication, in the 8th five-year plan, only 9% of enterprises had plans of social development affirmed by the ministry; by the 10th plan, this figure had

blame on ministry power for a range of problems, from chronic deficits, backwardness compared to other European countries, growing territorial differences of living standards, the absence of choice, the growing divide not of incomes but of privileges and consequent violations of social justice, the supremacy of producer interests, indifference and alienation.

The main reason for the existence of the above problems consists, in our view, in the discrepancy between the proclaimed social aim of increasing wealth as the main and priority task in relation to the economy, and the action of the *vedomstvennyy*-bureaucratic mechanism of administration, allotting social policy a subordinate role in relation to the economy.[13]

The trouble was that ministries administered the social policy, and, in the view of commentators, change would only be possible if there was

strengthened the role in social administration of those institutions which immediately answer to the well-being of people—local soviets, service sector organizations, health bodies, cultural groups, etc. The widening of their powers in resolving problems is connected with the creation of a fully valued life. At the same time, the role of enterprises, ministries, and departments must be relatively lowered in the sphere of material production in resolving the social problems of well-being.[14]

In some cases, as with protecting the environment of workers and residents, social measures were actively flouted. Even where funds were earmarked for social matters, ministries frequently cheated on the actual delivery of them, at the expense of other ministries, putting the local party in the position of constantly trying to impose honest trading on reluctant partners.[15]

increased to only 30%. Among the areas covered by the plans were: prevention and strengthening of health and raising of work-readiness of employees; improving conditions and safety at work; improving material stimulation and wages; improving social conditions; securing, for labour collectives of food products from farms attached to the enterprises; improving socialist competition and developing the creative activity of workers; and the organization of the administration of workers' social activity. It is also notable that social indicators were not included in ministerial plans for socialist competition; the focus lay entirely on production tasks. See V. Dinevich, 'Sotsialisticheskoe sorevnovanie v apparate upravleniya', in *Kommunist sovetskoy Latvii*, 6 (1972), 68–72.

[13] L. A. Khakhulina, 'Strategiya blagosostoyaniya v usloviyakh perestroyki', in *Postizhenie* (Moscow, 1989, 300–1). [14] Ibid. 303.
[15] Moskvichev, 'Gorod', 171–5.

Practice has shown that for industrial and agricultural ministries, services are subsidiary to technical-economic questions of the branch ... As a good example, one may cite the USSR Ministry of the Electro-Technical Industry. It built a complex of factories in the town of Minusinsk. According to the plan, it was necessary to spend in the first instance 77 million roubles on the non-productive [neproizvodstvennyy] sphere, but the ministry only allotted 44 million, as a result of which it excluded from the plan all medical facilities, trade organizations, canteens, clubs, libraries, and established only one school.[16]

Each branch pursued its own particular social policy, and, even within individual ministries, the complexities of size and age of enterprises, etc., meant that no single homogeneous policy operated.[17] For example, Gal'tsov's study of social policy in the Ministry for Light and Food Industry Machine-Building demonstrated that a positive correlation existed between an enterprise's size and the effectiveness of its social policy, and between the level of social services and rates of labour turnover.[18] The result in some ministries, where social policy was clearly secondary to branch output, was the continuing decline in the number of workers prepared to stay in it.[19] Where enterprises were old and relatively established, social policy worked fairly well; in new ones, however, there were great difficulties among workers because of the absence of established facilities. Similar discrepancies were evident in the so-called non-priority sectors of the economy.[20] What is evident, as has been shown by a survey of enterprises by Araslanov, is a very tenuous connection between levels of economic performance by the factory, or the individual worker, and the standard of social facilities available: the factors which *did* condition social development were the size of the enterprise, its age, its location, its branch affiliation, its own technical and constructions abilities, etc.[21]

This does not mean that ministries in favoured sectors, or enterprises with historically related advantages which operated successful housing policies, did not manage to achieve better results in economic performance. Again, according to Kostin, in the Ministry of Electro-Technical Industry productivity increased and labour turnover declined;

---

[16] M. N. Tarasenko, 'Vzaimodeystvie mestnykh sovetov i ministerstv', in *Sovetskoe gosudarstvo i pravo*, 8 (1980), 76.   [17] Ibid.

[18] See A. Gal'tsov 'Ukreplenie predpriyatii—vazhnyy faktor snizheniya tekuchesti kadrov', in *Sotsialisticheskiy trud*, 1 (1977), 33.   [19] Ibid.

[20] Ibid.

[21] K. M. Araslanov, 'Tri urovnya predpriyatiya i ego interesy', in *EKO* 4 (1978), 137–41.

and, where a ministry pursued the policy of building factories before providing social facilities, as was the case in the food industry ministry's factory in Brest, it was unable to obtain any workers to go there. Despite the notable inadequacies pointed out above, housing was, in fact, the highest priority area for ministry social performance.

The politically relevant point, however, is that the location of social policy primarily in the branch, and through the existence of favoured and unfavoured sectors, created circumstances affecting the rationality of social groups and individuals supportive of ministerial power. Justice, or legitimacy, was not the foundation of this power. As Stanislav Shatalin, interviewed in *Ogonek*, put it:

Let's take the limiting case: a good enterprise with a poor worker. Formally, he has there a better chance of receiving rewards, such as housing, socio-cultural facilities, and medical services, than a very good worker at a lousy enterprise. But who is to blame, that I work, let's say, at a bakery and not a 'ZIL', or some other giant.[22]

Despite this large variability in ministry social performance, the resulting inequalities and injustices, and the frequent failure and criticism of ministries for failing to perform adequately the social functions vested in them, it is notable that social services continued to develop in a direction that strengthened the role of ministries. For example, a further growth in the dimensions of the ministerial social fund was envisaged by the transfer of further powers to enterprises in 1979 to control the development of economic incentives to workers in the factories, in particular out of the socio-cultural funds.[23] Given the experience of previous measures in 1965 designed to increase enterprise control over their social funds, there is little doubt that the 1979 measure would effectively strengthen ministry control over overall social funding.[24] Ministries, therefore, appeared increasingly able to

[22] Interview with S. S. Shatalin, 'Skol'ko stoit dom postroit', in *Ogonek*, 43 (1987), 10.

[23] Tarasenko, 'Vzaimodeystvie', 77. On the importance of enterprise-based social policy to ministry power see also Kostin, 'Sotsial'nye rezervy', 6.

[24] After 1965 the ministries had argued successfully that economic efficiency demanded recentralization. For example, in Perm', Tomsk, and Vologda only paltry funds were allocated by the enterprises of the Russian Republic Ministry of Local Industry, with greater funds allocated in wages contrary to procedures. In addition, enterprises without ministerial authorization had used the social and housing fund to repair roads and bridges, maintain monuments, acquire office furniture and trucks for production, and build shops and vegetable cellars. One must doubt the minister's suggestion therefore, given the other evidence about the use of social funds, that first priority for centralized funds should be for use in housing, Young Pioneer camps, crèche facilities, canteens, etc. See *Sovetskaya Rossiya* (Feb. 10 1970), 2.

attack the existence of non-branch social services, on the grounds that they infringed against their abilities to provide economic stimuli to workers. Their success in this regard led not only to stronger ministries in the most direct sense, but also to the vastly important fact that there were generated forms of social inequality, and thus incentives, which were primarily branch based and, for that reason, channelled individual endeavour into distribution networks in ministerial control.

Before going on to assess the interrelation of the various forms of social inequality, and its impact on ministry power and the Soviet political system, it is important to identify in what main areas ministries affected social life and in what ways ministry-based inequality manifested itself.[25]

Housing

Housing in the Soviet Union was allocated along four main lines: at place of work, through ministry and enterprise; by place of residence, through the local soviet; through the co-operative sector; and through private ownership.

Government policy, from as early as the mid-1940s, formally favoured the transfer of housing in the state sector to the hands of a single master, the local soviet.[26] However, the transfer process went slowly between 1965 and the mid-1980s, if it happened at all. In the USSR in 1985, of the 72 per cent of housing in the state sector, ministries owned 46 per cent compared with only 26 per cent owned by the local soviets.[27] In the RSFSR, as a whole, 43.9 per cent of housing was in ministerial hands.[28] In Saratov in 1969, for example, only twelve buildings under ministry jurisdiction were transferred to the local soviets.[29] In the Talmenk region, where only the smallest part

[25] For further discussion of the impact of ministries on Soviet cities see: D. Cattell, *Leningrad: A Case Study of Soviet Urban Government* (London, 1968); S. Kotkin, *Steeltown, USSR* (London, 1991); H. W. Morton and R. C. Stuart (eds.), *The Contemporary Soviet City* (London, 1984); and W. Taubman, *Governing Soviet Cities* (New York, 1973). Though none of these authors takes ministerial power as the primary focus of research, the shadow of the ministries falls across many of the pages.

[26] See I. Andrianov, 'Vedomstvennyy zhilishchnyy fond', in *Khozyaystvo i pravo*, 3 (1986), 80.   [27] Ibid. 123.

[28] See A. T. Semushkin, 'Tsentralizm i mezhotraslevoy podkhod v upravlenii sotsialisticheskym khozyaystvom', in *Problemy mezhotraslevogo upravleniya obshchestvennym proizvodstvom* (Moscow, 1977), 38–40.   [29] See *Izvestiya* (Feb. 21 1970), 5.

of housing and communal construction actually rested with the local authorities, in 1981 and 1982 not one apartment changed hands organizationally.[30] In the Vladimirovskaya *oblast'*, according to the chairman of the local soviet executive committee, ministries remained the main house builders, controlling almost 74 per cent of the housing stock; house construction brigades worked for them almost exclusively, and funds for other local activities were released by the ministry only after it had satisfied its own needs in multiple ways.[31] According to Bessanova's calculations, in Novosibirsk the transfer of funds from ministerial to soviet jurisdiction was under way at the rate of 2 per cent per annum; this meant that government decrees would be fulfilled in fifty years.[32] Indeed, as a result of the 1983 Law on the Labour Collective, the rights of local soviets in respect of housing distribution could be said to have been limited rather than expanded, with the transfer of enterprise housing to the local authority prohibited except with the permission of the labour collective itself.[33]

The evidence suggests that, in general terms, ministry construction and administration of housing compared unfavourably to that of the local soviets. For example, ministry expenditure on housing repair totalled only 0.5 per cent of its total value, in comparison to 1 per cent in the soviet sector.[34] Because of the absence of expertise in house building, ministry apartments cost on average 20 per cent more than those of the local soviets, with lower quality services.[35] The expenditure of resources earmarked for housing was often very haphazardly organized. The absence of any branch department for housing in the Ministry of Light, Textile and Food Industry was quite typical of ministries in general. Only two-thirds of allotted sums for housing were actually allocated in the late 1970s.[36] Where ministries spent

[30] See M. K. Shishkov, 'Vedomstvennaya razobshchennost' v rayone: kak ee preodolet'', in *EKO* 11 (1983), 76–77.

[31] See interview with Yu. A. Dmitriev, 'Khotya slovo ne ochen' uyotnoe', in *Ogonek*, 43 (1987), 9–10.

[32] See O. E. Bessanova, 'Zhiloy fond goroda: neobkhodimost' i vozmozhnost' ego ob"edineniya', in *EKO* 7 (1988), 126.

[33] See *Argumenty i fakty*, 34 (1988), 8. Rules for the distribution of housing within the enterprise were extremely complex, and depended, where they were not abused, on a points system favouring management personnel, families, the sick, etc. The criteria for awarding housing was also decided within the ministry or the enterprise, in some cases by the the labour collective. See ibid. 38 (1988), 8.

[34] Semushkin, 'Tsentralizm'.

[35] See V. Z. Rogovin, 'Nekotorye voprosy sotsial'noy politika v sfere zhil'ya', in *Sotsial'nye garantii i problemy sovershenstvovaniya raspredelitel'nykh otnosheniy* (Moscow, 1979), 99. [36] See Tarasenko, 'Vzaimodeystvie', 76.

their funds on housing they did so inefficiently; 35 per cent less was spent out of the housing fund on actual housing in comparison to the local soviet, with 30 per cent higher administration costs.[37]

Ministries not only controlled the financing and administration of house building, but in many cases they controlled the extremely complex construction process as well, in a way which left Soviet citizens in the worst of all possible worlds: dependent on the ministries for poor housing, which they were frequently forced to build for themselves. In Saratov, eighty ministries acted as housing clients.[38] In Surgut, the city's general construction agent was the Ministry of the Petroleum Industry. Other ministries were required to transfer to it their central allocations for architectural planning, construction, and installation. According to the chairman of the city soviet, however, 'no matter how hard we campaign and cajole, they either do not do this or else put it off for a long time'.[39] The Ministry of the Coal Industry had responsibility for constructing the new town of Neryungri in South Yakutia, but was well behind in building houses.[40] In Kishenev in Moldavia, 'following the example of the Vibration Instruments Plant and the Zorile Footwear Association, every resident has decided to work 100 hours at construction projects'.[41] It even happened that the work credited to construction bodies was actually carried out by workers in the factory themselves or by workers from other locations, which must in some measure have accounted for the very low quality of building.[42]

The corollary of poor construction and administration, of course, was the hardship of many people dependent on ministry services. At one factory under the Ministry of the Machine Tool Industry in the Krasnodarsk *kray*, which had significantly increased its share of profits and other indicators, the ministry did not allot to the enterprise resources for house building, thus increasing the waiting list for houses by 1.7 times, even though more than 600 workers left the industry for lack of any prospect of obtaining accommodation. But, despite the hardship, there existed no large-scale organized alternative to ministry power in this area, and seeking accommodation, however poor in quality, through ministerial channels, whether by seeking employment in privileged sectors, or by contributing to its physical construction in

[37] See R. Obert, 'Zhilishchnomu fondu—edinogo khozyaina', in *Khozyaystvo i pravo*, 1 (1978), 22–3.   [38] See *Izvestiya* (30 June 1972), 3.
[39] See ibid. (5 Sept. 1975), 3.   [40] See *Pravda* (18 Sept. 1980), 2.
[41] See *Izvestiya* (27 June 1972), 2.   [42] See *Pravda* (12 Jan. 1981), 3.

brigades organized at places of work, certainly remained one of the key means of obtaining it.

Transport

There is further evidence of the ministerializing of society in the vast departmental transport networks which exist in many towns. Leaving his ministry apartment, *en route* to a job in the ministry's factory, the Soviet worker might well depend on the ministry to get there on time. Not only were the bulk of passenger cars controlled by economic agencies, causing the most inefficient and polluting use of petrol,[43] but even the bus service was often in ministry hands. In some measure reflecting the interests of the branch in getting people to work on time and in a fit psychological state, though more likely because of their regularly observable interests in maximizing control and resources in general, ministry-controlled transport increased at a far faster rate than the civic system in the period 1971–5, and, given all the other evidence about ministry power, probably thereafter as well. In Chelyabinsk *rayon*, for example, enterprises acquired over 1,600 buses in this period as compared to only 160 for the public network. The picture was identical throughout the republic. The average departmental bus driver carried forty to fifty passengers per day, so a large enterprise with 60,000 employees required at least 3,000 drivers. This resulted in further inflated costs in fuel and repairs.[44] However, the system was obviously preferable for drivers and passengers alike when compared with conditions available in the public sector, and must have created a further degree of social organization and rationality conducive to ministerial power.

Infrastructure

In all the areas servicing the housing, transport, and factories of the Soviet citizen, the performance of the ministries made an appreciable difference to life. The priorities of the predominant ministry in a given

---

[43] See M. Lemeshev, 'Ekonomicheskie interesy i sotsial'noe prirodopol'zovanie', in *Inogo ne dano* (Moscow, 1988), 257.   [44] See *Sovetskaya rossiya* (8 Oct. 1978), 2.

location made a difference to the quality of roads in that area.[45] Where goods had to be transported and preserved on these frequently appalling roads, which made such a difference to the quality and quantity of consumer goods available to the public, the departmentalist tendencies of ministries were often cited for failing to produce the necessary quality of preserving equipment and sacrificing everything to quantity.[46] In the Talmenk Altai *kray*, the existence of over eighty regional subdepartments of central economic organizations, each pursuing its own *vedomstvennyy* purposes, meant that there existed no single, unified system for gas or water supply, or for sewage and waste disposal.[47] In Surgut, there were forty-three boiler plants built by different ministries.[48] In Yalta, seven different organisations were engaged in rubbish disposal; one department was held to dump its collection on to the other's premises.[49] In Minsk, the Ministry of the Motor Vehicle Industry refused for three years to be involved in a *pro rata* contribution to the building of a central heating complex, preferring instead to build a large assembly shop, an administration building, and a dining-room, which could not be operated because of lack of heat.[50] Altogether, in the Soviet Union as a whole, nearly 4,000 enterprises controlled their own water-lines; 2,700 were in charge of sewers; and 700 maintained hotels that could accommodate 100,000 guests.[51]

Material well-being

As pointed out by Shatalin, the notion that workers should have their material incentives organized not only in wage payments, but in direct physical supply of goods at place of work, had a long history in the Soviet Union from the time of the creation of the departments of workers' supply, *otdeleniya rabochego snabzheniya* (ORS).

For example, the trade services in Kustanai, a region with 35,000 population, was run by the ORS of an asbestos-refining combine, subordinate to the Ministry of the Building Materials Industry, as part

---

[45] See G. Tartarovskiy, 'Uchastie predpriyatiy v dorozhnykh rabotakh', in *Khozyaystvo i pravo*, 2 (1978), 88.
[46] See A. O. Shatbalin, 'Effekt razvitiya infrastruktury', in *EKO* 11 (1986), 98–101.
[47] Shishkov 'Vedomstvennaya', 76.   [48] See *Izvestiya* (5 Sept. 1975), 3.
[49] See *Izvestiya* (10 June 1972), 3.   [50] See ibid. (6 Aug. 1975), 3.
[51] See *Pravda*, (18 Sept. 1980, 2.

of its then recently established national ORS; there were at least fifteen such local ORSs across the country. A similar organization, under the Ministry of Non-Ferrous Metallurgy, supplied workers in the medium-sized city of Rudny. In the Tatar Autonomous Republic, retail trade and restaurants were handled by light industry ministries, as well as the Ministry of Trade. In Karelia, it was handled by the ORS of the Ministry of Lumber and Wood-Processing; in Chechen-Ingush, by the Ministry of Petroleum-Extracting Industry; in Chita, by the Ministry of Non-Ferrous Metallurgy; on the Transbaikal railway, by the Ministry of Communications.[52]

As in other areas in which they intervened in social provision, there is strong evidence that many of these departments functioned badly, or had negative consequences on economic performance. However, the important political point is to note how even in doing so, the overall effect of such provision was to provide the organizational basis for branch-based social inequalities and incentives. As one commentator put it:

There is, in the first place, the transition to a category of worker having immediate professional access to the movement of deficit goods. Here it is possible, holding in one's hand one deficit good, to periodically exchange it for another deficit good or service. There are chances to increase money incomes through speculation or extortion. In the worst case, a worker can economize on inputs, and carry out the material as a free consumer product. All this is supported by the facts of sociological research . . . In the second place, the so-called 'closed forms of supply' should not be forgotten as these embrace a sufficiently broad strata of the population. The degree of attractiveness is directly proportional to the degree of goods deficit. Departmental supply, not available to the ordinary person, raises the buying power of money for those who use its services, such as the ordering of shortage goods at low state retail prices. From here it works out that the worker, transferring from one enterprise to another, in principle may increase his real income even if he takes a cut in his nominal wages. In this, the categories of departmental supply differ from one another by the level of availability of products of high demand.[53]

In Vilnius, for example, after continuous industrial growth had led to the exhaustion of labour resources, ministries established special conditions for their enterprises, including housing, higher pay, etc.

[52] See ibid. (11 Jan. 1970), 3.
[53] I. A. Glebov and V. G. Makharov, *Novyy sotsial'nyy mekhanizm* (Moscow, 1990), 187.

Not only was this, as could be predicted, detrimental to public facilities and, therefore, alternative social organizations; but, in the more subtle way that ministry power often built unwitting social support, it also led to the diminution in the value of education, with increased turnover, especially among the young. As the secretary of the Vilnius party committee noted, loss of interest in education and training had a subsequent effect on the ability of poorly trained workers to cope with complex technology, which, in turn, strengthened the ministry in its use of extensive techniques.[54] The application of the ministerial reward system, in other words, made society adapt itself to conditions which made it most fit for ministerial control. This occurred even where services were poorly organized. In Kamyshin, where ministries competed strongly for workers by offering social facilities,

the fact that housing, crèches, and stadiums belong to enterprises creates a great many inconveniences. A woman who lives at one end of the town must bring her youngster to the proper departmental day-care at the other end of town (though there may be a nursery, belonging to a different department, right next door).[55]

Ministerial activity extended to the provision of facilities for rest and recreation, often by joint arrangement with local councils. Legislation governing ministerial contribution to the provision of recreational facilities, either with local soviets or branch-based trade unions, was not highly developed, and ministries also frequently cheated in terms of their contribution to the local budgets of towns where they located their rest facilities.[56]

If ministerial control over the distributive network was one of the main planks of its social power, poor performance was not penalized. Indeed, ministerial control was strengthened further with the establishment of the so-called network of firm-based shops (*set' firmennykh magazinov*) which by-passed the regular trade network and local authority control, and acted as direct outlets for enterprise and branch products in the consumer sector. Though intended to allow ministries to improve their knowledge of the Soviet market, the factory outlet must have strengthened ministry control over the consumer sector.

[54] For a discussion of this, see article by the First Secretary of the Vilnius City Party Committee in *Pravda* (7 Jan. 1970), 2.

[55] See N. Aitov, *Literaturnaya gazeta*, 34 (1975), 10.

[56] See A. M. Serebryakov, 'Pravovye problemy sochetaniya territorial'nykh i otraslevykh nachal v upravlenii rekreatsionnymi resursami', in *Sovetskoe gosudarstvo i pravo*, 2 (1987), 43–50.

The Ministry of Communication, for example, ran the retail outlet for televisions and electrical equipment, Orbita.[57] Where *firmennye magaziny* existed, and when cities wanted consumer deliveries of scarce commodities, the ministries were in a position quite directly to comply or otherwise, creating the classic conditions for the extraction of favours and the exercise of power.

Cities

The urbanization of the Soviet Union was a factor of immense significance, not only to the personal lives of those who underwent the experience, but to the sources of support for the ministerialized society. As Vishnevsky puts it:

Soviet society became urbanized only very recently. Even in 1926, town dwellers comprised only 18 per cent of the population of the country, within which inhabitants of cities of over 100,000 people made up only 6.5 per cent. By 1987, 66 per cent of the total lived in the towns, and 40 per cent of those in towns of over 100,000. Between the two dates there are six decades, a term shorter than one person's life.[58]

Large bodies of new, low-skilled labour were continuously available for industry, and their prospects of improving their lives in material, training, and educational terms were highly linked to the branch of employment. Their very entry into the city was through the auspices of and in thrall to the ministry. Their lack of social organization in the new circumstances in which they found themselves probably contributed to the ease with which ministerial control was established over the population; added to this was the fact that, though the peasants who stayed in the countryside were the biggest losers of ministry-based industrialization, the peasants who moved to the towns, and especially their children, achieved huge degrees of social mobility. Furthermore, as Vishnevsky puts it, the recruitment of a large pool of former peasants in many ways created a cultural basis for ministerial power:

the rural [*derevenskaya*] system is oriented on natural economic indicators, on the equalization of distribution, on tradition, on collectivism, on external

---

[57] See *Pravda* (29 Sept. 1978), 3.
[58] A. G. Vishnevskiy, 'Sotsial'nye regulyatory i chelovek', in *Postizhenie* (Moscow, 1989), 62.

control over the social conduct of the person, on command methods of administration, on bureaucratic administration and so on.[59]

In perhaps less perceptible and measurable ways than with housing, goods, and services, the dynamics of ministerial interests and power had a complex and varied impact on the development of Soviet towns and cities. The physical environment, the geographical balance of population, the growth of industry and wealth in regions—in all these areas ministerial power was of the utmost significance to the lives of Soviet citizens. One of the most important demographic factors in Soviet life from the mid-1960s to mid-1980s, was the growth and movement of population from smaller and middle-sized towns to the main cities. A consequence was growth in the area of urban land and of land under construction. For example, population growth in the twenty-two largest Soviet cities comprised over 60 per cent of total population growth in the country as a whole.[60] The interests and attitudes of the industrial ministries, and, as a consequence, of the population as a whole who were drawn into these interests, were largely responsible for these demographic changes.

The subtle interplay of ministerial power and social interests through a combination of demographic, educational, infrastructural, and social service factors is evident in the following example. Ministries focused on established towns because of the existing infrastructure which tended to decrease their expenditures in this area, together with the unremunerated use of certain resources available in towns.[61] For example, the Ministry of Construction, the Ministry for Industrial Construction, and the Ministry for Construction of Heavy Industry Enterprises, in the first three years of the 1971–5 plan, put only 16 per cent of capital investment into small or medium-size cities.[62] However, the other side of concentration in large industrial towns was that established inhabitants, who had already gravitated to the advanced sectors, were able to use their advantages and privileges to raise their

[59] Ibid. 55. The evidence presented in this chapter casts doubt on Vishnevskiy's more hopeful interpretation of social development. 'The second, the urban [gorodskaya] system, arises in the main from the corner of market mechanisms, of money income, of payment by labour, of individual labour abilities of the person, of free choice, founded on a person's internal responsibility, the conscious solidarity of people, of the combination of common interests and so on.' Urban life, however, did not exist as a structural phenomenon independent of ministerial influence.

[60] See I. Barabanov, 'Territorial'naya struktura promyshlennogo proizvodstva i razvitie gorodov', in Voprosy ekonomiky, 8 (1988), 127–8.   [61] Ibid.

[62] See Pravda (9 Sept. 1975), 2.

educational and other ministry-relevant qualifications further. For certain production tasks, therefore, ministries were then forced to recruit workers from further afield.

The second factor conditioning the cycle of ministry–society–demographic developments arose from the technological implications of population concentration. With most industry and labour concentrated in them, large Soviet cities frequently contained networks of enterprises with the whole cycle of productive activity. Naturally, as will be discussed below, this impacted on the environment. The use of small towns and specialized production, which would improve all these indicators, however, did not favour ministry interests. This, in turn, created a vicious cycle, as towns lacking industry lacked infrastructure; these then lacked educational facilities to educate workers, which made them even less attractive to ministry investment.[63] Indeed, the social dimension of qualification in its branch form, which will be discussed in greater detail below, provided one of the main reasons for the failure of any demographic policy controlling the numbers of workers employed by ministries, and created pressure for improvement in inter-branch labour resource planning.

As important, of course, to demographic development, was the direct power of ministries in this field. In the sphere of regulation of labour resources, despite some formal powers residing with the local soviets, effective power really lay with the ministries. For example, ministries were entrusted with drawing up balances for labour needs within their branch, and for defining their requirements in qualified labour and for specialists with higher or secondary education. Local soviets were rendered powerless to define local needs, even had they found themselves in the unlikely position of seeking to turn away ministerial investment.[64] Because ministries sought informally to expand their allocations by increasing capital construction, even the little centralized planning that did occur was made irrelevant by unforeseen ministerial expenditure which required greater labour allocation.[65] In any case, enterprises and ministries simply broke regulations.[66]

For example, in the Siberian town of Omsk, population growth was expected to exceed the plan by over 300,000 as a result of the refusal

[63] Barabanov, 'Territorial'naya struktura', 128–31.
[64] See N. Tolstykh, 'Sochetanie otraslevogo i territorial'nogo planirovaniya truda i kadrov', in *Voprosy ekonomiky*, 7 (1986), 78.   [65] Ibid. 79–80.
[66] See Barabanov 'Territorial'naya struktura', 128.

of the ministries to site industry in smaller towns. Those ministries that did settle in Omsk, however, showed little interest in housing or other social, cultural, or service facilities, only considering it when bad conditions directly affected production. Enterprises built facilities only for themselves; where the local authority was able to secure agreement on an eighteen-ministry plan of co-operation on new sewage and water facilities, it still found it necessary to apply to each ministry separately to squeeze money out.[67] Even in completely new towns like Balakovo near Saratov, based around a hydroelectric station and a chemical factory, where central planning ought to have worked and where Gosstroy drew up the plans, departmental competition impacted on the physical characteristics of the city and on the lives of its inhabitants.[68] For example, the Ministry of the Petroleum-Refining and Petrochemical Industry, which was responsible for constructing pipes for industrial and drinking water mains, was extremely tardy about its task, preferring to concentrate on the construction of its own enterprises. Heating, which ought to have been provided by the Ministry of Power and Electrification, was delayed when the ministry insisted that its allocations were not enough for the task, and demanded the participation of other ministries. The Ministry of the Meat and Dairy Industry gave similar reasons for postponing construction of a factory with strong inter-branch ties in the area.[69]

Ministerial power and interests had a huge impact on the physical and social characteristics of Soviet cities, especially those of the new industrial towns. In the ministry or *glavk* headquarters in Moscow, Leningrad, or Kiev, where the branch staff timetable was worked out, all of the social indicators for even the remotest cities were decided. For example, in Kostroma, over thirty organizations, 'some of them thousands of kilometres away, are involved in the designing of industrial installations'.[70] Myasnikov's complaint that 'the city is not a mechanical conglomerate, but a living organism with its own face, with its own requirements',[71] did not make considerable difference to ministerial deliberation on issues within their jurisdiction. The result was a social geography far from conducive to the well-being of citizens. For example, the same coefficient of children's schools and play

[67] See *Izvestiya* (1 Mar. 1972), 3.
[68] Similar haphazardness was evident in the design of new towns in Nizhnevartovsk and Surgut. See *Izvestiya* (2 Sept. 1972), 2.   [69] See *Pravda* (25 Aug. 1972), 2.
[70] See *Izvestiya* (2 Sept. 1972), 2.
[71] A. Myasnikov, 'Khozyain dolzhen byt' odin', in *EKO* 4 (1977), 124–7.

facilities existed in Voronezh and Bratsk, despite the fact that the birth rate was three times greater in the latter. As a result, children went to school in three shifts. Furthermore, norms ignored not only the geographical factors of the town, but also the national, social, demographic characteristics of the population. Everything was focused on the average all-Union indicator, drawn up in branch headquarters.[72]

The Fourth Plenary Session of the USSR Architects' Union in 1972 noted that because of the refusal of ministries to build enterprises with common facilities, factory complexes took on extremely ugly appearances, as well as being more expensive to build and operate. In Krasnodar, 130 factories occupied 160 industrial sites. The role of city planners usually consisted of nothing more than assigning a sector of the city for building.[73] According to one engineer, the consequence of the vast increase in use of urban space resulting from industrial growth and the peculiar version of urban sprawl which ministerial interests caused, was that virtually no land in towns was free for further building. The result of the search for industrial land was a further decline in the area of settled land under agriculture. In Saratov,

each ministry was concerned only with its own interests, creating a city within a city, so to speak. That is why this part of Saratov reminds one of a layer cake. Industrial buildings alternate with apartment houses. As a result, there are breaks in utility and transportation lines. The same thing can be observed in Bryansk, Kostroma, and Shchekino.[74]

Ministries frequently used land with profligacy, seeking much larger tracts than were necessary, and tying them up before any plans for their use had been devised to prevent other ministries doing the same. Again, the local soviet proved to be of little counter-value, since, despite the complications this anarchy caused for town planning, the 'chief architects and their staffs, whose functions it is to conduct the implementation of the general plans, cannot influence the pace and quality of industrial build-up. Their authority extends only to the "plant's gates".'[75] In Surgut, according to the chairman of the city soviet executive committee,

industrial branches have built wherever they felt like building. It could perhaps be called the model for the departmental approach to city planning. In the

---

[72] Ibid.   [73] See *Izvestiya* (2 Sept. 1972), 2.
[74] See *Pravda* (5 Aug. 1975), 3.   [75] Ibid.

centre is an old village with its ancient log cabins. Next there are hastily thrown-together wooden buildings of the geologists, then a settlement of two-storey flats for the oil workers, and finally a five-storey residential district for the power industry workers.[76]

These descriptions point to the politically significant fact that the multidimensional cityscape in which Soviet people lived, though very far from satisfactory from the point of view of their needs, was none the less still a social construct of ministry power. In an important sense, the cities belonged to the ministries, and to get around in them, to get ahead in them, meant walking the corridors of the ministries and its enterprises where civic decisions were largely taken.

Environment

Finally, the behaviour of industrial ministries had an enormous impact on the environment in which Soviet citizens worked and lived. In this area more than any other, it is difficult to see how society could have been ministerialized to accept high levels of atmospheric and other pollution, and low levels of work safety; as Koptyug put it, 'there has developed a disquiet about ecology in social opinion . . . in the Soviet Union, so far as it is more strongly raised to consciousness as a result of the *vedomstvennyy*-egoism in the activity of a number of ministries'.[77] Even in this area, however, the dependence of the worker and the resident citizen on the jobs and goods the ministries distributed must have balanced to some extent the damage done by their provision. This notwithstanding, however, environmental policy stands out as a case demonstrating the inability of politicians, state bodies, and the public to act contrary to ministry interests, and of the callousness of ministry power regarding the needs of Soviet citizens.

After 1965, there were a number of legislative measures enacted directed at improving the environment for workers and residents.[78] These did not, however, meet with notable success; it remained the case that 'special danger for the health of people and for the national economy is presented by the pollution of the atmosphere in towns and

[76] See *Izvestiya* (5 Sept. 1975), 3.
[77] V. Koptyug, 'Ekologiya: ot obespokoennosti k deystvennoy politike', in *Kommunist*, 7 (1988), 25.
[78] For a detailed list of measures see Lemeshev, 'Ekonomicheskie interesy', 254–5.

industrial centres'.[79] One of the greatest contradictions between branch and territorial authorities lay in the inability of the latter to enforce ecological protection measures, which led, as a direct result, to the worsening of living conditions and, in turn, of industrial performance as well. The powerlessness of local authority had its corollary in the concentration of responsibility for environmental protection in the hands of the industrial polluters. As Lemeshev put it, 'in the branch which exploits natural resources, is lodged also the function of its protection . . . Not one of these departments in practice safeguards nature from pollution and exhaustion of its resources. In the best case, they only fix their negative influence on nature.'[80]

The attitude of the industrial ministries is evident in an example cited by Ikonnikov and Krylov in an article in the Communist Party's journal *Kommunist*.

In reviewing the question of the reconstruction of the metallurgical factory 'Red October', the Ministry of Ferrous Metals guaranteed the diminution in pollution of the atmosphere from their powerful electric steel furnace ovens. In fact, this very production had become one of the sources of emissions of harsh, harmful substances in the atmosphere in the central part of the town, in the region of the central sports complex and memorial to the heroes of the city of Stalingrad. It was necessary for the Ministry of Ferrous Metals to realize measures for the reduction in emissions by 1982. At the present time [1984], out of five noted measures, only one has been fulfilled. It has also delayed for an unspecified period the construction in the factory of a system of circulating water supply. The Ministry of Ferrous Metals has not even allotted the necessary resources for the conducting of highly necessary nature defence measures. There are similar interrelations of the *oblast'* with the majority of other ministries and not only in environmental problems, but with house construction, creches, hospitals, and objects of the productive infrastructure.[81]

Environmentally, some of the worst damage was done by ministerial activity to the industrial towns of Siberia. 'The general ecological situation in [Siberia] is already today strongly complicated and has clearly expressed tendencies to worsening.'[82] The environmental problem in Tyumen was staggering. Each year 57 million cubic metres of untreated waste were produced, almost half going immediately into the lakes and rivers. There were 698 major breaks in oil pipelines in

[79] Ibid. 255.   [80] Ibid. 258.
[81] V. Ikonnikov and S. Krylov, 'O sochetanii otraslevogo i territorial'nogo upravleniya', in *Kommunist*, 4 (1984), 52.   [82] Koptyug, 'Ekologiya',

1988 alone, leading to 12 million tons of oil spillage. Some 580,000 hectares of forest were destroyed between 1964 and 1985; In 1988 alone 108,000 hectares went. During twenty years, 450 billion roubles of damage was done to the Tyumen environment; 346 billion by the former Ministry of the Petroleum Industry, 68 billion by the former Ministry of the Gas Industry. Meanwhile, the standard of living was very low. On the Yamal Peninsula, despite allocation of 32 billion for housing and social facilities, less than 1 per cent was actually spent.[83]

In Armenia, the Ministry of the Chemical Industry was warned twice by *Pravda* about pollution from its chemical plant in Kirovakan, where it was discharging over twenty-five tons of harmful substances per day, and 18,000 cubic metres of polluted liquids. In order to avoid closing the plant, as had been ordered by the Armenian Ministry of Health, the ministry in Moscow agreed to install protection equipment by the beginning of 1978. The order, however, had not been carried out by November of that year, nor was it known when it would be.[84]

Minvodkhoz (the Ministry of Water Resources and Amelioration) was a notorious offender, as is well known, but other ministries were as bad. In Karelia and other regions of the north-east, over the course of many years the Ministry of Forestry, Pulp, and Paper practised deforestation. In reply to enquiries by the local party organization, the minister Busygin replied that he had formulated a programme, which, it transpired, would be introduced by 1991 and which would only begin to deal with the 'criminal activity' of the ministry to a small extent in the fourth year.[85] Not surprisingly, chemical pollution and other industrial pollution caused damage not only to residents but to workers in the industry as well, resulting in high rates of labour turnover. Over 70 per cent of production workers in the chemical industry, according to one survey, were at risk from unhealthy production processes.[86] Criticism of ministries for poor safety records for workers in industry was also forthcoming from the Health and Social Security Committees of the Supreme Soviet in 1985. The committees noted that the Ministry of Power and Electrification had not built a single anti-pollution device in ten years, despite clear instructions.[87] The Ministry of Power Machinery was singled out for its failure to set sufficient

[83] *Dialog*, 6 (1990), 50–8.   [84] See *Pravda*, 29 (1978), 3.
[85] Lemeshev, 'Ekonomicheskie interesy', 256.
[86] See I. I. Dovgalevich, N. V. Zavriyeva, V. P. Plisko, and N. M. Shulga, in *Sotsiologicheskiye issledovaniya*, 4 (1980), 115–17.
[87] See *Izvestiya* (3 Jan. 1986), 3.

safety standards, and for failing to train workers in production discipline and safety rules, most notably at a big factory of Atommash (Atomic-Power Machinery Association) and other sites, where cover-ups took place in the investigation of accidents. Medical care for workers in the branch was dilapidated; in the first four years of the 1981–5 five-year plan, the ministry built only one medical and first-aid facility instead of the five planned, and one polyclinic instead of nine. The construction of sanatoriums was no better.[88]

The complex relationship between the *de facto* property rights of ministries, their economic interests, their power to dominate other institutions including their nominal superiors, and the issue of environment pollution neatly and clearly indicates the extent to which policy developments and social expenditure from 1965 to 1985 followed the ministries' agenda. As Lemeshev puts it, 'this anti-social and anti-state activity of the ministries and departments', founded on the distribution of resources through the plan,

enabled the adoption of the practice of evaluating their work on the 'cultivation' by them of the resources at their disposal, that is, by expenditure. The branch departments of Gosplan, the Council of Ministers, the Central Committee, and their corresponding organs in the localities, co-operated in this ministerial *diktat* ... The branch, bureaucratic-*vedomstvennyy* plan of growth in production became the main destructive force in the economy and in nature.[89]

Lemeshev cites food production as a good example of the nexus of problems—economic, political, environmental—connected with ministry power.

How is the Food Programme resolved, or more exactly not resolved. Minvodkhoz confirms that it is necessary to broaden the field of irrigated and drained land, and annually spent tens of billions of roubles of the country's money, salinating, ruining the ground, destroying its fertility. The Ministry of the Chemical Industry, on its side, considers that without increasing production of mineral fertilizers and pesticides we cannot manage, and received their billions, producing millions of tons of chemicals, polluting the soil and water of the whole country. The Ministry of Agricultural Machine-Building proves that, without energy-saturated machines, the food problem will be unresolved, and received their share of the social pie [*piroga*], producing every year

---

[88] See ibid. (28 May 1985), 2.

[89] M. Lemeshev, 'Priroda i ekonomika: vedomstvennost' i perestroyka', in N. P. Federenko (ed.), *Perestroyka upravleniya ekonomikoy: problemy, perspektivy* (Moscow, 1989), 259–60.

hundreds of thousands of super-heavy tractors which destroy the structure of the soil and lead to its overcompression [*pereuplotnenie*] and erosion. The Ministry of the Biological Industry confirms that livestock production without artificial fodder will not grow, and produces thousands of tons of albimum-vitamin concentrate from paraffin oil, poisoning not only animals but people. Gosagroprom not simply sanctioned all this but also insisted on broadening the destructive activity of its neighbours . . .[90]

In housing, transport, infrastructure, material rewards, social geography, and the environment, Soviet society bore, and bears, the marks of ministerial power; it was organized to reflect ministerial power, and the behaviour of social groups was adapted to it. A range of inequalities and irrationalities arose from this social organization, and, as Stanislav Shatalin and others have rightly pointed out, the only way of breaking the grip of the ministry power in general was to transfer control over services, in the broad sense, out of their hands, and into the public domain of politics, especially through the local soviets, and the market. However, in challenging ministry power head on, this prescription only begs the important questions to be addressed in the next two sections: about the failure of local soviets in the first place, and about the rationality, organization, and skills of the citizens who would enter into the political struggle to secure change.

MINISTRIES AND LOCAL SOVIETS

As has been shown above, ministries made a huge difference to the form of life experienced by the average Soviet citizen. Before generalizations can be made, however, about the importance of ministerial influence to the politics of citizens, it is necessary to see how ministries related to local bodies which sought to organize and provide services for the local population. The weakness of the soviets *vis-à-vis* the ministries has already been touched upon in a number of areas: over environmental control, over housing, distribution of goods, transport, infrastructure, labour resources, and urban development. This section, while not intended to be an exhaustive analysis of the role of local soviets, will focus on other aspects of their relationship to industrial ministries with the aim of demonstrating that they failed to realize their potential as an organizational alternative to the ministerialized structuring

[90] Ibid.

of Soviet society. The failure of the local soviets in this regard will be shown to result from the direct power of ministries to override their authority and structure their interests.

The problem of ministry–soviet relations was not new in Soviet politics; they were regulated in Article 10 of the 1918 Constitution. However, writing in 1980, Tarasenko remarks that despite the enactment of many separate pieces of legislation, 'there is today no single normative act which orders the spheres, principles, and mutual rights and responsibilities in relations between ministries and soviets'.[91] A great number of measures, however, had been taken over a period from 1965 to 1985, designed to increase the power of local soviets. Among these can be mentioned: the decision of the Council of Ministers of the RSFSR in 1966, to increase the role of local soviet executive committees in overseeing ministries, and to give them the right to contribute to decisions about the siting of industry, and to participate in the building of communal facilities;[92] a decree of the USSR Council of Ministers in 1967 which supported this;[93] a decree of the USSR Council of Ministers on 1 March 1978 which concentrated in the hands of the local executive committees the sole power to order the construction of homes and socio-cultural facilities;[94] the Law on the Basic Powers of Soviets, which was passed by the Supreme Soviet in 1980, following the adoption of the 1977 Constitution, in which it was foreseen that 'soviets lead on their territory state and cultural-social construction; affirm plans of economic and social development and the budget';[95] and a decree issued in 1981 by the Presidium of the Supreme Soviet and the Council of Ministers, 'On the further raising of the role of soviets in economic construction', which essentially repeated what had been in the 1978 law.[96]

The previous section provided some evidence by which to judge the impact of all these measures on ministry–soviet relations. In large measure, the various bits of legislation were observed purely formally, and local soviets had no facilities for taking advantage of their rights even had they wanted to. For example, despite having broad powers extended to them in respect of labour resources, territorial balances,

---

[91] Tarasenko, 'Vzaimodeystvie', 74.
[92] See A. E. Lunev, 'Puti sovershenstvovaniya deyatel'nosti apparata upravleniya khozyaystvom', in *Pravovedenie*, 6 (1970), 33.
[93] See Bessanova, 'Zhiloy fond goroda', 124.
[94] See S. Andreev, 'Prichiny i sledstviya', in *Ural* 1 (1988), 111.   [95] Ibid.
[96] Ibid.

etc, according to Yermin, first vice-chairman of the RSFSR Council of Ministers, 'local soviet executive committees do not know how to use their power'.[97] In respect of planning rights, by 1986 over sixty plan indicators were handed down from the ministry, through the enterprise, and then on to the local soviet executive committee for review. However, the vast majority of these indicators were purely technical, and those relating to social factors, such as, for example, population, work-related income, and distribution of various enterprise funds on socially related construction projects, were absent.[98] Where social indicators were made available to the local soviets, they were intended purely for informational purposes, and there existed no formal mechanism regulating ministry–soviet interactivity in this regard. In any case, suggestions from local soviets about branch social policy, according to Vishnyakov, were a rarity, and 'the existing structure of the central apparatus of the branch ministries, the rights and functions of its multiple departments and administrations, the knowledge and psychological make-up of its workers, is not adapted to taking an interested overview of recommendations coming from the local soviets'.[99] The power of territorial departments in the ministry was small. In comparison, however, the branch departments of the soviets were no stronger. In any case, sociological research carried out in the industrial Urals in the mid-1970s indicated that work in the departments of the local soviets was in many instances a very good career move for those seeking advancement in the ministerial hierarchy.[100] Tying promotion in the ministry to performance in the soviet can only have rendered the latter bodies even more compliant.

Aitov, in his study of the town of Kamyshin (the water-melon capital of the Soviet Union), also took exception to the view that ministries govern industry and soviets the territory. 'Of course, the local authorities do not and cannot lay claim to the administration of plants of all-Union subordination. But the ministries and enterprises not only lay claim to the administration of the population's living conditions, but actually do administer them.'[101] However, a further factor governing the failure of soviet authority *vis-à-vis* ministries arose as a direct result of its inability to control inter-branch labour resource planning. Where

[97] See *Pravda* (18 Sept. 1980), 2.
[98] V. G. Vishnyakov, 'Otraslevoe i territorial'noe upravlenie: opyt i problemy', in *Pravovedenie*, 3 (1988), 13–17. [99] Ibid.
[100] See A. Litvinov, *Literaturnaya gazeta* (28 Jan. 1976), 11.
[101] See *Literaturnaya gazeta*, 34 (20 Aug. 1975), 10.

there was evident competition among ministries for skilled workers, with the best moving into the ministerial system, local soviets were unable to recruit and keep good personnel.

> Enterprises strive to create better conditions for their own personnel, some-times even enticing valuable workers from their neighbours by promising to give them an apartment quickly or a place in kindergarten for their child. And they get them! After all, relatively speaking, there are 'rich' and 'poor' enterprises. Differences in the degree of availability of housing in the same city are quite considerable. Sometimes a plant has twice as many apartments as its neighbours ... What can the soviets do about this? Almost nothing, despite the expansion of their rights.[102]

The absence of local control over job placement, lamented by Aitov, provides the explanation.[103]

In purely financial terms, local soviets could not compete. For example, in Bratsk, the difference between the city budget to be spent on capital investment and communal infrastructure and the ministerial budgets was between 21 million roubles and 105 million.[104] Even when the government ordered the ministries to put 542 million roubles into construction work in Bratsk, they initially refused to comply, and in the end gave only half the amount with great reluctance.[105] This common occurrence happened despite the fact that the Law on City Soviets began by describing them as the 'organs of state power in the town, or in the city region [which] resolve within the limits of their rights, established by law, all questions of local significance, arising from the general state interests and of the people of the town, with account of the historic, economic, geographical and other peculiarities'.[106] Even where industry was almost entirely locally based, the soviets had little success in controlling resource allocation, as Serebryakov noted of the capital of Soviet health resorts, Sochi.[107]

Gennady Fil'shin, then working in the Novosibirsk Institute of Economics before becoming an important political figure during *perestroyka*, discussed the inadequacies of the performance of soviets in western Siberia, where the rate of investment in the non-productive sphere was barely two-thirds of an already low average in the Soviet Union as a whole, and where the local soviets were described as

---

[102] Ibid.
[103] Aitov suggested an expansion in the control of local job placement agencies.
[104] See Myasnikov, 'Khozyayn', 126.   [105] Ibid. 127.
[106] Ibid. 128.   [107] Serebryakov, 'Pravovye problemy', 46.

evincing a 'passive attitude' in relation to the big ministries. This, in turn, had a bad effect on the level of life and the morale of workers. The Ministry of the Chemical Industry was again singled out for particular criticism.[108] Even at the republic soviet level, similar problems were manifest. In Lithuania, for example, despite the existence of a 'scientifically substantiated long-range plan for the development of cities and the siting of industry in the republic', which was confirmed in 1965, the ministries were able to override the soviet. The Ministry of Light Industry, for example, ignored housing when locating industry. The Ministry of the Food Industry allocated no funds for general services for a period of several years. The Ministry of Geology did the same. Indeed, the chairman of the Lithuanian Gosplan, Drobnys, commented that the procedures for capital and other construction was so complex, wherein there was provision 'for such a great variety of forms for the transfusion of funds from one branch to another that only very knowledgeable people can find their way around'.[109] Over half of capital investments were formed inside the branch, while the rest were made up from deductions from the ministries.[110]

All this did not mean that initiatives taken by local soviets met with no success. There is evidence that, when their power was combined with high-level state and party support, the soviets could function more effectively. For example, following a Gosplan decree in 1984, in Perm an inter-branch commission for goods for public consumption was formed whose regulations were obligatory for all enterprises in the region, and it worked to regulate the activity of subordinates of 200 ministries and departments.[111] The worst position of all for the local soviet, however, arose not because of excessive ministerial intervention, but in those towns where the ministry has forsaken interest altogether. As Shevardnadze was aware when first secretary of the Georgian Party, where enterprises were too small to be effectively supervised or supported by the ministry, they could still 'play an enormous role for the region where it was located and required constant attention'.[112] It was probably this awareness that led him to

[108] See G. I. Fil'shin, 'Sochetanie otraslevykh i territorial'nykh interesov pri formirovanii investitsionnykh programm', in *EKO* 2 (1971), 39–52.

[109] See *Pravda* (14 July 1975), 2.   [110] Ibid.

[111] See Vishnyakov, 'Otraslevoe', 17–18.

[112] Comment of Shevardnadze in *Ekonomicheskaya gazeta*, 21 (1982), 8.

support the establishment of the Poti experiment linking the non-all-Union enterprises in a single local economic association.[113] For bodies with no independent resources, therefore, and without research facilities which could enable them to offer a realistic alternative, their best possible institutional strategy was to become, in Gavriil Popov's words, the 'territorial co-ordinators of ministry activity'.[114] As with the Communist Party, and high state bodies, described in the previous chapter, so the local soviets became ministerialized institutions, whose best chance of succeeding even within narrow confines, lay in playing the game according to the ministries' rules.

SOCIAL INTERESTS AND INDUSTRIAL ORGANIZATION

In this section, closer attention will be paid to the impact of ministerial power on occupational structure and on occupational interests. As was the case with the social geography of the Soviet city, the available evidence suggests that the structure of employment, and the interests of the vast majority of the urban population who worked in ministry establishments, reflected ministry power and interests. The jobs people had, and how they acted in them, in other words, were stamped with the imprint 'ministry'.

Arguments about the relationship of the occupational structure, the institutional arrangements of the Soviet economy, and worker attitudes have been expressed most cogently by Tatyana Zaslavskaya. In her famous leaked position paper, which became known in the West as 'The Novosibirsk Report', for example, Zaslavskaya advanced the claim that,

Important changes have also taken place in the social type of worker in the socialist economy. The level of his education, culture, general information, and awareness of his social position and rights has grown enormously. The main body of skilled workers, on whom above all the effectiveness of the production process depends, nowadays has a rather wide political and economic horizon, accurately recognises his own interests and can defend them if necessary.[115]

---

[113] See *Pravda* (18 Feb. 1983). 2. See also D. Slider, 'More Power to the Soviets? Reform and Local Government in the Soviet Union', in *British Journal of Political Science*, 16 (1986), 495–511.

[114] G. Kh. Popov, *Sovershenstvovanie otraslevoy i territorial'noy struktury upravleniya proizvodstvom* (Moscow, 1986), 30–1.

[115] T. I. Zaslavskaya, 'The Novosibirsk Report', in *Survey*, 28 (Spring 1984), 91. For a similar argument see M. G. Voropaev, 'Khozyaystvennoe upravlenie i partiynoe rukovodstvo', in *EKO* 1 (1973), 98–104.

The difficulty with Zaslavskaya's argument, however, is that it contains a number of equivocations. In the quotation just given, there is a move from 'worker', as the true bearer of modernity, to 'skilled worker', which materially affects the reliability of the answer: who, after all, were the skilled workers in the ministerial system? The most serious equivocation in Zaslavskaya's argument, however, comes later in the article when she says,

the system of production relations which has been in operation over the course of many decades has formed a predominantly passive type of worker, who bears witness to the famous principles of 'I need no more than anybody else' and 'that's no concern of mine.'[116]

To be clear: whereas in the first quoted passage, Zaslavskaya insists on the potency of formal educational qualifications, training, and culture over the institutions of the economy, in the second passage she insists that quite the opposite is true. Instead, the institutional structure—the 'production relations'—are reflected in an unskilled, uneducated, and anti-social labour force. The same contradiction is evident in other work by Zaslavskaya. For example, in a 1972 article she declares that socialism was ever less capable of operating through administrative measures.[117] At the same time, on the basis of research in farms in Siberia in 1980, she held that given the lack of material incentives, or fear from hunger or unemployment, Soviet workers and managers simply wanted a quiet life.[118]

It may be that there is no way round the apparent contradiction; if only one alternative had to be sustained, the evidence presented below would suggest that the second was more likely than the first. However, the evidence will also support a more synthetic outlook. On the one hand, social passivity *was* the consequence of social disorganization; low skill and training resulted from the poorness of the education system. On the other hand, an ability to defend their interests through personal activism and the search for advancement through education and other socially desirable criteria was widespread, but organized by the very same institutions, often the industrial ministries, which caused social passivity in the first place. Ministry power, in other words, closed

[116] Ibid. 99–100.
[117] T. I. Zaslavskaya, 'Sotsiologicheskie issledovaniya trudovykh resursov', in *EKO* 1 (1972), 50–1.
[118] T. I. Zaslavskaya, 'Ekonomicheskoe povedenie i ekonomicheskoe razvitie', in *EKO* 3 (1980), 15–33.

the circle on social attitudes, defining the terms of advancement and activity, while at the same time constraining it to public inaction.

Given this, it should not be surprising, for example, that workers in the great many enterprises with historically established social facilities and assured output should have accepted what Andreev has described as 'drunkenness and sleep' as the main goals in life. Having their wages fixed from the achieved level,[119] and being given their so-called thirteenth-months' pay,[120] with a declining number of new workers, there was little motivation for existing ones to perform.[121] Large numbers of employees in any case received wages for doing nothing productive at all.[122] As Ponomarev and Shinkarenko put it, social passivity was one of the 'columns of bureaucratism'. In a survey of 13,200 workers and collective farmers, for example, passivity in terms of life position was noted as characteristic of almost 60 per cent. Almost 82 per cent claimed to encounter unconscientious attitudes to work and duties, and 67.6 per cent suggested that they encountered efforts to take more from society than they gave.[123]

The point is also made simply by looking at certain aspects of the employment and educational structure. Not mentioning the vast numbers of drivers and chauffeurs in the ministerial network, who derived great benefits from their private illicit use of their vehicles,[124] Polyansky has estimated that, of workers in industry, almost 50 per cent were engaged in manual work and individual labour in auxiliary workshops. Effectively, they performed service work, and the level of demand for it was very difficult to reduce given the departmentalist interests of production.[125] Very many workers were simply involved in repairing defective machinery.[126] Aitov suggests that workers using simple hand labour produced only 600 roubles in value of their output per annum, but received about 2,000 roubles in income.[127] Even the physical characteristics of production, Soviet-style, in many cases in

[119] See S. Andreev, 'Struktura vlasti i zadachi obshchestva', in *Neva*, 1 (1989), 145–7.

[120] See L. I. Abalkin, 'Trudnaya shkola perestroyki', in *Uroki gor'kie, no neobkhodimye* (Moscow, 1988), 265.

[121] See G. Kh. Popov, *Effektivnoe upravlenie* (Moscow, 1976), 17.

[122] See B. P. Kurashvili, *Bor'ba s byurokratizmom* (Moscow, 1988), 20–1.

[123] See L. Ponomarev and V. Shinkarenko, 'Kto kogo? Chem silen byurokrat?', in *Uroki gor'kie, no neobkhodimye* (Moscow, 1988), 158.

[124] Zaslavskaya interview, Moscow, July 1989.

[125] See V. G. Polyansky, 'O sisteme spetsializirovannogo obsluzhivaniya v otrasli', in *EKO* 6 (1972), 100.

[126] V. P. Rassokhin, *Mekhanizm vnedreniya* (Moscow, 1985), 13.

[127] See interview with N. A. Aitov, *Sots. iss.* 1 (1989), 121.

small enterprises in towns with weak soviets and few other sources of employment, must have influenced the possibilities for anti-ministerial social action in the absence of defined organizational alternatives.

Shubkin mentions the connection between continued low qualifications among workers and ministerial interests; low qualified workers necessitated easy plan targets.[128] Furthermore, in Shubkin's view, the education system itself effectively trained children to operate on bureaucratic criteria.[129] Evidence presented in an earlier chapter supports the view that the technical and other training qualifications of ministry workers themselves made them highly adapted to the functioning of the existing system. It is also evident that the training structure of personnel for the administration of ministries, state, and territory was accomplished, if at all, within the very boundaries of the existing structure of the society. Each educational link 'prepares specialists for definite categories of organs of administration or for the fulfilment of defined administrative functions'.[130]

The penetration of the interests of the ministries into the interests of social and professional groups was further evident in a great deal of management behaviour, wherein they showed little interest in pursuing economic reform without other changes in the economic structure.[131] Not only were management interests and behaviour antithetical, in many cases, to increased marketization, but they also opposed the sort of efficiency-seeking typical of technocratic planning reformers as well. As early as 1967 there were reports of management hostility to the introduction of the so-called automated systems of administration, no doubt the result of the loss of control and confusion which resulted from their introduction.[132] Even in 1985, managers continued to oppose such a system because they believed they would be unable to manœuvre the plan to their advantage.[133] Further evidence for the corruption of professional standards, and for doubts regarding the naïve view that education and occupational structures implied the creation of social attitudes and an organization which

[128] V. Shubkin, 'Byurokratiya: tochka zreniya sotsiologa', in *Uroki gor'kie, no neobkhodimye* (Moscow, 1988), 119.   [129] Ibid. 113–14.

[130] See V. G. Vishnyakov, 'Podgotovka i povyshenie kvalifikatsii gosudarstvennykh sluzhashchikh', in *Sovetskoe gosudarstvo i pravo*, 6 (1971), 76–9.

[131] See M. I. Piskotin, 'Izmenenie kompetentsii i sovershenstvovanie form i metodov raboty ministerstv v usloviyakh ekonomicheskoy reformy', in *Organizatsiya raboty ministerstv v usloviyakh khozyaystvennoy reformy* (Moscow, 1969), 26.

[132] See *Pravda* (26 May 1967), 3–4.

[133] See N. P. Fedorenko, *Ekonomicheskaya gazeta*, 1 (1985), 14.

would oppose ministry power, was manifest in the behaviour of professionals such as ministry accountants. 'When departmental auditors expose malpractices in [report padding], they risk running into a lack of understanding towards their over-scrupulous attitude.' Consequently, the 'absolute majority of report-padding and other violations have been disclosed not by managements themselves, but by oversight agencies outside the department proper'.[134] Over 3,000 accountants were arrested in 1987.[135]

The peculiar combination of ministry power and interests, the Soviet occupational structure, and the black economy is neatly packaged in the following case of the control, or absence, of industrial theft. Despite an order from the Council of Ministers in 1965 for the transfer of security of all non-defence enterprises to the regular police, the Soviet Union continued to employ over 400,000 ministerial security guards, employed in seventy branches, dressed in sheepskin coats, and armed with nineteenth-century rifles. In an interview conducted by the *Pravda* correspondent, Chernenko, with the chief of the Ministry of Internal Affairs department for non-ministerial security, Maj.-Gen. Popov, it emerged that ministries were refusing to introduce electrical alarms or use police departments to guard their premises. As Popov put it,

I think most economic managers avoid contact with police agencies because they prefer their own departmental security guards for carefully calculated reasons. They don't want anyone 'poking his nose into their business' figuratively speaking ... In the course of departmental check-ups, each enterprise in the meat, dairy, and food industries unearths an average of fewer than a hundred instances of petty theft committed by pilferers each year. By contrast, in spot checks our own guards arrest up to a hundred pilferers in a single shift.[136]

Getting on in life, which was so clearly related to the work-place in terms of the formal reward structure, was even more evident in the widespread informal and illegal reward structure. Indeed, the black economy, fused with the official ministerial one, functioned as a further means whereby individual rationality and occupational interests were fused with ministerial power. First, as the last chapter has shown, the direct support of ministry officials was often necessary if successful black economy arrangements were to be achieved. 'As with the leaders,

---

[134] See report by USSR Prosecutor A. Rekunkov, in *Pravda* (18 Jan. 1986), 3.
[135] See *Pravda* (1 June 1988), 6. [136] See ibid. (1 June 1988), 6.

so were ordinary workers, or at least part of them, drawn into the shadow economy.[137] Thus was established a direct vertical economic link from top to bottom. Secondly, workers were able to benefit from ministry power more indirectly by utilizing for themselves the market advantages which accrued from the monopoly structure on which ministerial power as a whole was based.[138] Just as ministers were able to control resources for their private or institutional aims, so workers in enterprises were able to do the same.[139] *All* managers, for example, were involved and could not begin to do their jobs without participating in the building up of favours to secure supplies which the shadow economy demanded.[140]

MINISTRIES, POLITICS, AND THE PUBLIC

The general argument of this chapter has been that part of the answer to such questions as, why was there relative stability in Soviet politics from 1965 until the late 1980s?; why did soviets not function as viable institutions?; why did reforms fail?; and why were politicians so weak?, lies in the complex structuring of social interests. As Kordonsky argues,

The social structure is the key concept in explaining our reality . . . Every Soviet person has his social status, that is, his place in the social structure, so far as he is assigned to a definite social group . . . Stability and definedness are the basic features of the new social structure.[141]

A further claim, however, has been that because these interests emerged out of the organization of distribution and rewards, the organizational vehicle—in the Soviet case, the industrial ministries— was crucial. To understand industrial ministries as political institutions, therefore, required society to be brought back in.

Not all commentators agree on the nature of the Soviet social structure, or its impact on politics. There are those like Batkin, for example, who fundamentally deny that the causes of stability in the Soviet Union can be found in the interests of its social groups. For

---

[137] S. Men'shikov, 'Ekonomicheskaya struktura sotsializma: chto vperedi?', in *Novyy mir*, 3 (1989), 197.   [138] Shubkin, 'Byurokratiya', 120–1.
[139] Men'shikov, 'Ekonomicheskaya struktura', 198.   [140] Ibid.
[141] S. G. Kordonskiy, 'Sotsial'naya struktura i mekhanizm tormozzheniya', in *Postizhenie* (Moscow, 1989), 37–8.

Batkin, the problem lay in the amorphousness of Soviet society, which consisted only of those who stood in queues, those who used their privileges, and those in the grey economy who used connections. The vast majority were in the first group.[142] Klyamkin expresses a similar argument in a more cogent form. For him, the process of the formation of individual and group economic interests is only beginning in the Soviet Union. Until it is achieved, to speak of the role of interests in Soviet politics would be premature.[143]

While Batkin's and Klyamkin's points seem to run counter to the general direction of argument of this chapter—though their views on the irrelevancy of the social structure ultimately do not accord with reality, as earlier sections have shown—they are concordant with it in two important ways. First, amorphousness *is* quite compatible with the social disorganization which results from the reward structure. Given the verticalization of inequalities and incentives, social groups will not exist in the same sense in Soviet society as they do in countries where horizontal organization is commonplace. Secondly, interests will not be defined in a developed way by social groups or individuals, in such circumstances, independently of the criteria which are established by those who control the reward structure. As Kordonsky puts it:

The character of consumption is defined by social-accounting parameters, such as internal passports and place of residence, social duties, employment in more or less important branches of industry. The formation of norms, quotas, systems of bonuses and compensation comprised the content of state social policy, closely connected with production. These very forms were the equivalent in conditions of real socialism of market mechanisms of regulation ... The very deficit of material goods, which accompanied the ranging of distribution, created special centralizing forces and structures the population and its labour force, and also those employed in administration, in forms of social activity, specific for real socialism.[144]

Once social interests and rewards have been made administrative rather than political questions, in the sense that they cease to be issues decided in the context of the public space of democracy, the main issue then revolves around which organizations and institutions are dominant. The three most important distributive channels in the Soviet Union were by territory, by appointment, and by branch.

[142] See Batkin's comments in the round-table discussion in 'Perestroyka: kto protiv?', in *Ogonek*, 50 (1988), 10–14.　　　　[143] See Klyankin's comments, ibid.
[144] Kordonsky, 'Sotsial'naya Struktura', 39–40.

In the territorial aspect, the social-accounting status of the individual is defined by his registration in a concrete territory, his right to a house which is realized by an order for an apartment, and, if he is a conscript soldier, then by an army account in a defined army commissariat. The norms and sanctions, defining the social situation in its territorial aspect, are called the administrative regime. Control over the observance of the administrative regime is realized by organs of the Ministry of Internal Affairs, the executive committees of local soviets, and by army commissariats.[145] . . . there exists the hierarchy of appointments, founded on the principle of the *nomenklatura* . . . At every stage in the *nomenklatura*, beside responsibilities are also handed out rights, in particular rights to additional supplies of foodstuffs, industrial goods, place in medical institutions, etc. The range of levels and quality of life in dependence on the situation of the *nomenklatura* hierarchy, creates a definite gradient, compelling people to compete for responsibility.[146]

It is not suggested that these two channels of distribution were unimportant, or that the mechanism of social competition to achieve rewards distributed through these channels, whereby social inequalities, in Kordonsky's words, 'compel people to compete', are not central to social processes. However, the evidence presented in this and earlier chapters suggests that, in comparison to the ministerial network which, through its control not only of distribution and consumption, but production as well, was able to dominate territory and even party appointments, they were diminished. Kordonsky suggests that:

Each of these new social groups is heterogeneous. Inside each group are visible ranges in dependence on the importance of the strata or sub-group to the functioning of the whole structure . . . The real hierarchy of ranks is far from being as straightforward as it appears to be. Protectionism, corruption, and criminality in state appointments destroy the strictness of the hierarchy and act counter to the system of selection and upbringing of cadres.[147]

But this does not amount to an objection. Clearly, as has been shown above, the second economy tied the worker even more closely to the ministerial system. Furthermore, it was precisely the existence of social inequality, formed on the basis of ministerial criteria, and resulting in large measure from inter-ministerial competition, and generating social mobility and improvement through ministerial channels, that supported ministry power.

The support social inequality offered to ministerial power even extended to an Alice-in-Wonderland aspect of Soviet life, the need to compete for the privilege of spending one's hard-earned roubles.

---

[145] Ibid. 40–1.   [146] Ibid. 42.   [147] Ibid.

The point about the buying power of money is that it is essentially dependent on the social status of its possessor. According to the strength of the rank of the territory, branch, or appointment, and corresponding division of wealth, the buying power of money grows with an elevation in service position, with a migration from a low rank to a high rank, and with a transition from an enterprise or organization of a low prestige branch to one of high prestige. Employment in a branch with high status, which has connected to it specialized ORSs, systems of social consumption, and other privileges, facilitates the possibility of obtaining goods at lower prices.[148]

Arguing that the interests of social groups were structured primarily by ministerial power is not to suggest that the interests of workers and ministries were identical. Nor does it mean that social groups identi-fied with the sectoral hierarchy in which they worked, or accepted the legitimacy of its decisions. On the contrary, in many respects interests diverged. Mark Mikhaylov raises the question directly in an article in the Communist Party's journal *Kommunist*:

Whose interests are properly reflected by the existing narrowly departmentalist tendencies? Is it always the case that the interests of the ministry can be assimilated to the collective interests of all workers of a given branch? It is certain that it is absolutely not so, because, first, the interests of the ministry are one thing, but *vedomstvennost'* is something altogether different; and second, all damage to all-people and all-state interests are turned against the core interests of each of the multiple ranks of workers who are employed in branches of the national economy.[149]

For example, ministries, and the Ministry of the Coal Industry in particular, were upbraided by the Central Committee for breaking labour laws by dismissing workers illegally, changing working days without consultation, and ordering workers to do jobs outside their job description.[150] Ministries were also criticized for their role in destroy-ing labour discipline.[151] When the minister of the Ministry for Ferrous Metals tried to shift responsibility on to the labour collectives, the workers responded by attacking ministry incompetence in setting plans and for their indulgence in useless business trips.[152] In a conversation

---

[148] Ibid. 45–6.

[149] M. Mikhaylov, 'Po povodu vedomstvennosti', in *Kommunist*, 8 (1981), 105.

[150] See A. E. Lunev, 'Puti dal'neyshego sovershenstvovaniya deyatel'nosti promysh-lennykh ministerstv na osnove leninskoy teorii gosudarstvennogo upravleniya', in *Organizatsiya raboty ministerstv v usloviyakh ekonomicheskoy reformy* (Moscow, 1972), 18.

[151] See V. N. Smirnov, 'Sotsial'no-pravovye voprosy ukrepleniya trudovoy ditsipliny', in *Pravovedenie*, 1 (1984), 5.   [152] See *Pravda* (13 *Mar.* 1983), 2.

between a minister and a shop-floor worker in a factory producing
obsolete refrigerators, the minister indicated his awareness that the
fridge could not be taken out of production immediately because 'what
would there be for the collective to do?' But, he went on, 'at the same
time you must understand—and tell your comrades—that I, as a
minister, am unable to take your collective and make it happy. All of
us are in very strained circumstances.'[153] Relations between managers
and ministries also betrayed signs of strain. Certainly, there was a
complex bargaining process and ministries frequently intervened to
make the life of the manager more difficult. In a survey of 1,064
Siberian enterprise directors carried out over ten years to 1973, over
80 per cent blamed ministries for violating their rights. In one year,
ministries changed plans 1,554 times without changing financial
values.[154]

While noting that the interests of occupational groups and of the
ministries often diverged, a fact of some consequence to the prospect
of ministerial reform, the authors Buzgalin and Kolganov seem closer
to the truth than Mikhaylov's rhetoric when they suggested that

it is reasonable to say that there existed a sufficient coincidence of interest,
given the structure of power which favoured the ministries and the absence
of organizational forums for worker opposition, between ministers and workers
in the given situation. Workers concerned themselves primarily with their
private problems, and left general issues to higher up bodies; this then became
the mutual relationship between top and bottom.[155]

The answers to the questions posed at the beginning of this section,
therefore, are interrelated. Political stability, in the sense of the
absence of public action in pursuit of distributive goals, was secured
by keeping organizational control of the process within the bounds of
the ministerial system as a whole. The social passivity which resulted
in the disorganized society, where workers tended to their private
business, should not be confused with inactivity; but it did close the
space for social support for change, be it at the level of limited

---

[153] See *Izvestiya* (9 Oct. 1983), 6–7.
[154] However, the ambivalence in the managers' position is evident from the fact that
though 90% of those surveyed believed that an expansion in the rights of managers was
necessary—the majority favoured increased control over wages and bonuses—44%
were worried about the difficulties in supply which might result from this, and only 26%
cited deficiencies in the rights of managers. See *Pravda* (12 Nov. 1973), 2.
[155] See A. V. Buzgalin and A. I. Kolganov, *Anatomiya byurokratizma* (Moscow, 1988),
13–15.

marketization, institutional reform in the soviets, progress through professionalization, and even in party control through its *nomenklatura* system. If politicians, therefore, were to be successful in reforming the Soviet system, the whole nexus of ministry power—their hegemony— over their own structure, in the economy, over the state and the party, and over society, would need to be broken. The battle against ministry power, for that reason, was at the heart of *perestroyka*.

5
Ministries and the Failure of the Surrogate Civil Society

THE book so far has described the influence of industrial ministries on the Soviet political system as it existed until 1985. To use the spatial language of state and civil society, the Soviet political system was highly fused without developed autonomous spaces between politics, economics, and society. Industrial ministries were the organizational basis of this fusion, and their powers and interests were therefore critical to the character and functioning of state, politics, and society as a whole.

This chapter and the next will investigate *perestroyka* as an attempt by Soviet politicians to improve their control and power. It will be suggested that not only was ministerial reform necessary for economic reasons, but for political reasons as well, and that this was connected with the desire of at least some leading politicians to remove the constraints imposed by ministerial power on the efficacy and scope of their decisions. Two main stages in this process will be delineated: first, the attempt to deal with ministry power by creating a surrogate state and civil society distinction, wherein, by means of structural, economic, and legal reform, space would be opened up between political, economic, and social spheres in which greater authority could be exercised; and, consequent upon the failure of this first approach, there occurred a decisive shift in the politicians' legitimation strategy involving radical changes in ideology and political reform in the direction of democracy and market liberalization. For both approaches, however, ministerial power was central to explaining the politicians' failure.

A SURROGATE STATE AND CIVIL SOCIETY

When addressing the question, 'What inspired us to launch *perestroyka*?', Gorbachev made clear the centrality of the leadership's authority crisis and the power of industrial ministries:

the narrow democratic basis of the established system of [economic] management began to have a highly negative effect . . . Public property was gradually
fenced off from its true owner—the working man. This property frequently
suffered from departmentalism and localism, becoming no-man's land and
free, deprived of a real owner . . . *This was the major cause of what happened* . . .
The braking mechanism in the economy, with all its social and ideological
consequences, led to bureaucracy-ridden public structures and to expansion
at every level of bureaucracy. And this bureaucracy acquired *too great an
influence in all state, administrative and even public affairs.* (Author's italics)[1]

The ideas expressed by Gorbachev in this passage support the view
that the difficulties which motivated the political leadership to launch
perestroyka were not so much defined by the purely economic consequences of ministerial power, as by the implications of that power for
the regime as a whole. The narrow base of the regime's constituency,
with control over the economy lying in the hands of economic
organizations, whose power in this area led to their domination of the
state—these were the main causes of difficulties which required
perestroyka. While not entirely discounting Gorbachev's democratic
credentials, it should be remembered that he had made his political
career within the old system; for this reason, it seems reasonable to
substitute 'the political leadership' for the 'common man' in the
passage quoted above. If we regard the 'true owner' as the Communist
leadership, Gorbachev's concerns become clearer.

The strong dissatisfaction of the leadership with the behaviour of
industrial ministries had been evident as early as the XXVII Congress in
February 1986, when in his speech Gorbachev went as far as to suggest
that ministries' behaviour ran counter to the central planks of communist
power, the socialization of the means of production. He reminded them
that their true function was to serve as instruments of the leadership.

Ministries, departments, and territorial organs are not the owners of the means
of production, but only institutions of state administration, responsible before
society for the effective utilization of public wealth. And we cannot allow
vedomstvennost' or localism to hinder the realization of the advantages of
socialist property.[2]

These anti-ministerial concerns were evident, as the next chapter
will show, at all stages of the *perestroyka* campaign. In the initial period,

---

[1] M. Gorbachev, *Perestroika* (London, 1987), 47–8.
[2] *Uskorenie sotsial'no-ekonomicheskogo razvitiya stranu—zadacha vsey partii, vsego naroda*
(Moscow, 1987), 34.

however, the reform-minded politicians operated no doubt in an environment heavily constrained by ministerial power, and this made them cautious. It is no objection to the arguments of this book to say that, if ministries were so powerful, *perestroyka* could not have been launched at all. In the first place, *perestroyka* took a long time to launch. But, secondly, there is no reason to deny that politicians had *some* room to manœuvre via institutions which the ministries did not control directly—like the coercive agencies and the press—or via institutions in which the ministries only participated, like the party. All that is being argued, and which the evidence supports, is that industrial power severely constrained the politicians, and radical anti-ministerialism was both difficult and dangerous for all actors.

Initially, then, the politicians sought to control ministry behaviour by changes which did not go beyond the bounds of the existing system. The term 'surrogate' in the title of this chapter, therefore, is used to denote the attempt to create space for the differentiation of political, state, economic, and legal powers in the Soviet system, without abolishing the central legitimating claims of the various institutions of the Soviet élite—the leading role of the party, socialism, planning, all-round economic development, equality, and so on. The logic of the reform strategy was to put ministries in a changed strategic position *vis-à-vis* both subordinates and superiors, and, as a result, ensure that ministry personnel acted more like state bureaucrats than economic agents, and became more dependent and malleable to political control.

However, as shall be shown, the defeat of this strategy is largely explained by the continued ability of industrial ministries to control the implementation process, and affect the interests of other relevant actors against the spirit of reform. In an important sense, the ability of the ministries to control the reform process, even when directed by energetic and serious reformers like Gorbachev and his entourage rather than the compromised and weak politicians of the Brezhnev era, is final proof of their centrality within the old system and their strength in dictating the interests of other actors at many levels of the political system.

ANOTHER ROUND OF STRUCTURAL REFORM

The most immediate response of the political leadership was to seek to improve control through changes in the ministries' internal structure. Structural reform had two main ambitions: to devolve economic management from ministries to autonomously functioning structures beneath them; simultaneously, to force ministerial personnel to operate not on the basis of direct economic control—not, in other words as economic agents—but as actors far more like bureaucrats or regulators. The adoption of this strategy was probably reflective of the constraints which the leadership inherited ideologically, institutionally, and economically. As a reform measure, it was predictably also the weakest and least effective in securing improved malleability or instrumentality from the ministries, though it probably did have the effect in the long run of weakening ministry control even at the expense of reduced central control in general.

Changes in personnel

The first element in the anti-ministerial strategy was to restrain its power and redirect its activity by controlling the number of personnel directly employed. By controlling their numbers, ministry officials, who had previously operated direct control on the economy, would be forced to use different methods, and behave more like state officials than economic actors. According to official figures provided by the Moscow Labour Research Institute, between 80,000 and 120,000 were to be cut from ministries and departments during the five-year plan 1986–90, and the staffs of branch and academy research institutes were to be reduced by more than 50,000.[3] By 1989, Pankov, the First Deputy Minister of Finance, revealed that 82,000 people worked in the central apparatus of ministries and departments, with a total budget, including wages, of 2.9 billion roubles, or 7.5 per cent of all expenditure on administration, or 0.6 per cent of the total state budget. In three years from 1986, he claimed, 200 ministries and departments had been liquidated at the Union and Union–republic level, and among the central apparatus of ministries and departments, 63,000 people were dismissed, saving 450 million roubles.[4] In addition to cuts centrally, 50 per cent of employees in the republican ministries,[5] and 30–5 per cent in *raion* administration were due to go.[6]

---

[3] *Nedelya* (29 Feb.–6 Mar. 1988), 8.

[4] *Pravitel'stvennyy vestnik*, 5 (1989), 4–5. For every 100 people employed in the USSR, 15 worked in some form of administration compared to 27 in the USA.

[5] For details see 'Postanovlenie Tsentral'nogo Komiteta KPSS i Soveta Ministrov SSSR' (28 Apr. 1988), No. 588 (Estonia), No. 686 (Turkmenia), and No. 824 (RSFSR); as well as *Izvestiya* (27 Feb. 1988), 2 (Turkmenia); ibid. (5 Apr. 1988), 2 (Tadzhikistan); ibid. (12 Apr. 1988), 3 (Uzbekistan); ibid. (13 Apr. 1988), 3 (Kirgizia); ibid. (17 Apr. 1988) 3 (Kazakhstan); and *Pravda* (21 Apr. 1988), 1–2 (RSFSR).

[6] See *Pravda* (21 Jan. 1988), 2.

It is clear that the personnel cutting campaign struck political chords among some members of the public. A letter from a disgruntled veteran in Moscow was probably quite typical: after citing his war record, the correspondent asserted that 'there's no reason to get all soft-hearted about those people who wore out the seats of their pants sitting around in chief administrations and offices during the years of stagnation—they should be laid off! They had a comfortable life while the economy was going steadily downhill.' However, in what may have been an admission of the reality of this sort of reform, *Pravda* added the comment that 'at present, all ministries and departments are working feverishly to demonstrate ... their need to exist with the maximum number of employees. The second concern is how to hold on to one's position within the ministry—whatever the cost.' To this end, the old-style solutions of 'clever inter-departmental manœuvring' in which nothing more changed than the sign on the door were much in evidence. Or worse, as a letter from a ministry worker suggested, lay-offs were targeted on technical specialists, leaving the executives intact. 'And just what is a department head at a ministry? As a rule, he is someone with connections who learned about the branch only during armchair intervals between trips abroad.'[7] The Moscow State Research and Design Institute for Engineering Problems, for example, turned out to be just an extension of the staff of the Ministry of Machine-Tool and Tool Industry. The head of the investigation team found that this was quite a common manœuvre among the ministries. Five of the nine institutes of the ministries investigated were supposed to have been closed, and the Ministry of the Machine Tool and Tool Industry refused to close its institute even after the State Committee for Science and Technology (GKNT) inspection instructions, and only complied after being ordered to do so by a special decree of the Council of Ministers. The members of the commission found themselves subject to threats of retaliation.[8]

Frequently, the form taken by staff cuts preserved general staff levels, and maintained organizational integrity. There were a large number of vacancies in the total of staff cuts, for example, out of 536 job losses, 144 were vacancies.[9] When the Ministry of Heavy and

[7] Ibid. (4 Mar. 1988), 2.

[8] Ministers were given the right to set base salaries for personnel within limits of a total number and the wage fund. Up to 70% of savings were to remain at the minister's disposal. *Moscow News*, 27 (1987), 10. In an interview, Silayev claimed that mergers would save 1,226 staff. See *Pravda* (21 Sept. 1987), 2.

[9] *Moscow News*, .7 (1988), 8–9.

Transport Engineering and the Ministry of Power Engineering were merged, the head of department came from one ministry, his deputy came from the other. The Ministry of Machinery for Light Industry, the Food Industry, and for Household Appliances was abolished from 1 March 1988,[10] and its personnel and functions were dispersed into the apparatuses of eight other machine-building ministries. A further deputy minister was created in each of them, with the transfer of 500 staff. A new department of the Council of Ministers State Commission was created to co-ordinate the complex, which was headed by the old minister, who retained his rank.[11] The Deputy Minister for Personnel had already been given an identical post in another ministry.[12] Not surprisingly, according to reporters, 'many people in the former ministry sincerely believe . . . that everything will return to what it was before'.[13]

Ministries were also instructed by a resolution of the party, Council of Ministers, and Central Council of the Trade Unions to seek cuts in employment among factory workers in their branches.[14] One official—Prostyakov, vice-chairman of the Council of Ministers' Bureau on Social Development—suggested that there were 16 million such superfluous personnel. 'But if an employee finds himself outside a plant gate . . . today, he won't vanish. I just got a phone call: industrial enterprises and construction urgently need 1 million workers. This is in just two branches. To develop the BAM zone, several million will be needed in the next few years. And take the service sphere'.[15] At least the chairman of the State Committee for Labour and Wages, Gladky, admitted to being deeply worried about the 'emotional turmoil and disappointments' and that 'a serious psychological restructuring is necessary and unavoidable' especially among older workers who must move to other cities, particularly since labour resource management was often done by guesswork.[16] Some evidence suggests, however, that the injunction to cut workers was taken more seriously in certain ministries than the injunction to cut themselves. In an economic experiment in the Belorussian Ministry of Railways,

[10] *Izvestiya* (22 Feb. 1988), 1. [11] Ibid. (2 Mar. 1988), 3.

[12] *Moskovskiye novosti* (13 Mar. 1988), 4. For further articles on this subject see *Pravitel'stvennyy vestnik*, 5 (1989), 7.

[13] *Izvestiya* (2 Mar. 1988), 3. In the foyer of the ministry on the day it was abolished, a large electronic board displayed plan performance throughout the country; 17 cars stood in the parking lot, and the canteen was functioning normally.

[14] See *Pravda* (19 Jan. 1988), 1–2. [15] See ibid. (21 Jan. 1988), 2.

[16] See *Trud* (28 Jan. 1988), 1–2.

12,000 people were cut from the labour force and wage increases granted to those remaining, averaging 35 roubles per month. This system was then extended to a third of the railways in the country— 125,000 jobs were cut across the country in 1987. However, some argued that it adversely affected the volume of rail stock shipped. Managers were largely unaffected. The ministry also appears to have used the situation as a pretext for an attack on the Ministry of Transport Construction, using the released workers to form brigades of building workers.[17]

There is little evidence that those released from the ministry apparatus were made available for production, which had been one of the reasons given for the cuts. In the abolished Ukrainian Ministry of the Coal Industry, of 744 former officials, 255 were re-employed in the Donetsk State Coal Industry Production Association which was set up to replace it. Almost all of the rest went into other jobs in economic administration. Very few went into production, and none into the co-operatives, though one co-operator made it clear, 'we are very much interested in former ministry personnel. After all, these people are very sociable, as a rule, they know how to get through to someone, and they have considerable connections.' It may be a mark of the attractiveness of the perks of ministry life that there were apparently at that time no takers, despite the prospect of 500 roubles per month salary—a nominal increase of more than 300 per cent.[18] Those who left ministry employment retained their pay for a year,[19] and one former head of a department demanded that he be made redundant rather than pensioned off—to get twice the pay-off.[20] The biggest problem groups were those near retirement, and those in the housing queue who needed to be found jobs in the same sectoral trade union.[21] Officials in Moscow job placement agencies maintained

that the hardest thing of all is finding jobs for specialists who are relatively inexperienced, have never seen production, and, for all practical purposes are not specialists at all. Paradoxically, it is these people who make the greatest claims when it comes to future work, claims that, as a rule, are not very practical: they want jobs that will entitle them to special food deliveries and cut-rate manufactured goods, and they want a fixed-length working day and a clean and quiet working environment.[22]

[17] *Moscow News*, 10 (1987), 11.
[18] See *Izvestiya* (28 Jan. 1988), 2.
[19] Ibid. (2 Mar. 1988), 3.
[20] *Moscow News*, 11 (1988), 4.
[21] Ibid. 7 (1988), 8–9.
[22] *Moskovskaya pravda* (2 March 1988), 2.

There is little evidence to suggest that the reforms changed power relations or the style of work within the ministry. An investigation by sociologists of the Academy of Social Sciences under the Central Committee of the Communist Party into activity in four union ministries—finance, bread production, chemical industry, and water industry—revealed that the new demands of the party for a *perestroyka* of the style and methods of administration in the ministries was practically unfulfilled. As before, there was a wealth of paper creation and a slow decline in the number of unnecessary, useless tasks. These facts were attested to by 43.7 per cent of those in the Ministry of Finance, 69.5 per cent in the water industry, by 80.4 per cent in the bread industry, and by 92.4 per cent in the chemical industry.[23] The problem was well expressed by Gavriil Popov in an article in 1987, in which he described how the continuity of ministry interests predominated over personnel factors.

One of my acquaintances was named to an executive position in a ministry. In his previous job at a factory, he had fought for many years for a new type of economic accountability. But within a few months of joining the staff of the ministry, he began saying that enterprises could not be given broad powers. Strange as it may seem, this metamorphosis occurred because of his conscientiousness.[24]

While not wishing to discount personal honesty as a motivation for pro-ministerialism, the evidence presented here and in other chapters suggests that the most likely and consistent reason for this Damascus experience lay in the dominant work ethos and reward structure of the ministry itself.

Changes in the internal structure

The second prong in structural reform was directed at changing the internal structure of the branches supervised by the ministries. As an attempt to increase central control and improve economic performance, this reform was an extension of the earlier *ob'edinenie* reforms in the mid-1970s, though again with greater scope and, given the degree of distinction in forms and administration of state enterprises by 1990, resulting in greater confusion as well. As was the case in the

[23] L. Ponomarev and V. Shinkarenko, 'Kto kogo? Chem silen byurokrat?', in *Uroki gor'kie, no neobkhodimye* (Moscow, 1988), 157. [24] *Pravda* (20 Jan. 1987).

mid-1970s, the operative control of high ministerial officials over the structure beneath them prevented success. Several important facets of structural reform can be listed.[25]

Ministry mergers and redesignations

In July 1987 a new all-Union Ministry of Farm Machinery and Tractors was formed from the then existing Ministry of Tractors and Farm Machinery and the Ministry of Animal-Husbandry and Feed Production; and the all-Union Ministry of Heavy, Power, and Transport Machinery was formed by combining the Ministry of Heavy and Transport Machinery and the Ministry of Power Machinery.[26] In December 1988, the Presidium of the Supreme Soviet formed a Union Ministry of Motor Vehicles and Farm Machinery from the existing Ministry of the Automotive Industry and the Ministry of Farm Machinery and Tractors.[27] The same wave of structural reforms saw many Union–republican ministries transformed into all-Union ones— including the Ministry of Power and Electrification, the Ministry of Ferrous Metallurgy, the Ministry of Non-ferrous Metallurgy, the Ministry of the Coal Industry, the Ministry of Geology, and the Ministry of Petroleum-Refining and Petrochemical Industry. But the degree to which such structural change was likely to succeed may be judged from the fact that ministers themselves were given the power to affirm the table of organization for their departments.[28]

Indeed, the difficulties in policy were highly reminiscent of earlier reform efforts of this type, and are to be explained by the continuing domination of the formation and implementation process by ministerial input at all decision-making levels. The former Ministry for the

---

[25] A further example of structural reform inside the ministries in this period was the attempt to create branch councils, comprised of directors of leading enterprises, advanced workers, representatives of the branch trade unions, major scholars, and specialists, to review aspects of the economic, scientific and technical, and social development of the branch. The intention was to make ministries more democratic and collegial in their decision-making, procedural reforms which, it was hoped, would increase the effectiveness of related economic reform. Ministries were instructed to inform labour collectives of the content of their activity—without it being clear how this was to be accomplished. The body would meet 'not less than twice per year' and would elect a presidium. See Yu. Perelygin, 'Tsentral'ny otralevoy sovet', in *Khozyaystvo i pravo*, 5 (1988), 49–50; and *Izvestiya* (30 Aug. 1988), 2.

[26] *Izvestiya*, (21 July 1987), 2.   [27] Ibid. (3 Dec. 1988), 3.

[28] Interview with Silaev, then deputy chairman of the Council of Ministers, *Pravda*, (21 Sept. 1987), 2.

Construction of Heavy Industry Enterprises was transformed into the USSR Ministry for Construction in the Urals and Western Siberia, and became a cross between a ministry and a regional economic council. The minister explained that it remained in Moscow to make it 'easier to manage'. This also made it expensive—77,000 roubles were overspent on travel costs, and total spending on the central apparatus was 3 million roubles. Regionalization did not stop the ministry's interest in capital spending, or make producer–client relations better: 'The problem, according to the clients, is that the revamped ministry has lost the ability to shift resources and labour from other parts of the country that are now outside their region.' All four of the new regional construction ministries had the same structure, despite different conditions.[29] Furthermore, ministry mergers were used as convenient ways to infringe the rights of subordinate enterprises. For example, in 1987, the country's only producer of low-capacity tractors was given a target to carry a planned loss of 8 million roubles with a promise from the ministry to compensate all losses. However, following the merger, the guarantee was lost, and the enterprise was soon 25 million roubles in debt. The experience, in fact, led one observer to conclude that these super-ministries were even less capable of improving anything than their predecessors.[30] As one author put it, the problem with merging ministries was that the absolute number of bad enterprises under one management was actually higher, thereby increasing the chances of the ministries which were exercising operational control to take over the responsibilities of the good ones, thus diminishing the chances of their concentrating on scientific and technical policy and perspective development.[31]

Towards a two-link system and functionalism

There was initially considerable enthusiasm in some academic writings for these changes, wherein the structural middle-link, be they *glavki* or industrial association, would be abolished and greater power inside the ministry would accrue to its functional apparatus. Great potential

[29] See ibid. (18 Jan. 1988), 1–3.

[30] *Moscow News*, 30 (1989), 12. Indeed, as shall be shown in various sections below, they were almost certainly worse from the point of view of entrenching economic power over political authority.

[31] A. Omel'chenko, 'K effektivnomu upravleniyu', in *Khozyaystvo i pravo*, 10 (1989), 3–12.

was seen in vastly reducing the size of the administrative apparatus by this means, as well as strengthening ministry performance.[32] In particular, the old industrial associations (VPOs) and *glavki* were to be replaced by state production combines (GPOs), which were supposedly not administrative agencies, dependent for their funds on deductions from enterprises: their officials' pay would relate to the profit of enterprises; and the apparatus of the GPO would take decisions only in the interim between meetings of the Council of Directors. On this basis, it was hoped, tiers of wasteful administration would be removed, leaving the ministry apparatus free—and, hopefully, compelled—to concentrate on the general directions of the branch. At the same time, inside the ministry power was to devolve on the so-called functional departments for whom the rationality, as Paul Gregory has pointed out, ought to have been regulative rather than operational.[33]

The new system, with its attendant problems, had already been in place in the machine building sector since 1986, when the majority of large enterprises were directly subordinated to the ministry. All 108 industrial associations were liquidated and *glavki* created in their place. However, the new structure bore a certain resemblance to the old one, with the strengthened functional departments exhibiting a mixed (*smeshnyy*) character—meaning that they preserved operational control powers. The production *glavki* continued to exercise the most general control over subordinate enterprises, though they were also in many cases juridical persons with their own accounts. Of the officials in the old VPOs, 70 per cent were transferred into the ministries. As one commentator put it in the typical euphemism for failure: 'There were evident certain difficulties in the redrawing of boundaries of functions, rights, and responsibilities of the structural subdivisions of the apparatus.'[34]

Forty new subdivisions were to be created in the Ministry of the Forestry Industry, where it was planned to concentrate '40 per cent of the general volume of work of the branch'.[35] The old industrial

[32] See *Pravda* (21 Sept. 1987), 2. V. K. Pokrovskiy mentions the cut in the number of ministerial subdivisions by 65% and the concentration of all planning economic work in one department. See V. K. Pokrovskiy, 'Ministerstvo: puti k novoy kontseptsii', in *Khozyaystvo i pravo*, 1 (1989), 12–21.

[33] See P.Gregory, 'Soviet Bureaucratic Behaviour: Khozyaistvenniki and Apparatchiki', in *Soviet Studies*, 4 (1989), 511–25.

[34] See D. Levchuk, 'Na osnove novykh general'nykh skhem', in *Khozyaystvo i pravo*, 2 (1987), 54–8.

[35] D. Levchuk, 'Manevry so srednym zvenom upravleniya', in *Khosyaystvo i pravo*, 9 (1988) 17.

associations would be transformed into these new bodies, with expanded rights *vis-à-vis* the enterprise, where they would 'play the very role of the central apparatus of the ministry in relation to the basic link, being administered in a two-link system'.[36] Given what has already been said concerning the organization of work inside the ministry, however, there is probably ample reason to be suspicious about the reality or effectiveness of such proposals when they reached ministerial level. Indeed, as might have been expected, ministries not only defeated the thrust of the proposals to change their strategic interests, but actually used the changes to increase their power over subordinates. By the time of his speech to the XIXth Conference, Gorbachev had admitted that the creation of the so-called state production associations (GPOs) had amounted to nothing more than 'an effort to give rise to the system of former bureaucratic ministerial *glavki*, in which the swollen apparatus was repartitioned (*peregorodka*)'. 'Life showed that they [GPOs] did not turn out to have sufficient rights for the realization of real *khozraschetnyy* [cost accountable] forms of activity and their transformation into single economic complexes.'[37] Employees of a production combine in the Ministry of Petroleum Refining and the Petrochemical Industry testified to the formal nature of changes, wherein the *glavki* were unable to prevent all problems being solved at the ministerial level.[38]

By the autumn of 1988, therefore, the promised move to a two-link system had clearly not occurred. The middle link was preserved in many branches by the production *glavk*, which functioned to administer the large combines. There had been no major decrease in the number of Union ministries. Attempts to create large territorial associations, including scientific institutes in the state production combines (GPOs), simply led to the creation of yet another level of superfluous middle

[36] Ibid.

[37] *XIX vsesoyuznaya konferentsiya Kommunisticheskoy Partii Sovetskogo Soyuza* (Moscow, 1988), i. 31.

[38] The informers ended by asking that their names not be published. *Izvestiya* commented: 'Perhaps these fears are not so unfounded. The protection of narrowly departmental, parochial interests to the detriment of state interests, blind patriotism at the level of the given division, and the persecution of those who want to break out of some outmoded routine—all these things are, sad to say, holdovers from days past (*Izvestiya* 26 Oct. 1986), 2). Bondar' points out that in almost all cases, the general schemes worked out by the ministries after 1987 contradicted the law on the enterprise in so far as they directively forced enterprises to enter combines. See L. Bondar', 'General'nye skhemy upravleniya: protivorechiya i tendentsii', in *Khozyaystvo i pravo*, 12 (1989), 3–11.

administration, which was useful only to the strategic position of the ministry concerned. The abolished Ukrainian Ministry of Ferrous Metals, for example, was preserved in the form of a GPO. The GPOs in fact became useful means whereby the ministries transmitted state orders, limits, and other indicators to the enterprises supposedly voluntarily beneath them. Where the middle link was formally abolished, there were created co-ordinational–technological or technological administrations within the apparatus of the ministry which also took on sub-branch leadership functions.[39]

Similar reservations must be expressed about the attempt to create effective industrial organization by forming combines of enterprises outside ministerial subordination—the so-called inter-branch production combines (MGOs).

The peculiarity of the combines is that, in their organizational plan, they are not subordinate to their former ministries. The function of the highest organ of state power is exercised by the Council of Directors who are elected on a democratic basis. Each combine has its own share bank, which allows it essentially to broaden the economic independence of all its parts. These combines differ from those of the previous generation which, on the contrary, limited the independence of those enterprises which made the combine up.[40]

On analysis, however, the MGOs, which were formed in the energy and chemical machine-building sectors on the basis of enterprises in Leningrad were far from independent actors and required a high degree of central support. Reminiscent of the experience of the *sovnarkhozy*, plans and supplies were received from Gossnab and Gosplan direct. Far from enhancing enterprise autonomy,

the apparatus of the MGO passes on defined indicators to every enterprise. In fact, these functions are analogous to those of the ministry. The difference consists in the sweeping away of all intermediate stages of administration between the MGO and central economic departments. However, this situation is possible only where there are few MGOs.[41]

Making the point that, unless the operating principles were changed, nothing else would, Omel'chenko said of the MGO Energomash in Leningrad, 'it fulfils all the routine work which before was carried by the ministry, as they were forced to function in conditions of limits and normatives'.[42] In other words, MGOs quickly assumed the powers

[39] Levchuk, 'Manevry so srednym zvenom upravleniya', 16.
[40] Glebov and Marakhov (gen. eds.), *Novyy sotsial'nyy mekhanizm*, 230–1.
[41] Levchuk, 'Manevry so srednym zvenom upravleniya', 16.
[42] A. Omel'chenko, 'K effektivnomu upravleniyu', in *Khozyaystvo i pravo*, 10 (1989), 5.

and interests of ministries themselves, and probably posed the central leadership the same difficulties.

The leasing of factories

Formally, *arenda*, or the leasing of factories, went beyond mere structural change within the ministries as it put an additional legal barrier between the ministry and the operational management of the enterprise. Many writers saw this form of reform as an opportunity for far more anti-ministerial changes.

The transition to leasing arrangements will not be formal if it decisively changes the situation of the enterprise in the ministerial system. This does not exclude a more radical approach: the transition of the enterprise to leasing arrangements must be accompanied by its removal from ministerial sub-ordination with the aim of liquidating the majority of economic ministries from the perspective of seeing them as the rudiments of the command economy.[43]

In practice, however, ministries were largely able to deal with *arenda* and use it in the same way as they had other forms of structural reform. Leasing was, in any case, prohibited in defence, transport, and certain other basic branches, including coal, metallurgy, chemicals, timber-processing, and many other enterprises;[44] it is worth remembering that most consumer goods came from the defence sector.

Pavel Bunich, the reforming economist and radical deputy, pointed out the problems of giving ministries the power to decide on leasing arrangements with enterprises they were used to calling their own; there would be arbitrary differences between branches in the details of leasing arrangements, on the degree of implementation, and the prices charged.[45] The Moscow deputy Aleksei Yemelyanov argued that leasing, or state co-operatives, was made available only to dying enterprises; the enterprises still had no protection from departmental *diktat*—whether it was via a direct violation of adopted laws and decisions, or by correction through departmental instructions.

But still the main lever of administrative pressure is control over the work collectives' life support. If you want independence, take it, legally it is granted. But economically there is no independence since there is no free trade with

---

[43] Glebov and Marakhov (gen. eds.), *Novyy sotsial' nyy mekhanizm*, 183.

[44] *Izvestiya* (26 May 1990), 1–2.

[45] *Ogonek*, 47 (1989), 1–3. He thought Gosarbitrazh should have the power to intervene.

resources. Rationed, centralized supply is the best antidote for the independence dream, the lease system, the co-operatives, people's enterprises, and joint ventures.[46]

It is clear that leased enterprises had little freedom from ministries on the basis of the leasing arrangements concluded. The collective had to maintain machinery, update the machinery, and 'satisfy the economy's requirements for necessary output'. As a deputy minister said, 'If these contractual requirements are not met, we are entitled to cancel it, with appropriate compensation for damage.'[47] The Orsk-Khaililovo Combine had been refused permission by its ministry to enter into a leasing arrangement. In reply, the minister stated that seven enterprises were already working on leasing arrangements but 'a changeover to any form of economic accountability does not relieve an enterprise of its obligations to the budget and to the state in general'.[48] Since *arenda* occurred within the framework of *goszakazy* (state orders) and other ministry powers to determine rates of profits, amortization payments, central budget investment allocations, and other fund payments, it was rendered highly ineffective, at least in this period.[49]

ANOTHER ROUND OF ECONOMIC REFORM

As was argued in earlier chapters, the position of industrial ministries was an ambiguous one, even in the language of Soviet administrative theory. On the one hand, they possessed state powers to issue binding decrees on subordinates; on the other, they were enjoined from 1965 onwards to interact with their subordinates on the basis of economic levers and through the medium of interests. This ambiguity in the ministries' position was not abolished by legislation governing the role of ministries and their relations to subordinates passed in 1987; indeed, it was, if anything, strengthened.

Economic reform had two main aims relative to ministry power: first, it sought to affect the ministry's ability to interfere in the rightful activity of enterprises; and second, it entrenched the view that the basis

---

[46] *Moscow News*, 44 (1989), 8.   [47] *Izvestiya* (27 Oct. 1988), 2.

[48] Ibid. (6 July 1989), 1, 3.

[49] N. Grineva, A. Umanskiy, and A. Votsko, 'Organizatsionnye i ekonomicheskie problemy vvedeniya arendy na gospredpriyatiyakh', in *Voprosy ekonomiki*, 11 (1989), 28–34.

of their interaction was to be principally economic. The experience of economic reform from 1987 to 1990, however, suggested that ministerial power was the main obstacle to its success. Far from having successfully created a distinction between politics and economics, and given greater autonomous space for both the state and civil society, economic reform measures foundered on the very fusion that existed in Soviet society between the two.

Two important pieces of legislation passed in 1987, the law on the state enterprise and the decree on the activity of the ministry, ought to have strengthened the distinctness of the economic sphere and more clearly delineated the scope of ministry action. The Law of the USSR on the State Enterprise (Combine) strengthened its property rights, and sought to establish ministries' rights to interfere only as specified in the law.[50] Though ministries were still held responsible for much enterprise activity, Article 9 of the law gave enterprises the right to go to *gosarbitrazh* (state arbitration) in the event of a ministry issuing an illegal departmental norm.[51] The corresponding decree on the activity of ministries continued to hold them responsible for implementing the broad tasks of party policy.[52] The main thrust of change was to construct ministry–enterprise relations on the basis of economic methods: state orders, long-term economic norms and limits, and control figures. However, it is evident that these pieces of legislation were not effective in creating space between the ministry and the enterprise, did not effect the ministries' powers and interests, and did not, therefore, fundamentally alter the ministry's bargaining position in the state structure.

[50] Glebov and Marakhov (gen. eds.), *Novyy sotsial'nyy mekhanizm*, 311.

[51] The issue of arbitration will be discussed in greater detail in the section on legal reform below.

[52] These comprised: the conduct of a progressive scientific–technological and investment policy; the realization of the balanced and proportional development of the branch; the rational location of production and products comprising the branch profile; the effective resolution of inter-branch tasks in co-operation with other interested ministries and local organs; the working out of annual plans with the enterprises, and of five-year plans with Gosplan; the realization of anti-monopoly policy; the stimulation of the effective use of enterprise resources; the development of internal and inter-branch co-operation; the supervision and improvement of the use of enterprise funds; and the resolution of branch social questions. Broad powers were also retained in the area of capital construction, material–technical provision and wholesale trade, prices, finance, and credit. See 'Postanovlenie TsK KPSS i Soveta Ministrov SSSR' (17 July 1987), No. 823, 'O perestroyke deyatel'nosti ministerstv i vedomstv sfery material'nogo proizvodstva v novykh usloviyakh khozyaystvovaniya', in *O korennoy perestroyke upravleniya ekonomikoy* (Moscow, 1987), 191–207. The other major form of ministerial control lay in its ability to form, merge, split, and dissolve enterprises. See R. E. Ericson, 'The New Enterprise Law', in *Harriman Institute Forum*, 1/2 (1988), 1–8.

State orders and wholesale trade

The idea of state orders (*goszakazy*) was to introduce a measure of profitability to enterprises while allowing the state to regulate the economy in priority areas. *Goszakazy* were intended to be used for social policy reasons only when either the consumer could not afford to buy or the producer could not afford to produce.[53] The obvious corollary of state orders over a proportion of output was the development of direct ties and wholesale trade in non-state order production. However, it quickly became evident that these reforms would not prove effective in breaking the ministries' habits of holding operational economic control of their subordinates' activity, for the following reasons:

1. The lion's share of production was included, transforming state orders into a rechristened nomenclature plan, in which, as in the past, output was specified in natural, physical indicators.[54]

2. The supplier remained in a dependent position with regard to his customers, especially if they had had relations for more than two years; since there were high degrees of inherited interdependence among enterprises, the existing ministerial chain was not threatened.[55]

3. *Goszakazy* were conceptualized in the 1987 act in a way that allowed almost any item to be conceived as legitimate for *goszakazy*. The very idea of the state order should allow a choice of directions; none the less, the unthinkable happened, where priorities were defined so broadly that they included everything.[56]

4. Furthermore, the state, and the ministry, could not go bankrupt, which made its role of orderer highly dubious. As Figurnov put it: 'The state organ, not having its own money, must be allowed the right to order from the producer only those products which can be purchased not at the account of the enterprise but at the account of the state budget.'[57] This condition, however, was not satisfied.

5. Ministries discredited the social aspects of *goszakazy*, for example, in terms of the politicians' aims to give every family a home by 2000. In

---

[53] See V. V. Maslennikov and V. I. Slobodnik, *Gosudarstvennyy zakaz* (Moscow, 1990), 69–70.
[54] L. I. Abalkin, 'Trudnaya shkola perestroyki', in *Uroki gor'kie, no neobkhodimye* (Moscow, 1988), 267.
[55] See P. G. Bunich, 'Goszakazy ili gosprikaz?', in *Ogonek*, 12 (1988) 5.
[56] Abalkin, 'Trudnaya shkola', 267.
[57] Glebov and Marakhov (gen. eds.), *Novyy sotsial'nyy mekhnaizm*, 178–9.

one ministry, by using *goszakazy* to order an enterprise to produce low-profit goods, and by controlling deductions from the residuals into the social fund, the ministry prevented the possibility of meeting the housing programme.[58]

The second thrust of this stage of reform, therefore, was directed at limiting the volume of state orders and specifying the range of goods over which they could be exercised.[59] As a corollary of cuts in this area, the number of centrally distributed goods was also to decline markedly, except in some key sectors such as energy, and wholesale trade was to increase. Enterprises were enjoined to enter into direct ties to secure supplies. By the end of 1988, however, after two years of economic reform, only 3 per cent of trade in means of production was wholesale.[60] Ministerial power played a central role in a number of ways in the continuing failure of a rational system of state orders and developed wholesale trade to emerge.

1. A considerable portion of the wholesale market was envisaged to be in ministerial hands anyway. The network of *firmennye magaziny* (ministry-based distribution centres), which existed in only five ministries, was to realize wholesale trade of up to 40 billion roubles by 1990, compared to 90 billion for direct links, and 70 billion through Gossnab.[61]

2. Many enterprise directors said they were in favour of continuing 100 per cent state orders, in order to find a market for their output.[62] In responding to questions regarding his nomination for minister,

[58] 'Perestroyka i apparat', in *EKO* 3 (1988), 47–58.

[59] The volume of *goszakazy* in 1989 was lowered by a factor of two to three times. Ministries lost the right to use *goszakazy* in matters of series production, intra-ministerial trade, the enterprise's production for its own needs, and some industrial services; changes in state orders had now to receive Gosplan approval. The production of goods of national consumption, (except in the Ministry of Light Industry), programmes and tasks connected with the acceleration of scientific and technology revolution, and basic energy and fuel resources were the only areas where 100% *goszakazy* were to be allowed. In machine-building, for example, *goszakazy* were to comprise only 35% of output, while the remainder was to be sold on direct contracts. Out of the 108 enterprises of the Ministry of Heavy and Transport Machinery, 45 were not to be subject to state orders at all. State orders were to cover 1,000 as opposed to 15,000 products in 1989 compared to 1988, and could be set only by Gosplan. See 'Gosudarstvennyy zakaz: garantii, stimuly, otvetstvennost'', in *Khozyaystvo i pravo*, 11 (1988), 10–15; Glebov and Marakhov (gen. eds.), *Novyy sotsial'nyy meckhanizm*, 176; and *Izvestiya* (3 Jan. 1989), 2.   [60] *Izvestiya* (3 Jan. 1989), 2.

[61] L. Voronin, 'Razvitie optovoy torgovli', in *Planovoe khozyaystvo*, 3 (1989), 3–13.

[62] *Izvestiya* (21 July 1988), 2.

Kulpakov at metallurgy said that he had had no takers among enterprise directors for the offer of complete independence. As he put it, 'intra-branch co-operation consists of hundreds of thousands of ties. What would happen to it?'[63]

3. The system of state orders effectively tore the fabric of the market anyway, by introducing priorities. Though the volume of state orders was being steadily reduced, it was immediately reborn, either in the list of items required by Gosplan or Gossnab, or in the form of ministry control figures. 'What is obligatory ceases to be an element of trade and becomes an element of allocation.'[64] Wholesale trade was effectively a rationing system which gave more power to the ministerial link; the ministries were therefore getting stronger.[65]

4. Wholesale trade was hindered by ministerial monopolism,[66] where monopoly control over output meant that wholesale trade was effectively a non-starter.[67] New ministries, such as the Ministry of the Automobile Industry, Tractor, and Agricultural Machinery, produced almost 50 per cent of the country's machine-building, according to its minister.[68] In these circumstances, there were strong barriers to the emergence of markets in capital goods. Masol, then chairman of the Council of Ministers of the Ukraine, argued that there were significant problems resulting from the extension of wholesale trade to monopoly enterprises in conditions of scarcity, since they sought to operate on-barter arrangements even for goods covered by contractual obligations.[69]

5. Big questions remained about the relationship of ministries to Gosplan where regulation of *goszakazi* was concerned, after Gosplan was made responsible for affirming orders. 'Can Gosplan independently define the priorities of the branch, or must it, as in the past, adopt decisions on the basis of the recommendations of the ministries?'[70] As Viktor Prozorov said, putting all responsibility for

[63] Ibid. (6 July 1989), 1, 3.   [64] Ibid. (3 Jan. 1989), 2.

[65] *Ogonek*, 10 (1989), 15.   [66] *Izvestiya* (3 Jan. 1989), 2.

[67] As was mentioned in Ch. 3, these tendencies had been strengthened by the decision to establish the juridical guarantees of the head ministry system as a means of adding to the ministries' structural advantages in particular product lines. In 1989 the system of head ministries was abolished. The ministries retained their specialization, but enterprises that wished to produce in any specific line could pay for information on the market from the head organization. See *Izvestiya* (14 Jan. 1989), 1.

[68] *Moscow News*, 30 (1989), 12.

[69] *Izvestiya* (16 Dec. 1989), 11–15. A system of 100% state orders, he considered, should be introduced for strategic goods like fuel and cement.

[70] V. V. Maslennikov and V. I. Slobodnik, *Gosudarstvennyy zakaz* (Moscow, 1990), 70.

goszakazy in Gosplan and Gossnab would not be easy, as the enterprise managers themselves understood; only the ministry knew how to do it.[71]

Normatives and enterprise deductions

Similar problems of continuing ministerial control were evident with the attempt to use economic normatives. These were supposed to provide a stable basis for enterprises to pursue profitability, but the power of ministries to define them made their nature and scope highly unstable and threatening to the enterprise. The ministry defined norms on budgets, wage funds, economic stimulation, and regional variations. 'For example, the Ministry of Light Industry defines and affirms for its enterprises norms on deductions of profits to the state budget, local budget, and to the ministry; the growth in the wage fund; the formation of the funds of economic stimulation; the correspondence between the growth of productivity of labour and average wages.' In the Ministry of Forestry, Pulp and Paper, norms were affirmed for twelve areas governing virtually all enterprise activity. Efforts were made to control this excessive ministerial interference by the passage of a special resolution of the commission for the improvement of administration, planning, and the economic mechanism, restricting the scope of ministries to redistribute profits.[72] As one commentator observed,

plan organs as in the past lower down their list of normatives, the ministries retouch and affirm them for every enterprise, but for the latter each normative frequently worsens their financial situation . . . Once again, but now in relation to economic normatives, there is being used the lexicon of the not too distant past: 'knock it out', 'reduce', 'correct'. . . . workers of the ministry continue to resolve problems arising not on the basis of economic norms but by the route of addressed communications and unbalanced tasks.[73]

---

[71] V. Prozorov, 'Pervye shagi i trudnosti reformy khozyaystvennogo zakonodatel'stva', in S. N. Bratus, *Sovetskoe zakonodatel'stvo: puti perestroiki* (Moscow, 1989), 288.

[72] S. Mogilevsky and S. Ayzin, 'Otnosheniya predpriyatiya s vyshestoyashchim organom', in *Khozyaystvo i pravo*, 2 (1988), 3–7.

[73] The Ministry of Oil Technical Industry gave one of its enterprises a normative for deductions from profits into the socio-cultural fund of 89.9% in 1988 and 19.1% in 1989. High-profit enterprises transferred 75–90% of profits to the ministry budget, with only a small part remaining in their hands. The opposite applied in low-profit industries. Norms of deductions from profits in the Ministry of Construction of Road

Normatives were not taxes, which were obligatory, but were supposedly mutually beneficial. However, it was clear that the right to establish normatives was lodged with the enterprises' superiors, without need for preliminary consultation and agreement with the labour collective. Normatives were arbitrary and changeable. The criteria for the choice of enterprises paying greater normatives were often their reliability and profitability to secure branch funds. Furthermore, the monopoly position of the ministry impinged on its attitude, both in the process of affirming a normative on distribution of profits (gross income), and in allocating funds for deductions from amortization to renovation. Monopoly profits accrued 'as a result of the monopolisation by the ministry of the right to establish normatives'.[74]

Limits

Similar ministerial interests were evident in the application of their responsibility to secure important material resources for enterprises, and in their use of their rights to resolve issues of sale of output, to organize agreements, and to make orders more precise to secure a supplier or consumer for a state order.[75] In the Council of Ministers' Temporary Resolution on the Order of Forming State Orders for 1989 and 1990 it was stated that 'the enterprise will realize independently only that production which is: first, not included in state orders; second, not distributed along limits of consumption; third, not to be transferred for sale in the order of the wholesale trade network through supply organizations'. The trouble was, as the experiment in the Ministry of Machinery for Construction, Road Building and

---

Machine-Building varied from 1% to 49% for 1988–90; for funds for the development of production, science, and technology, from 21.4% to 82.6%. In the Ministry of Agricultural Machine-Building, the normatives for funds for social development varied from 0.23% to 88.2%; for material stimulation, from 1.43% to 99.77% and for production, science, and technology from 0.9% to 95.91%. For example, the Ministry of Road-Building, affirmed norms according to which the growth of profits by 1990 should be 41% compared with 1987. Out of this, budget payments to the centre should grow by 2.1 times, while the remaining profits should grow by 13.7% and funds for social development by 12%. Projected profits were also envisaged to outstrip increased funds for material stimulation. See V. G. Vishnyakov, 'Ekonomicheskim normativam—pravovuyu osnovu', in *Khozyaystvo i pravo*, 6 (1988), 41.

[74] Ibid.

[75] See 'Gosudarstvennyy zakaz: garantii, stimuly, otvetstvennost'', in *Khozyaystvo i pravo*, 11 (1988), 10–15.

Municipalities showed, the mechanism for allocating resources did not change: those who turned down unneeded resources would not get the same amount next time.[76] The term 'limits of consumption in production' filled its old administrative role. The funds to production did the job of the ration system. Superior bodies effectively ordered enterprises, by thus using the notion of limits of consumption, to conclude agreements with customers. For the enterprise, however, getting rid of *goszakazi* could make things worse in so far as the ministry would then no longer be responsible for providing the necessary supplies; all responsibility then fell on its shoulders, though its independence had in no way increased.[77]

Control figures

These were quickly used by the ministry to maintain operational control.[78] There was little success in keeping down the number of branch indicators to the desired limits, as in the case of the Ministry of Forestry, Pulp, and Paper, the Ministry of the Gas Industry, the Ministry of the Oil Technical Industry, and the Ministry of the Automobile Industry, whose indicators to enterprises, in the period immediately after the ministries were themselves put on *khozraschet*, increased to as many as seventeen.[79] Although control figures were not supposed to have a directive obligatory character, ministries treated them as such.[80] A questionnaire to directors in 1988 indicated clearly that 80 per cent felt no reduction in the number of centrally established indicators.[81] Ministries sought to preserve daily reporting. As one writer put it, 'to tell the truth, one can judge enterprises' level of independence by the volume of such reports'. The Ministry of Ferrous Metallurgy demanded daily reports on the state of the coking by-products industry—signed by the deputy minister, in whose opinion, 'the ministry should know every 24 hours how many furnaces are operating in the country . . . The people in the Ministry of Ferrous Metallurgy sincerely believe that since no one has relieved it of its responsibility for supplying the economy with metal, it has the right to ask for any kind of information it wants from enterprises.'[82]

[76] *Izvestiya* (3 Jan. 1989), 2.　　　[77] Bratus *Sovetskoe zakonodatel'stvo*, 285–6.
[78] Glebov and Marakhov (gen. eds.), *Novyy sotsial'nyy mekhanizm*, 177.
[79] Mogilevsky and Ayzin, 'Otnosheniya predpriyatiya'.
[80] See P. G. Bunich, 'Goszakazy ili gosprikaz?', in *Ogonek*, 12 (1988), 5.
[81] 'Anketa direktora', in *EKO* 3 (1988), 59–75.　　　[82] *Izvestiya* (11 Jan. 1988), 2.

The following story is therefore typical. In the Ministry of Machinery for Construction, Road-Building, and Municipalities, at the start of 1988, the ministry instructed enterprises to seek their own partners; in April, it issued a new directive saying that materials for state orders would be allocated centrally, and what was left over offered for sale; in June it issued control figures; then it announced that contracts for 1989 would be the same as for the year before; then came the decision to conclude contracts for 100 per cent of control figures.[83]

MINISTRIES AND LEGAL REFORM

Soviet legislation, as Prozorov shows, was often badly thought out; it would be wrong just to blame the executors.[84] None the less, the law-making process was dominated by departmental interests favouring their own interests in framing legal regulations.[85] The central tenets of legal reform relating to industrial ministries involved increasing the standing of law (*zakon*), making it directly active without the need for departmental enabling legislation mainly issued in the economy by industrial ministries.[86] It was also deemed desirable to enact provisions allowing enterprises and other ministerial subordinates to appeal to state arbitration in the event that an act of the ministry was considered unlawful. However, once again, the continued existence of the ministries was one of the main reasons for the failure to create an autonomous legal sphere.

[83] Ibid. (3 Jan. 1989), 2.

[84] He singles out the phrase 'carries responsibility' for particular criticism. The law on ministries gave the ministry 'responsibility' for providing resources for enterprises to meet *goszakazy*, but no one was actually made responsible, nor was it clear how they could be made responsible for damage to the enterprise as the law claims. See Prozorov, 'Pervye shagi i trudnosti reformy khozyaystvennogo zakonodatel'stva', 272–8.

[85] This was the case, for example, in the creation of the GPOs. Prozorov also mentions the failure of the Commission on Improving Administration, Planning, and Economic Reform to bring forward what it was called to do in 1987, namely a law on ministries. Other examples were the failure of the commission charged with introducing legislation in correspondence with the law on enterprises and other decisions about the radical reform of administration of the economy to carry their brief through. The Commission was designing a law on juridical guarantees of the rights of enteprises when, without discussion, the project was shifted aside. See ibid. 281. For an article on the secretiveness of ministerial law-making, see A. S. Pigolkin and T. N. Rakhmanina, 'Demokraticheskie osnovy sozdaniya normativnykh aktov', in *Sovetskoe gosudarstvo i pravo*, 11 (1989), 10–18.

[86] Yu. A. Tikhomirov, *Zakon, stimuly, ekonomika* (Moscow, 1989), 98–100.

Subdepartmental acts

Criticism of the old system whereby departmental acts supplanted law was widespread.[87]

Departmental norm-making for many years was seen as the form of activity of organs of state administration. In the conditions of rigid-command systems of leadership, it came to be arbitrarily interpreted and to involve changing the law, to bring it into the world in departmental clothes.[88]

Following the package of resolutions in 1987, including the law on enterprises and the resolution on ministries, over 1,200 decrees of the government, over 7,500 analogous laws of the republics, over 33,000 instructions from different ministries and departments, and over 80,000 acts of republican authorities were struck down.[89] However, it quickly became clear that 'in the past as now, ministries and departments issued a multitude of instructions trying with their help to avoid reproach for mistakes in administration'.[90] Regarding the new law on the enterprise, commentators noted that

this resolution is to be realized by means of the raising of the independence of the enterprise, establishing the possibility of their participation in the preparation and adoption of decisions by the ministries. Ignoring this approach has resulted in the directing to enterprises of great numbers of *prikazy*, [ministerial orders] directives, and other documents, squashing their initiative. The Ministry of Electro-Technical Industry, for example, in the half-year from January 1985 issued 2,000 *prikazy*, and consultative documents from the minister, which contained almost 20,000 instructions on various aspects of production and socio-cultural activity of the enterprises of the branch.[91]

Prozorov argued that the law on enterprises was never operative, only temporary recommendations and sub-acts which comprised the apparatus's self-interested interpretation of every inexactitude in the law. He went so far as to describe the law on the State Production Association (GPO) as an act of economic sabotage on the part of the

---

[87] 'Departmental acts, and sometimes the very laws, expressed above all the group and departmental interests, and not infrequently the interests of the majority of the participants of regulated relations were left beyond the limits of juridical establishment. The consequence of this was the diffusion of mass legal nihilism, a lack of esteem for the law: normative acts, not founded in wide social interests, cannot be actively fulfilled . . .' See M. Yu. Tikhomirov, 'O mekhanizme obespecheniya zakonnosti upravlenii ekonomikoy', in *Sovetskoe gosudarstvo i pravo*, 7 (1990), 33.

[88] *Tikhomirov, Zakon, stimuly, ekonomika*, 100.   [89] Ibid. 101.

[90] Ibid. 105.   [91] Mogilevsky and Ayzin, 'Otnosheniya predpriyatiya, 3.

apparatus: 'With the adoption of the Decree on the GPO, the branch apparatus of administration received the legal normative base for the regular transfer of their workers from wing to wing without cutting their numbers.'[92] This was possible because the law was so inexact, allowing, in violation of the resolution on the ministry, for a general director with rights of one-man management to lead a council of directors drawn from enterprises which could be included in the combine against their will. When GPOs were abolished, ministries were then, by the same method of interpretation, able to safeguard their interests by turning the GPO into a scientific productions association.[93]

Gosarbitrazh

In the hope of making Gosarbitrazh more potent, it had been transformed in 1987 into an independent organ under the Supreme Soviet and its presidium. In terms of juridical status, in other words, it had been raised above the level of the ministries. None the less, despite having powers to declare void administrative acts, and to compensate enterprises for damages, the power of Gosarbitrazh did not increase greatly. Indeed, some commentators attacked the arbitration service for continuing to be an essentially administrative organ acting as a support for the command system.[94]

This was the result of a number of factors. There continued to be many cases in which judicial competence lay with departmental services; many issues continued to be solved administratively. Ministries in practice seemed to have the ability to forestall Gosarbitrazh by deciding on the charges which the enterprise would be allowed to bring against it.[95] As Lushchkov, deputy and arbiter in the Koma ASSR, argued in an interview, the problem of Gosarbitrazh was the basis on which it took decisions. 'By what is the arbiter to be governed when reviewing this or that dispute? By the civil code, by the all-Union code? In some measure yes, but basically, once again by the norm-making of various departments.'[96]

[92] Bratus, Sovetskoe zakonodatel'stvo, 292.   [93] Ibid. 295.

[94] I. Avilina, 'Arbitrazh ili sud?', in Khozyaystvo i pravo, 5 (1989), 90–8.

[95] T. Abova, 'Gosarbitrazh v usloviyakh perestroyki', in Khozyaystvo i pravo, 5 (1989), 99–107.

[96] 'Programma—pravovoe gosudarstvo', in Khozyaystvo i pravo, 7 (1989), 8; N. Sraubin, 'Rasshirit' polnomochiya gosarbitrazha', ibid. 80–8.

The arbitration expert Belova makes clear, from a number of examples, that the article in the 1987 Law on the Enterprise which gave enterprises the right to appeal to Gosarbitrazh had not been applied to state orders, though in her view this was how the law should have been interpreted.[97] A Tyumen factory tried to bring a suit against the ministry to declare its control figures inactive, but Gosarbitrazh declined to rule because the law only allowed it to declare invalid acts of the ministry with a directive character, which control figures officially were not.[98] The law on enterprises was also regarded by Gosarbitrazh as being insufficiently detailed on the precise divisions of competence between enterprises and ministries.[99] Furthermore, while disputes between a ministry and one of its enterprises were settled by Gosarbitrazh, those between enterprises within one ministry were settled by ministerial arbitration; and different ministries had entirely different responses to one and the same problem.[100] The Ministry of Ferrous Metals, for example, drew up sample agreements in 1988 designed to safeguard the right of suppliers to dictate the contents and quality of deliveries. These agreements also provided for disputes arising to be solved by ministry rather than state arbitration, and only after attempts to find an alternative variant.[101] Furthermore, Gosarbitrazh should have been able to intervene in relations between enterprises and ministries on their own initiative and not just when involved by the enterprise.[102]

The main problem, however, with strengthening Gosarbitrazh seems to have resulted less from the ability of ministries to raise legal obstacles than in their ability to affect the rationality of the actors potentially involved. Studies showed that enterprises did not take great advantage of their right to appeal to Gosarbitrazh to declare invalid

[97] L. Belova, 'Rasshirit' polnomochiya gosarbitrazha', in *Khozyaystvo i pravo*, 3 (1989), 92–3.
[98] D. Lipnitskiy, 'Zashchitit' prava predpriyatiy', in *Khozyaystvo i pravo*, 11 (1989), 75–83.   [99] Ibid. 75–83.
[100] V. Zaragatskiy, 'A nuzhen li vedomstvennyy arbitrazh', in *Khozyaystvo i pravo*, 6 (1989), 151–2.   [101] Tikhomirov, *Zakon, stimuly, ekonomika*, 103.
[102] Zarubin, the chief state arbiter of the RSFSR, wanted article 163 of the constitution clarified to make clear that Gosarbitrazh was led only by law (*zakon*). He also noted that the Law on Gosarbitrazh gave it the right to declare departmental norms which contradicted higher legislation illegal, and favoured adding to the state arbitration's powers that of exercising control over the issuing by ministries of norms relating to economic matters. However, he considered it impractical to transfer the 800,000 disputes of Gosarbitrazh annually, and the 400,000 departmental arbitrations annually, to the court system.

ministry acts and to sue for damages. In a survey of directors in the Dnepropetrovsk and Donetsk regions, carried out by the department of economic and legal problems of the Institute of the Economics of Industry of the Academy of Sciences, to the question 'Would you go to court with your ministry if a conflictual situation arose?' only six answered 'yes' as opposed to seventy-two who said 'no'. For five months in 1989, there were only thirty suits in the Ukraine, and less than a hundred in the whole country, despite widespread infringements. Most suits were for recovery of fines from the ministry which the enterprise had incurred for failing to make deliveries to other enterprises, not direct anti-ministerial action. Replying to why they would not take the ministry to court, of ninety-two respondents, forty-three said they were frightened of retaliation by the ministry through its adoption of difficult normatives or unsecured limits. This rationalizing was probably affected by calculating the insignificant damages to be derived from a successful suit.[103] For example, an enterprise sued the Ministry of Agricultural Machine-Building in 1988 for damages resulting from failure to receive the necessary inputs for *goszakazy*. After a year, which was the regular waiting time for review, Gosarbitrazh awarded only 48,000 roubles, which the ministry paid out of its central fund for production and development. Had the demands for compensation of the enterprise been met in full, it would have taken up 7 per cent of the total ministerial development budget. The same sources for compensation were envisaged in the temporary changes to the rules for *goszakazi* for 1989 and 1990.[104]

Ministries were also, of course, anxious that suits against them should not become the norm. When Uralmash, Nikolai Ryzhkov's old plant, refused to accept the ministry's plan a reporter commented that:

people in the Ministry of Heavy and Transport Machinery were so openly and even emphatically unwilling to meet with us, the nervous tenor of the conversation and what they did end up telling us were all evidence of their one desire: that the Uralmash incident be forgotten, and, at the very least, not discussed in the press. In the view of those we spoke with, this could plunge not only the industry but the entire economy into chaos.[105]

---

[103] D. Lipnitsky, 'Zashchitit' prava predpriyatiy', in *Khozyaystvo i pravo*, 11 (1989), 75–83.

[104] V. Gazman, 'Partnerstvo po vertikali', in *Khozyaystvo i pravo*, 8 (1990), 15–23. Gazman was anxious that damages should be paid out of the ministry wage fund.

[105] *Izvestiya* (23 Mar. 1988), 3.

The main peculiarity of the case seemed to lie, however, in the fact that the

people at Uralmash never doubted for a moment that it was necessary to get their refusal [to accept the plan] approved by both the ministry and the State Planning Committee. And they, in turn, have no doubt whatsoever that they have the final say. Granted, that's not in the Law, but it's the way things have always been done, and the way they'll continue to be done. The ministry painted us downright apocalyptic scenes of enterprises refusing *en masse* to obey rules from Moscow. Can you imagine what would happen if every plant approved itself a plan that was below the control figures?[106]

The visions of apocalypse summoned up by the ministries were intended, of course, to create the sort of fears among actors at all levels of the political and economic system which would help ministries remain in power. As the next chapter will show, the difficulties in removing ministries from the central place they occupied in the Soviet system may well have justified fear of the consequences. What is also evident from the experience discussed above, however, is that the desire of politicians to exercise effective authority was highly attenuated by the ability of ministries to control the process. Other actors, who might have been useful to politicians had they been active in the political arena continued to be structured in their interests by ministerial power and effectively organized out of politics. It is clear from the evidence that even where politicians were willing to effect radical reforms, the strategy of doing so within a surrogate state and civil society, in which ministries straddled both, was clearly flawed. It is for this reason that the anti-ministerial campaign was broadened in an attempt to create genuine space for the emergence of authority.

[106] Ibid.

6

Industrial Power and the Crisis of the Soviet State

THE all-round failure by 1988 of the attempt to create a surrogate civil society posed for the politicians who had launched *perestroyka* the dilemma of either accepting the continued domination of industrial ministries in the Soviet system and retreating from their programme, or finding some more radical way of gaining political authority. Though the rhetoric of *perestroyka* had significantly raised the stakes so far as the Soviet and world public opinion was concerned, it is probably fair to say that had the *perestroyshchiki* retreated at this stage, a return to some form of the status quo ante would have been possible. However, Gorbachev and his allies in place in the highest reaches of the party apparatus, if not yet dominating the Central Committee, were willing to make use of their success, in placing the blame for the failure of reform on to the industrial apparatus, to deepen the reform process and to seek out a new source of authority.

As ministerialism held the old political and social system together, however, so did the next round of anti-ministerialism pull *perestroyka* and the Soviet Union apart. Though more radical political reform did diminish the power of ministries in many ways, this occurred for reasons not foreseen, and gave rise to consequences not desired by the politicians who launched it. Broadening the anti-ministerial campaign both worsened economic performance and widened the scope for independent economic action by industrial actors who were responding to the new strategic environment. New forms of industrial organization developed with interests and demands which were hard to accommodate. Political control over the direction of the economy declined even further. At the same time, in these undesirable and unpredictable circumstances, open competition among élites emerged which was increasingly supported by overt social action by the population. The public entered politics, however, in conditions of an economic crisis brought about, in part, by the reform programme itself. At the same time, the organizational forms of structuring the interests of the public and keeping them out of politics—the ministries—were both pulled apart and striking out on their own. Politicians, without authority or legitimacy, were then confronted with the latent crisis of the Soviet state made manifest. The collapse of the Soviet Union, then, was simply the revelation of the hollow heart of politics in what was supposed to be the most political of states.

THE REFORM PROCESS INTENSIFIES, 1988–1989

Following the failure of the first round of reforms, anti-ministerialism assumed an even more virulent character, most evidently in Gorbachev's speech and in the subsequent discussion at the XIXth Party Conference. Indeed, the anti-ministerial front was opened to include those institutions, including the Communist Party, which were regarded as under the domination of ministry interests. Gorbachev made clear in his speech that he was aware of the attempts by ministries to avoid making real changes, especially in their relations with the enterprises, and that this was made possible by lack of control and connivance by Gosplan and other standing organs of the Council of Ministers.[1] *Goszakazi* and normatives were being applied to even the largest of enterprises: 'many ministries try to establish such normatives, in order with their aid to preserve the possibility, as in the past, to redistribute funds from properly operating enterprises to ineffective ones.'[2] Gorbachev also made clear his understanding of the power of ministries to ruin the government's general control over the economy: 'The scope of unfinished projects in capital construction, rather than decreasing, as was envisaged by the decisions of the XXVIIth Congress, has considerably increased—by 30,000 million roubles. Both the USSR State Planning Committee and the USSR Committee for Construction yielded to the pressure of departments and local bodies while the government did not show due exactingness.'[3]

---

[1] See *XIX vsesoyuznaya konferentsiya Kommunisticheskoy Partii Sovetskogo Soyuza* (Moscow, 1988), 28–29.   [2] Ibid. 29–30.

[3] *Documents and Materials Congress of People's Deputies*, 25 May – 9 June 1989 (Moscow, 1989), 13–14. The Ministry of Petroleum Refining and Petrochemical Industry had construction projects under way in 1988 with a total value of 9.8 billion roubles, being on average five years behind completion, and, in the following five years, managed to use less than half its capital allocations; the Ministry of the Chemical Industry had construction projects under way worth 14.4 billion roubles, being on average six years behind schedule; the Ministry of Medical and Microbiological Industry had construction projects worth 3.2 billion roubles under way, with an average lag of

As Sergey Andreev put it:

one of the positive elements of the analysis of the situation [at the conference] was that there was a recognition of the actual *dependence* of party organs in relation to the organs of economic administration. Even in the Central Committee this [dependence] resulted in the adoption of half-hearted and sometimes also mistaken decisions, as was attested by the general-secretary ... From top to bottom, the party apparatus is entangled with the economic administration ... At the conference this question was raised in all its fullness. The conclusion drawn by the conference was entirely justified—it is necessary to separate economic and ideological functions, to be leaving administration to the administrators, but interaction on the masses to the party. (Author's italics)[4]

In support of Andreev's evaluation, the section of Gorbachev's conference speech entitled, 'Why is reform of the political system necessary?', argued that:

In the period of stagnation, the administrative apparatus, multiplying to almost one hundred union and eight hundred republican ministries and departments, *practically came to dictate their will* in both the economy and in politics. These very departments and other administrative structures held in their hands the execution of adopted resolutions, and by their activity or inactivity decided what would or would not be. (Author's italics)[5]

Speeches by delegates were even more clear and radical in blaming ministries for the political weakness of the party. Perhaps most famously, Kabaidze, a well-known abrasive enterprise director, asked:

Many conversations go: is it necessary to liquidate ministries, and how many of them should there be? Really, from one side, there is a paradox—nowhere in the world are there so many ministries as in our country, but business goes like dirt. [*Applause*] But don't wait for my suggestion: let's liquidate them tomorrow ... If I speak honestly, I don't need ministries. [*Applause*] We can do fully without them. Fodder we now get for ourselves, hard currency we get for ourselves. What can the minister give us? Absolutely nothing! But this doesn't mean that there isn't a need for a co-ordination centre. It is needed. But they must work, be fed from us, not from the state budget. Then the minister will be like the mouse and the trap—if he wants to eat ... [*Laughter, Applause*][6]

six years. 'In light of these facts, it is difficult to avoid the impression that the ministries needed these new multibillion rouble appropriations primarily to cover their failure to use the money they had received earlier and to avoid accountability for that failure.' See *Kommunist*, 2 (1989), 22–33; and ibid. 5 (1989), 75–81.

[4] S. Andreev, 'Struktura vlasti i zadachi obshchestva', in *Neva*, 1 (1989), 170.
[5] *XIX vsesoyuznaya konferentsiya Kommunisticheskoy Partii Sovetskogo Soyuza*, 46–7.
[6] Ibid. 240–1.

The existing political institutions were not effective instruments of the politician's reform strategy, and industrial ministries were the main negative influence. At the party conference, Logunov had noted that there was ample evidence that ministries and departments could not or would not introduce reform. 'But this means that our higher state organs do not fully administer the processes in the national economy.'[7] Saranskikh, first secretary of the Cherepovetski party city committee, insisted that 'the course headed by the party' in the economy had been

blocked by central organs—from ministries to the Council of Ministers . . . It is surprising that, being members of the CC and deputies of the Supreme Soviet, many ministers don't speed to change something in the activity of subordinates at their bureaucratic counter, and of the methods of the leaders of the branch. In this connection, there is a necessary and reasonable suggestion on the ending of the practice of automatic selection of ministers and other leaders to leading party and state organs.[8]

By the time of his report to the Congress of People's Deputies in 1989, Gorbachev had made even clearer the distinction central to the real position of ministries in the Soviet system: transferring control over the economy to the law and to enterprises, he said, *'does not mean belittling the role of the state, if, of course, one does not confuse it with ministries'*. (Author's italics)[9] The Politburo noted at its September 1989 meeting that 'the existing situation is the result of miscalculations, red tape, and an irresponsible attitude towards this matter on the part of top officials of ministries, departments, enterprises, and permanent bodies of the USSR Council of Ministers and Gosplan'.[10]

The more vigorous tenor of anti-ministerialism was also reflected in the comments of some of the most important politicians of the *perestroyka* period. Boris Yeltsin's demands in the debate in the Supreme Soviet on Ryzhkov's economic proposals of December 1989 were first for the abolition of ministries and branch monopolists, and then for fundamental reform of Gosplan, price reform, banking

---

[7] Ibid. 261–2.   [8] Ibid. 295.

[9] *Documents and Materials Congress of People's Deputies*, 25.

[10] Singled out for criticism were V. K. Gusev of the Council of Ministers' Bureau of the Chemical and Timber Complex, V. P. Lakhtin, first vice-chairman of the Council of Ministers' Bureau for Social Development and A. Ya. Yefimov, vice-chairman of Gosplan. The Politburo instructed the Central Committee to look into holding Gusev and Lakhtin 'accountable to the Party'. Yefimov was removed from his post by the Politburo—'a strict party penalty'. Further criticism at the meeting came for the Russian Republic construction ministries for failing to play a significant role in house building. See *Pravda* (10 Sept. 1989).

reform, including an independent state bank, monetary reform, and exchange of money.[11] Nikolay Petrakov, then an adviser to Gorbachev, noted that,

it would be a mistake to think that one can make the transition to a market with the help of the present industrial-branch structure of management. The branch ministry will not create a market. For the ministry, that is suicide ... We must eliminate the ministries or, at the very least, change their functions ... We got preoccupied with cutting ministry staffs, but what is needed are specialists of a fundamentally different sort. Why maintain the old labels? In the next year or two we need to transform 2,200 enterprises in various branches—enterprises that account for 70 per cent of our fixed assets—into joint-stock companies.[12]

When asked about the changes of the past three years, Stanislav Shatalin, one of the men charged with drawing up plans for economic transition, noted that, despite attempts at reform,

the former management mechanism was strengthened (intentionally or not, I do not know). The majority of ministries were left intact, some of them were consolidated through mergers, and they were told: you are now to co-ordinate only the activities of your own sector and nothing more. But all the material resources were left at their disposal, that is, even more gigantic monopolies were created, capable of surviving without any technical progress solely by raising prices. And meanwhile we were calling on them to combat the monopolism of their own enterprises.[13]

Gennady Fil'shin, who was soon to become chief economic adviser to Yeltsin, attacked the government for raising retail prices and doing nothing about the 'ministries and departments which are impeding all the new processes, and have no intention of dying off of their own accord'.[14] Larissa Piyasheeva, who was to take charge of privatization in Moscow in 1991, argued that, 'the state (departmental, ministerial, etc.) monopoly on the production of goods, on the right to create new production facilities and on control of the domestic market totally blocks the channels for improving the economic structure and turns a price increase into a direct attack on the people's standard of living'.[15]

The greatest achievement of the politicians in the period to the XIXth Party Conference and beyond, and perhaps Gorbachev's strength as a leader, was to steer the blame for the failure of reform

[11] *Izvestiya* (17 Dec. 1989), 13–15.   [12] *Pravda* (26 April 1990), 2.
[13] *Izvestiya* (21 April 1990), 3.   [14] Ibid. (25 May 1990), 1, 5.
[15] Ibid. (19 April 1990), 3.

on to the ministries and the institutions they dominated. This in turn opened up the possibility to deepen the struggle against them by seeking to find new political institutions in which the politicians could operate more effectively. The strategy of political reform, therefore, involved bringing new democratic legitimating principles to bear, through the creation of new political institutions and the democratization of old ones, which would give added authority to the politicians in their effort to secure compliance from the industrial economic apparatus. The guiding principle of political reform, that 'being freed from economic questions, the politician and the corresponding organs of the state and party would receive the possibility to realize leadership in developing the economy',[16] could be realized only when political institutions were separated formally from industrial ones.

Party reform

The idea that separating political from economic power would increase rather than decrease the power of the top party leadership explains the puzzle about why a general secretary, who had, in formal terms at least, enormous potential power over the secretariat and branch departments of the Central Committee and the *nomenklatura* system of appointments, should choose to abolish these branch departments— as happened after the Party Conference in 1988. Why should he wish to shift power from the party to new representative institutions?[17]

In the early stages of *perestroyka* Gorbachev had sought to use these traditional implements to achieve control over the ministries, or at least had paid lip-service to them. For example, he had threatened to revive the party's right of control via the primary party organizations.

The Central Committee of the CPSU considers it necessary to raise decisively the role of party committees of ministries and departments, to raise the level of their work in the *perestroyka* of the activity of the apparatus of administration and the branch as a whole. A review of the reports of the party committees of a number of ministries by the Central Committee demonstrates that they are

[16] V. P. Shkredov, *Ekonomika i pravo* (Moscow, 1990), 156.
[17] In large measure, of course, this may have been the result of a leadership competition in which Gorbachev chose to weaken institutions which strengthened his rivals. However, this must be regarded as unlikely given the level of control over appointments which Gorbachev had achieved.

still very timid with their right of control, do not act as catalysts of the new, do not struggle with *vedomstvennost'*.[18]

The reason for this timidity was explained by the first secretary of the Kirghiz Communist Party, Masaliev, who said directly: 'It is necessary . . . to sharply define the status of the secretary [of the primary party organization], to reduce his dependence, including materially, on the economic leader.'[19]

Material dependence was not the whole story, however. As was argued in Chapter 3, one of the main difficulties which faced reformers in the party seeking to use traditional methods was the presence of large numbers of ministers in the highest decision-making bodies. In a study of membership of the Central Committee and other standing organs of the party as of February 1990, it was noted that of the 560 people serving in the party's central bodies approximately 500 were officials: ministers, department heads, first secretaries of republic central committees, etc.

Ministers and deputy ministers make up a powerful group in the Central Committee—there are ninety-four of them (including chairmen and vice-chairmen of the Councils of Ministers) . . . Many people have probably noticed that, after the XIXth Party Conference, joint resolutions of the CPSU Central Committee and the USSR Council of Ministers stopped appearing. It seemed as if there had been a separation of party and state functions. Altogether, however, top-ranking officials of the party, of key sectors of the national economy, and of such departments as the Ministry of Internal Affairs, the KGB, and the Ministry of Defence account for almost two-thirds of the Central Committee, and this means that in essence, nothing has changed.[20]

Indicating that even the most conservative of communists held similar views, Ivan Poloz'kov, who emerged as leader of the hard-line Russian section of the party in 1990, testified to the same problem at the highest level.

Current ministries by themselves are not capable of decisive reorganization of their branches. For them, this is of equal force to their liquidation. But the branch departments of the Central Committee have also proved ill-equipped to overcome this conservatism. They, in my opinion, don't try to stand up against them [ministries]. (Applause) . . . The truth today is that many party

---

[18] For party documents on *vedomstvennost'* and ministry power 1985–7, see *Uskorenie sotsial'no-ekonomicheskogo razvitiya stranu—zadacha vsey partii, vsego naroda* (Moscow, 1987), 67.   [19] S. Andreev, 'Struktura vlasti i zadachi obshchestva', 170.
[20] *Argumenty i fakty*, 5 (1990), 6.

personnel, by years oriented on technocratic methods, are not ready to work in other ways. In the party apparatus we find . . . not political commissars, but workers in industry, construction and trade. Look at the structure of the apparatus of the Central Committee: in its departments are represented not only ministries and *glavki*, but even their subdepartments. This also in many ways predefines the structure and style of work of *kray, oblast'*, and *rayon* level party committees. We fully support the suggestion to get away from the construction of the party apparatus on the branch principle.[21]

One can only wonder, however, under these circumstances, about the seriousness or effectiveness of the work of the Politburo Commission on the *perestroyka* of the organizational structures of central economic organs, ministries, and departments when it was headed by Nikolay Ryzhkov, chairman of the Council of Ministers, Lev Zaykov, in charge of overseeing the military–industrial complex, Nikolay Slyun'kov, long-time industrial official in the secretariat, and Nikolay Talyzin, until that time chairman of Gosplan.[22]

The decision in 1988 to take political reform seriously, following the decisions at the party conference,[23] put the problem faced by the *perestroyshchiki* starkly: abandoning the traditional, albeit ineffective, form of political supervision of economic power, while *simultaneously* seeking to defeat the party apparatus whose interests were tied to the ministries, meant that Gorbachev and his allies were gambling heavily on the success of alternative institutions to expand their power and authority. It is a mark of the seriousness of the problems of reform that they felt it necessary to take this step.

Government reform

In the early stages of the reform process, the political commentator Boris Bolotin had suggested that

the Council of Ministers of the USSR is being made the general headquarters of the work for the fulfilment of the economic reform . . . It is the Council of Ministers that will set the national economic priorities to be translated by the State Planning Committee, the Ministry of Finance, and the Committee for Labour and Social Questions into concrete economic norms.[24]

[21] *XIX vsesoyuznaya konferentsiya Kommunisticheskoy Partii Sovetskogo Soyuza*, 231–3.
[22] See *Izvestiya Tsk KPSS*, 1 (1989), 68–73.   [23] Ibid. 81–5.
[24] *Moscow News*, 35 (1987), 3.

Despite this, however, the Council of Ministers and its apparatus had been subject to the same cuts and structural changes discussed in connection with the ministries in the previous chapter. Of 2,560 staff positions in Gosplan, for example, 1,095 went.[25] Cuts in the State Committee on Labour and Social Questions were to reach 30 per cent.[26] Great hope was also placed in the prospects of structural reform of the Council of Ministers, especially in a reformed Administrative Department (*Upravlenie Delami*), acting as the permanent organ of the chairman and the Presidium. Stress was put on its non-departmental influences, which, according to the department head, had been prevalent in the past.

The authority of the governmental apparatus is an affair at the heart of every one of its members. This truth is not yet clear to everyone. There have been cases, when our specialists have approved the accounts of ministries and departments on such and such a project when in fact its value turned out to be two to three times higher. Such incompetence is one of the causes of imbalances in the economy.[27]

That such incompetence or ministerial impropriety should have gone undetected in the apparatus of the Council of Ministers is not surprising given that the first attestation of Council of Ministry staff had taken place only in 1987. It resulted in a relative large number of dismissals, at least formally. In the pre-attestation period alone—for reasons of health and age, as well as 'insufficient preparedness'—167 were sacked; after attestation, one in ten was reduced in responsibility, and 117 were transferred. However, data in the biographies of the members of subdepartments of the Administration Department indicate that they continued to be products of the existing economic system. Few specialists worked there without a branch background; there continued to be great difficulties in even finding other kinds of specialists. In any case, the main basis of the departments' work continued to be suggestions from ministries and departments.[28]

Considerable hopes had also been placed in the bureaux of the Council of Ministers, set up mainly in 1986 and 1987 to resolve inter-branch problems and intended to unite a number of different ministries. The claim was that the ministries would decline in importance as a result of the existence of these bodies, which were supposed to

[25] *Moskovskiye novosti* (6 Mar. 1988), 9.
[26] *Moskovskaya pravda* (2 Mar. 1988), 2.
[27] Interview with A. P. Volgin, *Pravitel'stvennyy vestnik*, 4 (1989), 6–7.   [28] Ibid.

function as co-ordinators, relieving pressure on the apparatus of the Council of Ministers from which they were originally created.[29] For example, in the earliest stages of the Council of Ministers' reform, the Politburo in 1986 formed a Bureau for Social Development to co-ordinate the social powers of ministries which were charged with implementing the social programme;[30] along with this were created the Bureau for Machine-Building, the Bureau for Fuel and Power Complex, and the Council of Ministers' State Foreign Economic Commission.[31] The process was supposedly deepened by further decisions taken in 1988 when it was announced that the Council of Ministers was to liquidate its fragmented apparatus organized on narrow branch lines and in its place form structural subdivisions on the basis of the main lines of national economic complexes, with strengthened subdivisions.[32]

As has been shown in earlier chapters, the dilemma faced by politicians seeking to improve control by strengthening the state apparatus was between simply re-creating ministries within the Council of Ministers apparatus—that is, organs whose main interests lay in operative economic management—or, where operational management was left with the ministry, allowing ministries to dominate the subsequent bargaining relations. There is evidence that the same problems applied to the reformed Council of Ministers apparatus after 1987. Ryzhkov himself opposed creating any more Council of Ministers' bureaux on the grounds that it would lead to too cumbersome a system of management in the economy.[33] As the management theorist Rapoport put it,

attempts in recent years to overcome the departmental-branch diffusion of state administration, to realise inter-branch integration even if in the framework of national economic complexes, have been shown to be ineffective. The creation of standing organs of the Council of Ministers—bureaux and state production committees—formed without destroying ministerial hierarchical systems so far represent themselves as only the superstructure to the existing pyramid. The process of administration of the national economy is subordinated all the same to the rules of line subordination. An exactly similar situation is observed in attempts to create inter-branch integration in the central economic departments.[34]

[29] See interview with G. D. Margulov, *Pravitel'stvennyy vestnik*, 21 (1989), 2–3.
[30] *Pravda* (17 Oct. 1986), 1.   [31] *Izvestiya* (6 Nov. 1986), 2.
[32] Ibid.   [33] Ibid. (12 June 1989), 2–6.
[34] V. Rapoport, 'Printsipy i napravleniya perestroyki organizatsii otraslevogo upravleniya', in *Voprosy ekonomiki*, 10 (1989), 15.

For example, the liquidation of the Ministry of Machine-Building for the Light and Food Industry and the transfer of its functions to the defence sector led to nothing but the repetition of the old structure and departmentalist character, including the preservation of its links direct to the line leaders.[35]

The domination of its decision-making by ministerial interests, then, meant that both the Council of Ministers as a whole and its apparatus headed by Ryzhkov were increasingly identified by radical reformers as a buttress of the ministries and an obstacle to the reform process and thus, its credibility was effectively undermined. Leading figures in the Council of Ministers often acted irresolutely in the face of such criticism. Anatoly Denisov pointed out that, under attack, the strategy of the Council of Ministers after 1989 was to hand decisions to the Supreme Soviet in order to avoid responsibility: for example, the Supreme Soviet had to decide to hand power over the railways to the Ministry of Transportation under emergency conditions even though the Council of Ministers had competence to act.[36] The final blow to its credibility came in response to the Ryzhkov plan of mid-1990 which was characterized by Piyasheeva as a price freeze which would 'preserve the existing levers of plan-based regulation'. For this reason, apropos the government's April proposals to increase prices, they

will have no effect whatsoever on the scale of production, on the creation of new production facilities, or on an expansion of the market . . . It is clear that [the government's] measures will most likely have the temporary effect of partially reducing demand, but, in the near future, everything will go back to the way it was before. The Ministry of Finance will announce the size of the budget deficit and a new round of inflation will begin, shifting the cost of maintaining the expensive administrative system, with all of its scientific-administrative 'planners' on to the shoulders of the citizens.[37]

As the Ryzhkov plan fell, Fyodor Burlatsky, long-time moderate reformer and member of the Supreme Soviet, called for a new cabinet, quite separate from the Council of Ministers, in which the political ministries would be divided from the economic ones, and amalgamated under the control of the Supreme Soviet.[38] This does not suggest that the Council of Ministers did not actively defend itself against those deputies who were interested in turning the Council of Ministers into

35 Ibid. 14–24.   36 *Moscow News*, 44 (1989), 9.
37 *Izvestiya* (19 Apr. 1990), 3.   38 Ibid. (28 June 1989), 1–2.

a committee of the parliament; indeed, it demanded in turn that a new law on the Council of Ministers give it legal guarantees against the new Supreme Soviet and its committees. It resolutely opposed the idea that republics should be able to override Council of Ministers' decisions—in fact, it aimed to act as arbiter among republic Council of Ministers and all-Union ministries—and it sought to retain powers over guiding economic reform and social reorientation, changes to property and the creation of a market, the conduct of social policy, and the introduction of new technology.[39]

However, from being a potential headquarters of *perestroyka*, the pursuit of economic reform and anti-ministerial policies had by late 1990 revealed the Council of Ministers as a weak, ministerially dominated institution whose permanent apparatus did not function as a reliable buttress to the power of the reforming political leadership. Indeed, as was evident in the defeat of the Shatalin–Yavlinsky '500 Days' and, of course, in the 'constitutional coup' of June 1991 and the coup of August, the Council of Ministers functioned as a centre of opposition to radical reform and to the *perestroyshchiki*.

The new parliament

Scholar then parliamentary leader, Ruslan Khasbulatov, offered the following characterization of the role of the Supreme Soviet in the pre-*perestroyka* period:

The first secretary of the *obkom* of the party flies in. And ... he goes to the ministry, to knock out some funds. Then, to the corresponding branch department of the Central Committee. Then, to Gosplan and the Ministry of Finance ... Note that to the list of addresses to which the first secretary hurried, I haven't included the [Presidium of the Supreme Soviet]. The scheme of things is: ministry—Central Committee department—Gosplan—Minfin. In this quadrumvirate, and not in the [Presidium] or the Supreme Soviet, the important socio-economic decisions were adopted. In these very places were concentrated real power, the power of the government apparatus, incomparable to the representative organs.[40]

Following the decisions of the XIXth Conference, the old Supreme Soviet was transformed from the moribund institution described above

[39] Pravitel'stvennyy vestnik, 18 (1989), 2–3.
[40] R. I. Khasbulatov, *Byurokratiya tozhe nash vrag*... (Moscow, 1989), 75.

into an active institution with the sort of legitimacy which the frustrated reformists in the political leadership calculated would build their authority. The hope that bodies of the Supreme Soviet could act as counterweights to the ministerial power was not entirely new. The XXIIIrd Party Congress had allowed standing commissions to make recommendations to the ministries. Naturally, of course, the ministries paid little attention. Subsequent legislative acts allowed commissions to give ministries instructions to review standing commission recommendations, and required them to report back in a month.[41] The significance given to this requirement, however, may be judged from the report on the appearance in spring 1987 of Pugin, Minister of the Automotive Industry, before the Supreme Soviet Joint Committee on Science and Technology. The branch was rebuked for failing to meet world standards, but the minister was not said to have shown 'undue concern'.[42]

The shift of the forum for political struggle from the Communist Party and the Council of Ministers, where the industrial apparatus dominated, to the new institutions of parliament in which the ministries were excluded from direct representation was a huge breakthrough on the road to political reform. There were still those who thought that the new legitimation strategy could be combined with ministerial power in the economy,[43] but these voices were few and far between compared to the radical anti-ministerial rhetoric frequently heard on the floor of the Congress and the Supreme Soviet. As Abalkin argued at the first Congress, however, though everyone wanted the end of ministerial *diktat*, they also wanted the guarantee of material supplies.[44]

The most trenchant comment on the relationship of anti-ministerialism to *perestroyka* and political reform came from the radical Leningrad deputy, Anatoly Denisov, after the first Congress of People's Deputies. When asked in an interview whether he agreed with the view that all power lay with the party, Denisov said, 'I have another opinion. All power in our country belongs to the sphere of material production which dictates its conditions to the party and the soviets.' He noted that the structure of government consists of three elements: material production, governmental authority, and ideology.

[41] See L. T. Krivenko, 'Postoyannye komissii i ministerstva', in *Sovetskoe gosudarstvo i pravo*, 1 (1970), 32–40.   [42] *Izvestiya* (30 Apr. 1987), 2.
[43] See K. Khubiev, 'Sobstvennost' i ekonomicheskaya vlast'', in *Planovoye khozyaystvo*, 11 (1989), 92.   [44] *Ogonek*, 41 (1989), 1–2, 25–7.

In our state, the functions of these subsystems are intermingled. It's not that the party has arrogated to itself the basic function of government, as some believe, but that material production has subordinated to itself both governmental authority (that is the soviets) and ideology (the party). Otherwise, why is it that the party is so closely involved with agriculture, the output of goods, and other questions of material production?[45]

In order to introduce order into the issue of power,

it is necessary to separate the sphere of material production from the state, by establishing in it only the functions of defence of the interests of the population by means of regulating the economy as a whole system ... I foresee the way out of the gathering crisis situation in the country in the following, that there must be a division of production from the state. For this, it is necessary to close the industrial ministries.[46]

The main impetus to parliamentary anti-ministerialism came from its work in approving or rejecting ministerial appointments. Some committees of the Supreme Soviet were themselves accused of being under ministerial domination—nineteen of the thirty-eight members of the Committee on Defence and State Security, for example, were members of the military–industrial complex, including the chairman[47] —but evidence of a new-found activism can be seen in the refusal of one committee to nominate Bogomyakov as Minister of the Petroleum and Gas Industry.[48] In the Standing Committee on Transport, Communications, and Information Science, there was opposition to Pervishyn's nomination as Minister of Communications on the grounds that with the merger of the Ministry of Communication with the Ministry of the Communications Equipment Industry his position would represent a victory for the 2.4 million production workers over the public. Other deputies worried about Pervishyn's abilities, given that he had worked in the military sector before coming into the civilian sector.[49] Discussing Gusev's appointment to head the Council of Ministers' Bureau of the Chemical and Timber Complex, Deputy Yudin attacked the bureau for having no clear-cut, constructive programme: while claiming to want to cut back on timber cutting, this was the only indicator he could claim to have on the positive side.[50] Following the scandalous situation on the railways, Konaryov was first turned down as minister, only later to be reinstated.[51] There was also

[45] *Izvestiya* (28 June 1989), 1–2.
[46] *Argumenty i fakty*, 30 (1989), 1–2.
[47] *Izvestiya* (12 June 1989), 2–3.
[48] Ibid. (23 June 1989), 1–2.
[49] Ibid. (24 June 1989), 1–2.
[50] Ibid. (30 June 1989), 1–2.
[51] *Pravda* (11 July 1989), 1.

very strong criticism of the nomination of Busygin for his record in deforestation, poor housing facilities, hundreds of settlements being left abandoned after the trees were cut down, and for literally closing the door of the ministry to criticism from workers and settlers in forestry areas.[52] Panichev was approved by the Supreme Soviet as Minister of the Machine Tool and Tool Industry, despite being left off the initial list by Ryzhkov after support from his branch personnel.

The political scientist and deputy, Ambartsumov, noted that, of proposed candidates, Polod-zade at the Ministry of Water Resources was in charge of the ecological disaster in Central Asia; Bykov, at the Ministry of the Medical and Microbiological Industry was responsible for the disastrous ecological situation at the chemical combine in Kirishi; and Chirskov at the Ministry of Building Enterprises of the Oil and Gas Industry was morally responsible for the explosion of the gas pipeline at Ufa and the environmental damage in Tyumen.[53] Polod-zade was defended by Ryzhkov, despite being opposed by committee members such as Yeltsin on Construction and Architecture for having been deputy minister for fifteen years.[54] He was removed from the list of nominations and replaced by Loginov, who has headed the RSFSR Minvodkhoz for several years. Many deputies criticized this even more strongly, arguing that the RSFSR Minvodkhoz was the worst offender. Loginov did not get the number of votes necessary to get past the committee stage.[55]

Despite the great rhetoric of the Congress of People's Deputies and the Supreme Soviet, analysis of the changes in ministerial types does not strongly suggest a fundamental transformation, and perhaps demonstrates the relative weakness of the parliament in controlling an agenda which continued to be set by the old apparatus. In the three years from 1985 to 1988, sixty heads of ministries and departments were changed, almost 70 per cent of their number. Average age was reduced to 56, all had twenty years party membership and higher education. But their backgrounds revealed a continuation in the long tradition of selecting people with branch specialism—70 per cent from technical institutes, and only 7 per cent economists and 9 per cent humanists. Ministers especially had a line-production background.[56]

The new Supreme Soviet of 1989 did little to alter this bias. If we look at the jobs new industrial ministers had immediately preceding

---

[52] *Izvestiya* (11 July 1989), 1–2.   [53] *Moscow News*, 26 (1989), 8.
[54] *Izvestiya* (18 July 1989), 1–2.   [55] Ibid. (8 Oct. 1989), 1.
[56] *Ogonek*, 31 (1988), 6–8.

their appointment: thirteen had come from the same ministry; eight were from a related ministry (bear in mind the number of mergers and abolitions); one had moved from the apparatus of the Council of Ministers (the Bureau for Energy); and one had moved from the party. Looking back into their more distant career backgrounds: seventeen had made their careers inside the industrial apparatus; five had had a mixed party–ministry background; and one had had a mixed Council of Ministers–ministry career.

The evidence does not strongly suggest, therefore, that the degree of control over appointments, the organizational type and interests of ministerial appointments, or the potential degree of influence of industrial interests were altered much as a result of the government approved by the Supreme Soviet in 1989. Ambartsumov commented on the engineering, apparatus, and defence sector bias in the new government which had more experience with administration than the economy. Why use these people, he wondered, for the purpose of creating new types of ministries, as was Ryzhkov's declared aim? The new government structure remained monopolistic.[57]

Overall, therefore, the evidence suggests that though old political institutions were reformed and new ones created in 1988–9, the net result did not lead to the emergence of a stable new autonomous and authoritative political sphere. Rather, as the ministries and their high-level supporters fought back against the challenge, representative institutions and political rhetoric simply became opposed to ministerial power, and the crisis of institutions deepened. This was most particularly evident in the development of representative institutions as forums of anti-ministerial populism, as was the case with articles such as 'How much does a minister cost?', in which the author drew attention to work by the Supreme Soviet Commission on Privileges and Benefits showing that 5 million roubles annually was spent on maintaining Cabinet *dachas*, that ministers paid only for living space not utilities, and that each automobile assigned to a minister cost 60,000 roubles.[58] One of the Commission's members, Kozyrev, reported that 'so many abuses and violations of the law and of normative documents currently in effect were found that the Commission can unequivocally report to the USSR SS that the supreme executive power in our country obeys no laws. This is where legal

---

[57] *Moscow News*, 26 (1989), 8.   [58] *Kuranty* (14 May 1991), 5.

nihilism begins.'[59] The Supreme Soviet was not to become a vehicle for filling the vacuum of legitimacy. Further institutional reform was to take place in 1990 and 1991. However, it occurred against a background of such intense economic difficulties, overt conflict of interests, and the public failure of political authority that the crisis was only exacerbated.

THE RESPONSE OF THE MINISTRIES

If there is little evidence of the new political institutions producing drastic changes in the type or background of minister or in building effective authority against industrial power, the level of anti-ministerialism did change ministerial behaviour in some ways. One ministerial response was to abandon the apolitical camouflage which had suited them so well in the past, and begin to act as overt political actors against reform.

The press had become a major critic of ministerial action.[60] In response to a hostile press, ministry press centres burgeoned, and were told to produce, in the words of one commentator,

unrestrained glorification, advertising, advertising and still more advertising ... Press centres have proliferated in the capital's ministries—they are quite literally countless. Their number is also impossible to calculate because the glorification industry is the province of employees who exist on paper as researchers, engineers, etc., but are in fact graduates of the literature institute or of journalism departments. Moreover, the glib spokesmen of these centres are now accredited in republics, territories, and provinces. Thus, in Tyumen there are window-dressing production lines in operation in nearly all chief administrations (and there are ten of them in operation) and in many all-Union production associations. High salaries have been used to lure staff journalists away from regional newspapers and ministry house-journals ... Even in Moscow they are leaving editorial boards for the notorious press-centres,

[59] *Izvestiya* (8 July 1991), 1–2.
[60] e.g. a letter from six ministers—from the gas industry, the petroleum industry, the petroleum-refining and petrochemical industry, the mineral fertilizer production, chemical industry, and the medical and microbiological industry—which objected to an earlier article criticizing a project for a huge petrochemical complex in Tyumen on the grounds that it was completely unnecessary, was in turn attacked for saying that 'everything that is being done is for the good of the country ... In the given case—as usual, by way of exception—the ministries have been allowed to begin construction without troubling themselves with any preliminary gathering and analysis.' See the debate in *Kommunist*, 2 (1989), 22–33; and ibid. 5 (1989), 75–81.

where staffs often swell to twenty. They are expediters in the service of economic management. They kept the central press in constant supply of materials which it was forced to refute. Ministry press-centre staff are given the following instructions: 'You should forestall critical remarks in the central press with an abundance of positive articles about the achievements of our ministry. Head them off! And if you can't do that, you should see to it that the critical article is countered by several positive ones.'[61]

The Central Committee examined instances of gross interference in the work of, and suppression of, criticism by the editorial boards of the newspapers *Vozdushny transport* and *Vodny transport*. Instead of supporting well-founded critical articles in the newspapers, executives of the USSR Ministry of Civil Aviation, the USSR Ministry of the Merchant Marine, and the RSFSR Ministry of Inland Shipping, together with the trade unions in these industries, 'undertook to persecute the editors of the newspapers and the journalists who had published the critical materials. In this context, far-fetched measures were used for taking illegal measures against the newspapers' editors and other employees.'[62] In 1988, the Ministry of Railways organized a campaign against public criticism, in which a worker in a ministry research institute slandered 'authors of critical articles in order to curry favour with the minister'.[63] In other ministries, spokesmen complained that they were forced to sing the praises of dubious innovations and inferior equipment; they were pressured, leaned on, given orders. By 1989, the situation had reached a stage where the *Izvestiya* reporter was not allowed in to the Ministry of Nonferrous Metallurgy. 'Not so long ago—in fact before the start of the current restructuring—one could get freely into practically any government agency with an *Izvestiya* identification.' But, as the security guard said when refusing entry, 'if you were from *Pravda* or Tass. . .'.[64]

Ministries organized at the electoral level as well. In the election of delegates from the Kievsky area of Moscow to the XXVIIIrd Party Congress—the area takes in many ministries—'the meeting took place, as is said in protocol notes, in an atmosphere of exclusive good-will and mutual understanding . . . The departmental storm of the congress is continuing . . . The worry and anxiety is called forth by the attempt to transform the upcoming forum of communists into a congress of economic leaders and generals.'[65] Evidence of the willingness of

---

[61] *Pravda* (27 Feb. 1987), 3.   [62] Ibid. (11 Feb. 1986), 1.
[63] Ibid. (11 Dec. 1988), 3.   [64] *Izvestiya* (11 Apr. 1989), 8.
[65] *Argumenty i fakty*, 16 (1990), 3.

ministry officials to intervene in party elections—which must always have occurred—comes from the case of a first secretary of a district party committee in the horrible Siberian oil town of Nefteyugansk, who found, after mounting an anti-ministerial campaign, that she had been deselected. After her name did not even appear on the ballot for elections to the city committee, the comment was that 'our parasitic departments have grown accustomed to pocket easily controlled leaders'.[66] The Ministry of the Petroleum Industry replied denying all charges, but this was countered by a senior researcher in the Western Siberian Oil and Gas Industry Research Institute, who said the ministry, and not the Communist Party or the local soviets, was the absolute master in his area.[67]

However, the political conditions created by the reforming leadership —*glasnost'*, democratization, the shift from party to parliament—and the rising public anger at the material conditions which economic reform had helped create made democratic politics and public persuasion a difficult game for industrial actors to win. The *perestroyshchiki* may have put themselves at risk by seeking a new base of authority, but at the same time it was no longer possible for the industrial apparatus to utilize the camouflage of party power as a means of resisting reform. Boris Kurashvili, then head of the Centre for Political Research at the Institute of State and Law which analysed the campaign for election to the first Congress of People's Deputies, argued that the tactics of the economic administrators had been to advance candidates drawn from industrial managers to present the case for cautious reform. The overwhelming and politically decisive success of Yeltsin in running for the Congress of People's Deputies against the director of a large Moscow car factory, however, was an indication of the dangers of electoral politics.[68]

For industrial actors, therefore, the tactics to be adopted in the new environment where anti-ministerialism was ever more prevalent among both public and politicians needed to be complex. Pursuit of their interests in the open political arena was a difficult proposition. Ministries needed to find a defensible, legitimate, and, if possible, profitable position in a hostile environment. As Pavel Bunich has argued, though in the initial period of reform ministries had tended to oppose reform measures, such as co-operatives, by 1989 and 1990

---

[66] *Moscow News*, 1 (1989), 13. There were other cases of attempted ministerial blacklisting: e.g. the first secretary of the Kogalym party committee.
[67] *Moscow News*, 23 (1989), 4.   [68]Interview with the author, May 1989.

the strategic possibilities for gain, and the fear of punishment for remaining conservative had induced many of the so-called conservative-bureaucratic apparatus into support for market-type reforms which they hoped would both increase profits and legitimacy.[69] The dilemma for the ministries lay in choosing between the two alternatives—state or economy—that they had previously managed to bridge so success-fully, and which had defined the Soviet political system. The use of the state and protection by it gave considerable power and comfort. However, if the state collapsed or was lost to hostile democratic elements, economic agents were at risk. Was it best to remain state institutions while pushing for an authoritarian polity and leave economic power to devolve on other bodies? Or should ministries become economic actors, openly reliant on their economic muscle against what would then be revealed as a clearly emasculated state?

Many commentators, in fact, experienced the same difficulty about which way the ministries should jump or be pushed. Some perceived that putting ministries on a purely economic footing was tantamount to wanting the liquidation of public administration of the economy though they considered that directive-planning, distribution, normatives, and control were necessary in the transition period. Others wanted the role of ministries redefined and transformed to something much more modest. In discussion of the role of ministries in *Pravitel'stvennyy vestnik*, for example, the head of the Frunze factory in Sumsk said that he envisaged the ministry acting as the factory's helper in foreign markets.[70] Velikhov, the scientist and adviser to Gorbachev on scientific matters, remarked that it would be

a good idea eventually to turn over the restructuring or reconstruction of the ministries themselves and their apparatuses to the very enterprises that are forming *de facto* companies ... since they have a better knowledge of the functions that they need, they could retain the necessary ties that now exist in these ministries, and at the same time they could elect the board, perhaps even the minister, and they could finance this structure.[71]

Nikolay Petrakov saw three variations for the reformation of ministries: first, liquidate them, and in their place create associations, concerns,

[69] *Literaturnaya gazeta* (5 June 1991), 6.

[70] *Pravitel'stvennyy vestnik*, 20 (1989), 3.

[71] *Izvestiya* (12 June 1989), 2–6. Beginning in 1990, the Ministry of Light Industry of the RSFSR actually claimed to have reformed itself into just such a service centre, receiving funds from the enterprises in return for the provision of services to the enterprises beneath it; the problem was that the ministry also retained its juridical powers. See 'Ministerstvo perekhodit na khozraschet', in *EKO* 4 (1989), 59–64.

corporations, operating outside higher standing bodies; secondly, preserve the ministries, but transform them into branch marketing organizations; thirdly, turn the ministries into Gosplan subsidiaries, responsible for branch development strategy.[72] Fairly sharply contrasting views of the future were evident in the opinions expressed by Gosplan and ministry officials with regard to the choice to be made. Gorshkov, from Gosplan, took the view that the new role of ministries should fully exclude 'interference in the operative-economic activity of the enterprise, including the formation of plans of production, renewing of basic funds, and technical improvement of acting production'. By contrast, Pashkov, of the Ministry of Automobile and Agricultural Machine-Building, argued that the directors of large enterprises, such as KamAZ, ZIL, and Rostsel'mash, were interested in the maintenance of strong ministries, and that the ministry should retain a wide list of central powers, including the ability to enforce a single technical policy, and responsibility for the realization of state programmes, marketing, placing state orders, realizing a rational investment policy, and securing a balance in the use of inputs and resources, as well as cadre policy.[73]

In all this discussion, however, the strategic possibilities open to ministerial actors tended to be ignored. In the new environment, ministries did not want to return to the *status quo ante*; but to think that such powerful actors could simply be transformed into branch consultancies deprived of control of resources was also wishful thinking. Turning the ministries into sub-units of Gosplan was to risk repeating the failures of 1957–64, and would merely deprive the state of Gosplan's albeit limited regulatory abilities. The irony was that, in the new circumstances, it was the first of Petrakov's alternatives which was most likely to appeal to the ministries' own interests, though transforming them into openly economic actors was also just what the reformers who had so heavily criticized them were also calling for. Ministries, in other words, sought to exploit the possibilities open to them to become concerns, corporations, associations, supporters of co-operatives, joint-stock companies, and privatized. They did so, none the less, with one eye on preserving any advantages of the old order, and to surviving if the old order was restored. As Tatyana Zaslavskaya noted, ministries were becoming concerns, but they could become ministries again if political circumstances changed.[74]

[72] See N. Ya. Petrakov, in *Pravda* (23 July 1989).
[73] 'Ministerstvo. Kakim emu byt'?', in *Planovoe khozyaystvo*, 11 (1989), 34–51.
[74] *Izvestiya* (17 Dec. 1990), 3.

NEW INDUSTRIAL ORGANIZATIONS

Concern about political pressures and difficulties in maintaining economic control comprised part of the strategic thinking of ministerial actors. But the gains to be made from entry into a market so heavily skewed in their favour as a result of their inherited power induced ministries and their allies in the Council of Ministers and party apparatus to support the huge growth in the number of quasi-autonomous, non-state economic organizations after 1989: concerns, associations, corporations, joint-stock companies, privatized enterprises, and co-operatives (see Table 6.1).

TABLE 6.1 *New industrial organization in Russia*

	1 November 1990	30 April 1991
MGOs	36	58
Concerns	73	164
Consortia	66	92
Joint-stock companies	252	1,186
Associations	842	1,790
Unions	—	101
Commercial banks	—	1,181
Exchanges	—	63

The concept of the state concern or association, for example, was typical of the duality with which ministerial officials sought to proceed. The concern was to be both an economic and administrative body, where the apparatus would enter into contractual relations with member enterprises. In a sense, it resembled the industrial combines created after 1973, except, of course, that the ministry would no longer exist. The concern was also the source, at least initially, of considerable wishful thinking. 'If we succeed in properly organizing those forms of administration, such as associations, concerns, and so on, utilizing these forms in correspondence with the ideology of socialist economic activity, then it should not be excluded that we will be successful in showing the world a decisively original method of self-organization of social production.'[75] Boris Milner, a long-standing supporter of management reform, went just as far, saying that in the

---

[75] Ibid.

Soviet Union today the concern was more the 'urgent symbol of the non-ministerial system of administration, the way out of departmental *diktat*, the widening of the economic sphere, than its direct analogue in the Western form of administration of production'.[76]

The fact was, however, that concerns—like many of the other new forms of industrial management which emerged at this time—were far from non-ministerial in practice. Though there were examples of concerns and associations emerging which were beyond ministerial subordination—Energomash, Tekhnokhim, Chasprom, and Kriogenika[77] —they were also a means for ministries to have the best of all worlds. The former Ministry of Construction Materials was reorganized into eight concerns, which reunited into a single State Association of the Industry of Construction Materials.[78] In August 1989, the government affirmed the creation of an independent state concern, Gazprom, acting on full *khozraschet*, self-financing and self-administering. Into it went all the enterprises of the gas industry. The council of the concern selected the administration, numbers, and wages of workers and expenditures on them. The concern directly interacted with the Bureau of the Council of Ministers for the Fuel and Energy Complex.[79]

In June 1990, the Council of Ministers approved a resolution in which the Ministry of Construction of Enterprises of the Oil and Gas Industry abolished itself and became a state concern, Neftegazstroy.[80] The Minister of the Chemical and Petroleum-Refining Industry 'resigned' from his job in October 1990, citing pressure from society, from greens, from local government, low pay, and loss of personnel, to move into the corporations and concerns which would emerge from the ministry.[81] Minvodkhoz, which had already become Minvodstroy, and worked without a minister for six months, was also 'abolished' in

[76] B. Milner, 'Problemy perekhoda k novym formam organizatsii upravleniya', in *Voprosy ekonomiki*, 10 (1989), 3–13.

[77] Zapol'skiy, 'Khozyaystvennye assotsiatsii—novaya forma organizatsii proizvodstva', in *Khozyaystvo i pravo*, 9 (1990), 58–66. The most frequently cited case of a non-ministerial association, the Leningrad Association of State Enterprises formed by the Leningrad City Soviet, was notable in a number of respects. First, it was not an association of exclusively Leningrad enterprises; the apparatus was in Leningrad. Second, though the enterprises entering it retained their economic independence *vis-à-vis* the association, many of them remained under ministerial subordination, though there were hopes that the association might act as a buffer against ministerial power. See A. Vaksyan, 'Assotsiatsiya: umnozhenie sil', ibid. 1 (1990), 58–65.

[78] *Pravitel'stvennyy vestnik*, 24 (1989), 2.

[79] A. Omel'chenko, 'K effektivnomu upravleniyu', in *Khozyaystvo i pravo*, 10 (1989), 3–12.   [80] *Pravitel'stvennyy vestnik*, 24 (1990), 3.

[81] *Izvestiya* (1 Oct. 1990), 2.

June 1990, to be transformed into a state concern for water industry construction. The initiative for the abolition of the Ministry of the Production of Mineral Fertilizers came from the ministry itself, which turned itself into the State Agro-Chemical Association, Agrokhim, supposedly to deal with the growing democratization and independence of enterprises.[82] Many of its constituents came out of the abolished Gosagroprom, and included former ministry officials in its apparatus.[83] One of the most obvious cases of ministries transforming themselves into concerns to avoid political pressure—fear of cuts in the number of ministries by the Ukrainian government—and improve profits can be seen in the Ukrainian Ministry of Local Production. Contrary to claims about the voluntary and democratic nature of the new management structure, the ministry spent some time organizing the enterprise directors; only those who agreed were invited to the founding meeting in Kiev. The ministry did, however, feel some discomfort. The minister was not elected to the concern's presidency; the former first deputy minister got the job. However, as the chairman of the Ukrainian Council of Ministers, Fokin, put it, the concern is the ministry as chameleon.[84]

Because of these ministerial manœuvrings, many commentators, including Rapoport and Milner, expressed doubts about the concern from an early stage. Rapoport recognized that in 'creating concerns and associations, we are obliged to place in them certain command-administrative duties, that significantly weaken the effectiveness of their democratic interrelations and may transform these forms into analogs of the ministry'. For this reason, 'there is a fully justified fear, that the fulfilment of definite functions of state administration, by subjects having their own economic interests, is fraught with even more deformations than went on in the traditional *vedomstvennyy*-bureaucratism'.[85] In fact, for many people concerned about creating corporate industrial structures, the worry was that changing ministries into concerns or associations might make industrial actors even *more* powerful. Boris Milner argued that the 'weakening and liquidation of the monopolism of ministries and central economic departments with growing force will give rise to monopolism of large corporations,

[82] *Pravitel'stvennyy vestnik*, 17 (1989), 8.   [83] Ibid. 21 (1989), 5.

[84] *Ekonomika i zhizn'*, 6 (1991).

[85] Rapoport, 'Printsipy i napravleniya perestroyki organizatsii otraslevogo upravleniya', 14–24.

concerns, and other associations, differentiated by their great scale of production'.[86] The economists Krylova and Lykova argued that

the lawful process of forming structures, organically leading to a multi-structured economy with developed market connections, frequently in practice turns out to be the safeguarding of previous levers of monopoly power [*vlast'*] under the aegis of new organizational forms. An especially propitious [*blagopriyatnyy*] environment for the next twist in the strengthening of monopolism is the forming, on the basis of whole branches of production, of concerns like Gazprom, Agrokhim, etc. Enterprises, risking being cut off from channels of securing material-technical resources, were voluntarily press-ganged [*dobrovol'no-prinuditel'no*] into the composition of such combines. Their activity within the framework of the new structures was regulated, as a rule, with the help of traditional ministerial attributes (voluntaristic redistribution of the incomes of members of the association, price *diktat*, artificial priorities in the supply of resources, and sale of output and so on).[87]

Ministries were being transformed into concerns without the existence of proper legal regulations.[88] Leonid Abalkin's State Commission on Economic Reform in October 1989 had passed recommendations on the formation of concerns and associations, but these were considered to contain serious flaws. For one thing, they were only recommendations: and they relied on a traditional approach by sharply defining the internal structure of the new concerns, while ignoring the most important fact—that they must not be ministerial structures.[89] Despite the paper change, for example, concerns retained the right to issue subdepartmental acts of an administrative–directive character.[90] Gazprom, for example, like the old ministry has responsibility for gas supply, and used state orders to achieve it. Many enterprises had even less juridical independence than previously; they could not leave the concern, had to fulfil their given plan, and were subjected to central redistribution of profits. The concern Elektromontazh of Minmontazhspetsstroi, for example, was created by the ministry; and

[86] Milner, 'Problemy perekhoda k novym formam organizatsii upravleniya', 3–13. An interesting example of anti-monopoly policy is evident in the case of the state concern in the non-ferrous metals sector, Noril'sk Nikel', which was to have its monopolistic tendencies controlled by supervision of its acquisition of shares in other similar factories monitored by Gosplan. See *Pravitel'stvennyy vestnik*, 24 (1989), 2.

[87] N. Krylova and L. Lykova, 'Formy monopolizma v sovetskoy ekonomike', in *Voprosy ekonomiki*, 6 (1990) 46–53.

[88] Omel'chenko, 'K effektivnomu upravleniyu', 3–12.

[89] L. Bondar' and M. Bokareva, 'Kontsern po-ministerski', in *Khozyaystvo i pravo*, 4 (1990), 23–31.

[90] *Zakon, stimuly, ekonomika* (Moscow, 1988), 98–100.

though it was supposedly a voluntary association, the concern was the fund holder.[91] 'In essence, this reformation is not a step forward to the market economy but back to the command system. If in the past the ministry in practice acted like a single complex (in planning and supply) but formally recognized the independence of the enterprise, then now in Gazprom the idea of the command economy received its final incarnation.'[92] The same held for Agrokhim, where the very organizational structure of the old ministry was retained; the former minister, in this case, chaired the meeting of concern members.

Ministerial personnel, however, were quick to seize on the advantages of the new management structures. Officials must also have enjoyed being put on currency self-financing, given that their wages were now paid out of the concern's budget.[93] An official in the State Commission for Economic Reform claimed that Gazprom actually worked better because of high wages to management.[94] Others, however, argued that

the only innovation is that members of the apparatus received solid bonuses to their wages and were freed from fear of job cuts, while maintaining the appearance of democratic and voluntary procedures ... If in the past the ministry, being a superstructural administrative organ of state administration, was still in some measure accountable for the public interest, the interests of the consumer, then in becoming an executive *khozraschet* branch complex, containing the enterprises of the sector, it objectively will be the supporter only of producer interests.[95]

Or, as the head of an administration of Minelektronprom candidly said: 'What changes in principle? Nothing. But then, the ministry has more rights. The Ministry of Finance will not regulate its staff size. The enterprise will pay for the apparatus.'[96]

In many ways, a similar perspective emerges from the process of leasing, and forming joint-stock companies. Ministerial personnel had their *de facto* property rights over state enterprises recognized both in

[91] O. Gerchikov, 'Kontsern—Ob"edinenie dobrovol'noe', in *Khozyaystvo i pravo*, 4 (1991), 33–7.   [92] Bondar' and Bokareva, 'Kontsern po-ministerski'.
[93] *Pravitel'stvennyy vestnik*, 24 (1990), 3.
[94] Meeting with Pyotr Makarovich Katsura, first deputy chairman of the Commission for Economic Reform of the Cabinet of Ministers, Moscow, Apr. 1991.
[95] Ibid.   [96] Ibid.

their right to determine the value of leased property,[97] and in the need to bribe ministry officials to secure deeds and titles.[98] Clearly, as has been pointed out, with the collapse of centralized supplies—though supply considerations and ongoing state orders were still most frequently cited by managers as a reason for staying in concerns and ministerial networks—and the political fragmentation created by the August coup, ministries encountered difficulties in retaining control over their 'property', but even the doubters concede that ministerial power was and remains highly significant in the privatization process.[99]

Government acts allowing the formation of joint-stock companies came into force in June 1990, with one of the first decisions being taken in connection with the KamAz factory. However, as Melikyan, deputy head of the general department of Council of Ministers' Commission on Economic Reform, said:

The ministry does, in fact, receive the controlling interest for the time being, and along with it the right to impose its will to an even greater extent than before. The ministries saw this as a way of prolonging their existence. In order to avoid that situation, the following variant was adopted for KamAz: of the 51 per cent of the vote exercised by the ministry at stockholders' meetings, half are being delegated to the labour collective.

Despite this, in practice the ministry held more than 51 per cent of the stock.[100] Specialists also poured cold water on hopes that joint-

---

[97] See I. Filatotchev, T. Buck, and M. Wright, 'Privatisation and Buy-outs in the USSR', in *Soviet Studies*, 2 (1992). They cite a case in which the ministry was able to confiscate leaseholders' profits by increasing the leasing charge and then multiplying the asset charge by three. Ministries themselves sought to promote leaseholding and, for the same reason, some co-operatives, as a means of cashing in on the *arbitrazh* possibilities of running goods valued at state prices through leaseholding or co-operative enterprises which may then sell the goods at free prices. See *Moscow News*, 8–9 (1990), 19. After Aug. 1990, formal control on deciding the values of rented property was delegated to the State Property Fund. In practice, however, it delegated its powers to branch organs. Branches continued to have wide limits on the types of leased property permitted. See Yu. Khachaturov and A. Sheblyakov, 'Arenda: stanovlenie prodolzhaetsya', in *Khozyaystvo i pravo*, 3 (1991). 28–35.

[98] A. Shleifer and R. Vishny, 'Privatisation in Russia: First Steps', paper presented at Conference of Transition in Eastern Europe (Cambridge, Mass., Feb. 1992). The authors point out, however, that not only were ministry officials being bribed by managers to sanction privatization, but workers may have been bribed by both, in the form of higher wages, to consent to privatization taking place.

[99] S. Johnson and H. Kroll, 'Managerial Strategies for Spontaneous Privatisation', in *Soviet Economy*, 4 (1991), 281–316. The authors concede that their findings may have been affected both by the fact that they did not interview ministerial officials and by ministerial secrecy.   [100] *Izvestiya* (29 June 1990), 4.

stock companies would improve economic efficiency and foster non-departmental industry. One of the biggest problems with the development of joint-stock companies was the absence of any connection between the creation of joint-stock companies and an anti-monopoly policy. By turning themselves into concerns and state joint-stock companies ministries simply strengthened their monopoly position. At the same time, as the administrative lawyer Alekhin pointed out, party government control over them was entirely lost. 'As a result ministries, covered by a "fig-leaf" of stock certificates, are becoming even more powerful than before.'[101]

There were many economic dilemmas in pursuing anti-ministerial policies. The various efforts to find industrial structures wholly or partly outside the ministerial system led to a great welter of organizational forms: inter-branch combines (MGOs), scientific–technical complexes (MNTKs), enterprises and combines with participation of foreign enterprises, enterprises operating with the help of worker funding, territorial inter-branch combines, associations (*assotsiatsii*), inculcation (*vnedrencheskie*) organizations, consultancies, new banks, co-operatives, joint-stock companies, all-round (*vsevozmozhnye assotsiatsii*) associations, inter-branch state combines (MGOs), voluntary associations in agro-consortia.[102] Continuous organizational upheaval had disrupted ties and corrupted information networks. As one commentator put it, 'a simplified approach to the *perestroyka* of organizational structure and an unjustified forcing of action in this sphere may lead to costs significantly greater than the savings from cutting the numbers in the apparatus. Economic chaos and group interests will be strengthened when administrative levers are beaten off but the economic methods don't work.'[103]

There were also a number of exogenous economic pressures leading to the collapse of the command economy: Chernobyl, the Armenian earthquake, the falling price of oil, the collapse of regimes and trade relations in eastern Europe, the disruptions to supplies and deliveries resulting from separatist pressures inside the country. Ideological collapse also played a role; as Pavel Bunich put it, there had been economic reform only in the destructive sense of the word. 'We

[101] *Ekonomika i zhizn'*, 19 (1991).

[102] See L. Bondor', 'General' nye skhemy upravleniya: protivorerchiya i tendentsii', in *Khozyaystvo i pravo*, 12 (1989), 8.

[103] D. Levchuk, 'Ministerstvo v zerkale ekonomicheskikh metodov upravleniya', in *Khozyaystvo i pravo*, 5 (1989), 3–12.

ideologically destroyed the command economy. We have smashed it, spat on it. Removed its authority. And in such a way, we lost the whip. Into the space has come anarchy, disorder, ill-discipline.'[104] But the political leadership's biggest problem lay in the fact that anti-ministerialism itself produced an economic crisis, partly the result of the disruption caused by greater local independence, and partly the result of greater independence and power by ministries transforming themselves into corporate economic agents.

The problem politicians faced was in attacking ministries in a ministerial environment. On the one hand, this meant that politicians started off from a base of minimal authority with a population which, as Chapter 4 has shown, was influenced not by a belief in the legitimacy of its rulers' claims but by the manner in which ministerial power structured its interests. Society was extremely hard to move into action as a result. On the other hand, society had every reason to take up strongly anti-ministerial attitudes; the dilemma that faced the politicians with little authority was how to tap these interests without harming themselves. Moreover, anti-ministerial policies had short-term negative consequences, especially in the economy, while social activity, taking place against a background of economic crisis, tended to be organized around cleavages that the politicians could not choose or effectively control. The result, therefore, of anti-ministerial politics was political failure, the atomization of state and civil society, and the strengthening of social relations based not on authority but on economic interests.

THE RESPONSE OF SOCIETY

A good account of the social strategy of the ministerial system is provided by the sociologists Shkaratan and Kudyukin and the lawyer Permyakov in their response to the demand by the United Workers' Front for the reintroduction of an enterprise-based electoral system.

A maximum of attention needs to be devoted to the defence of working people's interests—we don't dispute that—but as citizens, not as members of specific labour collectives. It isn't a question of where deputies work but of their not being elected from enterprises and not being dependent on them. The problem of independence is by no means imaginary, since in our country

[104] *Ogonek*, 18 (1990), 1–2.

an employee, in essence, belongs entirely to his enterprise. He belongs to public organizations set up according to a production-based principle. The provision of housing by the enterprise, combined with the internal passport system and the residence permit, tie a person to his enterprise almost inseparably. The kindergarten, the Young Pioneer camp, special orders for foodstuffs, and scarce manufactured goods—they all come from the enterprise. The entire life (from day care to the grave) of the overwhelming majority of residents of cities, towns, and workers' settlements depends on where and for whom they work. And while, in territorial elections, they may use their secret ballot to support a person who has dared to put forth an acceptable programme and has managed to get nominated, they will be in a completely different situation when voting in their own enterprise . . . What is needed is in fact the depoliticization and deideologization of production and economic life in general.[105]

The social strategy of *perestroyka*, therefore, was strongly related to finding and establishing anti-ministerial forms of social organization, particularly by broadening market distribution principles and creating the concept of citizenship. Leonid Abalkin, for example, made an explicit linkage between the market and freedom, and moved from there to an attack on the limitations of not only élite but ordinary distribution through the factories which arose from the absence of market relations, and which was made attractive by the existence of deficits to all social groups.[106] Aleksandr Maksimovich Yakovlev of the Institute of State and Law, in his description of the qualities of the legal-based state or *pravovoe gosudarstvo*, made clear the links between anti-ministerialism in the political sphere, on the one hand, and the creation of markets and citizenship in the social sphere, on the other. Until people can enter into market relations to buy what they want, he argued, they will not have a feeling of economic dignity which is the basis of all dignity.

If there is no 'Ministry of Consumer Services', if we may be partners of equal right with the shoemaker, interested in one another, then this is a legal structure, we are led by supply, demand, and the law . . . If real power, all the levers of the economy are with the ministry, it is not understandable how we may realize in practice the slogan 'All power to the soviets'. The ministries have ignored and will ignore the demands of the soviets . . . Of course, the old truth is that the question of power is resolved in the sphere of the economy. Therefore, in order for ownership decisively to be transferred to the soviets,

---

[105] *Izvestiya* (25 Oct. 1989), 3.
[106] Interview with L. I. Abalkin, *Ogonek*, 13 (1989), 6–7, 18–20.

it is necessary, first that there be reform of the system of soviets, and second, I repeat, it is necessary to transfer power from the ministries to the producers. But the producer, that is the people, and it will, through its representatives, realise power in the soviets. These two things, in essence, are the singular road to the *pravovoe gosudarstvo*.[107]

So much, as it were, for the theory. The difficulty with the practice was that it occurred in precisely the context that the theory wished to replace, the context of ministry control. What emerged socially, as a result, was not a stable structure of autonomous horizontal, market-based ties among free and equal citizens under the rule of law; on the contrary, where there was not passivity, anti-ministerialism produced a definite tendency towards social and political anarchy.

Sometimes, changes in social policy failed because of direct ministry power; environmental policy is a good example. In the summer of 1987 the Central Committee and the Council of Ministers adopted a resolution on the design of a long-term state programme for the defence of the environment and the rational use of natural resources. However, the design of the future programme was drawn from suggestions made by the interested ministries. The result was a more or less useless programme 'On the radical restructuring of affairs of defence of nature in the country', where the very same ministries were given the responsibility for fulfilment. Once again, *vedomstvennost'* seems to be the explanation, and though a decision was then taken to create a State Committee for Nature, it was probably bound hand and foot to departmental indicators worked out in the earlier programme.[108]

Despite decisions not to start on the Siberian river diversion scheme, for example, the Russian Republic Ministry of Land Reclamation and Water Resources moved equipment and men, and built a settlement anyway at one of the main sites at the Volga–Chograi canal. Its tactics, in response to the academic commission which had been formed to investigate the situation, was simply to create a commission of its own, and promise to meet any environmental objections, including the impossible ones. The implicit threat behind the ministry's decision to go ahead with the project must surely have been the work

---

[107] *Ogonek*, 43 (1988) 14–16, 29–30.
[108] A. Yablokov, 'Ekologicheskoe nevezhestvo i ekologicheskiy avantyurizm. Zavaly na puti perestroyki', in *Inogo ne dano* (Moscow, 1988), 250–1. See also, on the departmentalism of the 1988 Act, M. Lemeshev, 'Ekonomicheskie interesy i sotsial'noe prirodopol'zovanie', in *Inogo ne dano* (Moscow, 1988), 264–6.

and people already invested in 'the project of the century'.[109] The power of the ministries to force down their supervisors is evident in the fact that 'a reduction by one-third in capital investment in only the water resource industry would release in all the interrelated branches 500,000 workers'.[110] 'So the Danube–Dnepr and the Volga–Chograi projects have been halted? No problem. We'll speed up construction of the Southern Omsk irrigation system and the Ob–Chany canal in Novosibirsk Province.' The first had a price-tag of 3.8 billion roubles, with a time-frame for completion of construction of thirty-five years. 'This means that there simply won't be any [officials] left in their posts by the time it becomes possible to ask "what have you done?"'! And this question will inevitably arise, since the project is being carried out on soil that, according to the conclusions of authoritative specialists, is simply unsuitable for irrigation.'[111]

As Chapter 4 has shown, although society may have been structured by the ministries, this did not mean that it lacked reasons for being anti-ministerial. None the less, social anti-ministerialism was slow to materialize, because of a continued belief that however bad ministerial lines of distribution were, they remained the most powerful and, all things considered, the best. A poll concerned with lines of distribution, for example, far from favouring marketization suggested that over half—50.7 per cent—favoured the introduction of rationing. When asked which form of consumption they found most convenient, the largest proportion favoured some form of work-distribution.[112]

Certainly there were some social developments which slotted into the mainstream of the *perestroyka* social strategy. In 1988, for example,

[109] *Izvestiya* (29 Aug. 1988), 2.

[110] I. A. Glebov and V. G. Marakhov (gen. eds.), *Novyy sotsial'nyy mekhanizm* (Moscow, 1990, 192. Similar threats were forthcoming to those whose opposition to nuclear power plants and construction of hydro projects led them to call the Ministry of Power and Electrification criminal: 'What will happen to the country in five or ten years if we don't come up with those 120 million kW? We'll be able to cross it off the list of the world's developed countries . . . Do we know what we're doing? The sober realization will come in the first cold winter, and this realization will be harsh and too late. Power plants can be shut down quickly, but it takes 10–15 years of tremendous work to build them' (*Pravda* (23 Aug. 1989), 1). Given these threats, is it any wonder that people blame ministry sabotage for all kinds of shortages?

[111] *Izvestiya* (7 Feb. 1990), 3.

[112] *Ogonek*, 5 (1990), 1. The sociologist Tat'yana Zaslavskaya points out, on the basis of materials gathered in her Centre for the Study of Public Opinion, that of those who favoured the introduction of rationing, 29% were unemployed, and had no access to departmental distribution, and the remainder were low-paid workers in small towns which received poor supplies. See *Moscow News*, 11 (1990), 10.

the Leningrad Consumer's Association was formed, citing as its *raison d'être*:

the creation of counter-weights to the *diktat* of the producers in the shape of united consumers. Emerging in the quality of alternative forces to departmental monopolism, they are the bearers of democratization, such that they are immediately interested in the growth of the economic functions of the soviets, the transformation of them into organs of popular power . . . Votes in the elections are votes for consumers. It is important that they were given to those who place their interests above the interests of departments.[113]

In 1989, the Twentieth-Century Association was formed with an avowedly anti-ministerial aim to support projects such as conversion of the military sector outside ministerial boundaries. It claimed members in dozens of Moscow enterprises and co-operatives.[114]

The effect of political reform in an economic crisis, however, was that social activity took place beyond politically controllable limits. The very reform measures which the leadership had adopted against the ministries, in other words, either worked *for* the ministries or *against* both ministries and politicians—although, as has been shown above, ministries and their officials may have found it easier to hide from ultimate social judgement. When economic crisis came as a result of the anti-ministerial strategy of the political leadership, and ministry interests could no longer structure social behaviour, social unrest and fragmentation erupted, with each unit pursuing its own interests—as it always had of course—but now in ways far from conducive or acceptable to the *perestroyshchik* politicians.

For Rapoport, the miners' strike of 1989 was a key breakthrough, where action was taken 'to defend the interests of workers from departmental and localist tyranny', and when decisive differences between the state, the ministries, and the workers emerged.[115] The trouble in Donetsk started with the rumour that its output was too expensive and that cheaper coal from Kuznetsk would be imported into the Ukraine. Then, in late April, some mines were closed, with the first deputy minister confirming that future closures would occur, especially among the twenty-one older mines in the province. An additional large category of mines had an uncertain future in the

[113] Glebov and Marakhov (gen. eds.), *Novyy sotsial'nyy mekhanizm*, 191.

[114] *Moscow News*, 48 (1989), 8.

[115] Rapoport, 'Printsipy i napravleniya perestroyki organizatsii otraslevogo upravleniya', 15.

ministry's plans. However, the division of mines into profitable and investable-in, was not discussed at all at the local level, but hatched entirely in the ministry.[116] At the Supreme Soviet to discuss the way out, Gorbachev noted that it was clear that the reason for the strike was that the ministry had continued to handle all questions, and refused to allow the law on the enterprise to be effective.[117] The fact that the industry was subsidized to the tune of 5.4 billion roubles in 1988 had done nothing for branch social policy or productivity. The 'excessively inflated staffs of the managerial apparatus' from ministry to *glavki* were also blamed. Occupational health had declined. The ministry cheated workers on the output.[118]

Similar problems were evident in the oilfields when, after the failure of the ministry to ensure supplies, strike action was threatened. 'Our main wealth is in oil and gas. In order to successfully resist departmental *diktat*, we are setting up oil and gas production enterprises as alternatives to the Ministry of the Petroleum and Gas Industry and the gas concern, so as to conduct an anti-monopoly policy not just in words but in deeds.'[119] A letter to the Council of Ministers and the All-Union Central Council of Trade Unions (AUCCTU) from oilfield workers threatening strike action in early 1990 had demanded proper social spending, a state order which would provide stocks and materials including food and manufactured goods, a proper brick allotment, the lowering or freezing at 1986 prices of the cost of engineering products, and the establishment of a new regional wage coefficient. Alternately, the government could choose to leave 10–15 per cent of oil at the workers' disposal for sale at home and abroad. This 'invitation to dialogue', however, was ignored; the minister, Filiminov, called the letter a 'provocation'. In a clear sign of the complex and interrelated character of the crisis, it was noted that the big problem in backing orders with resources had been the failure of deliveries of parts from Azerbaidjan—only 10–15 per cent of what they

---

[116] *Pravda* (8 July 1989), 2.

[117] Ibid (25 July 1989), 1–2. One deputy, Kirilov, a senior researcher at Voronezh polytechnic, responded by saying that the strike was a response to the dissatisfaction at the Congress of People's Deputies, and to the inadequate procedures for appointing deputies.

[118] *Izvestiya* (27 July 1989), 2. A year after the strike, there was evidence that little had improved. Certainly, the economic independence promised the mines and a new wholesale price for coal were not adopted. The life expectancy of the average Soviet miner was 49; 1,000 miners per year died on the job (*Literaturnaya gazeta*, 20 (1990), 13.

[119] *Izvestiya* (20 Mar. 1990), 3.

should have been. One way out of the crisis, to cut the level of the
state order and leave a greater proportion with the oil workers
themselves, however, was effectively blocked by the ministry which
insisted on raising the order.[120]

A range of fragmenting forces were now evident, as society in crisis
fell back upon the most basic units of economic control and advantage.
The video riots in Yaroslav are a (typically Soviet) case in point. After
Panasonic video recorders were delivered to the local store for
consignment to a labour collective which had raised the money to
import them from residual earnings on export orders, local citizens
(was this what the social strategists of *perestroyka* had in mind?), not
employed at the enterprise, demanded to see proof that the video
recorders were, in fact, the rightful possessions of the labour collective.
Three days of picketing followed, then a march on the local Communist Party and soviet headquarters. When, after proof was forthcoming, the management of the store delayed putting the goods on
sale, anxious consumers staged a hunger strike which in the end
produced the desired result. 'The next morning, the men and women
who had spent five sleepless nights defending their consumer rights
carried away their prized new Panasonics.' But, 'the effect is to divide
the city into two groups of citizens: those who have access to scarce
consumer goods and those who don't.'[121]

THE RISE OF THE REPUBLICS

Region and nationality, however, were the main organizational sources
of unrest, and for two reasons already discussed in Chapter 4. First,
ministerial power was, perhaps, most deeply felt in contradiction to
regional and national interests. Ministry interests dominated over
regional development and ethnic sensibilities, and reduced local and
republican government to the role of bystander. The motivation of
territorial actors to anti-ministerialism must have been considerable.
Secondly, territorial social organization, though weak in comparison
to all-Union, was none the less the single strongest alternative source
of institutionalizing social interests. Part of what it was to be a Soviet
citizen, as the holder of an internal passport, was defined in ethnic

[120] *Moscow News*, 13 (1990), 8–9.
[121] *Sovetskaya Rossiya* (7 Apr. 1990), 2.

terms; and many aspects of distribution were organized on this basis. Indeed, it is important that in comparison to other social cleavages and identifications, typical of Western industrial countries—class, occupation, party—which were highly underdeveloped in the Soviet context precisely because sector and the Communist Party stood as proxy for them, territorial and ethnic organization was always relatively strong. When ministerial organization was attacked and weakened, therefore, territorial and ethnic identifications were the first, and in many ways, the only foci for social action.

The relationship between anti-ministerialism, anti-Partyism and strong regional and national sentiment was evident even inside the Communist Party itself. The party's draft nationalities programme recognized the importance of ministries to national underdevelopment.

Many acute problems of the present day have been engendered by contradictions in industrial and economic development itself and disregard for its social and ecological consequences. Extensive damage to the general condition of national groups was inflicted by the predominance of the branch principle of management and the related departmentalism, as a result of which national conditions and traditions, ecological requirements, and the interests of the comprehensive development of areas were not always taken into account. Over a long period of time, republic, territory, and province agencies themselves pursued a line aimed at an unbalanced development of industrial potential.[122]

At the debate on the new nationalities bill at the Central Committee in September 1989, Khabibullin, first secretary from Bashkiria, attacked the party for failing to make any breakthrough; the injustices in the current Union, he said, arose because 97 per cent of industry was in Union or Union–republic subordination, with only 3 per cent locally controlled, though the latter accounted for almost 90 per cent of the local budget. Sokolov, the Belorussian first secretary, despite noting that republics had responsibilities inside the Union and that secession should be permitted only if it harmed no one else's interests, none the less thought that moves to increase republic autonomy might be defeated: 'After all, it is not ruled out that the centre in the form of ministries and departments, can determine principles that would turn the republics' rights into an empty formality.' Nazarbayev, then first secretary of Kazakhstan, said: 'The rigid centralization of management and the all-powerful *diktat* of central ministries and departments have turned our union essentially into a unitary state . . .

[122] *Izvestiya* (23 Jan. 1990), 3 and *Pravda* (24 Jan. 1990), 8.

Millions of hectares in Kazakhstan have been kept out of economic use by military departments alone.' The other side of the picture was given by Shatalin. 'We have created a totally abnormal *nomenklatura* economy: enterprises under Union jurisdiction, Union–republic jurisdiction, republic jurisdiction, and so on. Today, all the republics are bothered by their enterprises under Union jurisdiction. All right, let's turn them over to the republics. What will change? Not a thing! All that will happen is that they will have new bosses.'[123]

Where local and regional soviets functioned more effectively, however, they tended to oppose the centre, especially because of the economic crisis. The Lithuanian Council of Ministers decided to limit the export of goods from the republic beyond the limit of state orders.[124] At the end of 1988, articles began to appear opposing the shipment of scarce goods from one republic to another; for example, the shipment of foodstuffs from Latvia, with demands for the Council of Ministers of the republic to stop it. There were also demands for cards allowing rationed goods to nationals only.[125] The leader of the Dushanbe City Party Committee worried about water wars in the event that control over resources went to the regions; he concluded by agreeing with Masol, then chairman of the Council of Ministers of the Ukraine, that departmental *diktat* should not be replaced by geographical.[126] In February 1990, the Kirgizian Council of Ministers banned the export of consumer goods, even those that were not made there. In early March, the Kazakh Supreme Soviet prohibited the export of goods over the production of state orders. Responding to these developments in April, the new head of the Moscow city soviet, Gavriil Popov, argued in his inaugural address that the main question was how a gigantic city like Moscow was to manage the transition to a market economy:

After all, it's perfectly obvious that all the city's ties that were formed in the past will be unable to function in the new system. Recently Uzbekistan decided to halt exports of scarce goods to points outside the republic. Other independent soviets that crop up in various parts of the country may begin to act in the same spirit. And given that, we must immediately think about what Moscow can offer the country in exchange for what its residents need.[127]

[123] *Izvestiya* (21 Apr. 1990), 3.   [124] *Pravitel'stvennyy vestnik*, 13 (1990), 1.
[125] *Pravda* (4 Nov. 1988), 3.   [126] *Izvestiya* (16 Dec. 1989), 11–15.
[127] *Sovetskaya Rossiya* (7 Apr. 1990), 2. He added: 'There is yet another problem. For the whole country, the elimination of many industrial ministries will be a good thing. The whole country will begin breathing freely when they are eliminated in the course

The case of the closure of the Sloka Pulp and Paper Mill in Latvia was an interesting mixture of ecology, anti-ministerialism, and republic–centre conflict. The affair began with the continuous picketing of the mill on the grounds of its pollution, which was often explained as resulting from the *diktat* of union ministries. Some demonstrators insisted that the issue was 'whether power will be in the hands of the people or of the departments. Real power still belongs to the departments, who have in their hands the means of production, money, etc.' Fragmentation and conflict, however, were not just two-sided. Difficulties then arose between the legislative branch in the shape of the republican Supreme Soviet and the Jurmala city soviet on the one hand, and the executive and administrative branches of government in the republican and Union governments, and the ministries on the other. The former called for the mill to be closed on 1 January 1990. *Pravda* commented that power to the soviets in this case was just a new form of *diktat*. Stopping production, however, had enormous implications for other regions, given that the enterprise was the sole producer of many products. Many lay-offs were threatened, and the blame for resulting shortages was directed against the local party and Union press. Threatened consumers, especially other industries in other republics, responded by refusing to send materials; Lithuania refused to deliver cardboard, Moldavia to deliver consumer goods, and the Ukraine to deliver metallurgy products. There were threats recognized by the republic's prime minister, Gorbunov, to the sanitary condition of food. The republican Council of Ministers, perhaps because of this, was less enthusiastic about the closure, particularly after it was made clear, by Ryzhkov and Gusev, the chairman and deputy chairman of the Council of Ministers, among others, that no other parts of the country would supply the shortfall in pulp. Swedish barter terms could not be met. The creation of a world-standard pulp mill to ecological standards would take years and be extremely costly.[128]

Republican and regional authorities, in conditions of an economic crisis caused by the collapse of the ministerial economy, continued to press for local control of economic resources. The most immediate

of several months. But for Moscow, this means hundreds of thousands of people for whom new jobs will have to be found.' Given his declared aim of introducing markets, it is ironic that one of Popov's immediate acts as mayor of Moscow was to introduce rationing on a territorial basis.

[128] *Izvestiya* (23 Jan. 1990), 3 and *Pravda* (24 Jan. 1990), 8.

crisis was felt in the Union budget. Enterprises handed their tax bills to republican governments first, and, with the declarations of sovereignty in 1990, republics stopped paying budget transfers to Union programmes. By 1991, Yeltsin had stopped 50 billion of the 70 billion roubles the RSFSR was due to hand to central authorities. By July 1991, there had emerged a crisis in all three areas of federal fiscal policy: in the payment of republican contributions to Union programmes which were at a 40 per cent level; in the failure to hand over locally collected federal taxes; and in non-payment into the specially formed federal stabilization fund designed to solve the budgetary crisis.[129] The issue of republican support for federal budgets, despite progress on the Union treaty before the August coup, was never really solved.

The second area of regional and republican pressure, however, was over ministry property itself. In May 1991, for example, the Ukraine announced that 100 per cent of military and converted industry would be under its control by January 1992—it had 13 per cent of all such industry in the Soviet Union. Then, in June 1991, the Ukrainian prime minister, Fokin, announced that the Ukraine was taking all Union enterprises on its territory under its control because Union ministries without waiting for the Union treaty had decided to start creating joint-stock companies as a way of avoiding transferring subordination of enterprises through the state.[130] Following this, Kirgizia asserted its authority over all Union enterprises, while the pragmatic Nazerbayev signed a deal with ministries of coal, metallurgy, and the radio industry to transfer enterprises to Kazakh jurisdiction.

If *perestroyka* had started as an effort by weak politicians to build authority against powerful economic agents who controlled the state, the cost of battle had been an economic crisis in which authority collapsed even further, interests which had been structured became

---

[129] See J. Tedstrom, 'Soviet Fiscal Federalism in a Time of Crisis', in *Radio Liberty Report on the USSR*, 31 (1991), 1–5. Of 12 billion roubles due to be paid into the stabilization fund, by May 1991 only 1.8 billion had arrived.

[130] *Izvestiya* (7 June 1991), 1. The complexities of anti-ministerialism, however, were then evident in another statement in which Fokin said that the Ukraine was not taking *ownership* of the enterprises, simply asserting its jurisdiction over them. Taking over the coal enterprises had shown the Ukraine, in his view, that it could not afford to own all enterprises – Moscow had responded by cutting off enterprise access to central resources, research, and technology. Very careful negotiations were under way, particularly with the Ministry of Metallurgy, about the transfer of enterprises to republican jurisdiction.

opposed, economic agents who had been strong became—by a variety of means more powerful—and the state was exposed for what it had long since been, a hollow shell. It was in this context that the final efforts at *perestroyka* were made.

THE HOLLOW SHELL

The ministries in 1991

In his address to the Supreme Soviet in June 1989, Ryzhkov pointed out the dilemma they faced:

Some insist on the immediate and complete abolition of branch ministries as no longer having a relevant purpose and functions in conditions of the developing economic reform. Others hold a different opinion—they say that we cannot get along without the ministries in their present make-up, since otherwise control over the economy will be lost, and the management of the national economy on a countrywide scale will become impossible.

At that time, the number of industrial ministries was reduced drastically, but Ryzhkov did not move to clarify the issue posed above, despite insisting, in a way reminiscent of Kosygin in 1965, that 'we are talking about ministries of a totally new type, qualitatively different from the past ministries'. The problem was that the terms of their work continued to be set vaguely enough to allow a continuation of both economic *and* state interpretations of their powers.

They will be deprived of many of their economic functions, apart from one— vigorously promoting the formation of an economic environment that will make it possible to fully disclose the potential of the basic production unit. This is probably their chief task. They are called upon to put primary emphasis in their work on developing priority areas of scientific and technical progress, determining the prospects of the various branches, and conducting investment policy in the spirit of the requirements of the social reorientation of the national economy.[131]

By 1991, the issue of the role of the ministries had still not been clarified. Following constitutional changes in December 1991, in which the dual executive was abolished and the Council of Ministers— renamed the Cabinet—made subordinate to the executive president,

---

[131] *Izvestiya* (11 June 1989), 1, 4.

heads of republic governments were allowed to participate with a casting vote in the Cabinet's work. The role of the Cabinet was to ensure, jointly with the republics: money and credit, drawing up the Union budget, administration of all-Union programmes, fuel energy and transport, defence, space research, food and agricultural policy, and foreign policy. However, no agreement was reached on the precise activity of Union ministries, and a special consultative body, in which the directors of the respective republic agencies were members *ex officio*, was formed to resolve the matter.[132]

In March 1991, the new prime minister, Valentin Pavlov, indicated in an interview that the position of ministries, bureaux, and commissions had been carefully studied and a decision taken to liquidate links of immediate administration of production where he could be sure of no loss of control. No law on the ministries was ever passed, however, and the cabinet structure remained, in Pavlov's words, 'transitional': functional ministries, he thought, would always be part of the state; 'market-type' ministries would be created for the reform period; old-style ministries would remain in energy, transport, nuclear power, and defence production; some ministries would be needed to maintain technical standards; and, among industrial ministries, only the Ministry of Automobile and Agricultural Machine-Building would remain because the heads of enterprises wanted it to survive. Intra-branch redistribution of materials and centralized distribution networks were to be eliminated, however—though these would remain intact inside the new concerns. So, he claimed, the old ministerial instruments of control already had ceased to exist though many directors recalled the system warmly.[133]

The theme of the transitional nature of the government was taken up by an official in the Cabinet of Ministers' Commission on Economic Reform who emphasized that a significant decline in the number of ministries awaited the conclusion of a new Union treaty. However, he thought, within two years, via the creation of concerns, etc., all industrial ministries would be gone. Inside the remaining ministries concessions were made to republican sensibilities by appointing representatives from corresponding republican bodies to the ministries' *kollegiya* (collegium).[134] However, as the deputy chairman of the Commission told me in April 1991, the ministries had not

---

[132] 'Constitution (Basic Law) of the Union of Soviet Socialist Republics', in W. E. Butler (ed.), *Collected Legislation of the USSR and Constituent Republics: Constitutions* (London, 1990).   [133] *Ekonomika i zhizn'*, 10 (1991).
[134] *Pravitel'stvennyy vestnik*, 16 (1991), 3.

been able to 'find their place' in the new government; ministries themselves were demanding more power, while changes in the law gave them less. Within two years, he envisioned, the number of ministries would need to be cut in half again.[135] In fact, by mid-June the Cabinet of Ministers announced a cut of one-third in jobs in all central ministries, with 36,000 jobs to go; some ministries were to be cut by 50 per cent. No solution, in other words, was found to the problem of the institutional form of the Soviet state, and the failure to resolve the problem of industrial ministries was, again, at the heart of it.

Authoritarianism without authority

In the midst of this deep crisis of the state, not surprisingly, voices for an authoritarian approach to reform began to be heard. Authoritarianism drew support from a number of strands, from those who wanted a return to the old order to those who saw the need for political stability if marketization and democratization were to be achieved.[136] But the main defect of the authoritarian approach was that it begged the question about the crisis: its successful implementation depended on the existence of the authority of political leaders, at least among the institutions of the state and, better yet, among sections of the population as well, and this had long since disappeared from Soviet life where interests and economic power were the dominant structuring forces in political behaviour. The crisis of the state lay precisely in the lack of authority and the divergence of interests, especially those of the economic agents from the political leaders. As societies hold together, so they fall apart; and the Soviet Union fell apart along the lines of the forces which had previously held it together.

All actors were seeking to place themselves in an advantageous position, and though some were more successful than others, given the level of uncertainty and the number of competing forces at the centre, in the republics, and among local agents, no actor could be sure of securing the desired outcome. In May 1990, Ryzhkov said:

[135] Interview with P. M. Katsura, First Deputy Chairman of the Commission for Economic Reform of the Cabinet of Ministers, Moscow, Apr. 1991.
[136] A. Migranyan, 'The Quality of Gorbachev's Leadership', in *Soviet Economy*, 2 (1990).

Enterprises, regions, and sometimes entire branches are pressing the government for the urgent resolution of social questions and thrusting on it demands for resource deliveries and additional capital investments. As a rule, this is done in the form of ultimatums and under the threat of strikes. One asks: is the government able to work with any efficiency if day after day ultimatum after ultimatum is placed on its desk.[137]

By November 1990 he was arguing:

Control has been totally lost at all levels of the state structure. Authority has been paralysed . . . situation has been created in which no one is in charge, and this has led to a complete or partial deterioration of all systems of administration.[138]

To some degree, the changes of December 1990 mentioned above (which Ryzhkov opposed), in which Gorbachev assumed direct formal control over the government, and other measures whereby he was granted temporary powers to rule by decree in the economy, were intended to strengthen the effectiveness of executive instruments. In conception, however, they were deeply flawed. On the one hand, they left Gorbachev even more in the grip of ministerial agencies to effect his will—more in thrall, in other words, to the very organs that he had begun *perestroyka* to struggle against. On the other, they could not redress the real deficiency in authority over economic and other agents. Decrees that were passed, such as the one in September 1990 on maintaining contract deliveries among all state enterprises regardless of territorial or departmental subordination, or the one in May 1991 on the operation of industry, were without effect.[139]

The turbulent circumstances, in which nationalist and democratic forces threatened the disruption of economic ties across the Soviet Union, intervened in the distribution of property which was already under way, and created power structures to rival those built by the ministries, caused calls to come from within the downgraded Cabinet for tougher measures, measures which the Cabinet itself was prepared to act upon. In February 1991, for example, Pavlov demanded that the Cabinet be given powers to resolve questions of a temporary nature in the economy. 'Can we allow ourselves to move towards complete elimination of branch agencies of management, as certain comrades

[137] *Pravda* (25 May 1990), 1–4.
[138] Radio Moscow domestic broadcast, cited in C. Ross, 'The USSR Cabinet of Ministers', in *Report on the USSR*, RFE/RL Research Institute, 3/26 (1991), 2.
[139] See *Izvestiya* (28 Sept. 1990), 1, and ibid. (17 May 1991), 2.

who consider themselves radical are proposing that we do? I am convinced that we cannot . . . Incidentally, there are no analogues abroad to a complete absence of state structures of economic management.'[140] Again, in mid-June, Pavlov asked the Supreme Soviet for more power for the Cabinet in legislative initiatives, in its dealings with the Supreme Soviet and local soviets, in the deployment of workers and setting state orders, and in banking and inflation, saying Gorbachev could not handle it all. The interregional deputy, Ryabachenko, called Pavlov's proposals 'a co-ordinated campaign to remove the USSR President from power'. In a constitutional rehearsal for the coup of August, Pavlov's proposal was supported by Pugo, Yazov, and Kryuchkov, but Pavlov kept his job, saying that he had been misunderstood.[141]

However, the interests of economic agents were also highly fragmented and often contradictory, so that authoritarianism of the Pavlovian type had difficulty in finding a constituency. There had been a dramatic growth in the formation of business associations in the period following 1989 which had been spurred on by the privatization process. As Peregudov, Semenenko, and Zudin have argued, Soviet business associations were not like those in the West, having a far more politicized role and a closer relationship to the state. The Agricultural Union (Peasants' Union), for example, acted through the parliamentary lobby system and was successful in getting the Council of Ministers to adopt measures requiring ministries to consult with the union on agricultural reform. The Science and Industry Union was the most powerful organization, and had been established by several dozen USSR Supreme Soviet members with an industrial background. It had a large membership representing 35 per cent of enterprises producing 60 per cent of all output. Forty smaller business associations become part of it, many of them with different political orientations, such as the conservative Association of State Enterprises, and the free market Union of Associated Co-operatives. A month after its establishment it was given permanent representation in the Council of Ministers, together with some of its collective members, including the Association of State Enterprises, the Union of Leaseholders, the Association of Young Enterprise Leaders, the Association of Joint Enterprises, and the Union of Associated Co-operatives.[142]

[140] Ibid. (21 Feb. 1991), 3.   [141] *Radio Liberty Report on the USSR* no. 26.
[142] S. Peregudov, I. Semenenko, and A. Zudin, *Business Associations in the USSR— and After: Their Growth and Political Role*, paper for IPSA Conference, 1991; revised and extended, Jan. 1992.

But despite the close relations between business and state, the pattern of interests had changed dramatically with the new circumstances. Where 'the expansion of organizations' rights in fact means the transfer of the rights of higher-level bodies of power to the top people in the organizations',[143] the building of power among politicians to direct this process in an orderly way was always going to be difficult to achieve.

Who are they, these new Soviet proprietors? In the first place, they are representatives of the *nomenklatura* (deideologized party officials and executives of enterprises and departments), especially those middle-aged or younger, the heads of co-operatives and joint-ventures, and newly elected Deputies to local soviets ... The Communist Party has just completed a division into a managerial class that has found advantageous places for itself in the new commercial structures and a relatively small group of 'ideologues' grouped around the Russian Communist Party.[144]

The drive for authoritarianism, favoured by part of the political class, did find some support among economic agents. At the December 1990 All-Union Meeting of Executives to the Fourth Congress of USSR People's Deputies, for example, a resolution was adopted calling for Gorbachev to stabilize the economy by decree.[145] Following the miners' strike in March and April, the First Deputy Minister of Metallurgy spoke threateningly of the disruption that democratization had brought: 'I don't oppose these democratic principles, but discipline and democracy must go together. I consider that the more democracy there is the more discipline there must be. There is no market here, so it is necessary to create discipline by another method.'[146] Following the swing to the right in the winter of 1990–1, there was speculation that managers might be induced to support authoritarianism because they then might rule the roost themselves. Echoing much of what was said in earlier chapters, one commentator noted:

After all, it is only [in the factory] that a person can earn a decent wage and turn the helpless rouble into a food order and buy clothes at closed sales— the shops will wither away. Kindergartens, transport, and housing—all this will necessarily come under departmental control. And the director, like the feudal lord, will joke in dead earnest about first night rights.

---

[143] *Izvestiya* (9 Dec. 1990), 2.   [144] ibid.
[145] *Pravda* (11 Dec. 1990), 2.
[146] Interview with the First Deputy Minister of Metallurgy, Leonid Vladimorovich Radyukevich, Moscow, Apr. 1991.

However, the author considered this a poor strategy for the manager, since a return to command methods would mean big deductions from enterprises to state budgets, and, using anti-managerial popularism, the party and ministry apparatus would turn the population against the director's privileges while getting power themselves.[147] Many economic agents may have agreed with this assessment, including the establishment leadership of the Science and Industry Union, which threatened Pavlov in the spring, however, with direct action by managers and directors against conservative action.[148]

By the end, therefore, the old Soviet state had become a hollow shell. Not only had the republics pulled away, and the public struck out in myriad directions, but the institutions of the economy, in response to the crisis and opportunities brought about by reform, had also changed form and changed tack. When the coup came in August 1991, therefore, there was no significant force left to support it, only the most vulnerable politically and socially. The problem since has been to cope with the explosion of interests and to build the political authority that might control and harmonize them. Since this is the problem at the heart of many aspects of Soviet power, we should expect to find similarities as well as innovations.

[147] *Moscow News*, 9 (1991), 9.
[148] See Peregudov, Semenenko, and Zudin, *Business Associations in the USSR*.

Conclusion
Industrial Power and the Post-Soviet State

PERHAPS the most significant general claim advanced in this book was that politicians and statesmen were weak actors in the Soviet system. In part, this conclusion is motivated by a definition of the political sphere. Political actors are those whose interests and power are based upon the exercise of authority rather than direct control over resources. Theory might suggest that, in the Soviet Union, where politicians were unencumbered by the constraints of private property, public accountability, or civil rights, political power would have reached its apogee. Through the authority of the party—the argument might go—the will of the politicians was done. Indeed, so powerful were politicians, it was almost impossible to separate politics and economics. However, the definition of 'politics' alerts us to the practical difficulties of turning the abolition of private property into effective authority, for the politicians had to delegate control over resources to agencies which they then had the problem of regulating. For most of the Soviet period after 1929, these agencies were industrial ministries—though changing the organizational face of industrial power, as successive leaders found, was no way to solve the problem of controlling it. The regulated, in the first stages of the game of Soviet politics, had become by the end the regulators. For the personnel who controlled the society's resources the front of communist power was indeed the perfect camouflage; the seemingly monolithic state offered those with operational control over the economy the added advantage of membership in the political committees guiding the state. To be a politician anywhere—to exercise authority—against the interests of those wielding economic power is a difficult task; in the old Soviet state, paradoxically, it was even more so. And it was in an effort to control their agencies and build authority that some of the political leaders launched *perestroyka*.

The failure of *perestroyka* has been explained in this book in the same terms as the stability of the Soviet state in the period which preceded it: interests, structured by ministries, held the old order together, so that changing interests by attacking ministries—while giving them more room to manœuvre—threatened the stability of the state as a whole. As ministries deserted the camouflage of the old order to enter a quasi-corporate economic existence and, as the economic crisis which change induced drove all actors to rely on economic power to secure their position, the last vestiges of authority in communist politics crumbled. The Soviet Union left a legacy, on the one hand, of a barren, weak, and corrupted state without institutional structure and, on the other, of a civil society dominated by the rush for property, and the more or less naked exercise of economic muscle among actors with very unequal builds.

THE END OF THE OLD STATE

Following the August coup of 1991, which only one industrial minister—Khadzhiev of the Ministry of the Chemical Industry[1]— publicly opposed, the institutional structures of the old state, which had been in transition for some time, finally collapsed. The Communist Party, of course, was the first to be suspended and then, effectively, killed when Gorbachev resigned citing its role in the coup. For a period, attempts were made to build an interim state structure of the USSR, and some actors hoped for a renewed federation. However, the institutions of the interregnum which included a number of ministries and committees—for defence, security, and foreign affairs, the Committee for the Operational Management of the National Economy (COMNE) and the Inter-State Economic Commission (ISEC)[2]—were dominated by republican leaders.

The Russian prime minister, and former Council of Ministers' bureau chief, Silaev, became the first head of the COMNE—he soon resigned his position in the Russian government. The committee struggled to exercise authority from the start. Almost immediately after the coup, the economy began to be transferred into republican hands. The USSR State Bank was immediately put under the jurisdiction of the Russian Rebublic—jousting over control of the State Bank continued in October and November[3]—and all precious metal and foreign

---

[1] He was reinstated at the ministry by Silaev in Sept. 1991.

[2] The ISEC was to take over the functions of the COMNE on the conclusion of a new economic treaty, when it would act as the executive of the economic community: to ensure co-ordinated economic policy in enterprises, marketing, transport, power engineering, information, monetary and banking policy, taxes and prices, capital and labour markets, finance, foreign policy relations, and currency policy.

[3] *Summary of World Broadcasts*, BBC (2 Nov. 1991).

currency transactions required RSFSR approval. At the end of August, Russia announced that it was taking over all operational and jurisdictional control of all-Union economic ministries. At first Silaev acceded to this demand, and only reasserted the Union's right to run all-Union ministries when he was rebuked by the head of the Science and Industry Union, Volsky. In late September, Silaev had to ask Yeltsin to rescind decrees proclaiming Russian sovereignty in economic affairs. In mid-October, Yeltsin went so far as to call the committee unconstitutional.

By October, it was clear even inside Union structures that the Soviet institutional framework had collapsed. Silaev announced that there was no need for the Ministry of Finance at an all-Union level; Union ministries would be retained only in railways, medium-scale engineering, atomic energy, and in a central cultural committee. He envisioned 37,000 job losses in the central ministries, though most were to get jobs in the newly created Russian equivalents.[4] At its meeting in early November, the State Council went further and agreed to abolish eighty Union ministries on 15 November, retaining ministries for foreign affairs, internal affairs, railways, power, atomic energy, and customs.[5] In early November, the Foreign Minister, Pankin, announced that his ministry would be staffed by between 2,000 and 2,500 personnel, a cut of one-third; Yeltsin responded by saying the cut would be of the order of nine-tenths.[6]

The ISEC would have comprised the rump of the whole former Union economic administration. It was envisioned that it would comprise 1,500 staff in 15–20 departments concentrated in five blocks, the largest to be the department of macro-economics, which would encompass the old ministries of economics, finance, and statistics. Some industrial ministries (unnamed) were to have been transformed into departments of the ISEC. At the meeting of the State Council in November, 'representatives of the Union ministries made a last stand'. Some managed to win an interim reprieve, and Volsky in particular argued for the retention of some administrative powers in new economic departments of the ISEC.[7] The committee was clearly a

[4] Ibid. (31 October 1991).

[5] Ibid. (4 Nov. 1991). There were to have been joint Union–republican institutions in industries at risk during the transition period—the merchant marine, communications, civil aviation, a currency commission, an inter-state pension fund, a committee on standardization, space research, and meteorology.

[6] *Summary of World Broadcasts*, BBC (5 Nov. 1991).

[7] *Izvestiya* (4 Nov. 1991); ibid. (6 Nov. 1991).

working body. Silaev and republican leaders worked on the union budget to be submitted to the Supreme Soviet; Silaev gave instructions to ministries on the need for fuel and energy, and to Gasprom, Neftgazstroy, and Rosvostkstroy on how to deal with the energy situation that winter; the committee recommended to the Russian Cabinet of Ministers that the Russian timber industry corporation should provide bonuses and consumer goods to timber workers. But its work was clearly massively hampered by the inability of the politicians to come to a settlement, and in mid-November its members threatened to resign if a Union treaty was not signed.

One of the biggest difficulties of the transition in industrial administration concerned the financing of enterprises which operated from central budgets, and it became clear that the part of the old ministries which dealt with financing would have to survive for some time to come. Abolishing the ministries was not proving to be so simple. Though they had been scheduled for complete elimination by 15 November, Silaev worked to extend this until 1 December in order to have time to create new structures. At least one suggestion was made to found inter-republican departments to support enterprises as part of the future Union government.[8]

The main difficulty, however, lay in getting a Union budget approved. Only 30–5 per cent of the revenue for the Union budget had actually been sent to the centre. Wages could not be paid, and there was a 300 billion roubles Union deficit.[9] A Yeltsin decree ended funding for central bodies on 20 November; and the USSR State Bank was then pronounced bankrupt according to the USSR Auditor. Following the Yeltsin decree, Russia then announced that all Union ministry property and that of its organizations and enterprises on Russian territory was subordinate to it. The budget and finance committees of the Union Parliament in late November agreed to support a 93 billion roubles emergency budget, and the Soviet of the Republics told Gosbank to lend 90.5 billion roubles to the Ministry of Finance, although the Soviet of the Union had been inquorate on this issue. But the RSFSR, in a meeting of the council of heads of government, voted against an emergency Union budget, saying it would finance all Union institutions itself. The Soviet Union, in other

---

[8] In mid-Nov., Silaev was confirmed by the State Council as head of the ISEC, although the body did not yet officially exist. He was effectively there on his own, awaiting a ministry of finance and ministry of the economy which were expected in the new year. [9] *Summary of World Broadcasts*, BBC, (18 Nov. 1991).

words, was in hock to the new Russian state and had no independent existence beyond Russia's interests.

The difficulty in constructing a new state structure was paralleled, as mentioned above, by the problems in finding a consensus among the republics. In late September, Yavlinsky announced that all fifteen republics had agreed to co-ordinate monetary policy through an association of central banks, and the Economic Community Treaty, which sought to create conditions for free movement of labour, goods, money, and capital, on the basis of a common currency and co-ordinated policy on finance, banking, and taxes, was signed by eight states in October. The treaty envisioned the existence of certain common funds for state internal and external debt, for emergencies, for targeted programmes, and a financial reserve, as well as envisioning institutions such as the Council of Heads of Government, the ISEC, the Banking Union, and a Court of Arbitration.[10] But in the discussion on the economic treaty a number of stumbling-blocks became evident. By mid-October, it was clear that the problem of getting an agreement on a banking union was becoming a major obstacle to the signing of the economic treaty. The Russian Republic, for example, supported the treaty in the main, but not the clause on a banking union. Nikolay Fedorov attacked the economic agreement as an infringement of Russian sovereignty leading to the re-creation of Union ministries. Though the agreement was signed, there remained 18–20 specific accords still to be worked out to fill in the details. Some progress was made, which enabled the Economic Community to agree a co-ordinated tax policy by early December. But, with the collapse of efforts to find agreement on a new Union treaty, with the signing of the agreement between Russia, the Ukraine, and Belorussia in early December, and the addition of other former republics a week later, the ground was effectively cut from under the ISEC's feet even before it had managed to get going. The locus of the interrelationship between state and industry moved effectively to Russia.

---

[10] Ibid. (21 Oct. 1991). 'Equal rights for entrepreneurs everywhere' was clearly a central issue, as was, with privatization set to accelerate, the issue of free movement of goods, labour, and capital.

THE EMERGENCE OF THE NEW STATE

The main problem inherited from the old order was that the state was disorganized, weak, and authorityless.[11] Significantly, Yeltsin put the blame for the delay in restructuring government and introducing economic reform on the long battle against the old Union ministries: 'the pressure of an enormous bureaucratic blanket comprising 80 union ministries obliged us to undertake a protracted trench warfare.'[12] However, Yeltsin also made clear his awareness of the problem of political authority—and a desire to avoid the fate that befell Gorbachev: 'I cannot imagine how one can implement a reform directed at democratisation and improvement of life in the future without having power. Vertical power. And we are creating this vertical power now, from the president and to executive power, to the very bottom. There should be responsibility.'[13]

The new structure of Russian government and in particular its relations with industry had, of course, been emerging for some time, but the process was accelerated by the emergency powers granted Yeltsin in November 1991, in which he acquired rights to decide on economic reform by decree, appoint members of government, and decide on the government's structure. Yeltsin himself was nominally prime minister as well as executive president, though the deputy prime ministers, on instruction from the first deputy, co-ordinated the activities of ministries. Ministers themselves were empowered independently to adopt resolutions on areas within their competence, apart from questions discussed at the meetings of the government. Within the government, there was also an advisory centre for the operation of economic reform comprised of government members sitting *ex officio*.[14] In a classic piece of anti-ministerialism, Yeltsin announced that he wanted fewer ministries, which he proposed to achieve in classic Soviet style by organizing them in five clusters with six to seven ministries in

---

[11] For an excellent discussion of the problems of the collapse of political authority in the face of economic power, see M. McAuley, 'The Regional Perspective: Electoral Politics, Economic Stalemate, and Élite Realignment', in *Soviet Economy* 1 (1992), 46–88.   [12] *Summary of World Broadcasts*, BBC (17 Dec. 1991).
[13] Ibid. (22 Nov. 1991). Yeltsin went on: 'And if somebody does not deliver the goods, he must be answerable. This is the case in any democratic civilised state. But we say: well, power in fact means a dictator. Why? Power is by the law and demands are in accordance with the law. If someone is criminal, he should be made answerable in accordance with the law. I have signed a decree on combating crime and corruption. Very tough measures will be taken now in this respect. But it does not mean that I am a dictator.'   [14] Ibid. (8 Nov. 1991).

each, with one executive in charge of each cluster to harmonize interests. On top of all, to harmonize all the clusters, would sit a first deputy prime minister.

In the new government which Yeltsin announced in mid-November, the number of ministries had indeed been reduced from forty-six to twenty-three. Industrial administration was concentrated in the Ministry of Industry, which consisted of twenty-one branch departments. There were few staff—3,000 did what 30,000 did before—compared not only with the Soviet past but—in the current vogue—with the 12,000 who worked in the equivalent Japanese ministry. According to the minister, Titkin, branch departments differed from the old Union ministries in that they had no redistribution functions. Their main task, he said, was the conversion of industry to the market.[15]

A new sort of state in which a radical break from the Soviet past had been achieved would need to rest on two principles: the absence of Soviet-style industrial ministries bridging government, the economy, and society; and, as a corollary, the publicization of politics, wherein space would be opened between industry and the politicians in which authority could be built. However, the process of building such a new state was complicated by disputes within the executive apparatus itself on industrial policy and administration, and by the response of Parliament to the economic difficulties of the transition.

A symptom of the problem was evident in the public disputes between Rutskoi, who opposed price liberalization and supported the conversion of the military–industrial complex, and the anti-communist and IMF-orientated positions held by Burbulis, Gaidar, and Shokhin.[16] But the heart of the disagreement lay in the dilemma of what to do about the Leviathan of industry, which retained enormous economic power. On the one hand, the autonomy of the state—the authority of politicians—depended upon its ability to take decisions independently of industry which would be effective even if it opposed industrial interests. Indeed, the power of industry was at the heart of the political and economic battle, crystallizing in the battle over the budget. The

[15] *Kuranty* (10 Mar. 1992), 3; *Summary of World Broadcasts*, BBC (10 Apr. 1992).

[16] At the end of November, the vice-president, Rutskoi, had come out against price liberalization and the disintegration of the military–industrial complex. In response, the first deputy prime minister, Burbulis, had attacked Rutskoi. Rutskoi then said he would not resign and attacked Burbulis, Gaidar, and Shokhin, saying the government lacked experience. At the next meeting of the Cabinet in early December, Gaidar called for Rutskoi's resignation.

achievement of a balanced budget, for example, would represent not only the victory of the new team's vision of sound economic policy but would be a manifestation of their ability to exercise authority independently of industrial interests. On the other hand, the new state structure was still ill-formed, its inherited symbiosis with industrial agents and its weakness in regulating economic behaviour still obvious. To try to accommodate industrial actors might so enfeeble the state that the old Soviet order would simply reconstitute itself: but to flout industrial power might lead to economic collapse.

The battle over the autonomy of the state against the inertia of the old order seemed to be progressively dissipated in 1992. The familiar pattern of growth in the apparatus, with each department in charge of—and captured by—a special interest re-emerged. In a speech at the end of March, Gaidar called for cuts in spending on the government apparatus, and a restriction in the growth of government departments such as one on defending the economic interests of the Russian federation. These, he said, had been created without powers or functions.[17] Sobchak described the new Russian state as corrupt, without a viable administrative structure, and consisting of duplicate and parallel administrations.[18] Indeed, a fascinating parallel with the Soviet past had emerged. Previously, the politicians in the party had sought to deal with the autonomy of the industrial ministries located in various buildings around Moscow by establishing their own departments in Central Committee buildings in *Staraya Ploshch'ad*. The reform team around Burbulis and Gaidar responded similarly to their fear of sabotage from the old apparatus, by establishing their own shadow structures located in the very same Central Committee offices.[19] Filatov, first deputy chairman of the Supreme Soviet, attacked the spread and disunity of the president's apparatus. Polozkov, former leader of the Russian Communist Party, commented that there were

[17] *Summary of World Broadcasts*, BBC (31 Mar. 1992). On 21 Jan. 1992 Yeltsin established a Russian Ministry of Nuclear Energy to co-ordinate nuclear enterprises that were acquiring some autonomy in their production tasks, though weapons technology would remain under total ministerial control. He appointed the former Soviet minister of the nuclear industry to head it. On the same day, a Russian Ministry of Science was established incorporating the State Committee for Science and Technology and other Soviet bodies. There was also a State Committee for Conversion created at the same time.   [18] Ibid. (5 Mar. 1992).

[19] This information was given to me by an official in the Russian Supreme Soviet. It is worth noting, as Ch. 3 has argued, that the independence of the branch departments of the Central Committee was not long preserved and the same question may be addressed to the present Russian government.

effectively three governments: presidential advisers, the president's apparatus, and the government itself. New ministries and departments, he said, were sprouting like mushrooms. Yeltsin was forced to agree that there were too many structures in the executive, and promised that they would be simplified. But, in response, he clouded the issue further by appointing another first deputy premier for industry.[20]

The difficulties the politicians faced in dealing with industry had also grown rather than diminished with the economic crisis and the break-up of the Soviet Union. The new government faced pressure from those who wanted a measure of justice against the old order via an attack on inherited industrial power. In his speech to the Congress of People's Deputies in late October 1991, Yeltsin had attacked *nomenklatura* privatization.[21] In September 1991, he had suspended the operations of all-Union ministries in coal, oil, gas, and nuclear power, as well as the all-Union part of Gazprom. Their subsidiaries were placed under the newly established Russian Fuel and Power Ministry. But, after the coup, the remnants of the all-Union ministries had continued their efforts to transform themselves into corporations and concerns based mainly in Russia. Roschermet—headed by the former minister—and Rostsvetmet—headed by the former deputy minister—replaced the Union Ministry of Metallurgy. Defence ministries dissolved in November were formed into corporations and their *glavki* made into concerns. Glavalmazzoloto became Rosalmazzoloto.[22] At the Congress of People's Deputies in April 1992, Yeltsin was asked by the chairman of the Supreme Soviet Committee for Industry and Power Engineering about changes in the structure of ministries: 'Such monsters have been created. Will the status of associations and concerns be defined, will their functional duties be clearly demarcated?' Yeltsin replied promising that the old structures would not be copied.[23]

However, a scandal broke out in the Russian government in early March 1992 after the deputy chairman of the Russian State Committee on Managing State Property, Yutkin, authorized the creation of a

[20] *Summary of World Broadcasts*, BBC (13 Apr. 1992).
[21] Ibid. (30 Oct. 1991).
[22] S. Johnson and H. Kroll, 'Managerial Strategies for Spontaneous Privatisation', in *Soviet Economy*, 4 (1991), 281–316. So far as the appointment of managers was concerned, the ministries seem to have stopped acting, and there was also a decline in transfer payments to the ministries. However, the ministry's approval was still needed for a change of an enterprise to leasing, for example, and following the coup, this became harder to obtain. [23] *Summary of World Broadcasts*, BBC (9 Apr. 1992).

joint-stock company which was then ruled illegal by the chief state inspector of the controlling department of the Russian president, Makharadze, as 'an attempt at illegal privatization by *nomenklatura*'. Yutkin was dismissed. The scandal arose in part because the investment by shareholders was in the form of intellectual property rather than money. For example, Leonid Kravchenko estimated his intellectual value to the company to be 10 million roubles and received shares of an equivalent value. Oleg Belyakov, former head of the defence industry department of the Central Committee, contributed his 'intellectual property' as well. In total, contributions of this sort amounted to 200 million roubles. The joint-stock company was founded to promote the potential of the military–industrial complex in the production of consumer goods. Aleksander Titkin, the Russian Minister of Industry, was forced to deny that he was the fixer in the *nomenklatura* privatization scandal, although he did sign the documents. He saw nothing wrong with the defence sector going into consumer goods, but insisted that he did not know that Kravchenko and others were involved. In response to the accusations, however, he made a public declaration on all concerns and associations set up by former ministries to disguise their true nature, saying most of them were now lining their pockets by selling Russia's raw materials abroad.[24]

But pressure for the revival of at least some aspects of the old order came from a number of quarters. Managerial autonomy continued to be limited by the same considerations which had long underpinned ministerial power; they wanted to be in big associations as a way of overcoming supply uncertainties. Though concerns did not always do much more than provide information, most managers surveyed by Johnson and Kroll were still receiving 100 per cent state orders.[25] In a meeting of Burbulis and Gaidar with industrial directors at the beginning of April 1992, the politicians were told that they needed to rethink the system of management and the role of ministries and departments in the reform process.[26] As the deputy chairman of the Supreme Soviet, Shumeyko—who was to become a deputy prime minister in May—put it:

Many deputies of the SS and, on the whole, specialists in commissions and committees are coming to the conclusion that thanks to the latest government

---

[24] Ibid. (4 Mar. 1992); ibid. (11 Mar. 1992).
[25] Johnson and Kroll, 'Managerial Strategies'.
[26] *Summary of World Broadcasts*, BBC (3 Apr. 1992).

decisions a super-monopolised, multi-link administrative and managerial monster, which in a number of aspects is looking more rigid than the old system, is being formed in the government. And the state enterprises have turned out to be the last in the chain of this five-link system: ministry, committee, department, concern, and enterprise ... These enterprises which, owing to a number of reasons, cannot be privatised or turned into joint-stock companies today have been practically left to the mercy of fate in their economic activity. There is such a view. I must say that it is not quite so. For example, departments of the Ministry of Industry are independent, they are run by very skilful specialists; they could be regarded as being of the same rank as the old industrial ministries ... Since the government cannot show a devil-may-care attitude to its property, to state enterprises, one should immediately revise such a system of running state industry. And a sensible combination should be found here, a combination of introducing new forms of running the economy—I have in mind inter-branch state associations, various structures of state commercial companies, the formation of regional and interregional associations, that is to delegate rights to them—and also a single link branch system having the rank of ministries should be preserved ... True, in our view, at the same time the government should give a clear annual task to these ministries for privatising a definite number of enterprises within each branch ... [but] a decision on obligatory preservation of at least 50 per cent of ties of last year's level should be adopted for state enterprises. Given the existing economic ties between state enterprises, command methods are permissible since this is state property ... We see this drop in production and we must not remain indifferent to it.[27]

Before his dismissal, Yutkin had said that his ministry needed to run the restructuring process. After agreeing that extra credits should be given to priority industries, Yeltsin announced that the ministries of economy, industry, and finance would work out the schedule. As a measure of the shift in policy, Gaidar himself confirmed that more money would go into conversion.[28] Although, after the appointment of Shumeyko and others from the old industrial staff to the government's inner cabinet, Yeltsin tried to blunt criticism of his U-turn by introducing his bankruptcy decree requiring enterprises to pay debts within three months or face being sold at auction, there was considerable doubt about whether, as in the case of Gorbachev, his decrees would be enforced.[29] Though Gaidar continued to threaten

[27] Ibid. (17 Jan. 1992). [28] Ibid. (9 Apr. 1992).
[29] *Guardian* (17 June 1992). Though none of the three appointed in June, according to Lloyd, had the label of 'conservative', they were all from industry. Shumeyko was a former plant manager; Khizha was a defence plant manager; Cheronmyrdin was Soviet gas minister. They displayed industry's success 'in counter-attacking against the charge Mr. Gaidar led against them'. After Mar. 1992 industry used its power. See *Financial Times* (12 June 1992).

bankruptcies, he had already granted extra credits, controlled energy prices, lowered taxes, issued more money, and delayed privatization. No one could know the extent of the budget deficit.[30] In the run-up to the Congress of People's Deputies in April 1992, Gaidar also announced the lifting of credit restrictions on some enterprises.[31]

If building an autonomous and authoritative state via a coherent set of institutions and policies out of the inheritance of the old Soviet ministerial order was already compromised by developments in the executive, then the other side of the equation, the 'publicization' of politics, was also under attack. Ironically, and probably unconsciously, it was the public itself and its representative institutions which were leading the way back towards political closure and insider privileges for industrial power. At one level, as one of the candidates for the chairmanship of the Supreme Soviet, Konstantinov, put it, Parliament remained too dependent on the ministries for their information. However, the problem is most evident in the fact that Parliament most feverishly attacked the executive for its actions at the height of the executive's autonomy against industry. When the government most actively pursued anti-industrial policies, designed to overcome the legacy of ministerialism, Parliament moved to set up its own structures to deal with the economy, claiming for itself the government's right to act, and threatening the government with dismissal. Parliament was demanding, as its chairman, Khasbulatov, put it, 'ministers who know real life, what real production is all about';[32] but the only people who could have had such experience were precisely those, like Shumekyo, who had worked within the old ministerial environment and who were then denounced for their *nomenklatura* connections.

With the retreat of the executive from its more ferocious attacks on the old industrial order, and with the granting of credits and allowances being made to prevent bankruptcies, it is to be expected that relations between Parliament and the executive may become easier. At the same time, in its desire to mitigate the effects of reform, Parliament can only create management structures which will allow a return to cosy insider arrangements. Parliament itself would be the biggest institutional loser from such a scenario. 'Ministerial society bites back' might read the headline, and the price of satisfying constituents might be the integrity of parliament lost to the exigencies

---

[30] Ibid. (12 June 1992).   [31] *Summary of World Broadcasts*, BBC (6 Apr. 1992).
[32] Ibid. (20 Jan. 1992).

of industrial power. The institutional form of the retreat may result, as Shumeyko suggested, in the formal re-creation of industrial ministries and a partial return to legitimate command methods. In such circumstances, concerns may, chameleon-like, become ministries again. If the old society is beginning to exert its influence, the new state is beginning to emerge too. As Gorbachev said in late November 1991: 'The military–industrial complex is convinced: no, they say, we have ruled this state and made decisions, and that is how we are to carry on.'[33]

[33] Ibid. (23 Nov. 1991).

SOURCES AND SELECTED BIBLIOGRAPHY

INTERVIEWS

Ye. P. Are'fev, Head of Sector, Commission for Economic Reform of the Cabinet of Ministers of the USSR, Moscow, April 1991.

P. M. Katsura, First Deputy Chairman, Commission for Economic Reform of the Cabinet of Ministers of the USSR, Moscow, April 1991.

Yu. M. Kozlov, Department of Administrative Law, Moscow State University, February, March, April, May 1989.

B. P. Kurashvili, Centre for Political Research, Institute of State and Law, Moscow, April 1989.

A. Ya. Maksimovich, Institute for State and Law, Moscow, April 1989.

L. V. Radyukevich, First Deputy Minister of Metallurgy, Moscow, April 1991.

V. G. Vishnyakov, Institute of Labour, Moscow, June, July 1989.

T. I. Zaslavskaya, Centre for Research into Public Opinion under the Institute of Labour, Moscow, July 1989.

PERIODICALS AND JOURNALS

Argumenty i fakty (1989–).
British Journal of Political Science (1982–).
Current Digest of Soviet Press (*CDSP*) (1965–).
Ekonomika i organizatsya promyshlennogo proizvodstva (*EKO*) (1970–).
Ekonomika i zhizn' (1990–).
Izvestia TsK KPSS (1989–).
Khozyaystvo i pravo (1979–).
Kommunist (1982–).
Moscow News (1987–).
Neva (1988–).
Novyy mir (1988–).
Ogonek (1987–).
Planovoe khozyaystvo (1982–).
Pravitel'stvennyy vestnik (1989–).
Pravovedenie (1965–).
Review of Socialist Law (1980–).
Sobranie postanovlenii pravitel'stva SSSR (*SPPSSSR*) (1964–).
Sotsiologicheskie issledovaniya (*Sots. iss.*) (1982–).
Sovetskoe gosudarstvo i pravo (1965–).
Soviet Studies (1964–).

Studies in Comparative Communism (1968–).
Vestnik MGU (1982–).
Voprosy ekonomiki (1982–).

BOOKS AND ARTICLES IN ENGLISH

AMANN, R., 'Searching for an Appropriate Concept of Soviet Politics: The Politics of Hesitant Modernisation', in *British Journal of Political Science*, 16 (1986), 475–94.
—— 'Soviet Politics in the Gorbachev Era: the End of Hesitant Modernisation', in *British Journal of Political Science*, 20 (1990), 289–310.
—— and COOPER, J. (eds.), *Industrial Innovation in the Soviet Union* (London, 1982).
BERLINER, J., *Factory and Manager in the USSR* (Cambridge, Mass., 1957).
BRAGINSKY, M., *The Soviet State as a Subject of Civil Law* (Moscow, 1988).
BROWN, A. H., *Soviet Politics and Political Science* (London, 1974).
—— 'Political Power and the Soviet State: Western and Soviet Perspectives', in N. Harding (ed.), *The State in Socialist Society* (London, 1984).
BRUS, W., *The Economics and Politics of Socialism* (London, 1973).
BUNCE, V., 'The Political Economy of the Brezhnev Era', in *British Journal of Political Science*, 13 (1983), 129–59.
CARR, E. H., and DAVIES, R. W., *Foundations of a Planned Economy* (London, 1969).
COLTON, T., 'The Politics of Systemic Economic Reform', in Ed. A. Hewett and V. H. Winston (eds.), *Milestones in Glasnost and Perestroika: Politics and People* (Washington, DC, 1991), 65–90.
CONYNGHAM W., *Industrial Management in the Soviet Union* (Stanford, Calif., 1973).
—— *The Modernisation of Soviet Industrial Management* (Cambridge, 1982).
DUNMORE, T., *The Stalinist Command Economy* (London, 1980).
DYKER, D., *The Process of Investment in the Soviet Union* (Cambridge, 1983).
—— 'Industrial Planning—Forward or Sideways?' in id. (ed.), *The Soviet Union under Gorbachev* (London 1987), 58–93.
—— 'The Power of the Industrial Ministries', in D. Lane (ed.), *Élites and Political Power in the USSR* (Aldershot, 1988), 188–204.
ELLMAN, M., *Planning Problems in the USSR* (Cambridge, 1973).
FOGELKLOU, A., 'Workers' Participation in the Management of Enterprises and Organisations in the USSR: The 1983 Law on Labour Collectives and its Implementation', in *Review of Socialist Law*, 12/2 (1986), 161–74.
FORTESCUE, S., *The Primary Party Organisations of Branch Ministries* (Washington, DC, 1985.
—— *The Technical Administration of Industrial Ministries* (Birmingham, 1986).

—— *Science and Technology Management Structures in Soviet Industrial Ministries* (Birmingham, 1986).

—— *Building Consensus in Japanese and Soviet Bureaucracies* (Birmingham, 1987).

—— 'The Regional Party Apparatus in the "Sectional Society",' in *Studies in Comparative Communism*, 1 (1988), 11–23.

GERNER, K., and HEDLUND, S., *Ideology and Rationality in the Soviet Model* (London, 1989).

GORBACHEV, M., *Perestroika* (London, 1987).

GORLIN, A., 'The Power of the Industrial Ministries in the 1980s', in *Soviet Studies*, 3 (1985), 353–70.

GRANICK, D., *Management of the Industrial Firm in the USSR* (New York, 1954).

—— 'Plant Managers and Their Overseers', in J. L. Nogee (ed.), *Man, State and Society in the Soviet Union* (London, 1972), 194–200.

GREGORY, P.R., *The Institutional Background of the Soviet Enterprise: The Planning Apparatus and the Ministries* (Cologne, 1989).

—— *Restructuring the Soviet Economic Bureaucracy* (Cambridge, 1990).

—— and STUART, R. C., *Soviet Economic Structure and Performance* (London, 1972).

HAMMER, D., *USSR: The Politics of Oligarchy* (Hinsdale, Ill., 1974).

HAUSLOHNER, P., 'Gorbachev's Social Contract', in *Soviet Economy* 1 (1987), 54–89.

HEWITT, ED. A., *Reforming the Soviet Economy* (Washington, DC, 1988).

HILL, R., 'Party-State Relations and Soviet Political Development', in *British Journal of Political Science*, 10 (1980), 149–65.

—— 'Soviet Political Development and the Culture of the *Apparatchiki*', in *Studies in Comparative Communism*, 1 (1986), 25–39.

HODNETT, G., 'Khrushchev and Party-State Control', in A. Dallin and A. F. Westin (eds.), *Politics in the Soviet Union* (New York, 1966), 113–64.

HOEFFDING, O., 'The Soviet Industrial Reorganisation of 1957', in F. O. Holzman (ed.), *Readings on the Soviet Economy* (Chicago, 1962), 475–87.

HOFFMANN, E. P., and LAIRD, R. F., *The Politics of Economic Modernization in the Soviet Union* (London, 1982).

HOHMANN, H.-H., and SAND, H.-B., 'The Soviet Union', in H.-H. Hohmann, M. Kaser and K. C. Thalheim (eds.), *The New Economic System of Eastern Europe* (London, 1975), 1–42.

HOLMES, L., *The Policy Process in Communist States: Politics and Industrial Administration* (London, 1981).

HOUGH, J., 'Reforms in Soviet Government and Administration', in A. Dallin and T. B. Larson, *Soviet Politics Since Khrushchev* (Eaglewood Cliffs, NJ, 1968), 23–40.

—— *The Soviet Prefects* (Cambridge, Mass., 1969).

HOUGH, J., *The Soviet Union and Social Science Theory* (London, 1977).
—— 'Understanding Gorbachev: The Importance of Politics', in Ed. A Hewett and V. H. Winston (eds.), *Milestones in Glasnost and Perestroika: Politics and People* (Washington, DC, 1991), 465–84.
—— and FAINSOD, M., *How the Soviet Union is Governed*, (London, 1979).
JOWETT, K., 'Soviet Neotraditionalism: The Political Corruption of a Leninist Regime', in *Soviet Studies*, 3 (1983), 275–97.
KATZ, A., *The Politics of Economic Reform in the Soviet Union* (New York, 1972).
KRYLOV, C. A., *The Soviet Economy* (Lexington, Mass., 1979).
KUSHNIRSKY, F. I., 'The New Role of Normatives in Soviet Economic Planning', in *Soviet Studies*, 4 (1989), 526–42.
LANE, D., *The Socialist Industrial State* (London, 1976).
—— (ed.), *Labour and Employment in the USSR* (London, 1986).
—— (ed.), *Élites and Political Power in the USSR* (London, 1988).
MCAULEY, M., 'The Ministerial System', in A. H. Brown (ed.), *The Cambridge Encyclopedia of Russia and the Soviet Union* (London, 1982), 309–12.
—— 'Soviet Political Reform in a Comparative Context', in *Harriman Institute Forum*, 2/10 (1989).
MORTON, H. W. and STUART, R. C. (eds.), *The Contemporary Soviet City* (London, 1984).
NOVE, A., *The Soviet Economic System* (3rd ed., London, 1986).
PAKULSKI, J., 'Legitimacy and Mass Compliance: Reflections on Max Weber and Soviet-Type Societies', in *British Journal of Political Science*, 16 (1986), 35–56.
PALEI, L. V., and RADZIVANOVICH, K. L., 'How to Carry Out Economic Reform: Points of View and Reality', in *Soviet Studies*, 1 (1990), 25–37.
PARROTT, B, *Politics and Technology in the Soviet Union* (London, 1983).
PHILP, M., 'Politics, Markets and Corruption', in R. Nick, M. Philp, and M. Pinto-Dushinsky (eds.), *Political Corruption and Scandals* (Vienna, 1990), 16–30.
RICHARDSON, J., *Organisational Affiliation and Leadership Selection in the Soviet Union: The Ministerial Élite under Brezhnev*, paper presented to the 25th Annual Conference of the Australasian Political Studies Association (Sydney, 1982), 8.
RIGBY, T. H., 'A Conceptual Approach to Authority, Power and Policy in the Soviet Union', in T. H. Rigby, A. H. Brown, and P. Reddaway (eds.), *Authority, Power and Policy in the USSR* (London, 1980), 9–31.
ROSS, C., *Local Government in the Soviet Union* (London, 1988).
RUTLAND, P., *The Myth of the Plan* (London, 1985).
—— *The Politics of Economic Stagnation in the USSR: The Role of Local Party Organs in Economic Management* (Cambridge, 1992).
RYAVEC, K., 'The Soviet Bureaucratic Élite from 1964 to 1979', in *Soviet Union/Union Sovietique*, 12/3 (1985), 332–45.

SABEL, C. F., and STARK, D., 'Planning, Politics and Shop-Floor Power: Hidden Forms of Bargaining in Soviet-Imposed State-Socialist Economies', in *Politics and Society*, 11/4 (1982), 439–75.

SLIDER, D., 'More Power to the Soviets? Reform and Local Government in the Soviet Union', in *British Journal of Political Science*, 16 (1986), 495–511.

SMITH, G., 'Bureaucratic Politics and Public Policy in the Soviet Union', in id. (ed.), *Public Policy and Administration in the Soviet Union* (New York, 1980), 1–17.

TAUBMAN, W., *Governing Soviet Cities* (London, 1973).

URBAN, M. E., 'Conceptualising Political Power in the USSR: Patterns of Binding and Bonding', in *Studies in Comparative Communism*, 4 (1985), 207–26.

VAN DEN BERG, G., 'The Council of Ministers of the Soviet Union', in *Review of Socialist Law*, 6 (1980), 293–324.

WINIECKI, J., *Resistance to Change in the Soviet Economic System* (London, 1991).

YELTSIN, B., *Against the Grain: An Autobiography* (London, 1990).

ZASLAVSKAYA, T. I., 'The Novosibirsk Report', in *Survey*, 28 (Spring 1984), 88–108.

BOOKS AND ARTICLES IN RUSSIAN

XIX vsesoyuznaya konferentsiya Kommunisticheskoy Partii Sovetskogo Soyuza, (Moscow, 1988), i and ii.

ABALKIN, L. I., 'Trudnaya shkola perestroyki', in *Uroki gor'kie, no neobkhodimye* (Moscow, 1988), 260–74.

ANDREEV, S., 'Prichiny i sledstviya', in *Ural*, 1 (1988), 104–39.

—— 'Struktura vlasti i zadachi obshchestva', in *Neva*, 1 (1989), 144–73.

BIRMAN, A. M., 'Otraslevoy printsip upravleniya: problemiy, perspektivy', in *EKO* 5 (1970), 60–8.

BISHER, I. O., 'Sovershenstvovanie otraslevogo upravleniya', in *Sovetskoe gosudarstvo i pravo*, 4 (1984), 27–34.

BONDAR', L., 'General'nye skhemy upravleniya: protivorechiya i tendentsii', in *Khozyaystvo i pravo*, 12 (1989), 3–11.

BORODKIN, F. M., 'Sotsial'naya politika: vlast' i perestroyka', in *Postizhenie* (Moscow, 1989), 241–63.

BUZGALIN, A. V. and KOLGANOV A. I., *Anatomiya byurokratizma* (Moscow, 1988).

DEMENT'ev, V. and SUKHOTIN, Yu., 'Sotsialisticheskaya sobstvennost' i upravlenie ekonomikoy', in *Obshchestvennye nauki*, 6 (1988), 66–80.

DZHAFARLI, T. M., KISTAURI, Sh. L., KURASHVILI, B. P., and RASSOKHIN, V. P., 'Nekotorye aspekty uskoreniya nauchno-tekhnicheskogo progressa', in *Sots. iss.* 2 (1983), 58–63.

FIL'SHIN, G. I., 'Sochetanie otraslevykh i territorial'nykh interesov pri formirovanii investitsionnykh programm', in *EKO* 2 (1971), 39–51.

FROLOV, E. S., 'O kharektere vzaimootnosheniy ministerstv SSSR', in *Vestnik MGU*, 3 (1973), 33–40.

GLEBOV, I. A., and MARAKHOV, V. G. (gen. eds.), *Novyy sotsial'nyy mekhanizm* (Moscow, 1990).

'Gosudarstvennyy zakaz: garantii, stimuly, otvetstvennost'', in *Khozyaystvo i pravo*, 11 (1988), 10–15.

GVISHIANI, D., 'Klyuchevye rezervy upravleniya narodnym khozyaystvom', in *Kommunist*, 4 (1984), 37–47.

IGNATOVSKIY, P., 'O politicheskom podkhode k ekonomike', in *Kommunist*, 12 (1983), 60–72.

IKONNIKOV, V., and KRYLOV, S., 'O sochetanii otraslevogo i territorial'nogo upravleniya', in *Kommunist*, 4 (1984), 48–58.

KALININ, N. G. (ed.), *Organizatsiya upravleniya v sisteme ministerstva* (Moscow, 1974).

KHALfiNA, R. O., 'Khozyaystvennaya reforma i razvitie teorii prava', in *Sovetskoe gosudarstvo i pravo*, 10 (1967), 79–87.

KHASBULATOV, R. I., *Byurokratiya tozhe nash vrag . . .* (Moscow, 1989).

KHUBIEV, K., 'Sobstvennost' i ekonomicheskaya vlast'', in *Planovoye khozyaystvo*, 11 (1989), 84–92.

KOLIBAB, K. E., 'O pravovom polozhenii ministerstv SSSR', in *Sovetskoe gosudarstvo i pravo*, 1 (1968), 15–23.

KONAVALOVA, L. F., 'Ispol'zovanie programmno-tselevykh struktur v promyshlennom ministerstve', in *Planirovanie i proektirovanie razvitiya sistem upravleniya proizvodstvom* (Moscow, 1977), 84–92.

KORDONSKIY, S. G., 'Sotsial'naya struktura i mekhanizm tormozheniya', in *Postizhenie* (Moscow, 1989), 36–51.

KOZLOV, Yu. M., 'Gorizontal'nye upravlencheskie otnosheniya', in *Sovetskoe gosudarstvo i pravo*, 12 (1973), 62–70.

KPSS v rezolyutsiyakh i resheniyakh s"ezdov, konferentsii i plenumov, 10–14 (Moscow, 1986 and 1987).

KRYUKOVA, K. S., 'Analyz chislennosti rabotnikov apparata promyshlennykh ministerstv', in *Trud i zarabotnaya plata*, 1 (1970), 16–22.

KURASHVILI, B. P., 'Gosudarstvennoe upravlenie narodnym khozyaystom', in *Sovetskoe gosudarstvo i pravo*, 6 (1982), 38–48.

—— *Ocherk teorii gosudarstvennogo upravleniya* (Moscow, 1987).

—— *Bor'ba s byurokratizmom* (Moscow, 1988).

LAZEREV, B. M., 'Sotsial'nye interesy i kompetentsiya organov upravleniya', in *Sovetskoe gosudarstvo i pravo*, 10 (1971), 86–94.

—— (ed.), *Upravlencheskie protsedury* (Moscow, 1988).

LEMESHEV, M., 'Ekonomicheskie interesy i sotsial'noe prirodopol'zovanie', in *Inogo ne dano* (Moscow, 1988), 254–69.

—— 'Priroda i ekonomika: vedomstvennost′ i perestroyka', in N. P. Federenko (ed.), *Perestroyka upravleniya ekonomikoy: problemy, perspektivy* (Moscow, 1989), 258–61.

LEVCHUK, D., 'Ministerstvo v zerkale ekonomicheskikh metodov upravleniya', in *Khozyaystvo i pravo*, 5 (1989), 3–12.

LOBASHEV, A. V., 'Ponyatie i priznaki zakonnosti normativnykh aktov ministerstv i vedomstv', in *Pravovedenie*, 3 (1987), 27–32.

LUNEV, A. E.. 'Sovershenstvovat′ pravovoy status i koordinatsiyu deyatel′nosti ministerstv', in *Sovetskoe gosudarstvo i pravo*, 1 (1966), 8–16.

MASLENNIKOV, V. V., and SLOBODNIK, V. I., *Gosudarstvennyy zakaz* (Moscow, 1990).

MAKSIMOVICH, A. YA., *Arbitrazh v sisteme ministerstva i vedomstva* (Moscow, 1987).

MEN′shikov, S., 'Ekonomicheskaya struktura sotsializma: chto vperedi? Opyt prognoza', in *Novyy mir*, 3 (1989), 197–8.

MIGACHEV, R. D., *Opyt sovershenstvovaniya upravleniya otrasl′yu* (Moscow, 1975).

MIKHAYLOV, M., 'Po povodu vedomstvennosti', in *Kommunist*, 8 (1981), 104–15.

'Ministerstvo SSSR i khozyaystvennaya reforma', in *Sovetskoe gosudarstvo i pravo*, 1 (1970), 82–5.

'Ministerstvo perekhodit na khozraschet', in *EKO* 4 (1989), 59–64.

'Ministerstvo. Kakim emu byt′ ', in *Planovoye khozyaystvo*, 11 (1989), 34–51.

MOGILEVSKIY, S., and AYZIN, S., 'Otnosheniya predpriyatiya s vyshestoyashchim organom', in *Khozyaystvo i pravo*, 2 (1988), 3–9.

MOSKVICHEV, N. P., 'Gorod, predpriyatiya i zhil′e', in *EKO* 7 (1982), 171–9.

Nauchnaya organizatsiya truda rabotnikov apparata ministertsv i vedomstv (Moscow, 1973).

NIKOLAEVA, M., 'Sistematizatsiya vedomstvennykh normativnykh aktov', in *Khozyaystvo i pravo*, 5 (1977), 47–53.

O korennoy perestroike upravleniya ekonomikoy (Moscow, 1987).

O strukture tsentralnogo apparata minugleproma SSSR (Prikaz ministra, 23.10.74), no. 370.

OBOLONSKIY, A. V., 'Formalnye i neformalnye gruppy v apparate gosudarstvennogo upravleniya', in *Sovetskoe gosudarstvo i pravo*, 5 (1983), 36–42.

—— 'Byurokraticheskaya deformatsiya soznaniya i bor′ba s byurokratizmom', in *Sovetskoe gosudarstvo i pravo*, 1 (1987), 54–8.

OKUN′kov, L., 'Periodicheskie attestatsii upravlennogo personala', in *Khozyaystvo i pravo*, 1 (1979), 21–24.

Organizatsiya raboty ministerstv v usloviyakh ekonomicheskoy reformy (Moscow, 1972).

'Partiynye organizatsii ministerstv v novykh usloviyakh', in *Partiynaya zhizn′*, 24 (1966), 25–36.

272   SOURCES AND SELECTED BIBLIOGRAPHY

Perekhod k rynku (Moscow, 1990).

PETROV, A. S., 'Ekonomicheskaya reforma: tendentsii organizatsii otraslevogo upravleniya promyshlennost'yu', in *Sovetskoe gosudarstvo i pravo*, 3 (1971), 12–21.

—— 'Ob osnovnykh napravleniyakh sovershenstvovaniya sistemy ministerstv', in *Organizatsiya raboty ministerstv v usloviyakh ekonomicheskoy reformy* (Moscow, 1972), 89–96.

PISKOTIN, M. I., *Sotsializm i gosudarstvennoe upravlenie* (Moscow, 1984).

POBEZHIMOVA, N. I., 'Nekotorye voprosy organizatsii kontroliya v deyatel'nosti promyshlenykh ministerstv', in *Voprosi sovetskogo administrativnogo prava* (Moscow, 1970), 66.

POKROVSKIY, V. K., 'Ministerstvo: puti k novoy kontseptsii', in *Khozyaystvo i pravo*, 1 (1989), 12–21.

PONOMAREV, L., and SHINKARENKO, V., 'Kto kogo? Chem silen byurokrat?', in *Uroki gor'kie, no neobkhodimye* (Moscow, 1988), 155–9.

POPOV, G. KH., *Effektivnoe upravlenie* (Moscow, 1976).

—— *Effektivnoe upravlenie* (Moscow, 1985).

—— *Sovershenstvovanie otraslevoy i territorial'noy struktury upravleniya proizvodstvom* (Moscow, 1986).

—— 'S tochki zreniya ekonomista', in A. Bek, *Novoe naznachenie* (Moscow, 1987), 187–213.

—— 'Sistema i zubry', in *Uroki gor'kie, no neobkhodimye* (Moscow, 1988), 93–105.

—— 'Perestroyka upravleniya ekonomikoy', in *Inogo ne dano* (Moskow, 1988), 621–33.

POPOV, V. V., 'Ekonomicheskaya rol' tsentralizirovannykh fondov i rezervov ministerstva v upravlenii otrasl'yu promyshlennosti', in *Materialy po voprosam planirovaniya i upravleniya proizvodstvom* (Moscow, 1972), 11–21.

Pravovoe polozhenie ministerstv SSSR (Moscow, 1971).

Pravovye problemy rukovodstva i upravleniya otrasl'yu promyshlennosti v SSSR (Moscow, 1973).

PRONINA, V. S., 'Sootnoshenie kompetentsii gosudarstvennykh komitetov i ministerstv', in *Problemy sovershenstvovaniya sovetskogo zakonodatel'stva* (Moscow, 1976), 89–98.

PROZOROV, V., 'Pervye shagi i trudnosti reformy khozyaystvennogo zakono-datel'stva', in S. N. Bratus, *Sovetskoe zakonodatel'stvo: puti perestroiki* (Moscow, 1989), 273–314.

RAPOPORT, V., 'Printsipy i napravleniya perestroyki organizatsii otraslevogo upravleniya', in *Voprosy ekonomiki*, 10 (1989), 14–24.

RASSOKHIN, V. P., *Mekhanizm vnedreniya dostizheniy nauki: politika, upravlenie, pravo* (Moscow, 1985).

—— 'Nauchno-tekhnicheskiy potentsial: tsentralizatsiya i svoboda tvorchestva', in *Sovetskoe gosudarstvo i pravo*, 1 (1987), 21–30.

—— 'Vedomstvennost' kak istoricheskiy fenomen Sovetskoy ekonomiki', in *Postizhenie* (Moskow, 1989), 463–71.

ROZENBAUM, YU. A., 'K ponyatiyu upravlenshskikh kadrov', in *Pravovedenie*, 6 (1975), 20–25.

RUBIN, A. M., 'Sovershentvovanie struktury apparata promyshlennykh ministerstv', in *Sovetskoe gosudarstvo i pravo*, 5 (1978), 30–8.

RUTMAN, L. M. and TSIMERMAN, YU. S., 'Normotvorcheskaya deyatel'nost promyshlennogo ministersva i upravlenie otrasl'yu' in *Sovetskoe gosudarstvo i pravo*, 4 (1972), 87–95.

SHABAYLOV, V. I., 'Soyuzno-respublikanskie ministerstva soyuznykh respublik', in *Sovetskoe gosudarstvo i pravo*, 9 (1984), 25–32.

SHIRYAEVA, I. V., *Sovershenstvovanie struktury i shtatov v otrasli promyshlennosti* (Moscow, 1975).

SHKREDOV, V. P., *Ekonomika i pravo* (Moscow, 1990).

SHUBKIN, V., 'Byurokratiya: tochka zreniya sotsiologa', in *Uroki gor'kie, no neobkhodimye* (Moscow, 1988), 106–30.

SIRENKO, V. F., *Interesy v sisteme osnovnykh institutov sovetskogo gosudarstvennogo upravleniya* (Kiev, 1982).

SOKOLOVA, I. F., and MANUIL'skiy, M. A., 'Kak stat' ministrom', in *Sots. iss.* 1 (1988), 16–25.

SPIRIDONOV, E., 'Zaboty golovnogo ministerstva', in *Khozyaystvo i pravo*, 11 (1981), 41–5.

TAKSIR, K. I., *Upravlenie promyshlennost'yu SSSR* (Moscow, 1985).

TARASENKO, M. N., 'Vzaimodeystvie mestnykh Sovetov i ministerstv', in *Sovetskoe gosudarstvo i pravo*, 8 (1980), 74–82.

TIKHOMIROV, YU. A., *Zakon, stimuly, ekonomika* (Moscow, 1989).

TOLSTOSHEEV, V. V., 'Sovershenstvovanie apparata ministerstv', in *Sovetskoe gosudarstvo i pravo*, 3 (1970), 75–82.

TSIMERMAN, YU. S., 'Promyshlennye ministerstva v usloviyakh khozyaystvennoy reformy', in *Sovetskoe gosudarstvo i pravo*, 10 (1969), 76–82.

—— 'Promyshlennye ministerstva v novykh usloviyakh otraslevogo upravleniya', in *Sovetskoe gosudarstvo i pravo*, 8 (1976), 19–27.

—— 'Khozyaystvennoe ministertvo i ob"edinenie', in *Khozyaystvo i pravo*, 8 (1979), 49–53.

—— 'Osobennosti mezhotraslevykh funktsiy ministerstva', in *Khozyaystvo i pravo*, 8 (1980), 28–31.

Uskorenie sotsial'no-ekonomicheskogo razvitiya stranu—zadacha vsey partii, vsego naroda (Moscow, 1987).

VASIL'ev, V. V., 'Nadvedomstvennye polnomochiya ministerstv SSSR', in *Sovetskoe gosudarstvo i pravo*, 4 (1977), 10–19.

VISHNEVSKIY, A. G., 'Sotsial'nye regulyatory i chelovek', in *Postizhenie* (Moscow, 1989), 52–69.

VISHNYAKOV, V. G., 'Povyshenie effektivnosti raboty apparata upravleniya promyshlennost'yu', in *Sovetskoe gosudarstvo i pravo*, 3 (1966), 33–43.

VISHNYAKOV, V. G., *Dvoynoe podchinenie organov upravleniya narodnym khozyaystvom* (Moscow, 1967).

—— 'Podgotovka i povyshenie kvalifikatsii gosudarstvennykh sluzhashchikh', in *Sovetskoe gosudarstvo i pravo*, 6 (1971), 73–81.

—— 'Sovershenstvovanie struktury i shtatov organov upravleniya v usloviyakh khozyaystvennoy reformy', in *Organizatsiya raboty ministerstv v usloviyakh ekonomicheskoy reformy* (Moscow, 1972), 106–16.

—— 'Sovershenstvovanie struktury promyshlennykh ministerstv', in *Pravovedenie*, 4 (1975), 26–35.

—— 'Problemy sovershenstvovaniya tsentral'nogo apparata promyshlennykh ministerstv', in *Konstitutsiya SSSR i pravovye problemy sovershenstvovaniya rukovodstvo narodnym khozyaystvom* (Moscow, 1979), 12–19.

—— 'Otraslevoe i territorial'noe upravlenie: opyt i problemy', in *Pravovedenie*, 3 (1988), 13–22.

—— 'Ekonomicheskim normativam—pravovuyu osnovu', in *Khozyaystvo i pravo*, 6 (1988), 41–5.

VOROTNIKOV, V., 'O neobkhodimosti i zadachakh dal'neyshego sovershenstvovaniya organizatsii upravleniya otraslyami promyshlennosti', in *Planovoe khozyaystvo*, 5 (1971), 29–39.

ZAMENGOF, Z. M., 'Vzaimootnosheniya po imushchestvu v sisteme promyshlennykh ministerstv', in *Organizatsiya raboty ministerstv v usloviyakh ekonomicheskoy reformy* (Moscow, 1972), 189–94.

ZASLAVSKAYA, T. I., 'Ekonomicheskoe povedenie i ekonomicheskoe razvitie', in *EKO* 3 (1980), 15–33.

ZASLAVSKAYA, T. I., 'Chelovecheskiy faktor razvitiya ekonomiki i sotsial'naya spravedlivost'', in *Kommunist*, 13 (1986), 61–73.

GLOSSARY

Apparatchiki: officials in administration, especially the Communist Party and the state committees, mainly concerned with regulation of other agencies.

Arenda: leasing, an administrative reform introduced in the late 1980s to allow enterprises or parts thereof to rent industrial capacity.

Diktat: the imposition of the will of higher organizations over the rights and interests of lower ones.

Glasnost': openness, a policy pursued by Gorbachev and his allies aimed at increasing public scrutiny of state administration.

Glavki: sub-units of industrial ministries responsible for line management.

Golovnoe ministerstvo: the head ministry, a legal framework wherein one ministry was given powers to determine policy in a particular product line across administrative boundaries.

Gosarbitrazh: the state arbitration service, located both inside ministries and at a supra-departmental level. Though arbitration had a judicial character, it remained primarily an administrative body charged with ensuring the public interest.

Goszakazi: the system of state orders to enterprises, supposedly on an economic basis, introduced in the late 1980s to replace the old system of directive plans.

Ispolnitel'nost: the unswerving fulfilment of instructions, considered a virtue among Soviet bureaucrats.

Khozraschet: the notion that enterprises and even state structures should be cost-accountable and self-financing.

Khozyaystvenniki: officials in economic administration, especially industrial ministries, mainly concerned with operational management. (See also *apparatchiki*.)

Kollegiya: the collegium of the ministry, formally an advisory body comprising the heads of departments and large enterprises.

Kontrol': control, in Russian designating supervision rather than operational responsibility.

Mestnichestvo: localism, a deviation wherein regional authorities put their interests above the party of state as a whole. (See also *vedomstvennost'*.)

Nomenklatura: formally, this refers to a list of state appointments for which party approval was required. The intention of the system was to ensure the political reliability of officials. The term also designates a social group held to have had privileges as a result of their position; in the latter sense, it comprises party as well as state officials.

Ob''edinenie: an administrative structure combining enterprises. (Plural: *ob''edineniya*.)

Perestroyka: the policy embarked upon by Mikhail Gorbachev and his allies (the *perestroyshchiki*), aimed at restructuring the Soviet political and economic system. The policy became more radical over time as it encountered resistance from both Communist Party officials and administrators in the economic agencies.

Pravo kontrolya: the right of control, held by primary party organizations, entitling them to supervise the work of management of enterprises and, after 1970, industrial ministries as well.

Prikaz: a legally binding order issued by the minister which put ministerial decisions into effect.

Soglasovanie: an administrative procedure wherein consensus on proposals needed to receive the agreement of relevant department heads to go forward. (See also *vizirovanie*.)

Sovnarkhozy: the system of regional economic councils introduced by Khrushchev in 1957 which lasted until the re-establishment of industrial ministries, which the *sovnarkhozy* had earlier replaced, in 1965.

Vedomstvennost': departmentalism, a deviation wherein officials in sectoral economic organisations put their interests above the state as a whole. (See also *mestnichestvo*.)

Vizirovanie: an administrative procedure wherein the heads of relevant departments affixed a seal (*viza*) indicating their agreement with a proposal.

Vlast': state power.

INDEX